BATMAN '66

VOL. 3

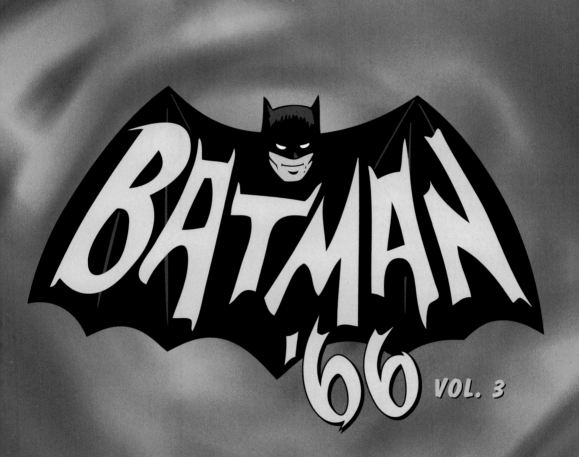

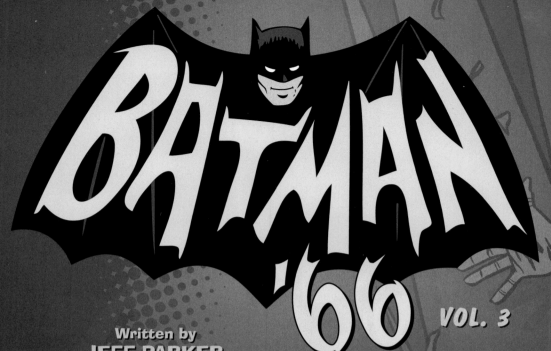

BATMAN '66

VOL. 3

Written by
JEFF PARKER
ART BALTAZAR
FRANCO
GABE SORIA

Art by
JONATHAN CASE
DARIO BRIZUELA
TED NAIFEH
DEAN HASPIEL
PAUL RIVOCHE
CRAIG ROUSSEAU
WILFREDO TORRES
BRENT SCHOONOVER

Colors by
JONATHAN CASE
TONY AVIÑA
ALLEN PASSALAQUA
PAUL RIVOCHE
KELLY FITZPATRICK

Letters by
WES ABBOTT

Cover Art & Original Series Covers by
MICHAEL & LAURA ALLRED

BATMAN created by **BOB KANE**

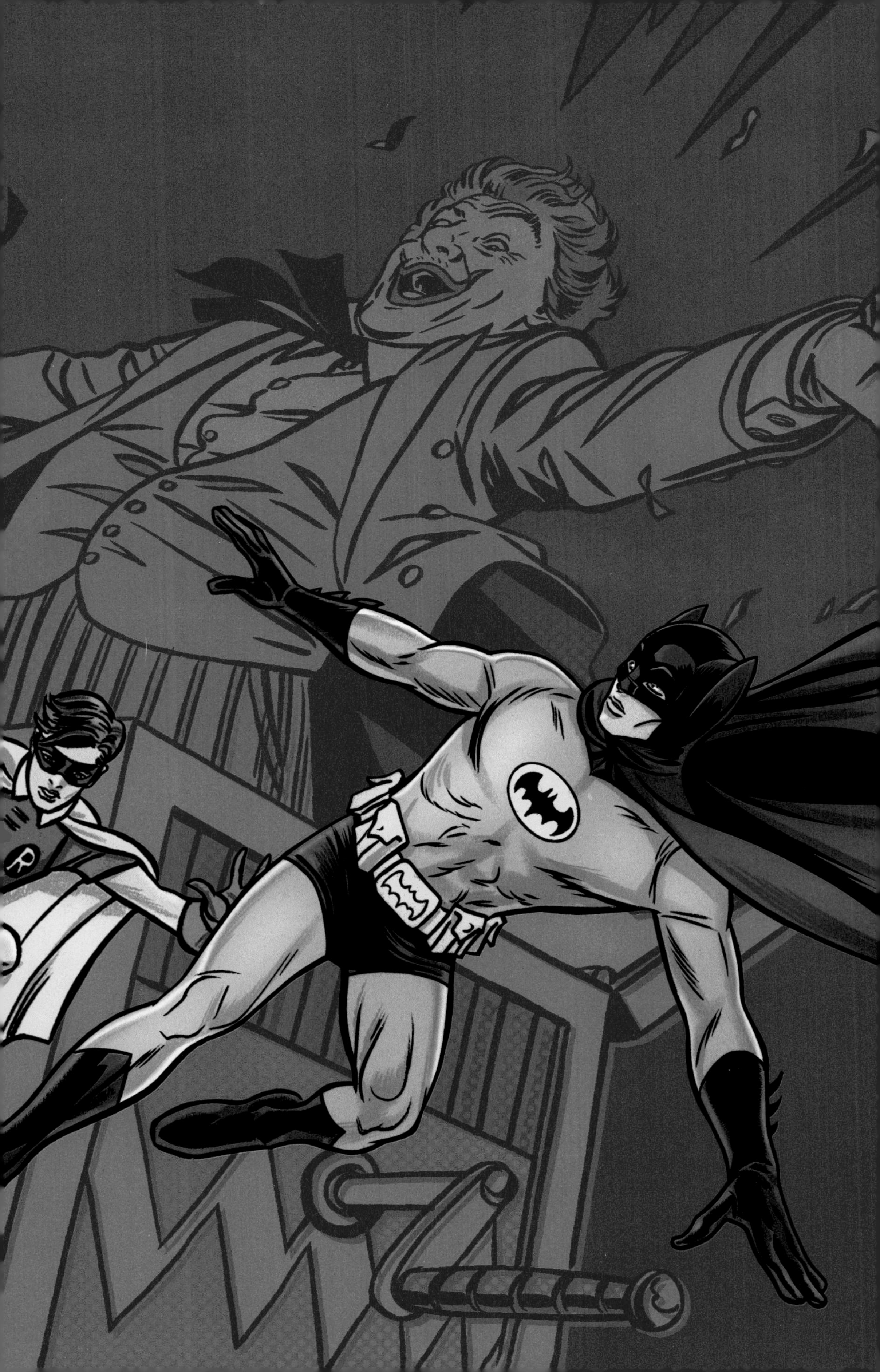

JIM CHADWICK
Editor – Original Series
ANIZ ANSARI
Assistant Editor – Original Series
JEB WOODARD
Group Editor – Collected Editions
SCOTT NYBAKKEN
Editor – Collected Edition
CURTIS KING JR.
Publication Design
BOB HARRAS
Senior VP – Editor-in-Chief, DC Comics

DIANE NELSON
President
DAN DiDIO and **JIM LEE**
Co-Publishers
GEOFF JOHNS
Chief Creative Officer
AMIT DESAI
Senior VP – Marketing & Global Franchise Management
NAIRI GARDINER
Senior VP – Finance
SAM ADES
VP – Digital Marketing
BOBBIE CHASE
VP – Talent Development
MARK CHIARELLO
Senior VP – Art, Design & Collected Editions
JOHN CUNNINGHAM
VP – Content Strategy

ANNE DePIES
VP – Strategy Planning & Reporting
DON FALLETTI
VP – Manufacturing Operations
LAWRENCE GANEM
VP – Editorial Administration & Talent Relations
ALISON GILL
Senior VP – Manufacturing & Operations
HANK KANALZ
Senior VP – Editorial Strategy & Administration
JAY KOGAN
VP – Legal Affairs
DEREK MADDALENA
Senior VP – Sales & Business Development
JACK MAHAN
VP – Business Affairs
DAN MIRON
VP – Sales Planning & Trade Development
NICK NAPOLITANO
VP – Manufacturing Administration
CAROL ROEDER
VP – Marketing
EDDIE SCANNELL
VP – Mass Account & Digital Sales
COURTNEY SIMMONS
Senior VP – Publicity & Communications
JIM (SKI) SOKOLOWSKI
VP – Comic Book Specialty & Newsstand Sales
SANDY YI
Senior VP – Global Franchise Management

BATMAN '66 VOL. 3

Published by DC Comics. Compilation Copyright © 2015 DC Comics. All Rights Reserved. Originally published in single magazine form as BATMAN '66 11-16 and online as BATMAN '66 Digital Chapters 31-45. Copyright © 2014 DC Comics. All Rights Reserved. All characters, their distinctive likenesses and related elements featured in this publication are trademarks of DC Comics. The stories, characters and incidents featured in this publication are entirely fictional. DC Comics does not read or accept unsolicited submissions of ideas, stories or artwork.

DC Comics, 4000 Warner Blvd., Burbank, CA 91522. A Warner Bros. Entertainment Company.
Printed by RR Donnelley, Salem, VA, USA. 10/30/15. First Printing. ISBN: 978-1-4012-5750-7

Library of Congress Cataloging-in-Publication Data

Parker, Jeff, 1966-
  Batman '66. Volume 3 / Jeff Parker, Jonathan Case.
    pages cm
  ISBN 978-1-4012-5750-7
  1. Graphic novels. I. Case, Jonathan. II. Title.
PN6728.B36P374 2015
741.5'973—dc23
                                    2014049021

TABLE OF CONTENTS

Cover art for BATMAN #11 by Jonathan Case.

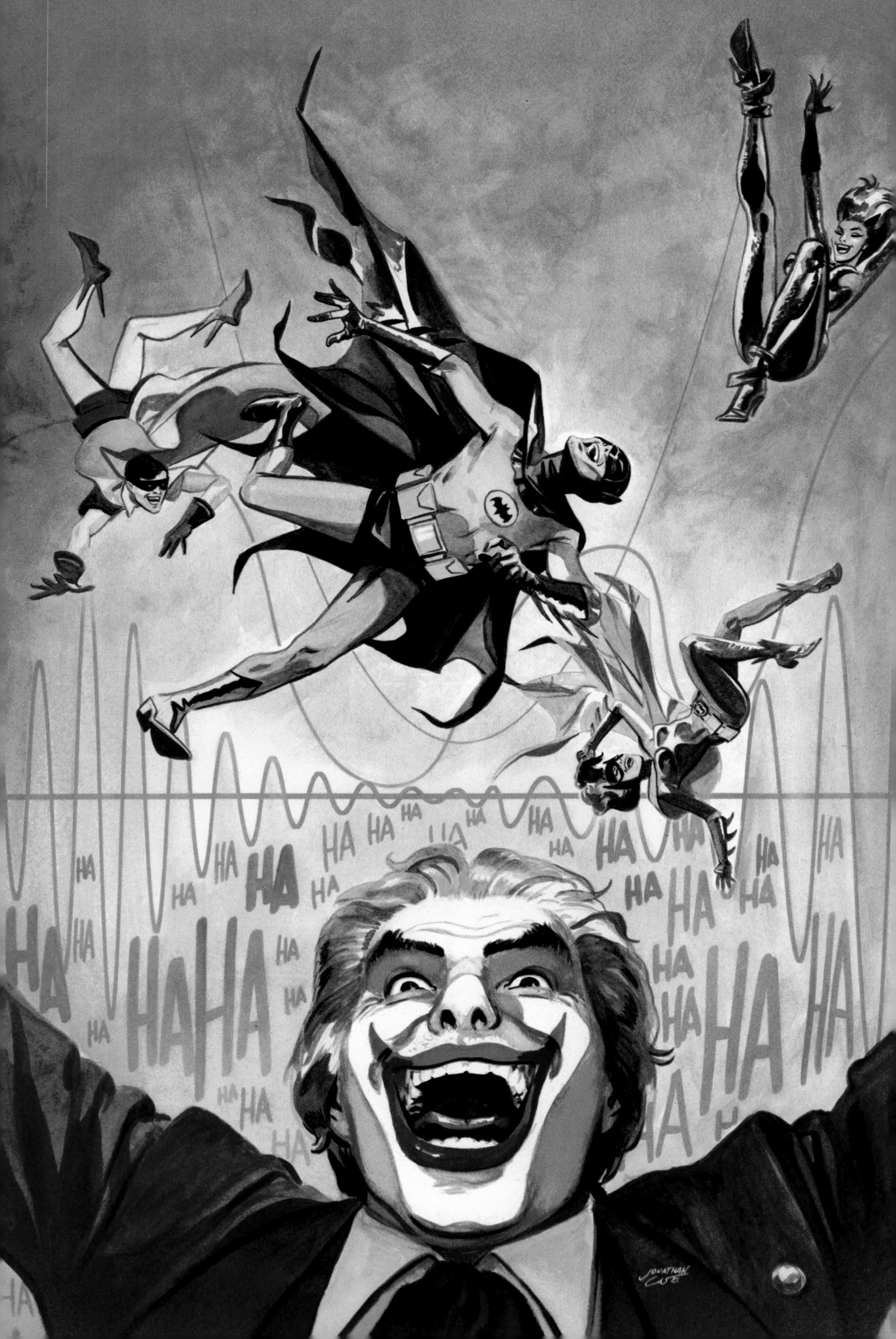
HA HA HA HA HA HA HA HA HA HA HA HA HA HA HA HA HA
HAHA
JONATHAN CASE

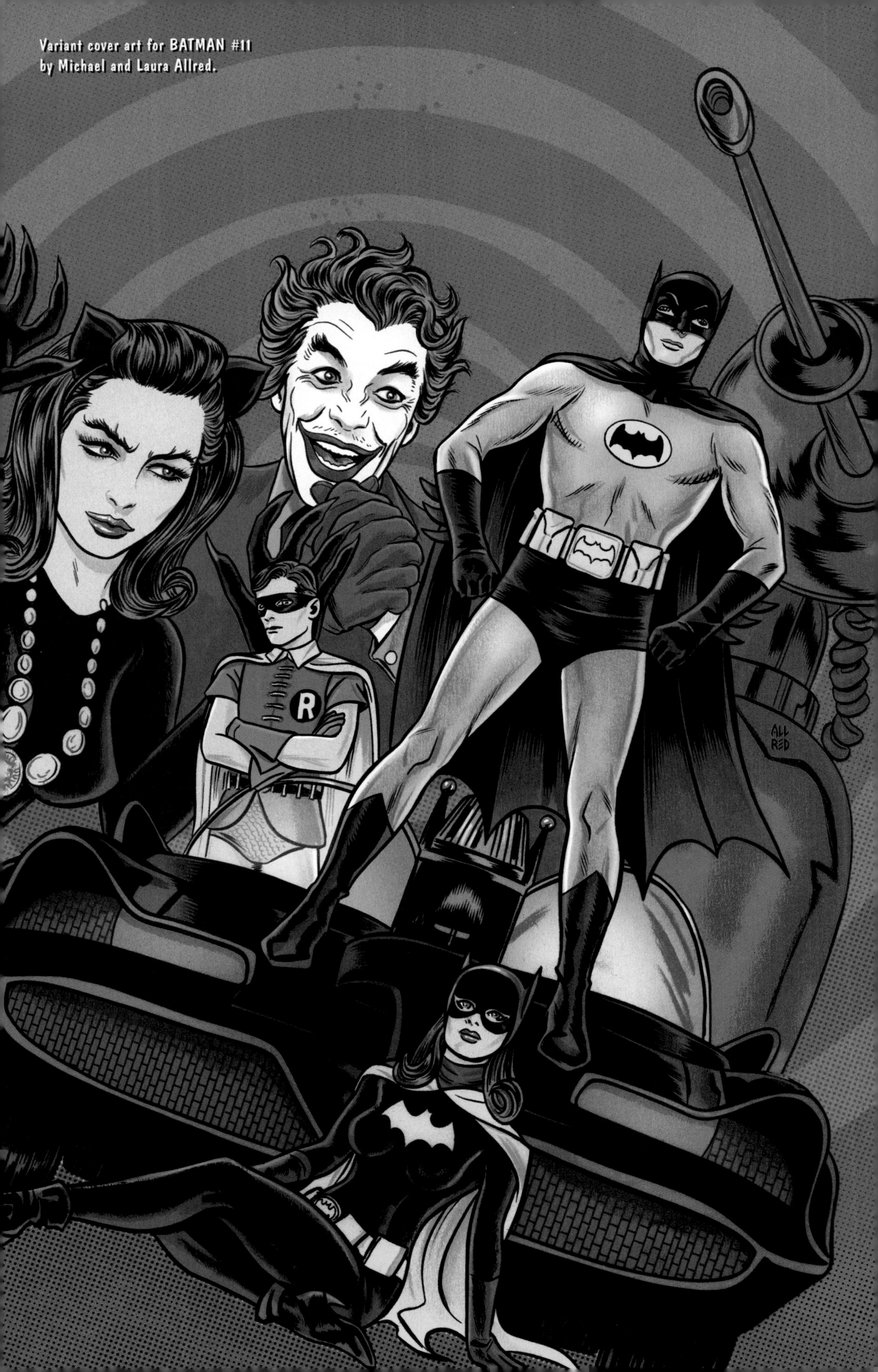
ALL
RED

Variant cover art for BATMAN #11
by Michael and Laura Allred.

KAPOW!!

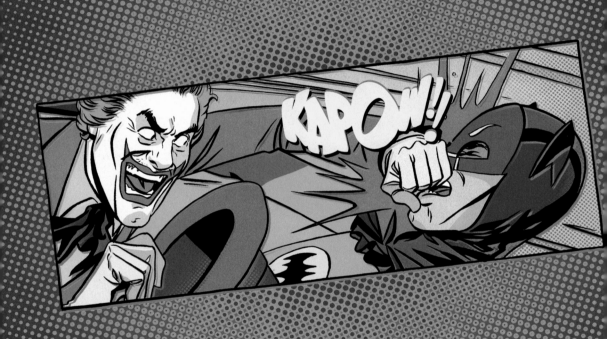

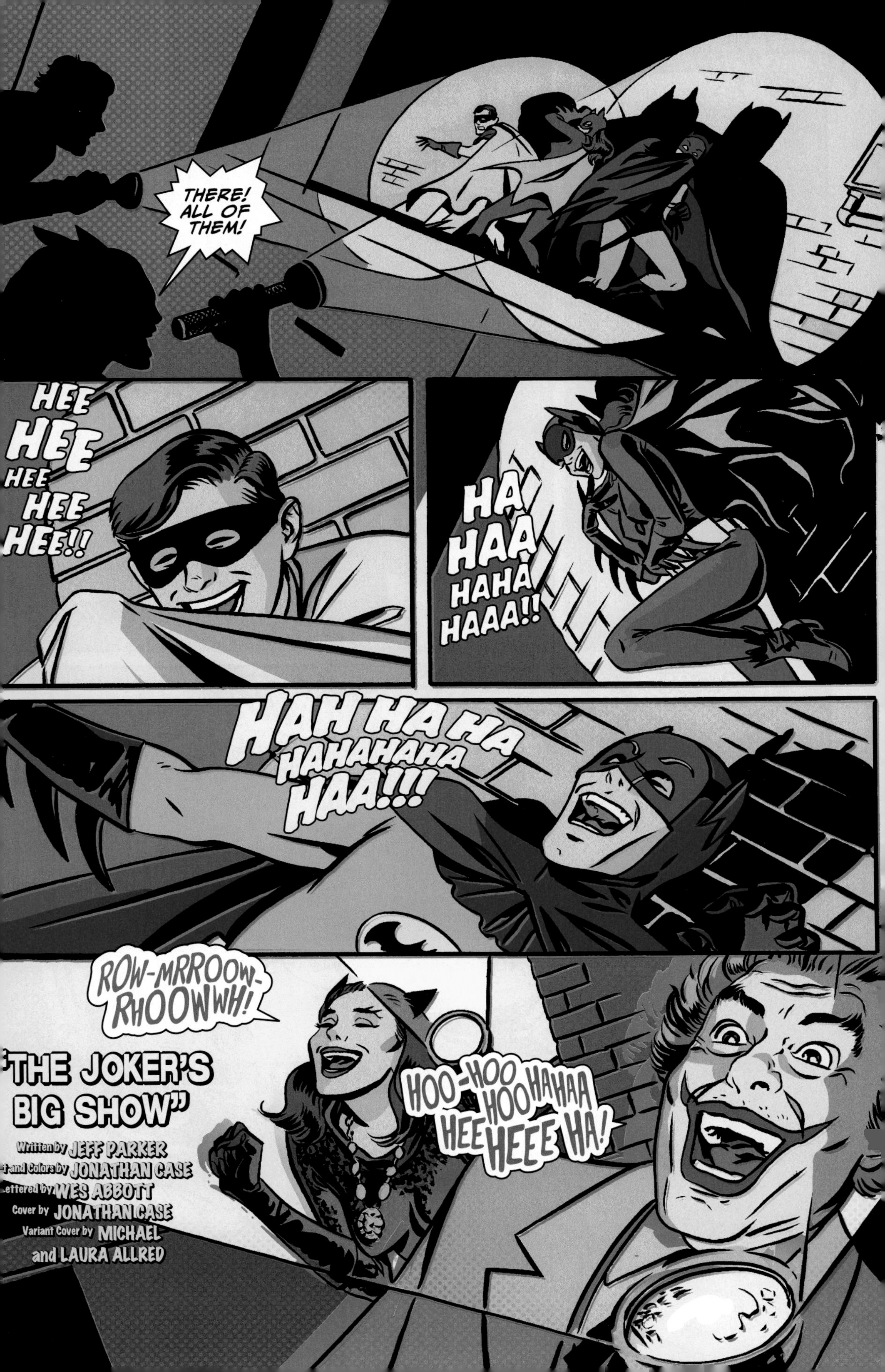
THERE! ALL OF THEM!
HEE HEE HEE HEE HEE!!
HA HAA HAHA HAAA!!
HAH HA HA HAHAHAHA HAA!!!
ROW-MRROOW-RHOOOWWH!
"THE JOKER'S BIG SHOW"
Written by JEFF PARKER
t and Colors by JONATHAN CASE
ettered by WES ABBOTT
Cover by JONATHAN CASE
Variant Cover by MICHAEL and LAURA ALLRED
HOO-HOO HOO HAHAA HEE HEEE HA!

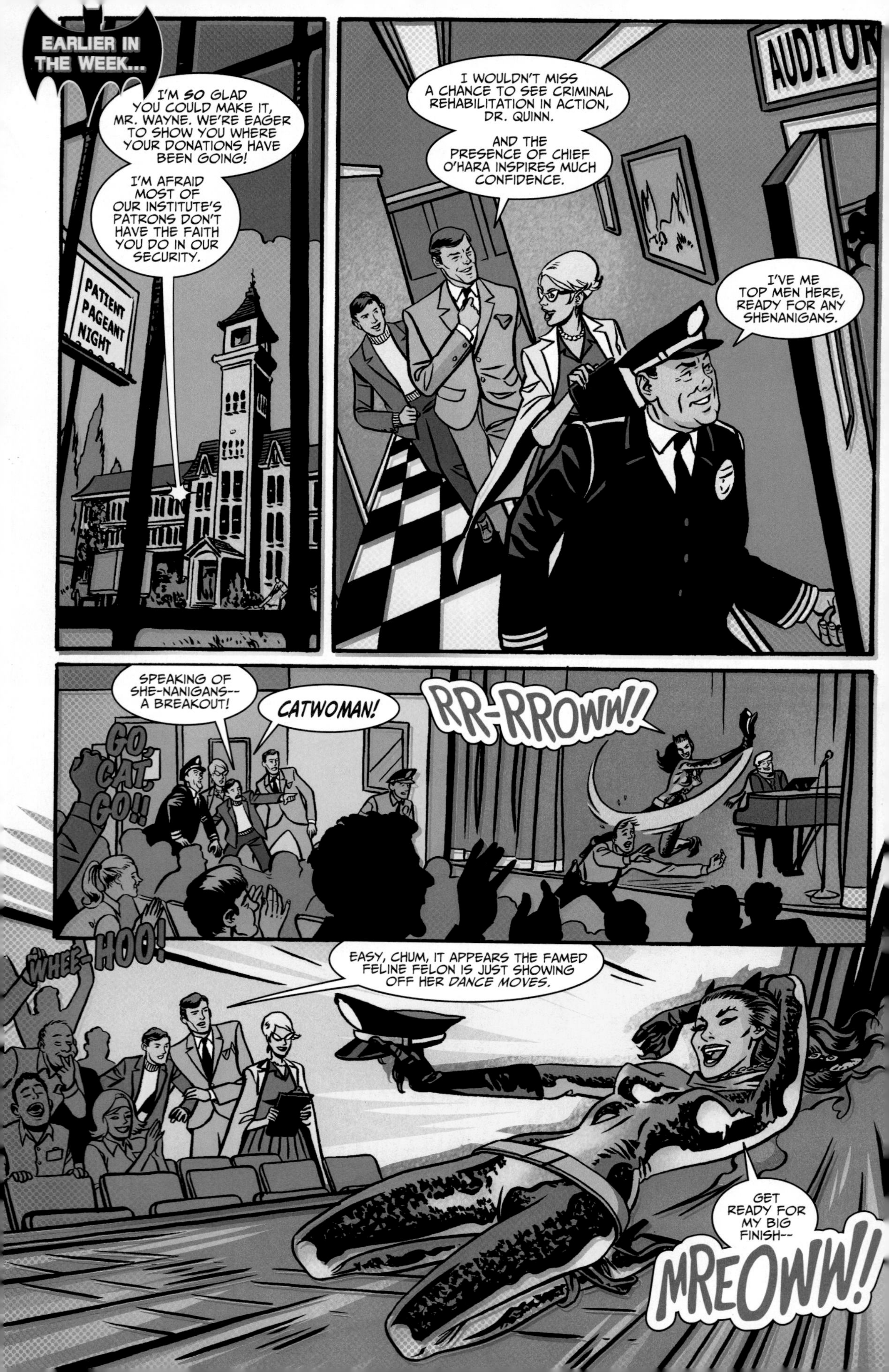
EARLIER IN THE WEEK...
I'M SO GLAD YOU COULD MAKE IT, MR. WAYNE. WE'RE EAGER TO SHOW YOU WHERE YOUR DONATIONS HAVE BEEN GOING!
I'M AFRAID MOST OF OUR INSTITUTE'S PATRONS DON'T HAVE THE FAITH YOU DO IN OUR SECURITY.
PATIENT PAGEANT NIGHT
AUDITOR
I WOULDN'T MISS A CHANCE TO SEE CRIMINAL REHABILITATION IN ACTION, DR. QUINN.
AND THE PRESENCE OF CHIEF O'HARA INSPIRES MUCH CONFIDENCE.
I'VE ME TOP MEN HERE, READY FOR ANY SHENANIGANS.
SPEAKING OF SHE-NANIGANS-- A BREAKOUT!
CATWOMAN!
RR-RROWW!
GO, CAT, GO!!
WHEE-HOO!
EASY, CHUM, IT APPEARS THE FAMED FELINE FELON IS JUST SHOWING OFF HER DANCE MOVES.
GET READY FOR MY BIG FINISH--
MREOWW!

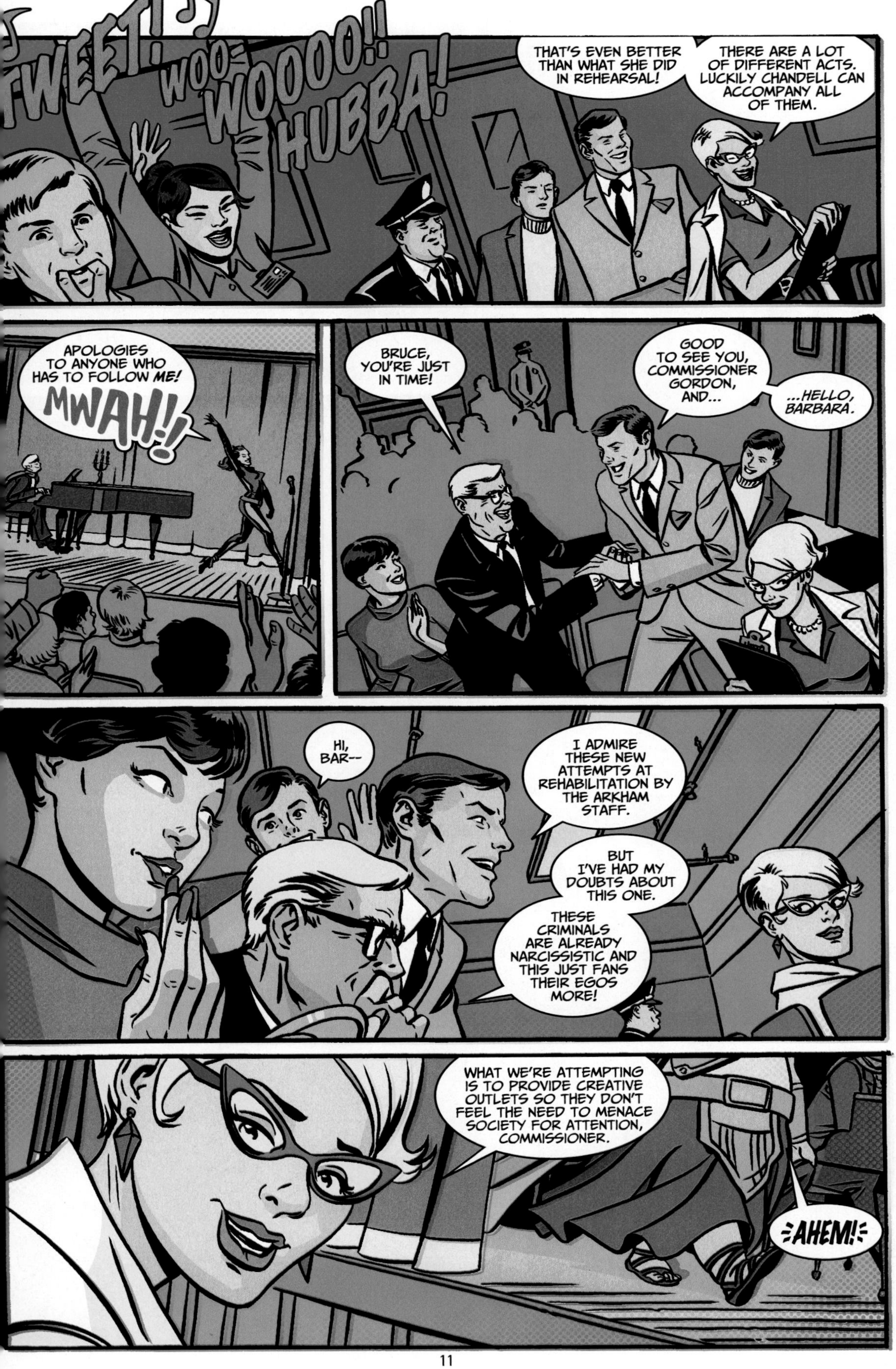
TWEET!
WOO-WOOOO!!
HUBBA!
THAT'S EVEN BETTER THAN WHAT SHE DID IN REHEARSAL!
THERE ARE A LOT OF DIFFERENT ACTS. LUCKILY CHANDELL CAN ACCOMPANY ALL OF THEM.
APOLOGIES TO ANYONE WHO HAS TO FOLLOW ME!
MWAH!!
BRUCE, YOU'RE JUST IN TIME!
GOOD TO SEE YOU, COMMISSIONER GORDON, AND...
...HELLO, BARBARA.
HI, BAR--
I ADMIRE THESE NEW ATTEMPTS AT REHABILITATION BY THE ARKHAM STAFF.
BUT I'VE HAD MY DOUBTS ABOUT THIS ONE.
THESE CRIMINALS ARE ALREADY NARCISSISTIC AND THIS JUST FANS THEIR EGOS MORE!
WHAT WE'RE ATTEMPTING IS TO PROVIDE CREATIVE OUTLETS SO THEY DON'T FEEL THE NEED TO MENACE SOCIETY FOR ATTENTION, COMMISSIONER.
AHEM!

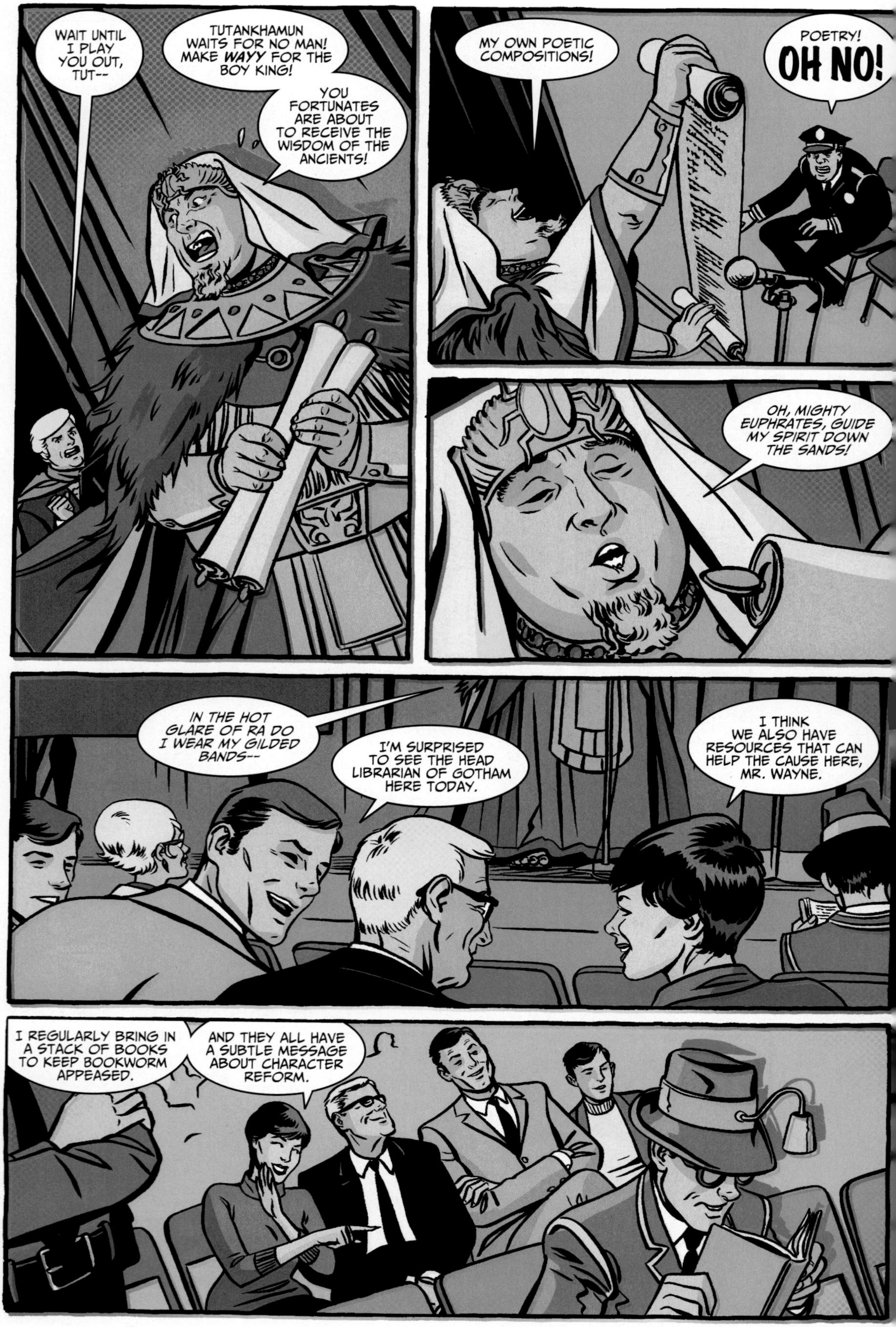
WAIT UNTIL I PLAY YOU OUT, TUT--
TUTANKHAMUN WAITS FOR NO MAN! MAKE WAYY FOR THE BOY KING!
YOU FORTUNATES ARE ABOUT TO RECEIVE THE WISDOM OF THE ANCIENTS!
MY OWN POETIC COMPOSITIONS!
POETRY! OH NO!
OH, MIGHTY EUPHRATES, GUIDE MY SPIRIT DOWN THE SANDS!
IN THE HOT GLARE OF RA DO I WEAR MY GILDED BANDS--
I'M SURPRISED TO SEE THE HEAD LIBRARIAN OF GOTHAM HERE TODAY.
I THINK WE ALSO HAVE RESOURCES THAT CAN HELP THE CAUSE HERE, MR. WAYNE.
I REGULARLY BRING IN A STACK OF BOOKS TO KEEP BOOKWORM APPEASED.
AND THEY ALL HAVE A SUBTLE MESSAGE ABOUT CHARACTER REFORM.

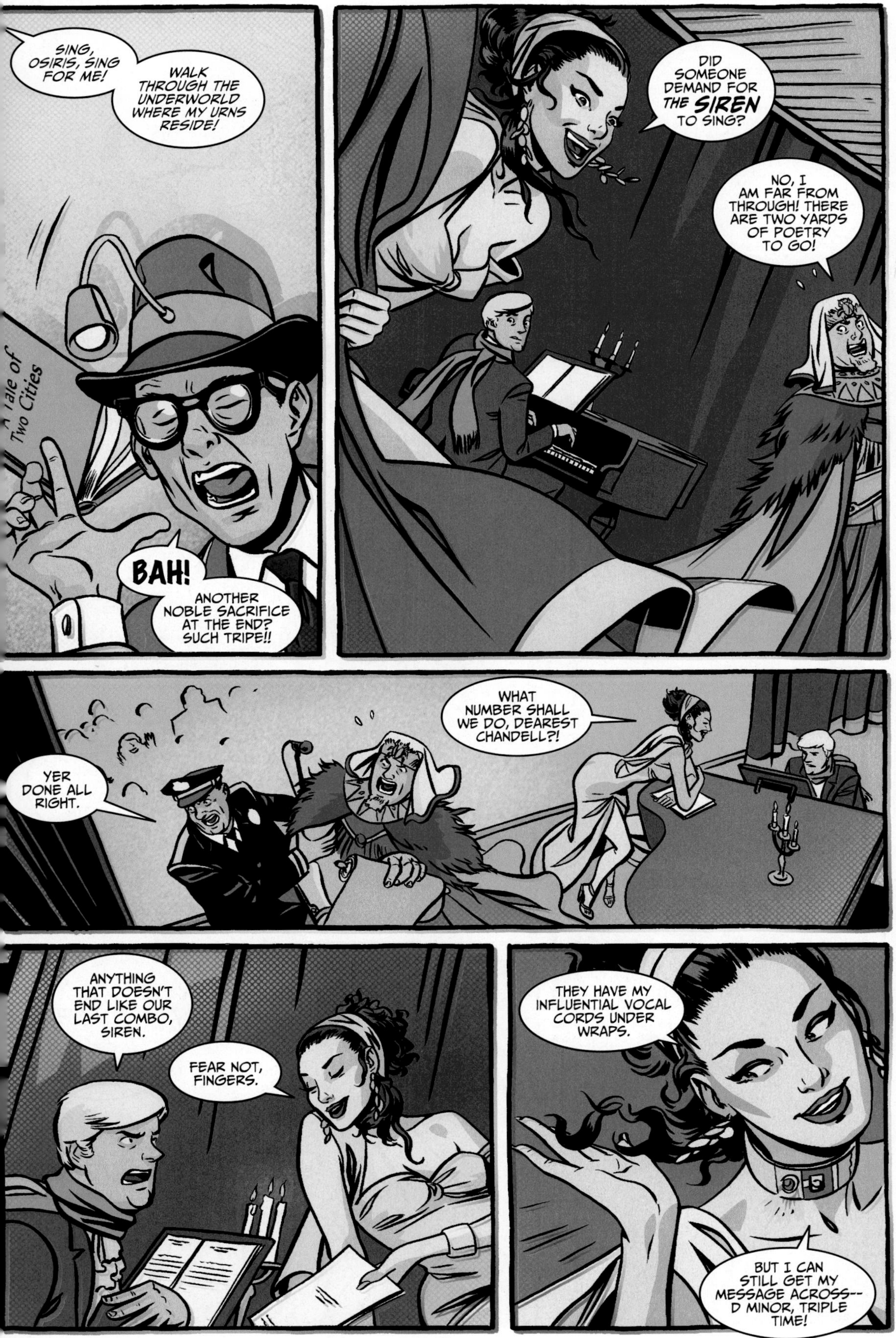
SING, OSIRIS, SING FOR ME!
WALK THROUGH THE UNDERWORLD WHERE MY URNS RESIDE!
A Tale of Two Cities
BAH!
ANOTHER NOBLE SACRIFICE AT THE END? SUCH TRIPE!!
DID SOMEONE DEMAND FOR THE SIREN TO SING?
NO, I AM FAR FROM THROUGH! THERE ARE TWO YARDS OF POETRY TO GO!
YER DONE ALL RIGHT.
WHAT NUMBER SHALL WE DO, DEAREST CHANDELL?!
ANYTHING THAT DOESN'T END LIKE OUR LAST COMBO, SIREN.
FEAR NOT, FINGERS.
THEY HAVE MY INFLUENTIAL VOCAL CORDS UNDER WRAPS.
BUT I CAN STILL GET MY MESSAGE ACROSS-- D MINOR, TRIPLE TIME!

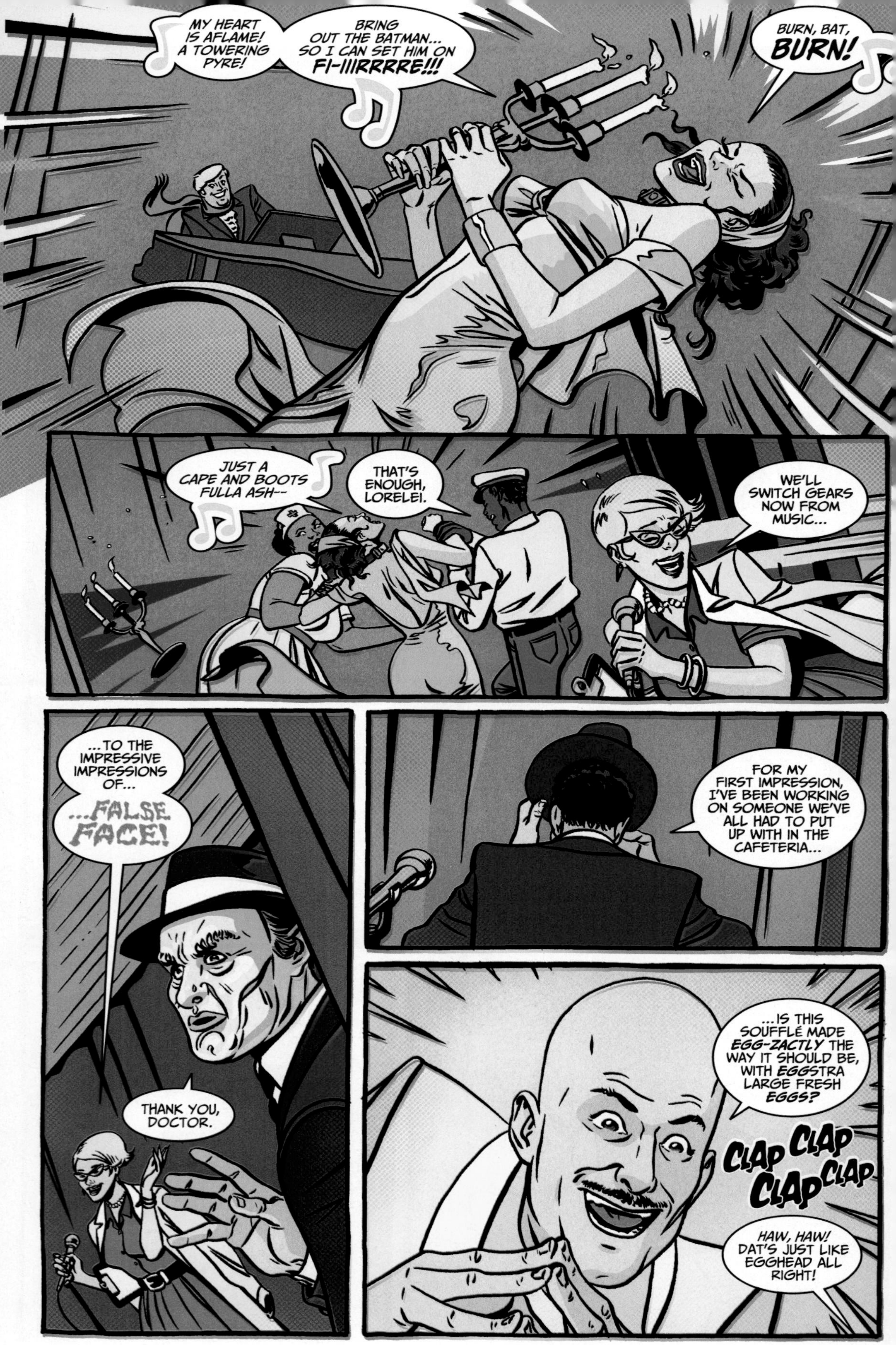
MY HEART IS AFLAME! A TOWERING PYRE!
BRING OUT THE BATMAN... SO I CAN SET HIM ON FI-IIIRRRRE!!!
BURN, BAT, BURN!
JUST A CAPE AND BOOTS FULLA ASH--
THAT'S ENOUGH, LORELEI.
WE'LL SWITCH GEARS NOW FROM MUSIC...
...TO THE IMPRESSIVE IMPRESSIONS OF...
...FALSE FACE!
THANK YOU, DOCTOR.
FOR MY FIRST IMPRESSION, I'VE BEEN WORKING ON SOMEONE WE'VE ALL HAD TO PUT UP WITH IN THE CAFETERIA...
...IS THIS SOUFFLÉ MADE EGG-ZACTLY THE WAY IT SHOULD BE, WITH EGGSTRA LARGE FRESH EGGS?
CLAP CLAP CLAP CLAP
HAW, HAW! DAT'S JUST LIKE EGGHEAD ALL RIGHT!

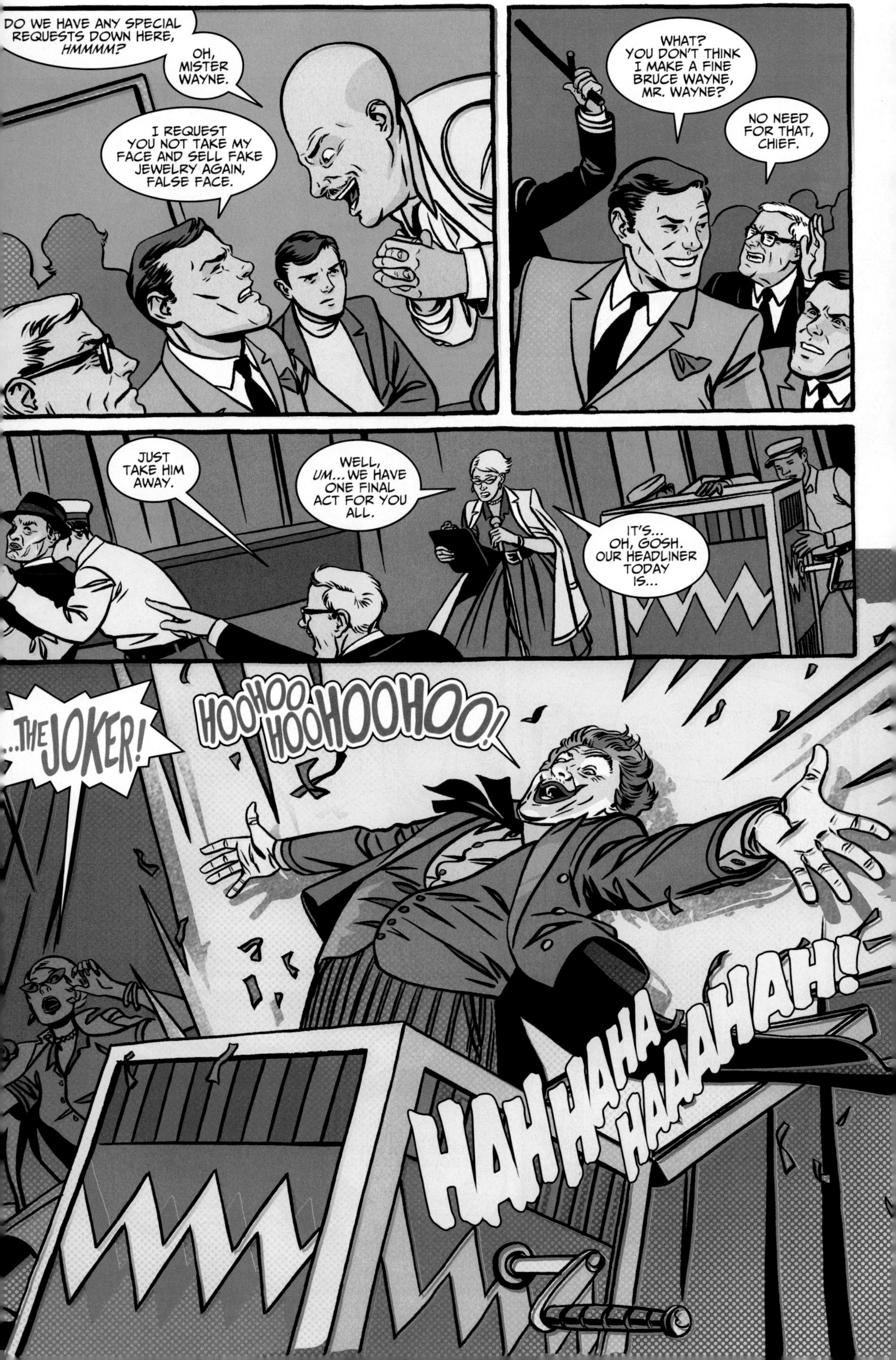
DO WE HAVE ANY SPECIAL REQUESTS DOWN HERE, *HMMMM?*
OH, MISTER WAYNE.
I REQUEST YOU NOT TAKE MY FACE AND SELL FAKE JEWELRY AGAIN, FALSE FACE.
WHAT? YOU DON'T THINK I MAKE A FINE BRUCE WAYNE, MR. WAYNE?
NO NEED FOR THAT, CHIEF.
JUST TAKE HIM AWAY.
WELL, *UM*... WE HAVE ONE FINAL ACT FOR YOU ALL.
IT'S... OH, GOSH. OUR HEADLINER TODAY IS...
...THE JOKER!
HOOHOO HOOHOOHOO!
HAHHAHA HAAAHAH!

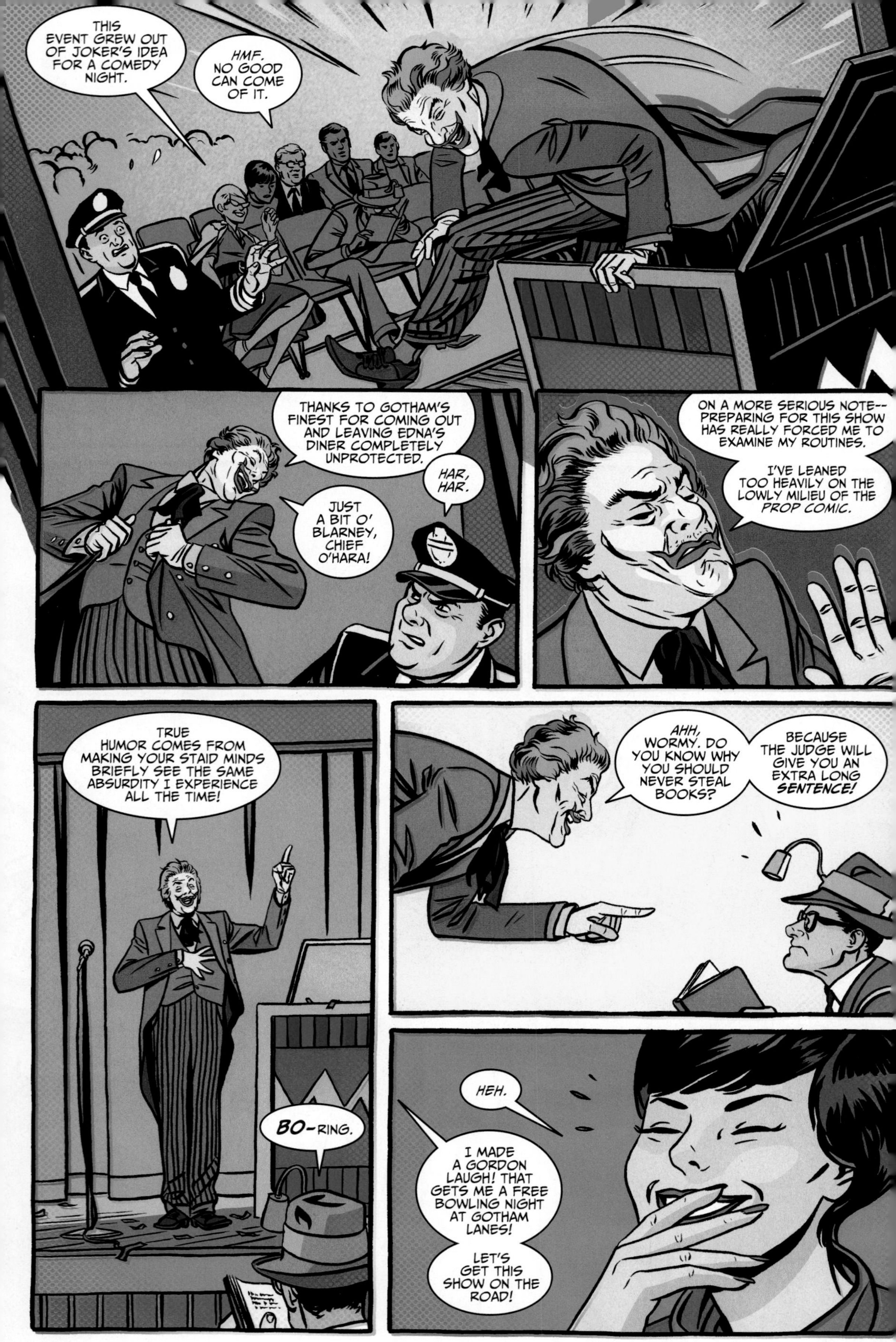
THIS EVENT GREW OUT OF JOKER'S IDEA FOR A COMEDY NIGHT.
HMF. NO GOOD CAN COME OF IT.
THANKS TO GOTHAM'S FINEST FOR COMING OUT AND LEAVING EDNA'S DINER COMPLETELY UNPROTECTED.
HAR, HAR.
JUST A BIT O' BLARNEY, CHIEF O'HARA!
ON A MORE SERIOUS NOTE-- PREPARING FOR THIS SHOW HAS REALLY FORCED ME TO EXAMINE MY ROUTINES.
I'VE LEANED TOO HEAVILY ON THE LOWLY MILIEU OF THE PROP COMIC.
TRUE HUMOR COMES FROM MAKING YOUR STAID MINDS BRIEFLY SEE THE SAME ABSURDITY I EXPERIENCE ALL THE TIME!
BO-RING.
AHH, WORMY. DO YOU KNOW WHY YOU SHOULD NEVER STEAL BOOKS?
BECAUSE THE JUDGE WILL GIVE YOU AN EXTRA LONG SENTENCE!
HEH.
I MADE A GORDON LAUGH! THAT GETS ME A FREE BOWLING NIGHT AT GOTHAM LANES!
LET'S GET THIS SHOW ON THE ROAD!

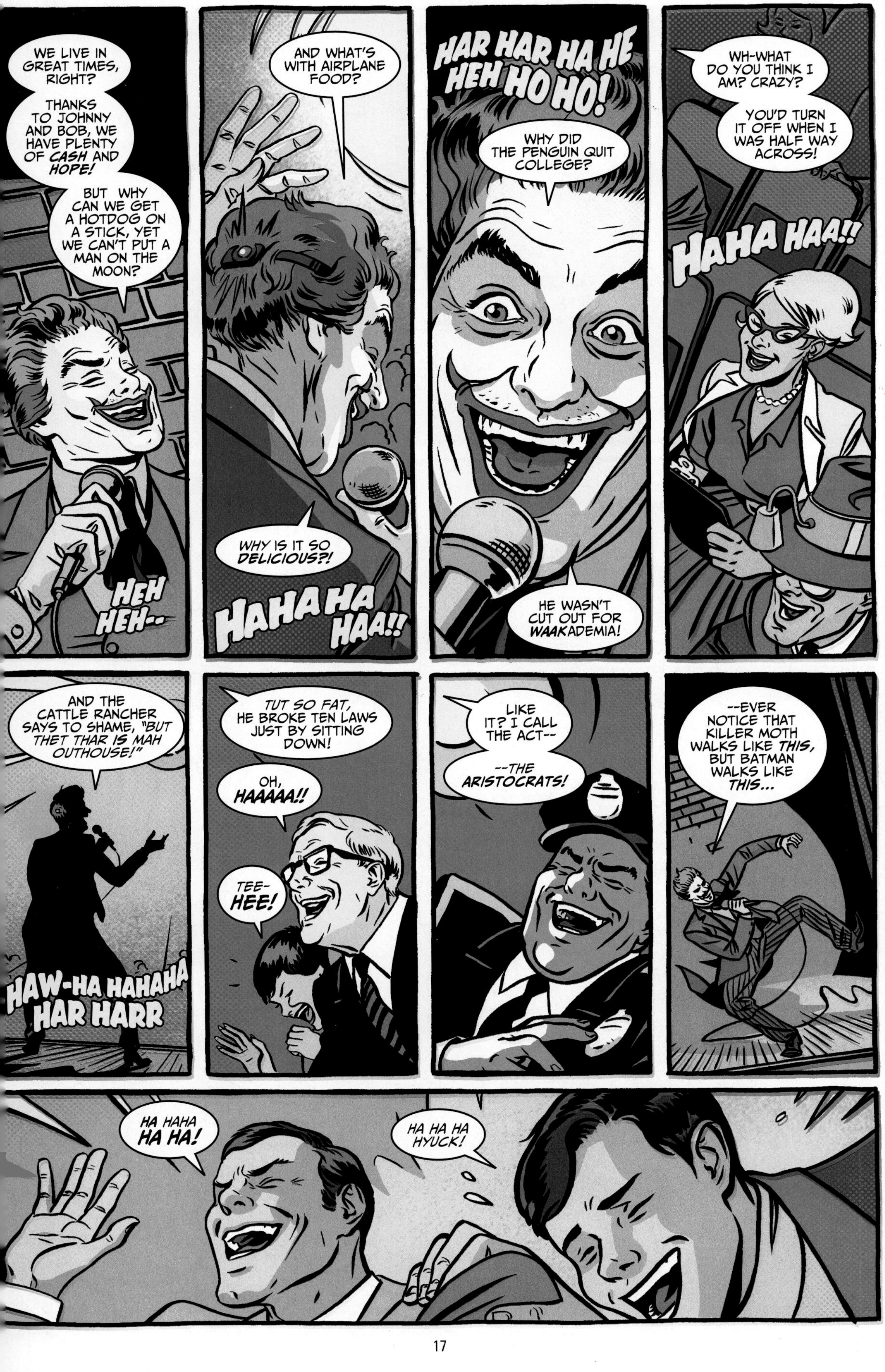
WE LIVE IN GREAT TIMES, RIGHT?
THANKS TO JOHNNY AND BOB, WE HAVE PLENTY OF CASH AND HOPE!
BUT WHY CAN WE GET A HOTDOG ON A STICK, YET WE CAN'T PUT A MAN ON THE MOON?
HEH HEH--
AND WHAT'S WITH AIRPLANE FOOD?
WHY IS IT SO DELICIOUS?!
HAHAHA HA HAA!!
HAR HAR HA HE HEH HO HO!
WHY DID THE PENGUIN QUIT COLLEGE?
HE WASN'T CUT OUT FOR WAAKADEMIA!
WH-WHAT DO YOU THINK I AM? CRAZY?
YOU'D TURN IT OFF WHEN I WAS HALF WAY ACROSS!
HAHA HAA!!
AND THE CATTLE RANCHER SAYS TO SHAME, "BUT THET THAR IS MAH OUTHOUSE!"
HAW-HA HAHAHA HAR HARR
TUT SO FAT, HE BROKE TEN LAWS JUST BY SITTING DOWN!
OH, HAAAAA!!
TEE-HEE!
LIKE IT? I CALL THE ACT--
--THE ARISTOCRATS!
--EVER NOTICE THAT KILLER MOTH WALKS LIKE THIS, BUT BATMAN WALKS LIKE THIS...
HA HAHA HA HA!
HA HA HA HYUCK!

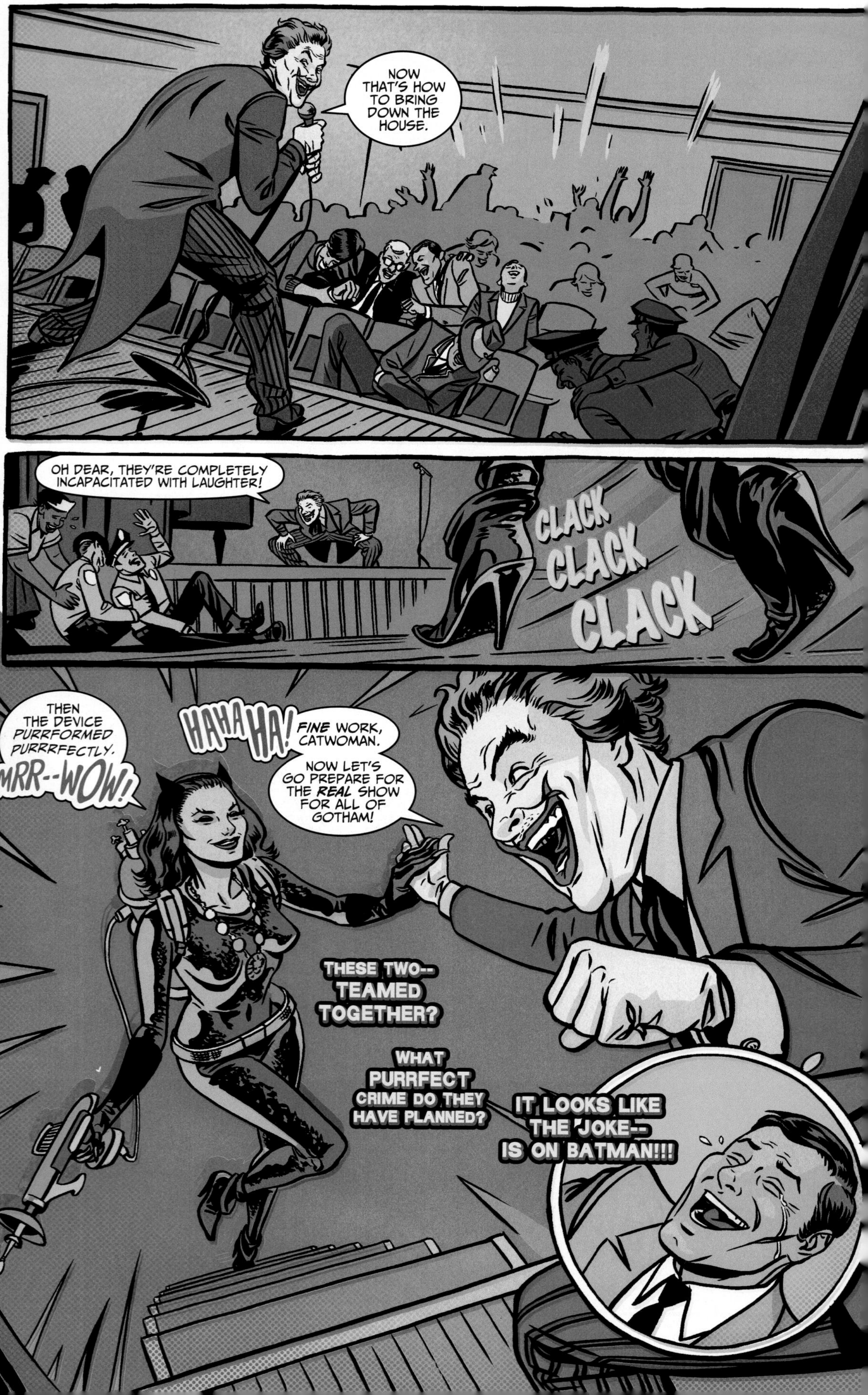
NOW THAT'S HOW TO BRING DOWN THE HOUSE.
OH DEAR, THEY'RE COMPLETELY INCAPACITATED WITH LAUGHTER!
CLACK CLACK CLACK
THEN THE DEVICE PURRFORMED PURRRFECTLY.
MRR--WOW!
HAHAHA!
FINE WORK, CATWOMAN.
NOW LET'S GO PREPARE FOR THE REAL SHOW FOR ALL OF GOTHAM!
THESE TWO-- TEAMED TOGETHER?
WHAT PURRFECT CRIME DO THEY HAVE PLANNED?
IT LOOKS LIKE THE JOKE-- IS ON BATMAN!!!

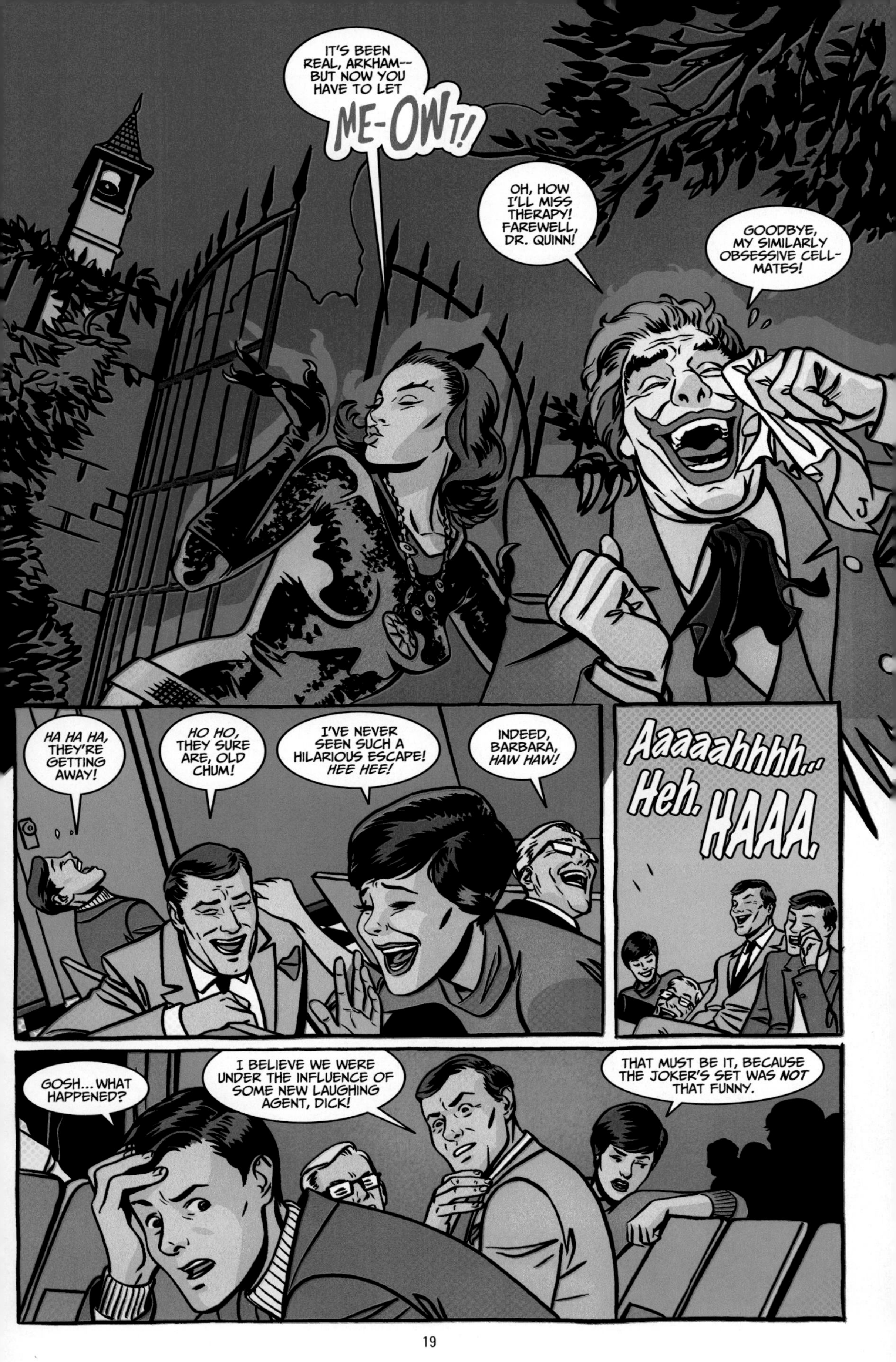
IT'S BEEN REAL, ARKHAM-- BUT NOW YOU HAVE TO LET
ME-OWT!
OH, HOW I'LL MISS THERAPY! FAREWELL, DR. QUINN!
GOODBYE, MY SIMILARLY OBSESSIVE CELL-MATES!
HA HA HA, THEY'RE GETTING AWAY!
HO HO, THEY SURE ARE, OLD CHUM!
I'VE NEVER SEEN SUCH A HILARIOUS ESCAPE! HEE HEE!
INDEED, BARBARA, HAW HAW!
Aaaaahhhh... Heh. HAAA.
GOSH...WHAT HAPPENED?
I BELIEVE WE WERE UNDER THE INFLUENCE OF SOME NEW LAUGHING AGENT, DICK!
THAT MUST BE IT, BECAUSE THE JOKER'S SET WAS NOT THAT FUNNY.

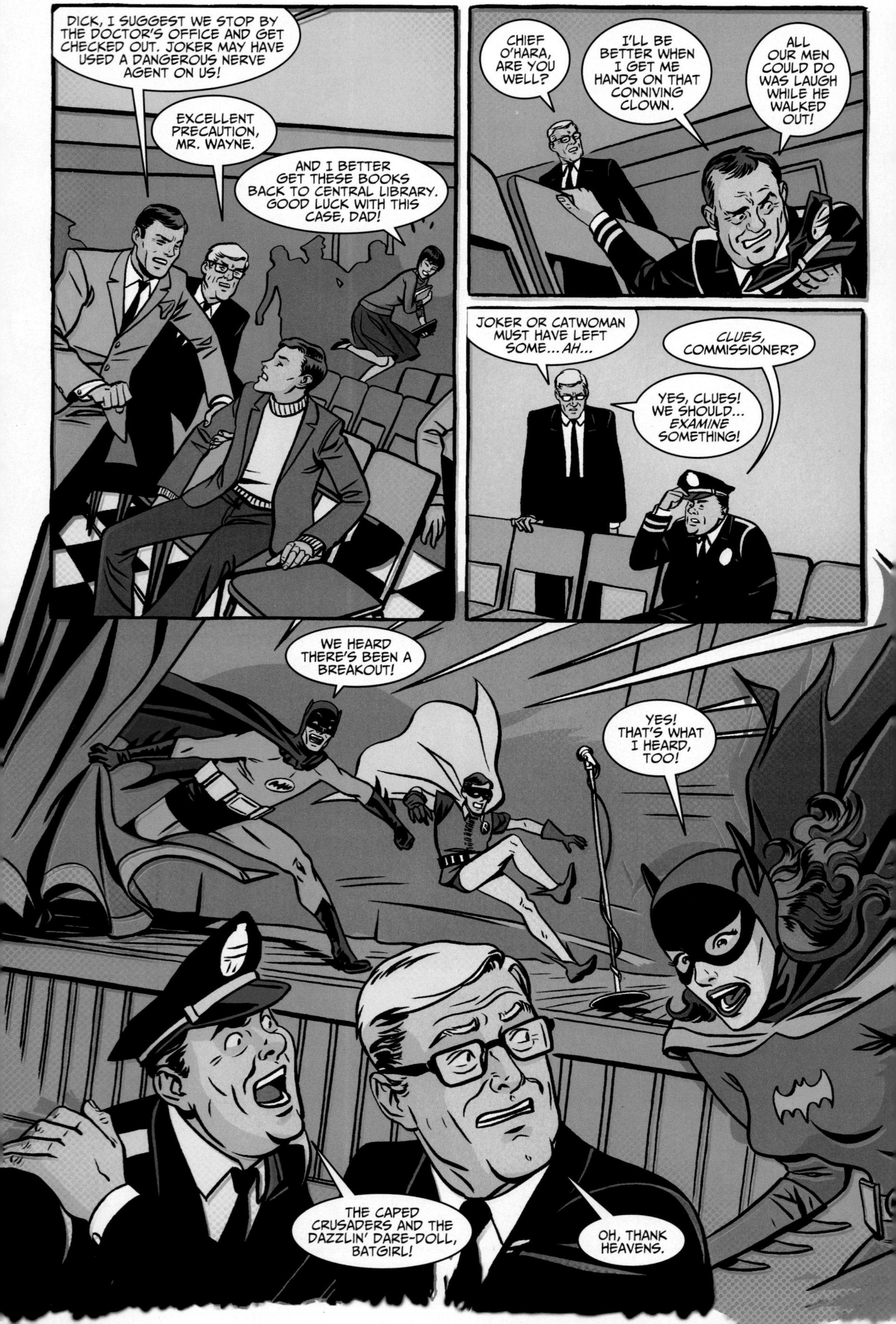
DICK, I SUGGEST WE STOP BY THE DOCTOR'S OFFICE AND GET CHECKED OUT. JOKER MAY HAVE USED A DANGEROUS NERVE AGENT ON US!
EXCELLENT PRECAUTION, MR. WAYNE.
AND I BETTER GET THESE BOOKS BACK TO CENTRAL LIBRARY. GOOD LUCK WITH THIS CASE, DAD!
CHIEF O'HARA, ARE YOU WELL?
I'LL BE BETTER WHEN I GET ME HANDS ON THAT CONNIVING CLOWN.
ALL OUR MEN COULD DO WAS LAUGH WHILE HE WALKED OUT!
JOKER OR CATWOMAN MUST HAVE LEFT SOME... *AH*...
CLUES, COMMISSIONER?
YES, CLUES! WE SHOULD... *EXAMINE* SOMETHING!
WE HEARD THERE'S BEEN A BREAKOUT!
YES! THAT'S WHAT I HEARD, TOO!
THE CAPED CRUSADERS AND THE DAZZLIN' DARE-DOLL, BATGIRL!
OH, THANK HEAVENS.

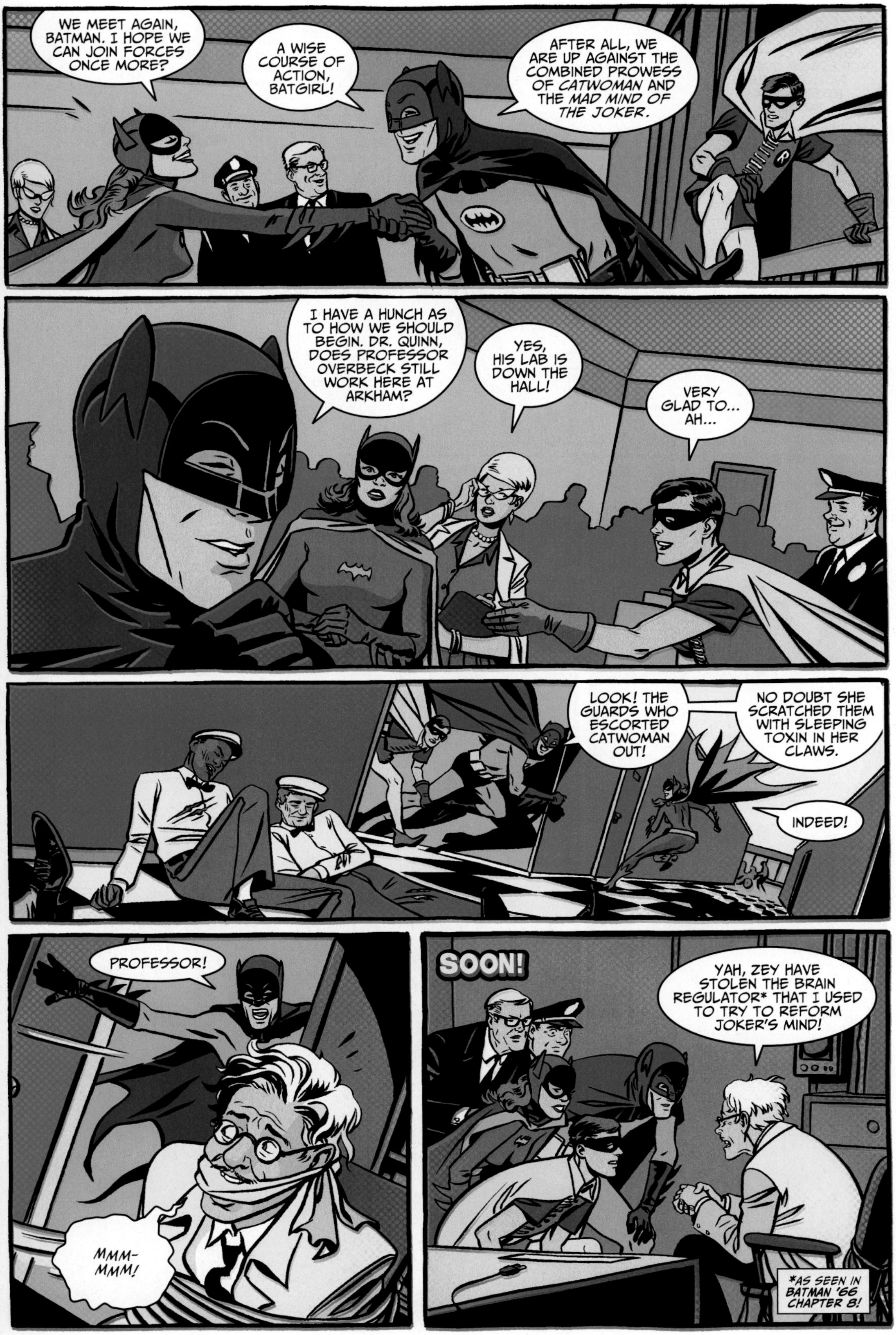
WE MEET AGAIN, BATMAN. I HOPE WE CAN JOIN FORCES ONCE MORE?
A WISE COURSE OF ACTION, BATGIRL!
AFTER ALL, WE ARE UP AGAINST THE COMBINED PROWESS OF CATWOMAN AND THE MAD MIND OF THE JOKER.
I HAVE A HUNCH AS TO HOW WE SHOULD BEGIN. DR. QUINN, DOES PROFESSOR OVERBECK STILL WORK HERE AT ARKHAM?
YES, HIS LAB IS DOWN THE HALL!
VERY GLAD TO... AH...
LOOK! THE GUARDS WHO ESCORTED CATWOMAN OUT!
NO DOUBT SHE SCRATCHED THEM WITH SLEEPING TOXIN IN HER CLAWS.
INDEED!
PROFESSOR!
MMM-MMM!
SOON!
YAH, ZEY HAVE STOLEN THE BRAIN REGULATOR* THAT I USED TO TRY TO REFORM JOKER'S MIND!
*AS SEEN IN BATMAN '66 CHAPTER 8!

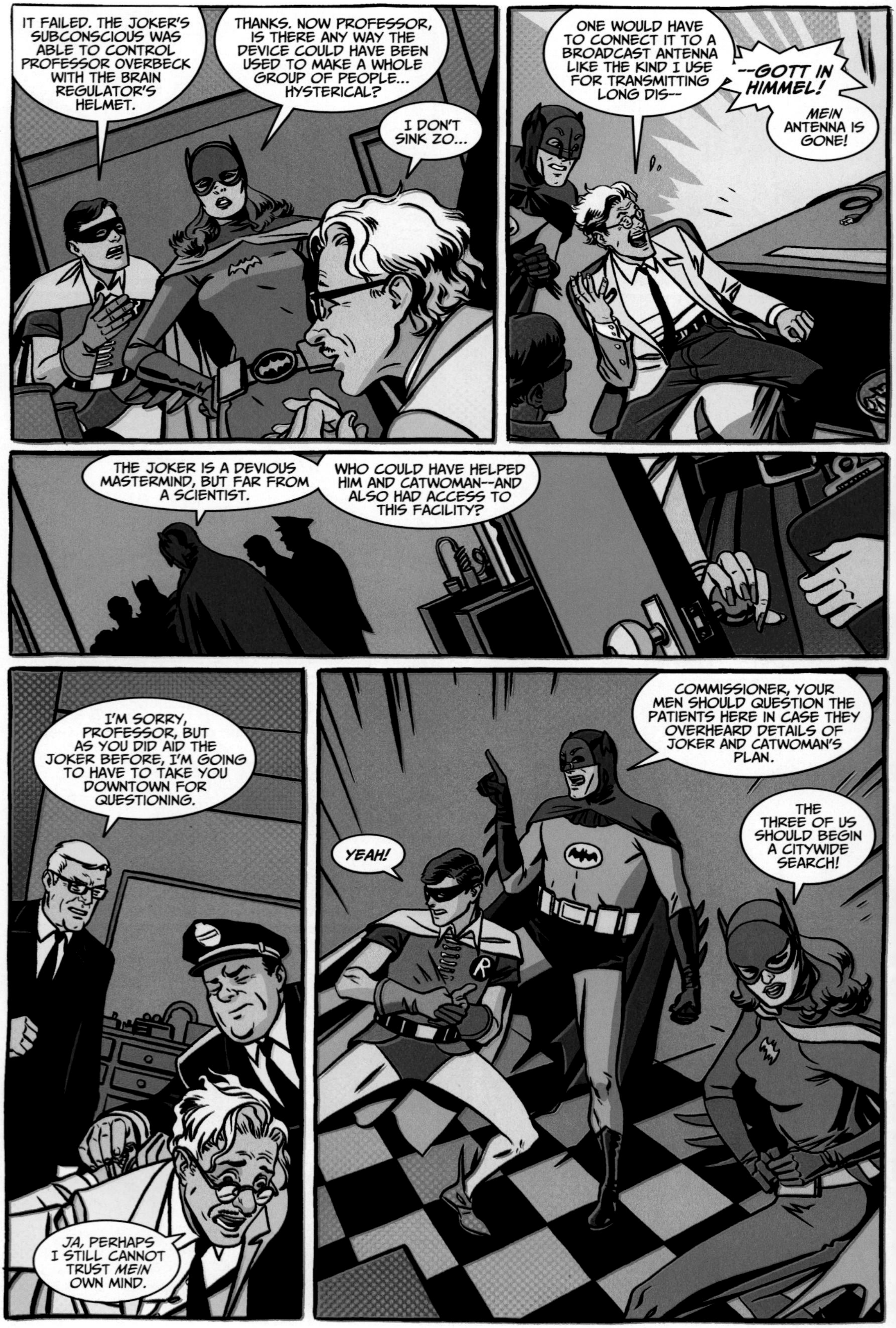
IT FAILED. THE JOKER'S SUBCONSCIOUS WAS ABLE TO CONTROL PROFESSOR OVERBECK WITH THE BRAIN REGULATOR'S HELMET.
THANKS. NOW PROFESSOR, IS THERE ANY WAY THE DEVICE COULD HAVE BEEN USED TO MAKE A WHOLE GROUP OF PEOPLE... HYSTERICAL?
I DON'T SINK ZO...
ONE WOULD HAVE TO CONNECT IT TO A BROADCAST ANTENNA LIKE THE KIND I USE FOR TRANSMITTING LONG DIS--
--GOTT IN HIMMEL!
MEIN ANTENNA IS GONE!
THE JOKER IS A DEVIOUS MASTERMIND, BUT FAR FROM A SCIENTIST.
WHO COULD HAVE HELPED HIM AND CATWOMAN--AND ALSO HAD ACCESS TO THIS FACILITY?
I'M SORRY, PROFESSOR, BUT AS YOU DID AID THE JOKER BEFORE, I'M GOING TO HAVE TO TAKE YOU DOWNTOWN FOR QUESTIONING.
JA, PERHAPS I STILL CANNOT TRUST MEIN OWN MIND.
COMMISSIONER, YOUR MEN SHOULD QUESTION THE PATIENTS HERE IN CASE THEY OVERHEARD DETAILS OF JOKER AND CATWOMAN'S PLAN.
YEAH!
THE THREE OF US SHOULD BEGIN A CITYWIDE SEARCH!

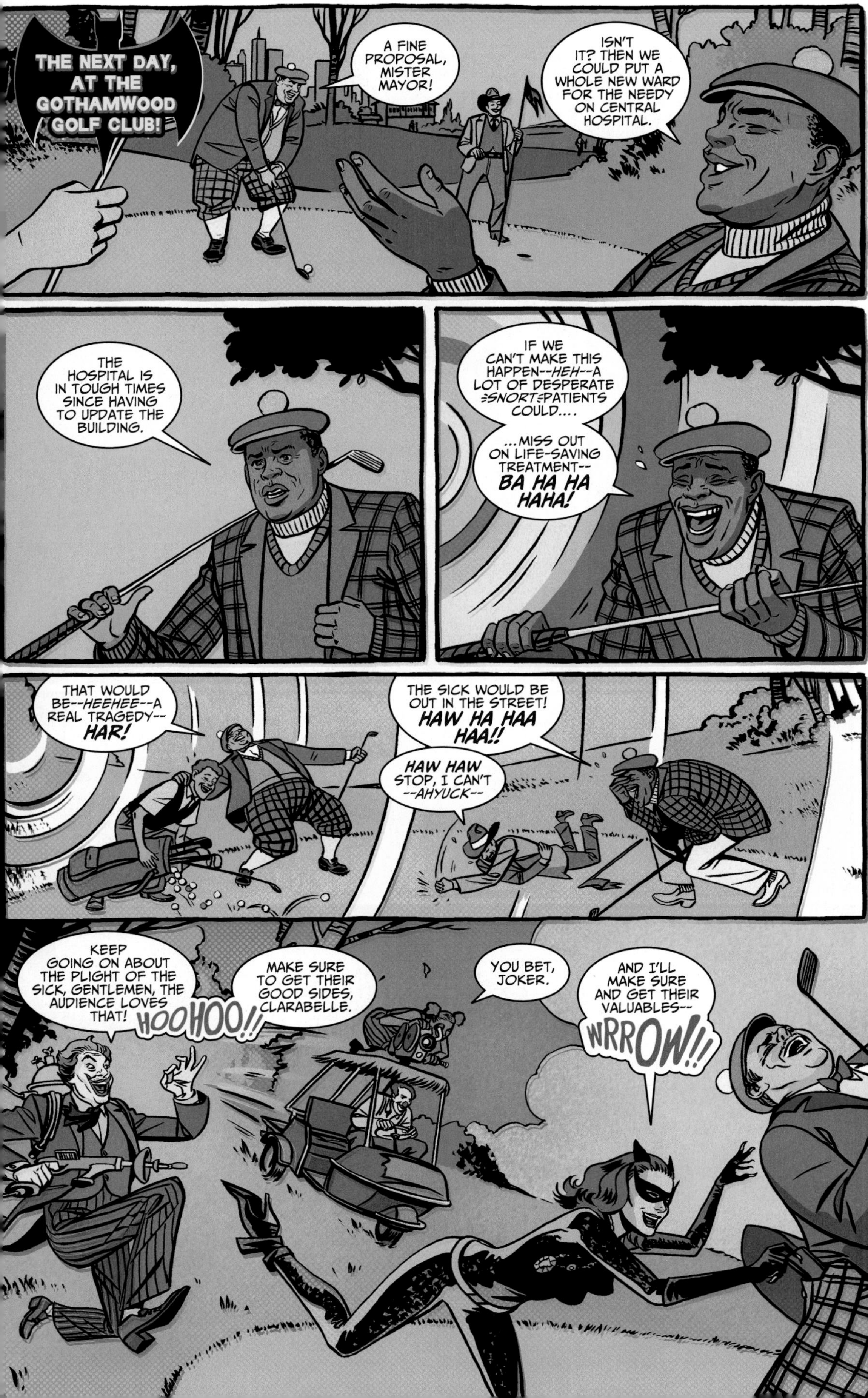
THE NEXT DAY, AT THE GOTHAMWOOD GOLF CLUB!
A FINE PROPOSAL, MISTER MAYOR!
ISN'T IT? THEN WE COULD PUT A WHOLE NEW WARD FOR THE NEEDY ON CENTRAL HOSPITAL.
THE HOSPITAL IS IN TOUGH TIMES SINCE HAVING TO UPDATE THE BUILDING.
IF WE CAN'T MAKE THIS HAPPEN--*HEH*--A LOT OF DESPERATE =*SNORT*= PATIENTS COULD....
...MISS OUT ON LIFE-SAVING TREATMENT-- **BA HA HA HAHA!**
THAT WOULD BE--*HEEHEE*--A REAL TRAGEDY-- **HAR!**
THE SICK WOULD BE OUT IN THE STREET! **HAW HA HAA HAA!!**
HAW HAW STOP, I CAN'T --*AHYUCK*--
KEEP GOING ON ABOUT THE PLIGHT OF THE SICK, GENTLEMEN, THE AUDIENCE LOVES THAT!
HOOHOO!!
MAKE SURE TO GET THEIR GOOD SIDES, CLARABELLE.
YOU BET, JOKER.
AND I'LL MAKE SURE AND GET THEIR VALUABLES--
WRROW!!

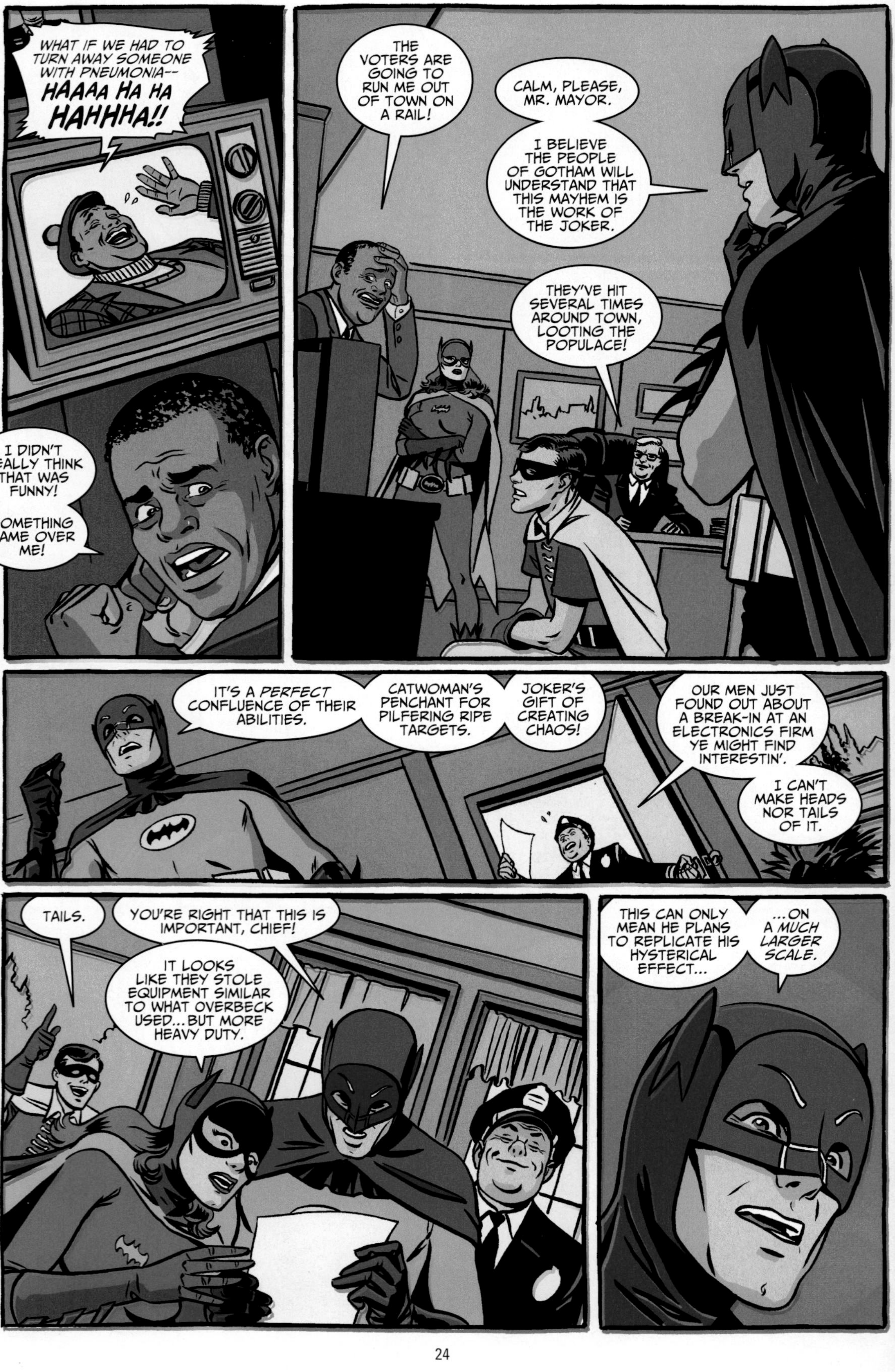

WHAT IF WE HAD TO TURN AWAY SOMEONE WITH PNEUMONIA-- HAAAA HA HA HAHHHA!!
I DIDN'T REALLY THINK THAT WAS FUNNY!
SOMETHING CAME OVER ME!
THE VOTERS ARE GOING TO RUN ME OUT OF TOWN ON A RAIL!
CALM, PLEASE, MR. MAYOR.
I BELIEVE THE PEOPLE OF GOTHAM WILL UNDERSTAND THAT THIS MAYHEM IS THE WORK OF THE JOKER.
THEY'VE HIT SEVERAL TIMES AROUND TOWN, LOOTING THE POPULACE!
IT'S A *PERFECT* CONFLUENCE OF THEIR ABILITIES.
CATWOMAN'S PENCHANT FOR PILFERING RIPE TARGETS.
JOKER'S GIFT OF CREATING CHAOS!
OUR MEN JUST FOUND OUT ABOUT A BREAK-IN AT AN ELECTRONICS FIRM YE MIGHT FIND INTERESTIN'.
I CAN'T MAKE HEADS NOR TAILS OF IT.
TAILS.
YOU'RE RIGHT THAT THIS IS IMPORTANT, CHIEF!
IT LOOKS LIKE THEY STOLE EQUIPMENT SIMILAR TO WHAT OVERBECK USED... BUT MORE HEAVY DUTY.
THIS CAN ONLY MEAN HE PLANS TO REPLICATE HIS HYSTERICAL EFFECT...
...ON A *MUCH LARGER* SCALE.

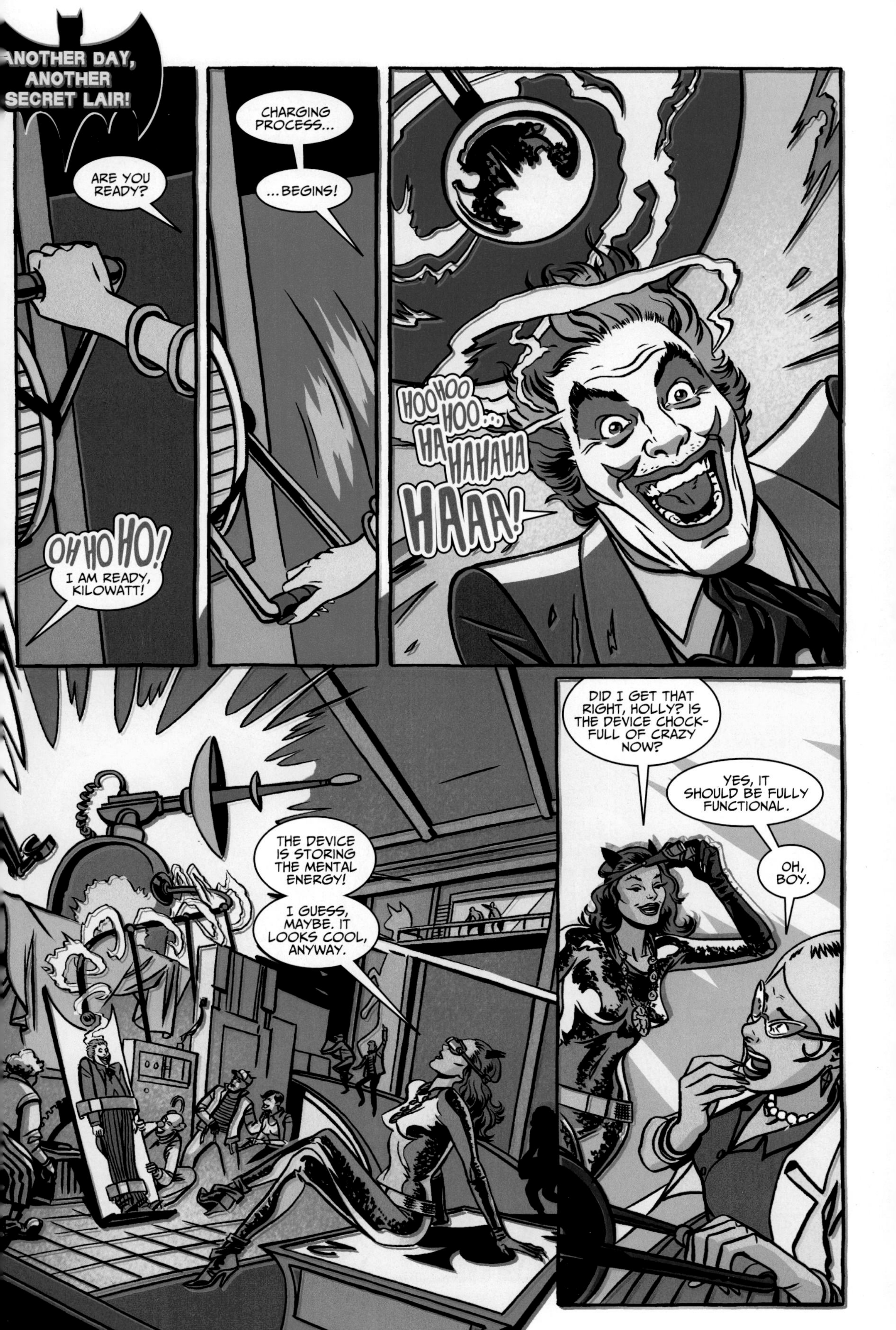
ANOTHER DAY, ANOTHER SECRET LAIR!
ARE YOU READY?
OH HO HO!
I AM READY, KILOWATT!
CHARGING PROCESS...
...BEGINS!
HOOHOO HOO...
HA HAHAHA
HAAA!
THE DEVICE IS STORING THE MENTAL ENERGY!
I GUESS, MAYBE. IT LOOKS COOL, ANYWAY.
DID I GET THAT RIGHT, HOLLY? IS THE DEVICE CHOCK-FULL OF CRAZY NOW?
YES, IT SHOULD BE FULLY FUNCTIONAL.
OH, BOY.

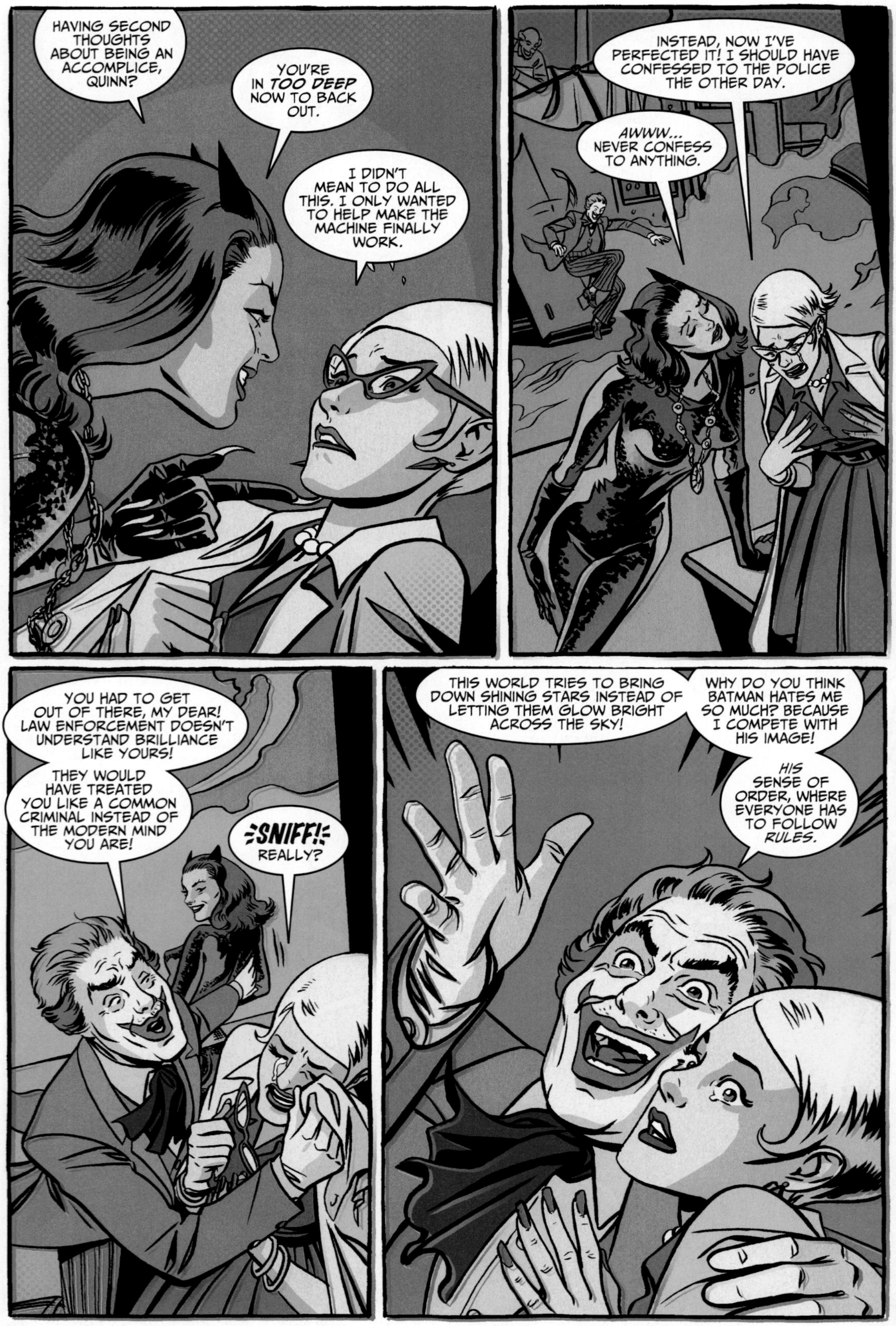
HAVING SECOND THOUGHTS ABOUT BEING AN ACCOMPLICE, QUINN?
YOU'RE IN *TOO DEEP* NOW TO BACK OUT.
I DIDN'T MEAN TO DO ALL THIS. I ONLY WANTED TO HELP MAKE THE MACHINE FINALLY WORK.
INSTEAD, NOW I'VE PERFECTED IT! I SHOULD HAVE CONFESSED TO THE POLICE THE OTHER DAY.
AWWW... NEVER CONFESS TO ANYTHING.
YOU HAD TO GET OUT OF THERE, MY DEAR! LAW ENFORCEMENT DOESN'T UNDERSTAND BRILLIANCE LIKE YOURS!
THEY WOULD HAVE TREATED YOU LIKE A COMMON CRIMINAL INSTEAD OF THE MODERN MIND YOU ARE!
SNIFF! REALLY?
THIS WORLD TRIES TO BRING DOWN SHINING STARS INSTEAD OF LETTING THEM GLOW BRIGHT ACROSS THE SKY!
WHY DO YOU THINK BATMAN HATES ME SO MUCH? BECAUSE I COMPETE WITH HIS IMAGE!
HIS SENSE OF ORDER, WHERE EVERYONE HAS TO FOLLOW *RULES*.

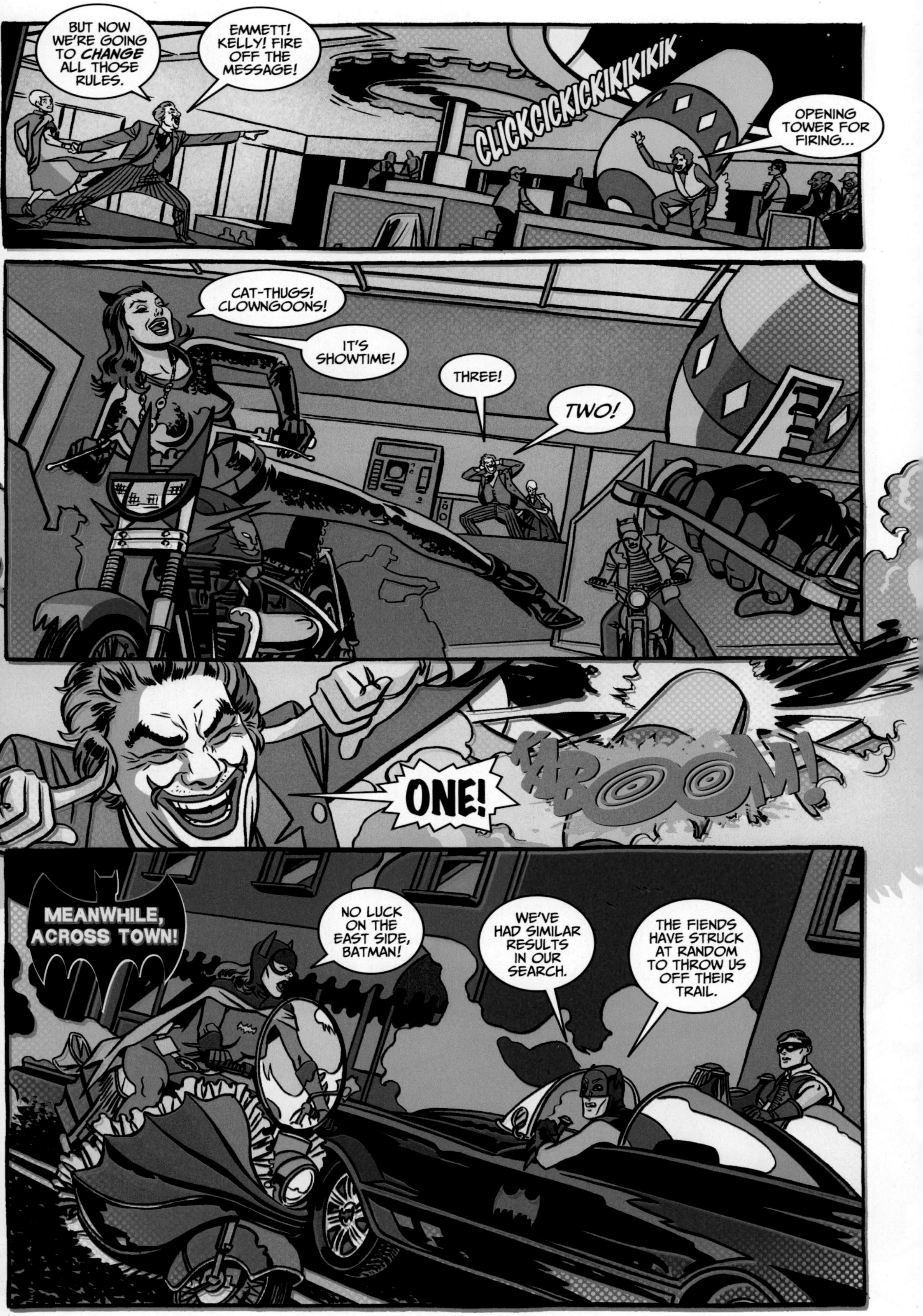
BUT NOW WE'RE GOING TO CHANGE ALL THOSE RULES.
EMMETT! KELLY! FIRE OFF THE MESSAGE!
CLICKCICKICKIKIKIKIK
OPENING TOWER FOR FIRING...
CAT-THUGS! CLOWNGOONS!
IT'S SHOWTIME!
THREE!
TWO!
ONE!
KABOOM!
MEANWHILE, ACROSS TOWN!
NO LUCK ON THE EAST SIDE, BATMAN!
WE'VE HAD SIMILAR RESULTS IN OUR SEARCH.
THE FIENDS HAVE STRUCK AT RANDOM TO THROW US OFF THEIR TRAIL.

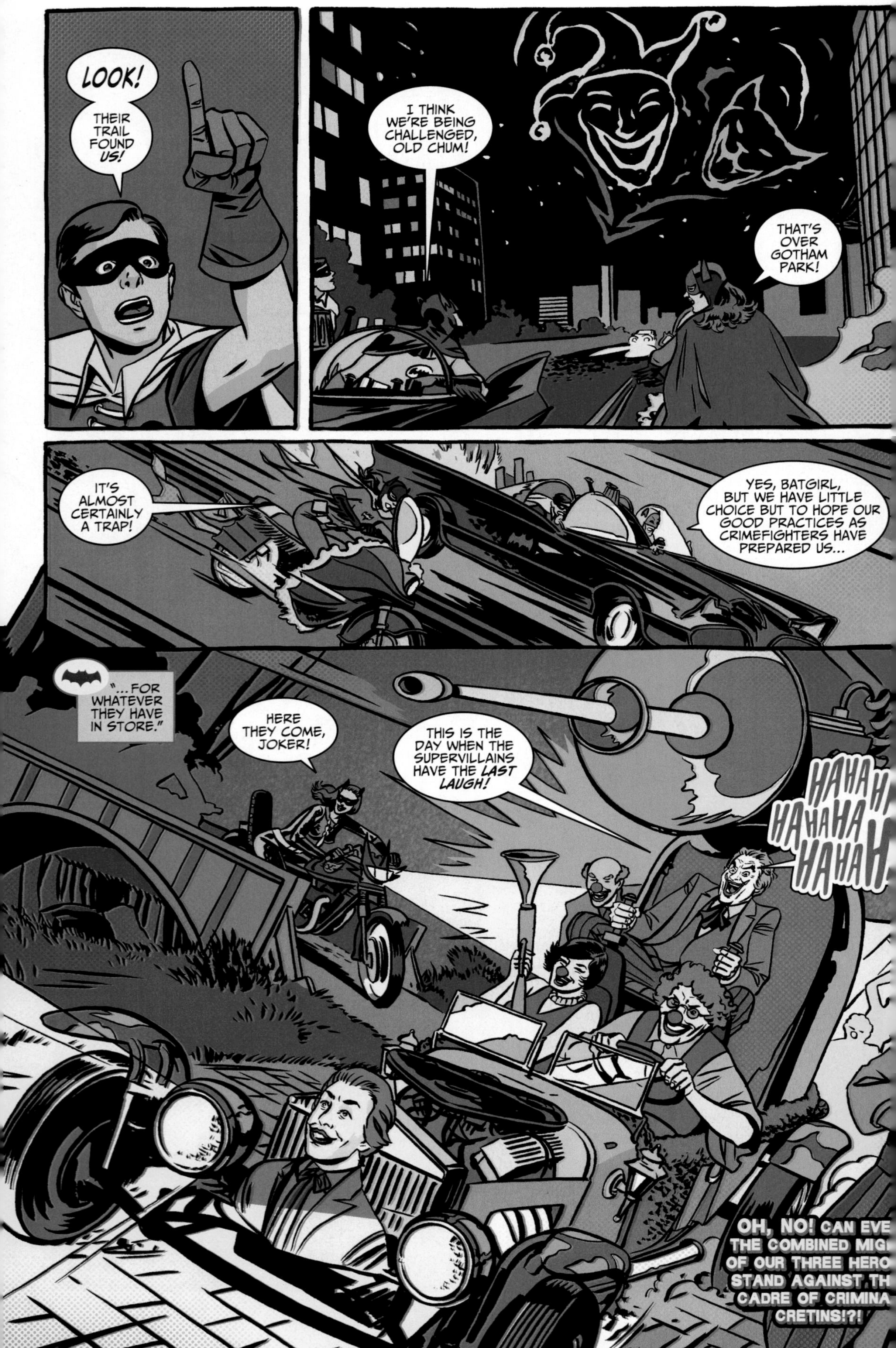
LOOK! THEIR TRAIL FOUND US!
I THINK WE'RE BEING CHALLENGED, OLD CHUM!
THAT'S OVER GOTHAM PARK!
IT'S ALMOST CERTAINLY A TRAP!
YES, BATGIRL, BUT WE HAVE LITTLE CHOICE BUT TO HOPE OUR GOOD PRACTICES AS CRIMEFIGHTERS HAVE PREPARED US...
"...FOR WHATEVER THEY HAVE IN STORE."
HERE THEY COME, JOKER!
THIS IS THE DAY WHEN THE SUPERVILLAINS HAVE THE LAST LAUGH!
HAHAHAHAHAHAHAHA
OH, NO! CAN EVE THE COMBINED MIG OF OUR THREE HERO STAND AGAINST TH CADRE OF CRIMINA CRETINS!?!

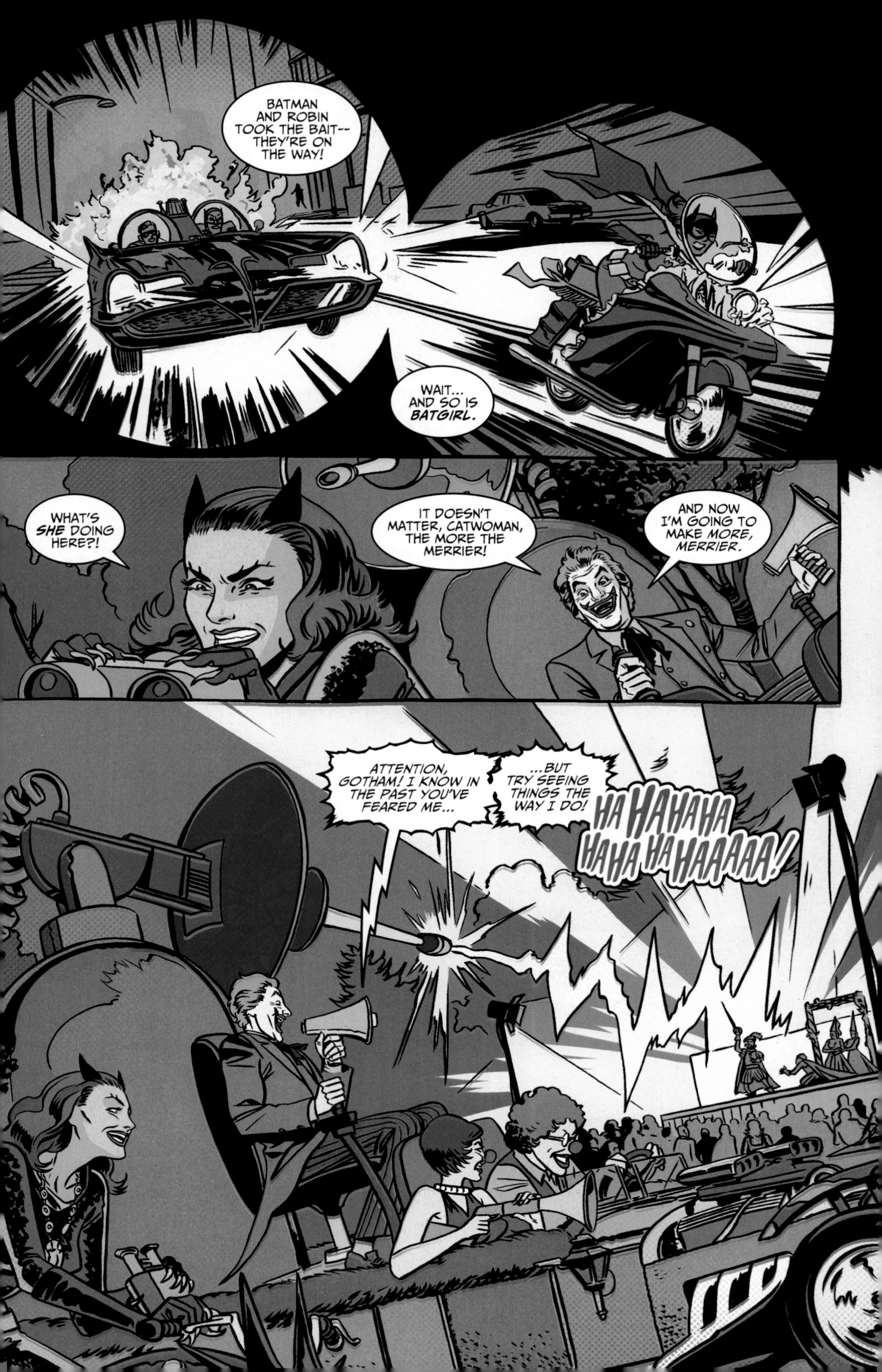
BATMAN AND ROBIN TOOK THE BAIT-- THEY'RE ON THE WAY!
WAIT... AND SO IS BATGIRL.
WHAT'S SHE DOING HERE?!
IT DOESN'T MATTER, CATWOMAN, THE MORE THE MERRIER!
AND NOW I'M GOING TO MAKE MORE, MERRIER.
ATTENTION, GOTHAM! I KNOW IN THE PAST YOU'VE FEARED ME...
...BUT TRY SEEING THINGS THE WAY I DO!
HA HAHAHA HAHA HA HAAAAAA!

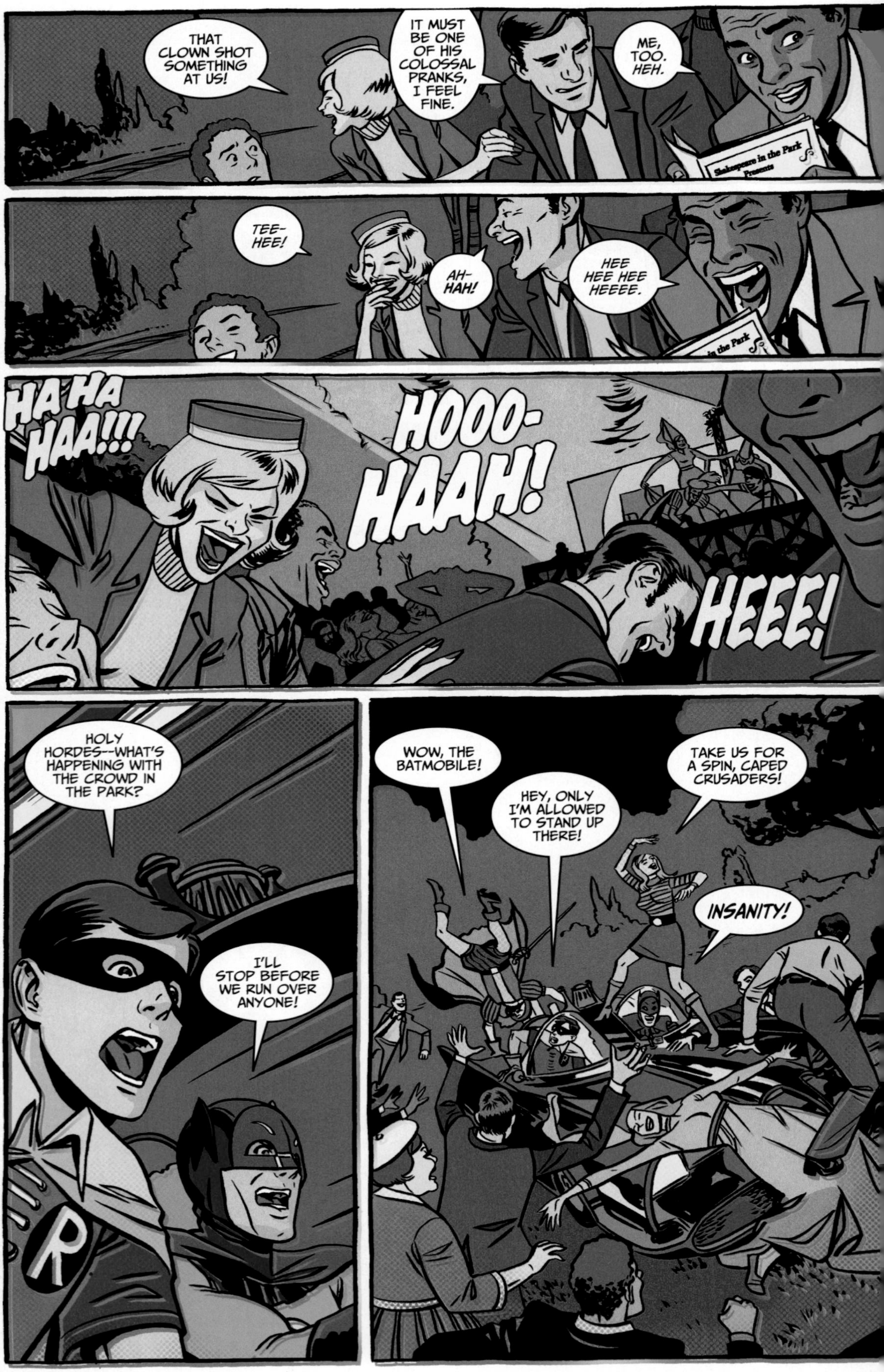
THAT CLOWN SHOT SOMETHING AT US!
IT MUST BE ONE OF HIS COLOSSAL PRANKS, I FEEL FINE.
ME, TOO. HEH.
Shakespeare in the Park Presents
TEE-HEE!
AH-HAH!
HEE HEE HEE HEEEE.
in the Park
HA HA HAA!!!
HOOO-HAAAH!
HEEE!
HOLY HORDES--WHAT'S HAPPENING WITH THE CROWD IN THE PARK?
I'LL STOP BEFORE WE RUN OVER ANYONE!
WOW, THE BATMOBILE!
HEY, ONLY I'M ALLOWED TO STAND UP THERE!
TAKE US FOR A SPIN, CAPED CRUSADERS!
INSANITY!

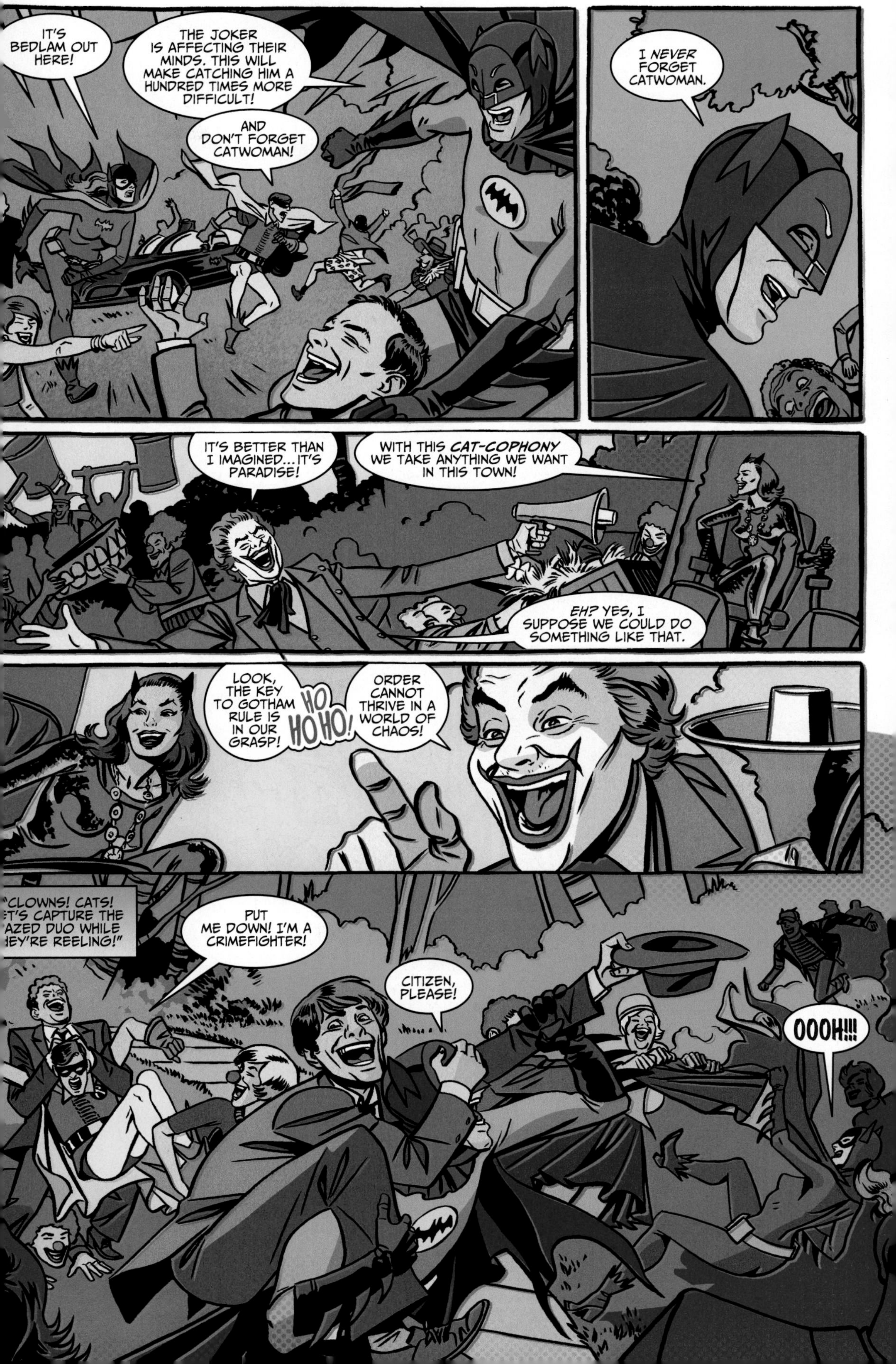
IT'S BEDLAM OUT HERE!
THE JOKER IS AFFECTING THEIR MINDS. THIS WILL MAKE CATCHING HIM A HUNDRED TIMES MORE DIFFICULT!
AND DON'T FORGET CATWOMAN!
I NEVER FORGET CATWOMAN.
IT'S BETTER THAN I IMAGINED...IT'S PARADISE!
WITH THIS CAT-COPHONY WE TAKE ANYTHING WE WANT IN THIS TOWN!
EH? YES, I SUPPOSE WE COULD DO SOMETHING LIKE THAT.
LOOK, THE KEY TO GOTHAM RULE IS IN OUR GRASP!
HO HO HO!
ORDER CANNOT THRIVE IN A WORLD OF CHAOS!
"CLOWNS! CATS! ...T'S CAPTURE THE ...AZED DUO WHILE ...HEY'RE REELING!"
PUT ME DOWN! I'M A CRIMEFIGHTER!
CITIZEN, PLEASE!
OOOH!!!

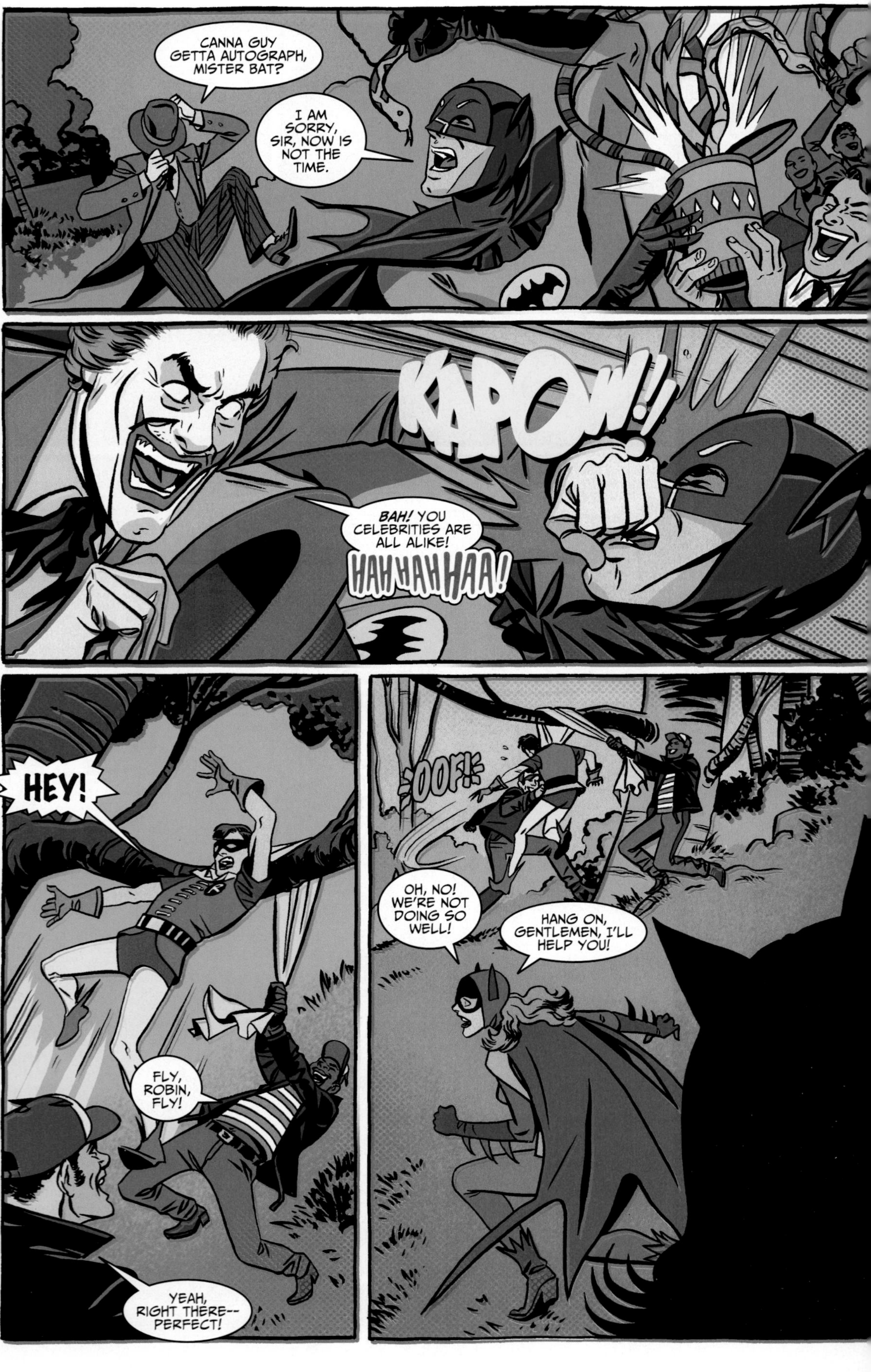
CANNA GUY GETTA AUTOGRAPH, MISTER BAT?
I AM SORRY, SIR, NOW IS NOT THE TIME.
KAPOW!!
BAH! YOU CELEBRITIES ARE ALL ALIKE!
HAH HAH HAA!
HEY!
FLY, ROBIN, FLY!
YEAH, RIGHT THERE--PERFECT!
OOF!
OH, NO! WE'RE NOT DOING SO WELL!
HANG ON, GENTLEMEN, I'LL HELP YOU!

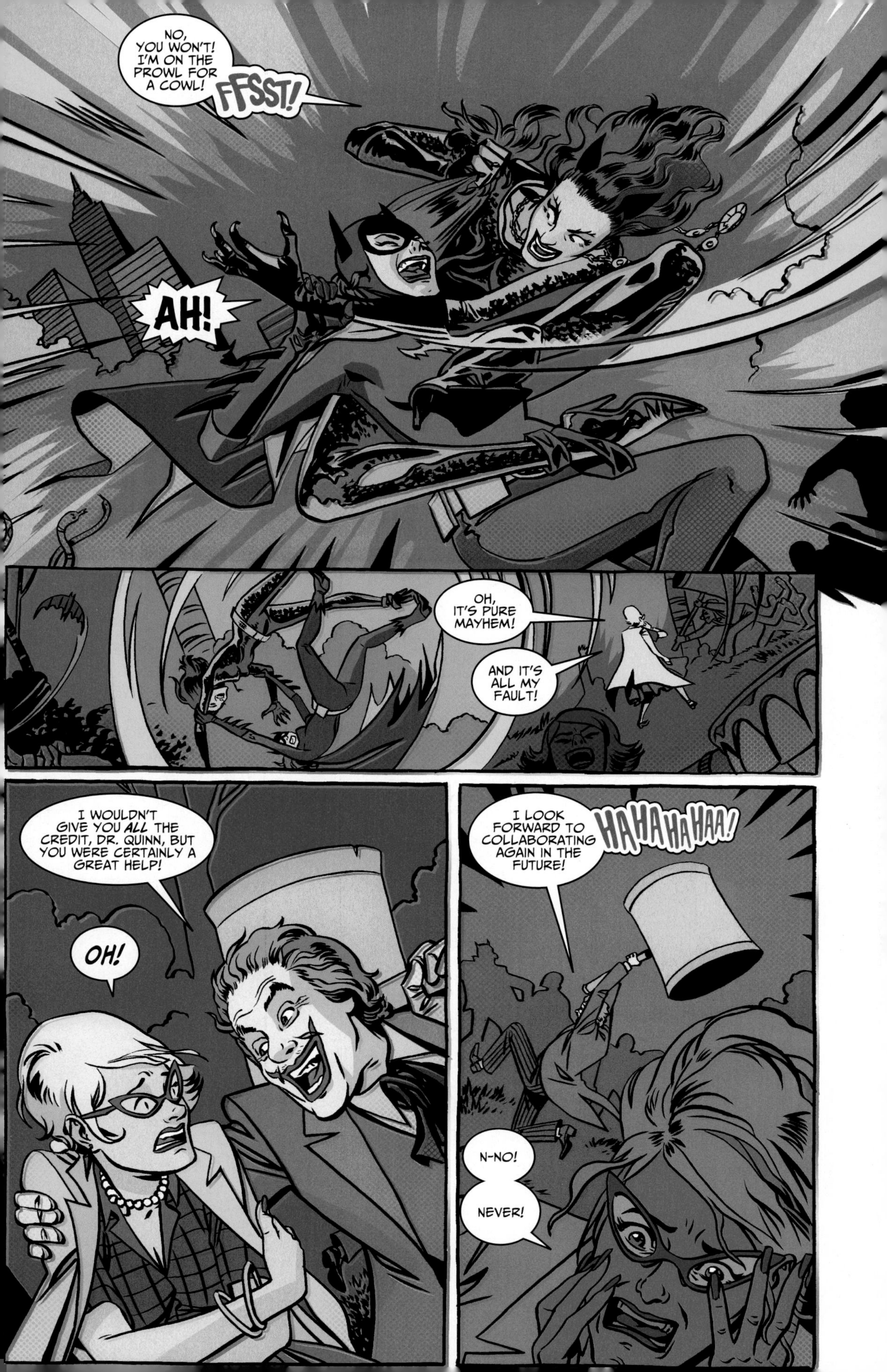
NO, YOU WON'T! I'M ON THE PROWL FOR A COWL!
FFSST!
AH!
OH, IT'S PURE MAYHEM!
AND IT'S ALL MY FAULT!
I WOULDN'T GIVE YOU *ALL* THE CREDIT, DR. QUINN, BUT YOU WERE CERTAINLY A GREAT HELP!
OH!
I LOOK FORWARD TO COLLABORATING AGAIN IN THE FUTURE!
HAHAHAHAA!
N-NO!
NEVER!

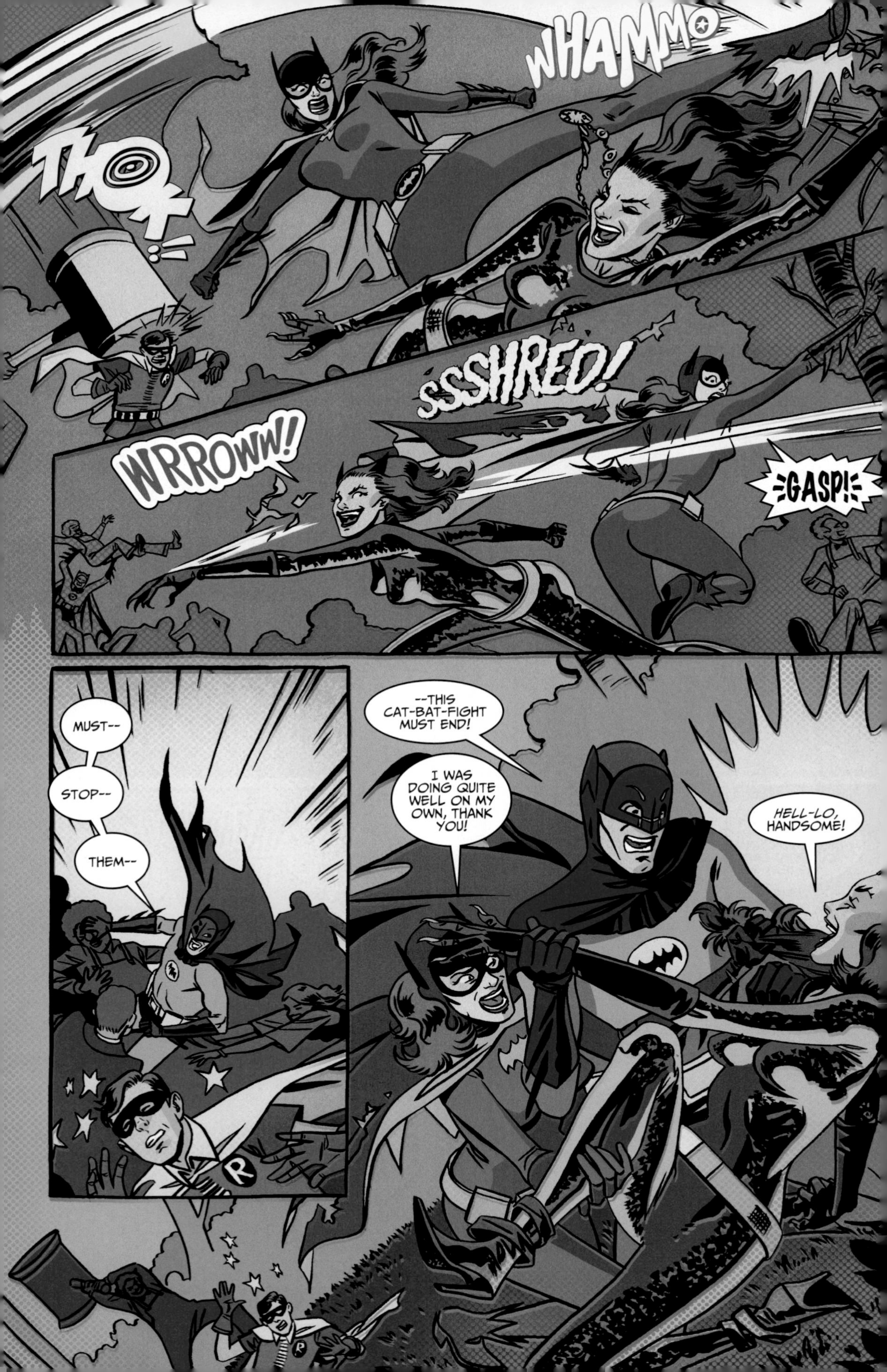
WHAMMO
THOK!!
SSSHRED!
WRROWW!!
GASP!
MUST--
STOP--
THEM--
--THIS CAT-BAT-FIGHT MUST END!
I WAS DOING QUITE WELL ON MY OWN, THANK YOU!
HELL-LO, HANDSOME!

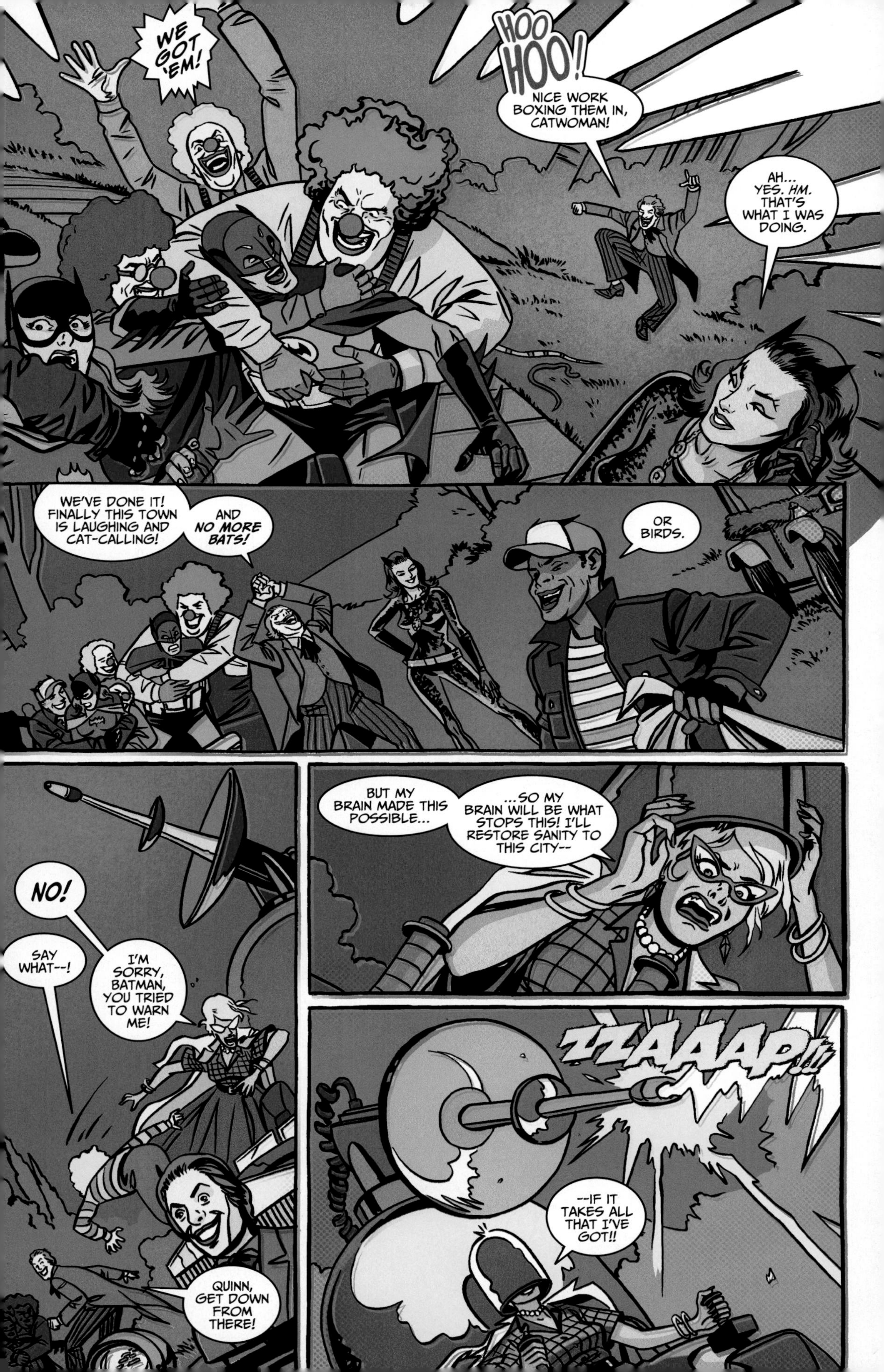
WE GOT 'EM!
HOO HOO!
NICE WORK BOXING THEM IN, CATWOMAN!
AH... YES. HM. THAT'S WHAT I WAS DOING.
WE'VE DONE IT! FINALLY THIS TOWN IS LAUGHING AND CAT-CALLING!
AND NO MORE BATS!
OR BIRDS.
NO!
SAY WHAT--!
I'M SORRY, BATMAN, YOU TRIED TO WARN ME!
QUINN, GET DOWN FROM THERE!
BUT MY BRAIN MADE THIS POSSIBLE...
...SO MY BRAIN WILL BE WHAT STOPS THIS! I'LL RESTORE SANITY TO THIS CITY--
ZZAAAP!!
--IF IT TAKES ALL THAT I'VE GOT!!

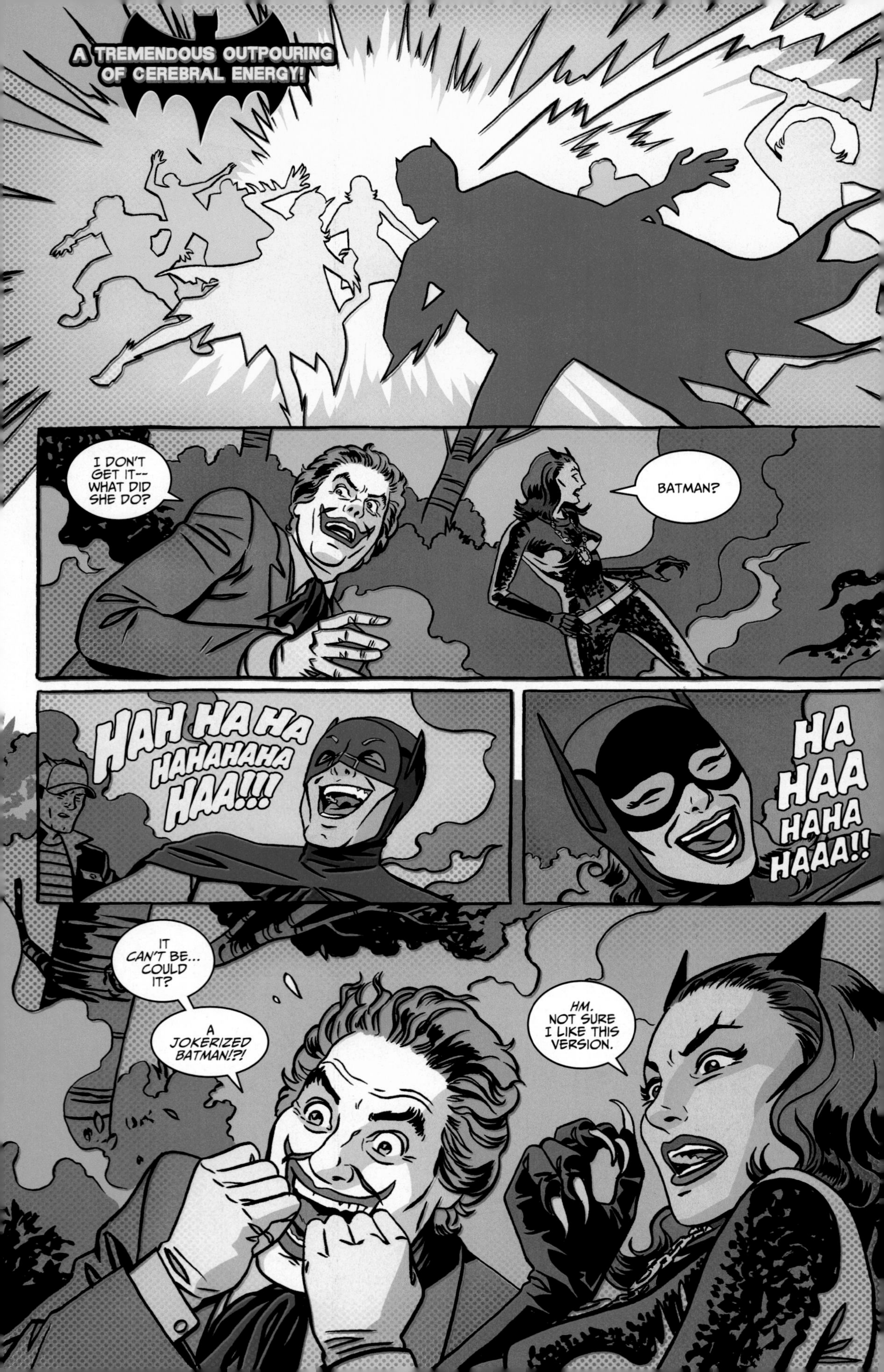
A TREMENDOUS OUTPOURING OF CEREBRAL ENERGY!
I DON'T GET IT-- WHAT DID SHE DO?
BATMAN?
HAH HA HA HAHAHAHA HAA!!!
HA HAA HAHA HAAA!!
IT CAN'T BE... COULD IT?
A JOKERIZED BATMAN!?!
HM. NOT SURE I LIKE THIS VERSION.

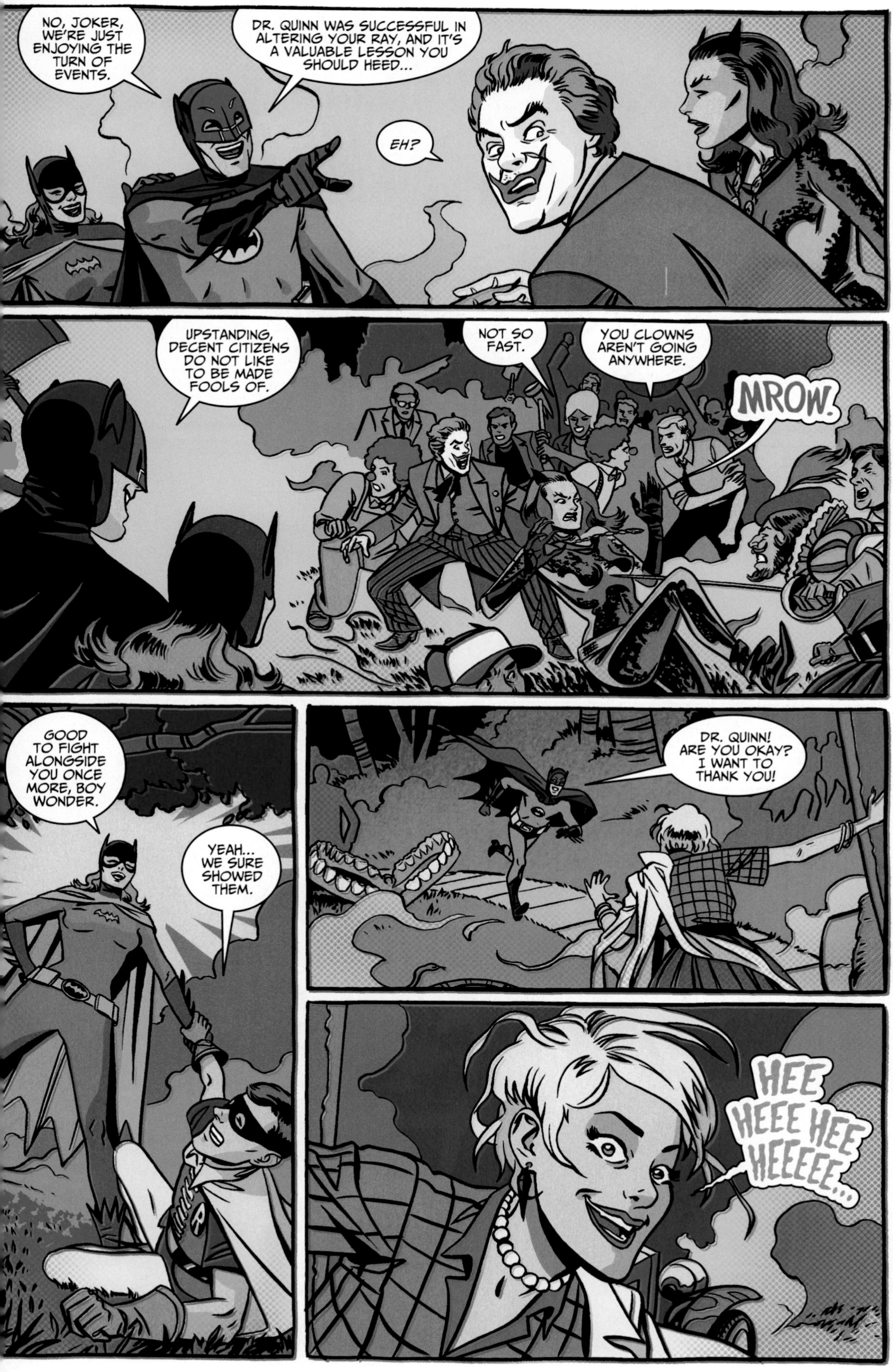
NO, JOKER, WE'RE JUST ENJOYING THE TURN OF EVENTS.
DR. QUINN WAS SUCCESSFUL IN ALTERING YOUR RAY, AND IT'S A VALUABLE LESSON YOU SHOULD HEED...
EH?
UPSTANDING, DECENT CITIZENS DO NOT LIKE TO BE MADE FOOLS OF.
NOT SO FAST.
YOU CLOWNS AREN'T GOING ANYWHERE.
MROW.
GOOD TO FIGHT ALONGSIDE YOU ONCE MORE, BOY WONDER.
YEAH... WE SURE SHOWED THEM.
DR. QUINN! ARE YOU OKAY? I WANT TO THANK YOU!
HEE HEEE HEE HEEEEE...

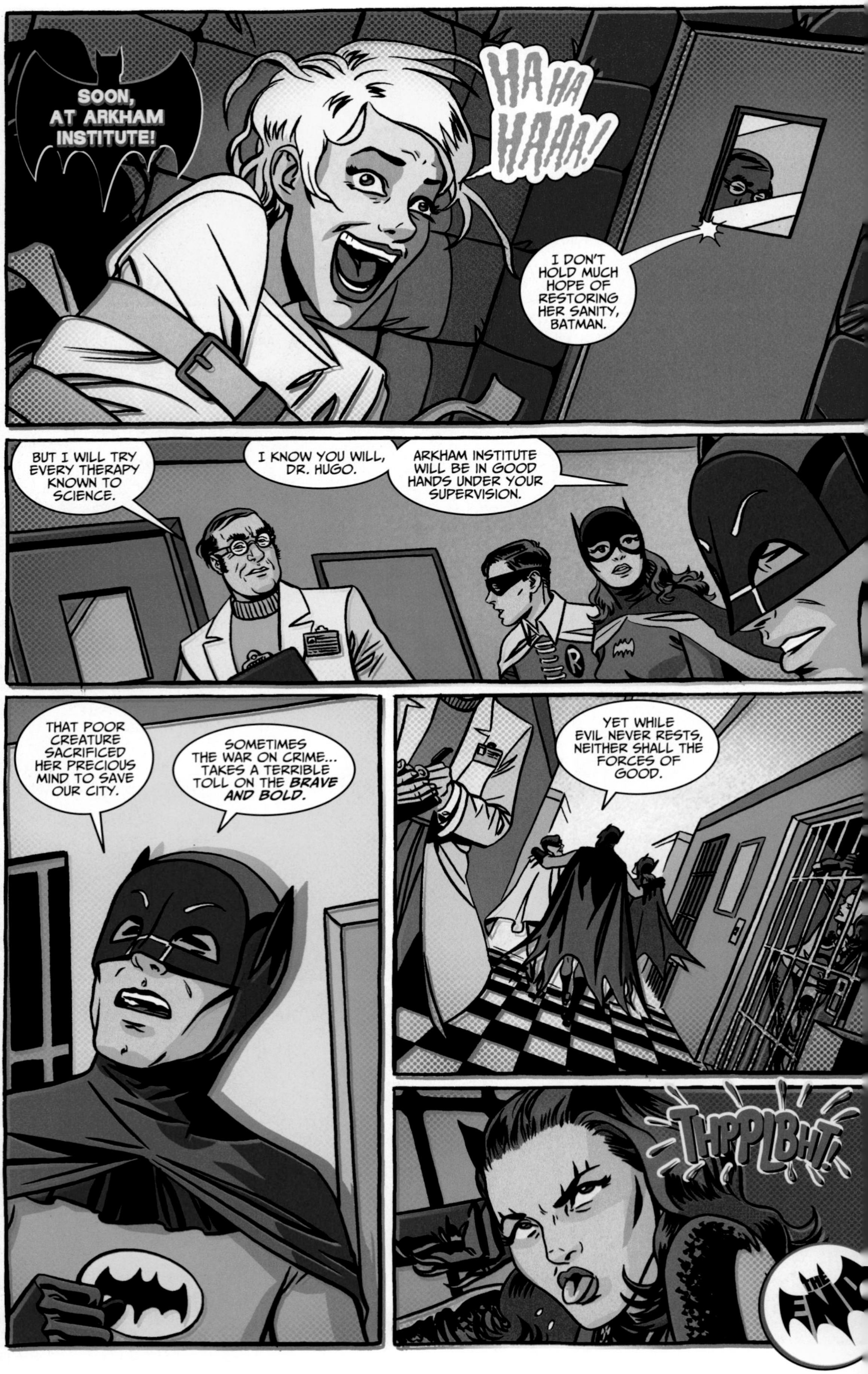
SOON, AT ARKHAM INSTITUTE!
HAHAHAAA!
I DON'T HOLD MUCH HOPE OF RESTORING HER SANITY, BATMAN.
BUT I WILL TRY EVERY THERAPY KNOWN TO SCIENCE.
I KNOW YOU WILL, DR. HUGO.
ARKHAM INSTITUTE WILL BE IN GOOD HANDS UNDER YOUR SUPERVISION.
THAT POOR CREATURE SACRIFICED HER PRECIOUS MIND TO SAVE OUR CITY.
SOMETIMES THE WAR ON CRIME... TAKES A TERRIBLE TOLL ON THE *BRAVE AND BOLD.*
YET WHILE EVIL NEVER RESTS, NEITHER SHALL THE FORCES OF GOOD.
THPPLBHT!
THE END

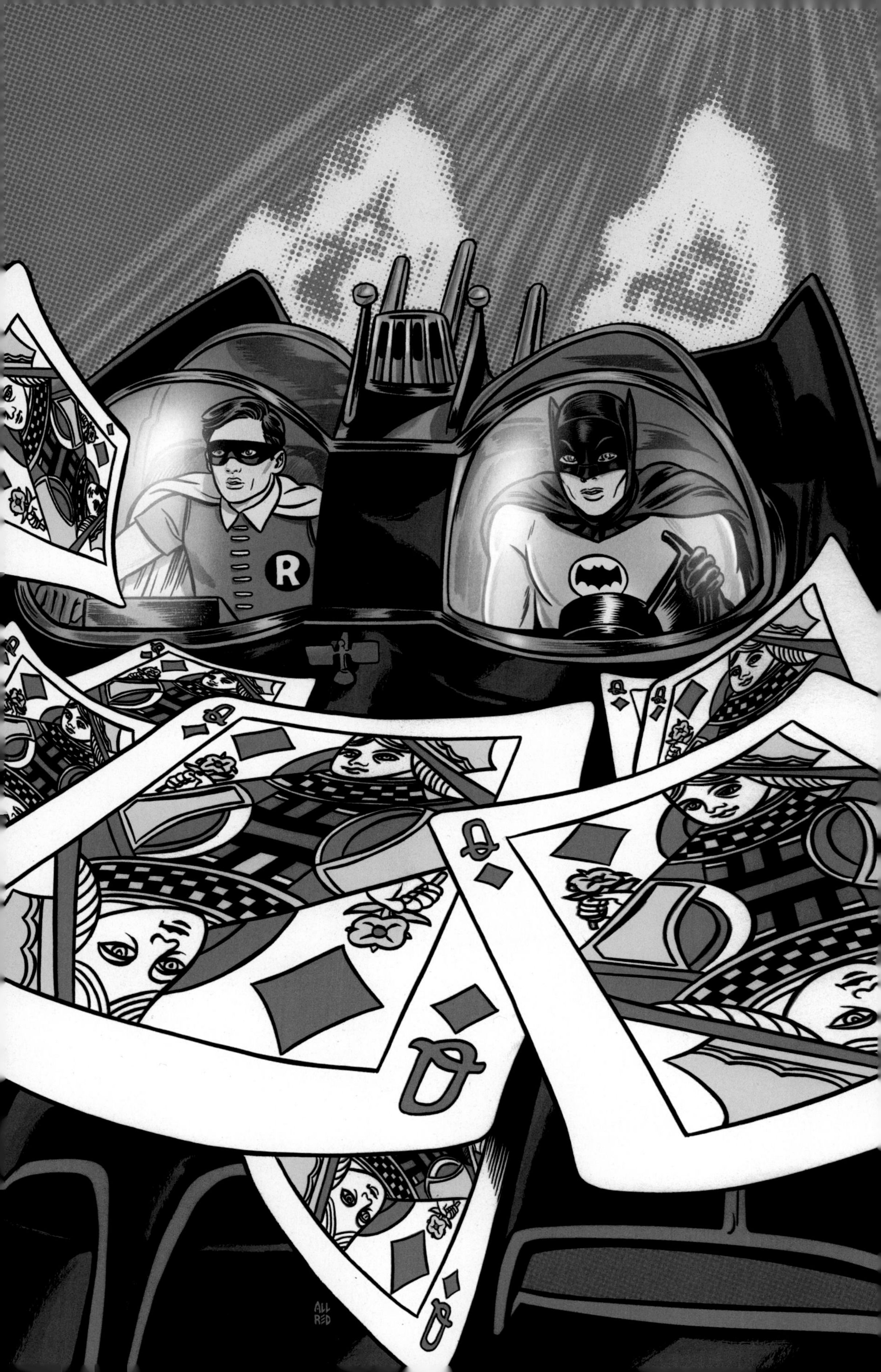

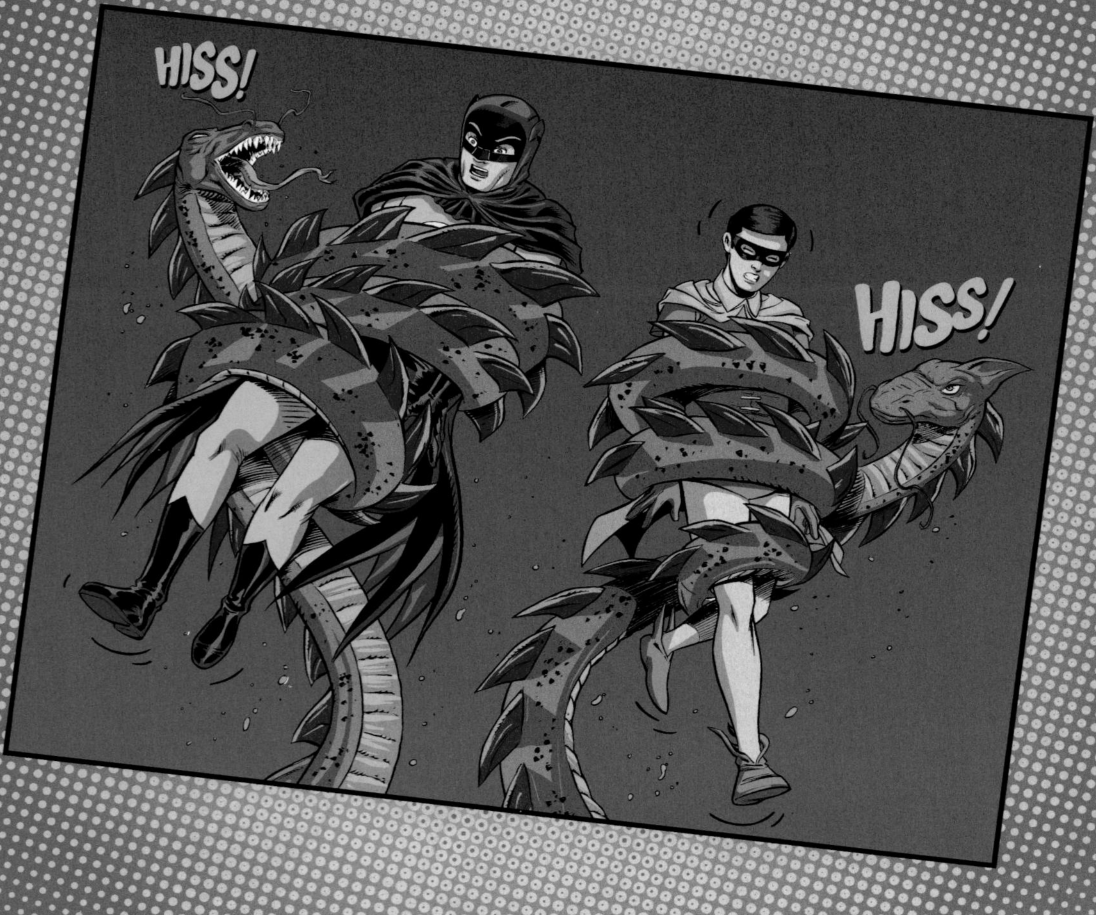
HISS!
HISS!

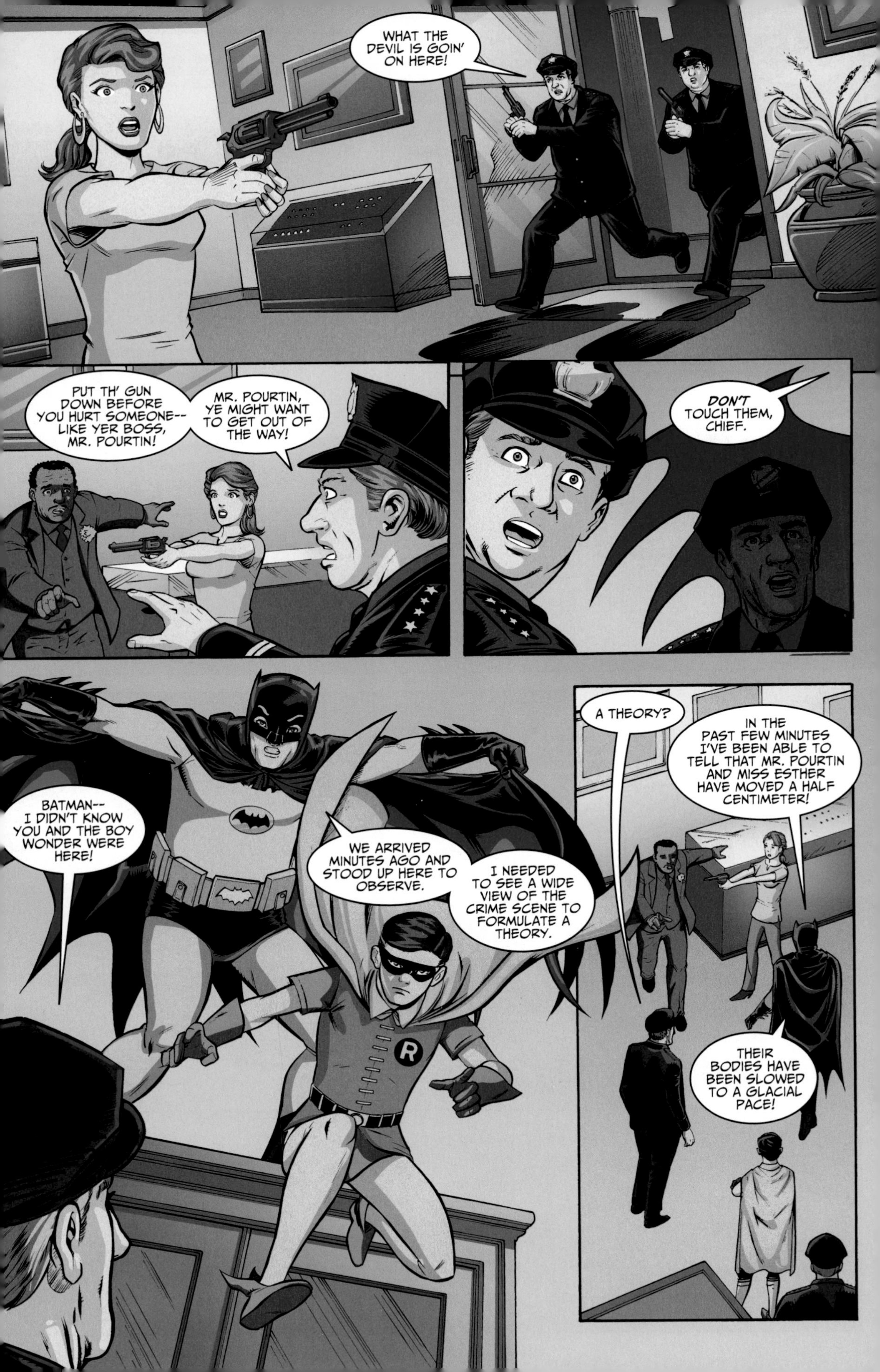
WHAT THE DEVIL IS GOIN' ON HERE!
PUT TH' GUN DOWN BEFORE YOU HURT SOMEONE-- LIKE YER BOSS, MR. POURTIN!
MR. POURTIN, YE MIGHT WANT TO GET OUT OF THE WAY!
DON'T TOUCH THEM, CHIEF.
BATMAN-- I DIDN'T KNOW YOU AND THE BOY WONDER WERE HERE!
WE ARRIVED MINUTES AGO AND STOOD UP HERE TO OBSERVE.
I NEEDED TO SEE A WIDE VIEW OF THE CRIME SCENE TO FORMULATE A THEORY.
A THEORY?
IN THE PAST FEW MINUTES I'VE BEEN ABLE TO TELL THAT MR. POURTIN AND MISS ESTHER HAVE MOVED A HALF CENTIMETER!
THEIR BODIES HAVE BEEN SLOWED TO A GLACIAL PACE!

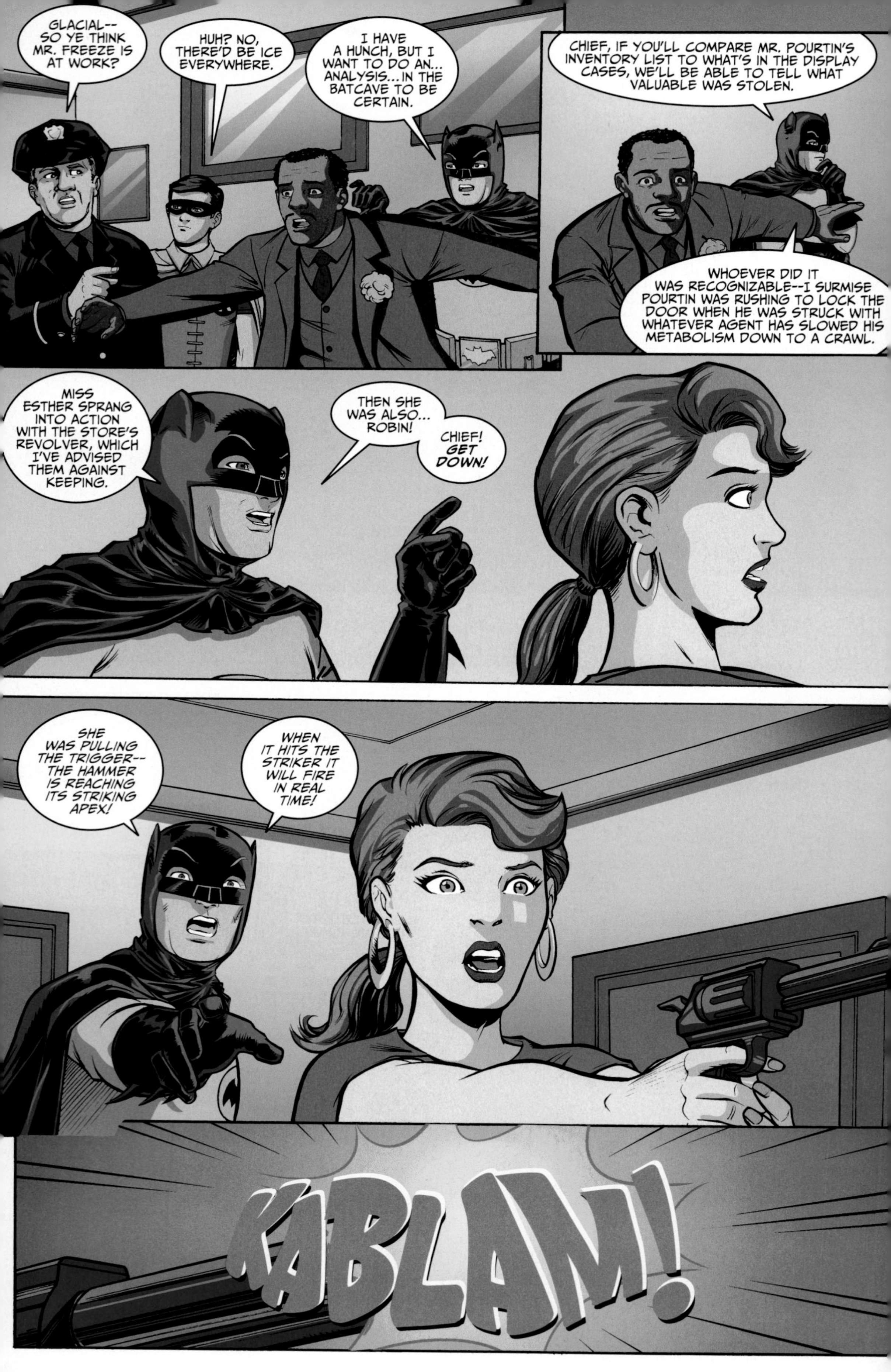
GLACIAL-- SO YE THINK MR. FREEZE IS AT WORK?
HUH? NO, THERE'D BE ICE EVERYWHERE.
I HAVE A HUNCH, BUT I WANT TO DO AN... ANALYSIS... IN THE BATCAVE TO BE CERTAIN.
CHIEF, IF YOU'LL COMPARE MR. POURTIN'S INVENTORY LIST TO WHAT'S IN THE DISPLAY CASES, WE'LL BE ABLE TO TELL WHAT VALUABLE WAS STOLEN.
WHOEVER DID IT WAS RECOGNIZABLE--I SURMISE POURTIN WAS RUSHING TO LOCK THE DOOR WHEN HE WAS STRUCK WITH WHATEVER AGENT HAS SLOWED HIS METABOLISM DOWN TO A CRAWL.
MISS ESTHER SPRANG INTO ACTION WITH THE STORE'S REVOLVER, WHICH I'VE ADVISED THEM AGAINST KEEPING.
THEN SHE WAS ALSO... ROBIN!
CHIEF! *GET DOWN!*
SHE WAS PULLING THE TRIGGER-- THE HAMMER IS REACHING ITS STRIKING APEX!
WHEN IT HITS THE STRIKER IT WILL FIRE IN REAL TIME!
KABLAM!

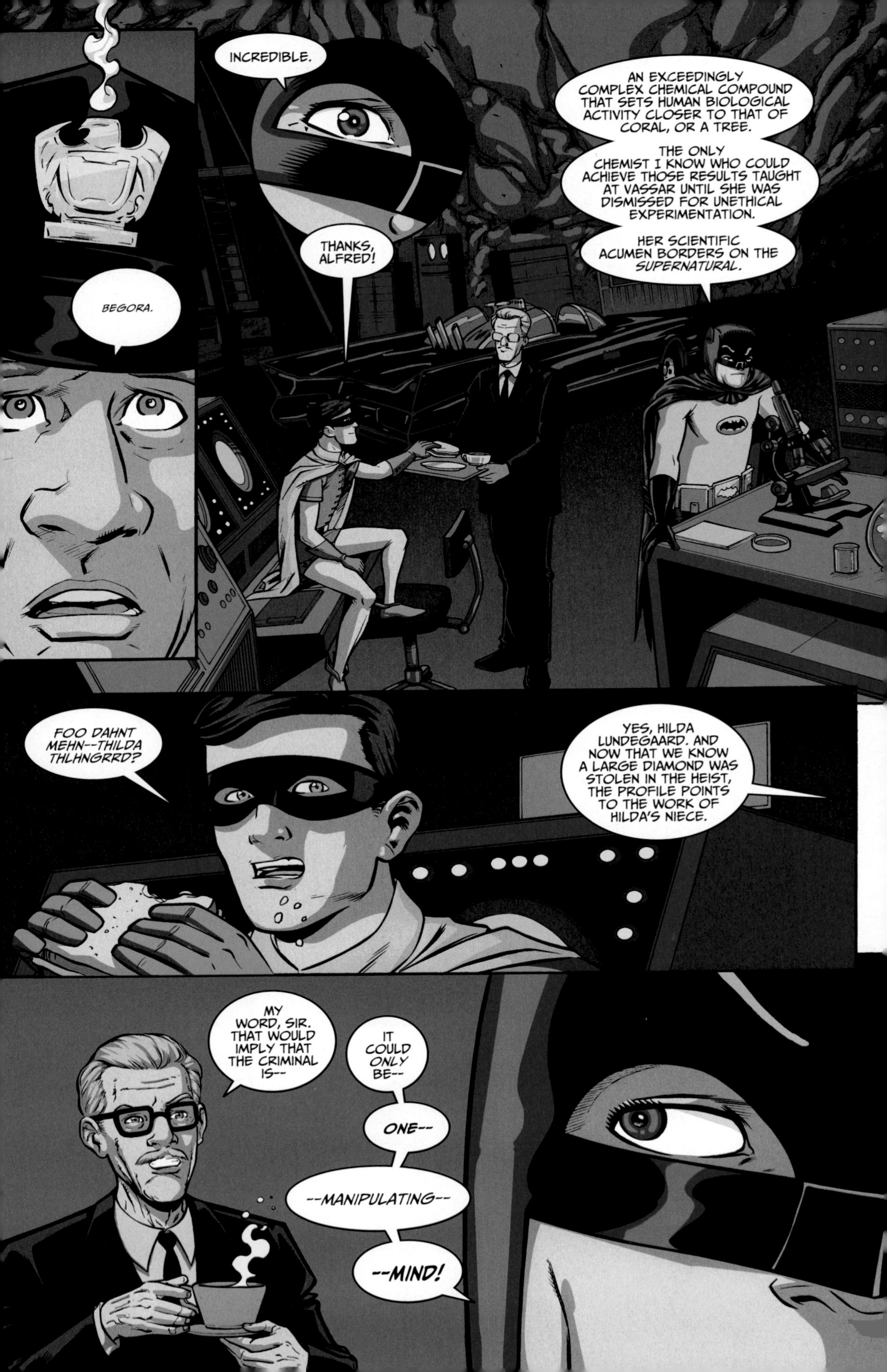
INCREDIBLE.
AN EXCEEDINGLY COMPLEX CHEMICAL COMPOUND THAT SETS HUMAN BIOLOGICAL ACTIVITY CLOSER TO THAT OF CORAL, OR A TREE.
THE ONLY CHEMIST I KNOW WHO COULD ACHIEVE THOSE RESULTS TAUGHT AT VASSAR UNTIL SHE WAS DISMISSED FOR UNETHICAL EXPERIMENTATION.
HER SCIENTIFIC ACUMEN BORDERS ON THE *SUPERNATURAL*.
THANKS, ALFRED!
BEGORA.
FOO DAHNT MEHN--THILDA THLHNGRRD?
YES, HILDA LUNDEGAARD. AND NOW THAT WE KNOW A LARGE DIAMOND WAS STOLEN IN THE HEIST, THE PROFILE POINTS TO THE WORK OF HILDA'S NIECE.
MY WORD, SIR. THAT WOULD IMPLY THAT THE CRIMINAL IS--
IT COULD ONLY BE--
ONE--
--MANIPULATING--
--MIND!

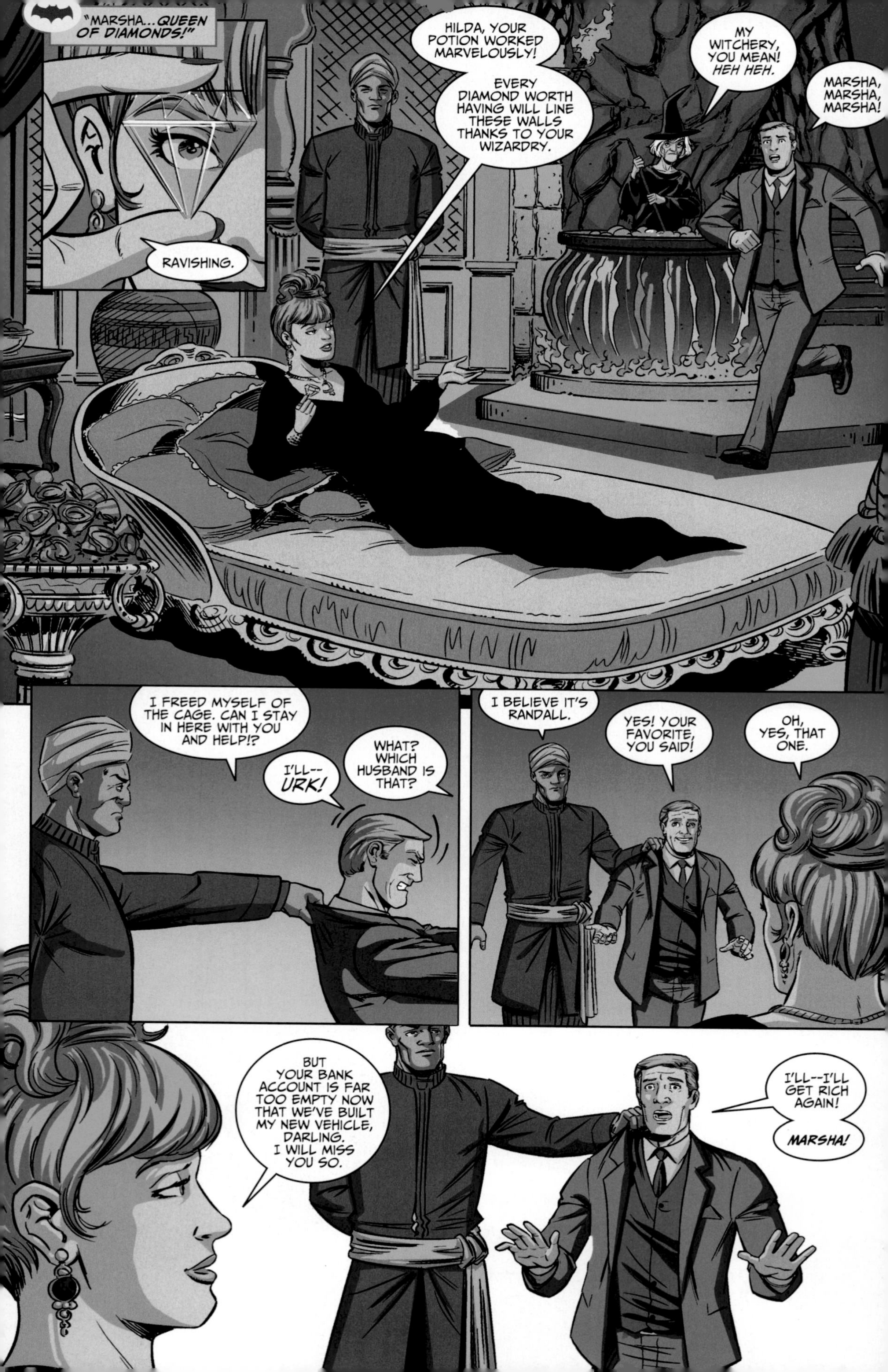
"MARSHA...QUEEN OF DIAMONDS!"
RAVISHING.
HILDA, YOUR POTION WORKED MARVELOUSLY!
EVERY DIAMOND WORTH HAVING WILL LINE THESE WALLS THANKS TO YOUR WIZARDRY.
MY WITCHERY, YOU MEAN! HEH HEH.
MARSHA, MARSHA, MARSHA!
I FREED MYSELF OF THE CAGE. CAN I STAY IN HERE WITH YOU AND HELP!?
WHAT? WHICH HUSBAND IS THAT?
I'LL-- URK!
I BELIEVE IT'S RANDALL.
YES! YOUR FAVORITE, YOU SAID!
OH, YES, THAT ONE.
BUT YOUR BANK ACCOUNT IS FAR TOO EMPTY NOW THAT WE'VE BUILT MY NEW VEHICLE, DARLING. I WILL MISS YOU SO.
I'LL--I'LL GET RICH AGAIN!
MARSHA!

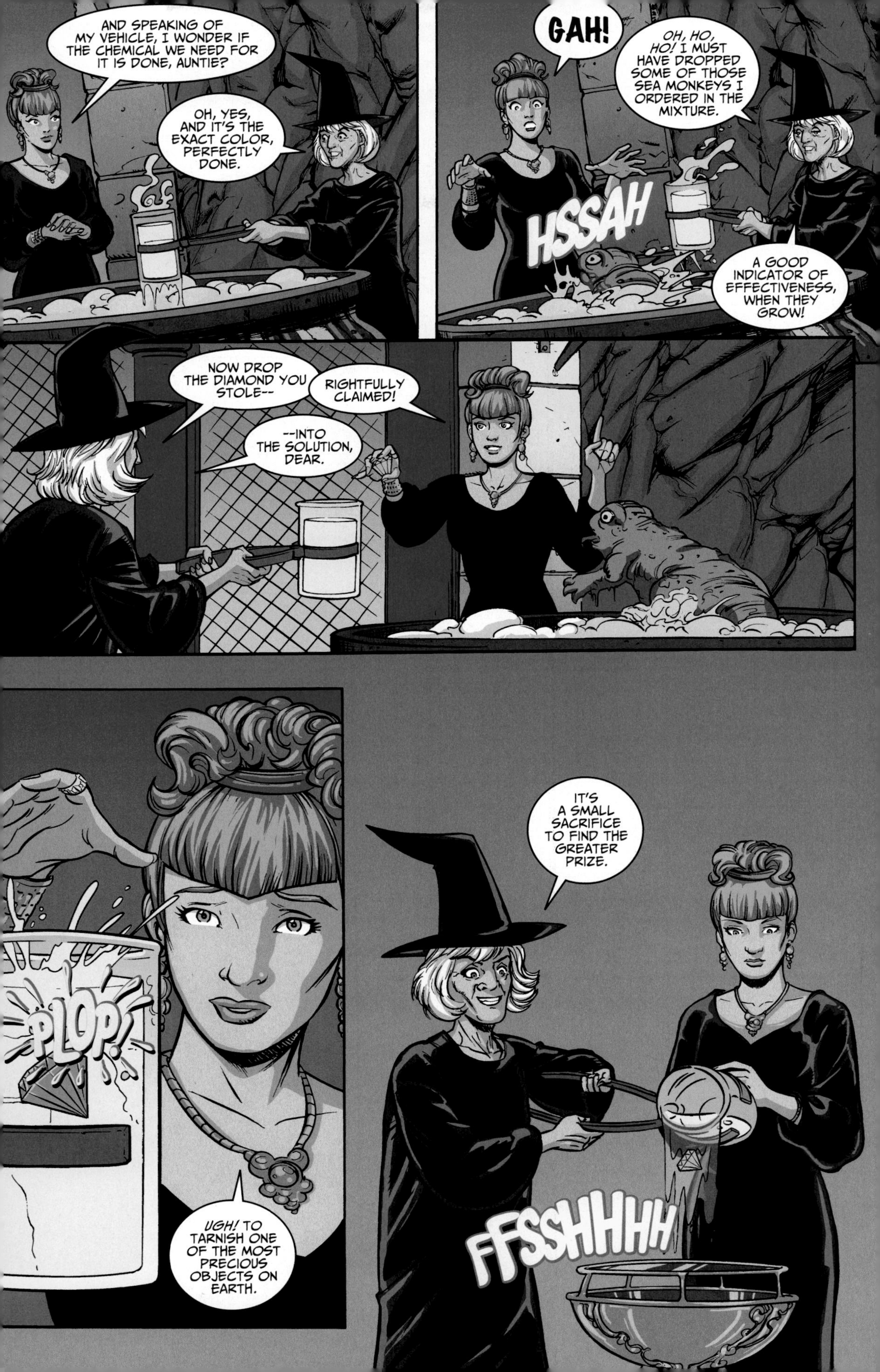

AND SPEAKING OF MY VEHICLE, I WONDER IF THE CHEMICAL WE NEED FOR IT IS DONE, AUNTIE?
OH, YES, AND IT'S THE EXACT COLOR, PERFECTLY DONE.
GAH!
OH, HO, HO! I MUST HAVE DROPPED SOME OF THOSE SEA MONKEYS I ORDERED IN THE MIXTURE.
HSSAH
A GOOD INDICATOR OF EFFECTIVENESS, WHEN THEY GROW!
NOW DROP THE DIAMOND YOU STOLE--
RIGHTFULLY CLAIMED!
--INTO THE SOLUTION, DEAR.
PLOP!
UGH! TO TARNISH ONE OF THE MOST PRECIOUS OBJECTS ON EARTH.
IT'S A SMALL SACRIFICE TO FIND THE GREATER PRIZE.
FFSSHHHH

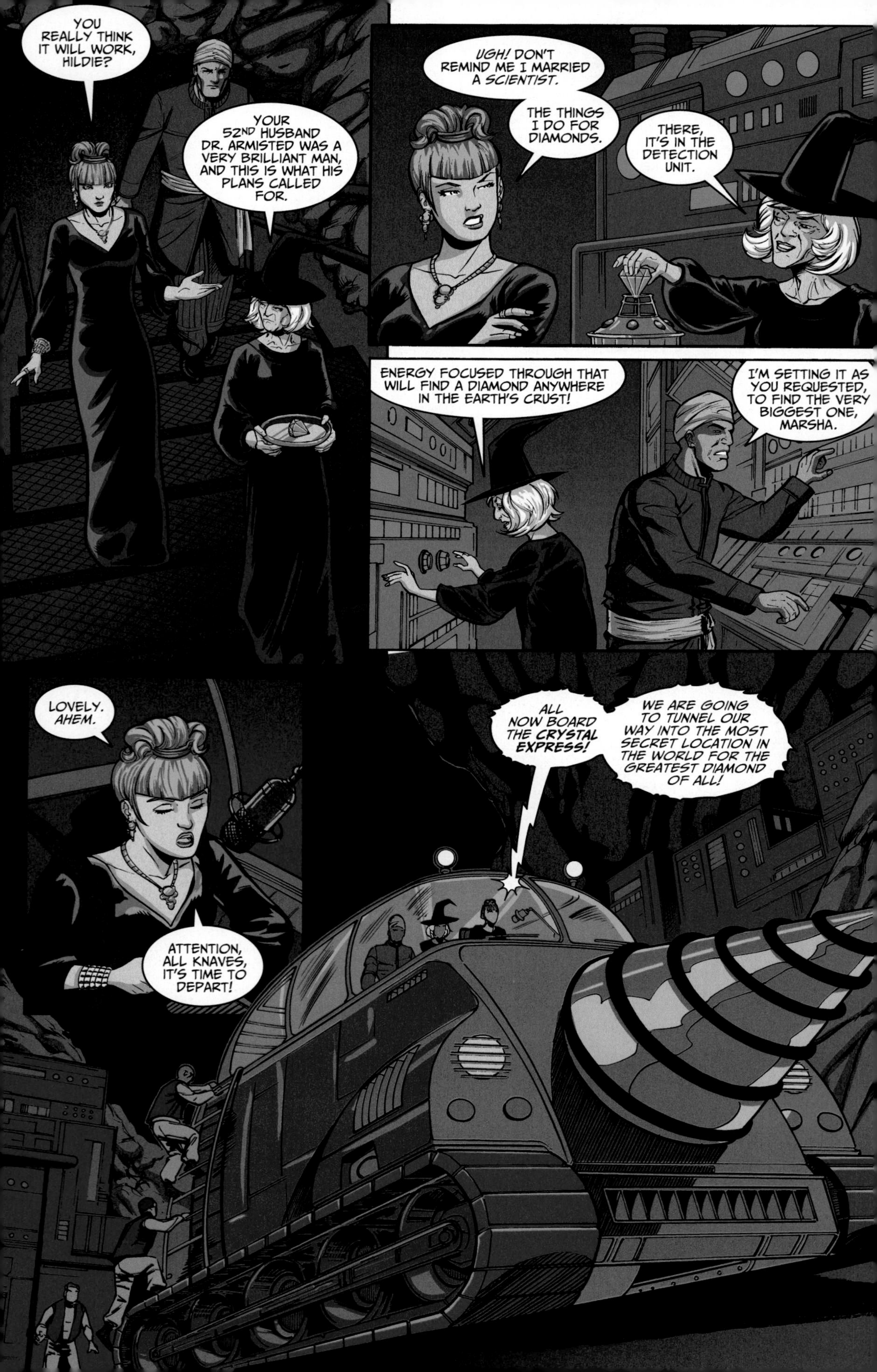
YOU REALLY THINK IT WILL WORK, HILDIE?
YOUR 52ND HUSBAND DR. ARMISTED WAS A VERY BRILLIANT MAN, AND THIS IS WHAT HIS PLANS CALLED FOR.
UGH! DON'T REMIND ME I MARRIED A SCIENTIST.
THE THINGS I DO FOR DIAMONDS.
THERE, IT'S IN THE DETECTION UNIT.
ENERGY FOCUSED THROUGH THAT WILL FIND A DIAMOND ANYWHERE IN THE EARTH'S CRUST!
I'M SETTING IT AS YOU REQUESTED, TO FIND THE VERY BIGGEST ONE, MARSHA.
LOVELY. AHEM.
ATTENTION, ALL KNAVES, IT'S TIME TO DEPART!
ALL NOW BOARD THE CRYSTAL EXPRESS!
WE ARE GOING TO TUNNEL OUR WAY INTO THE MOST SECRET LOCATION IN THE WORLD FOR THE GREATEST DIAMOND OF ALL!

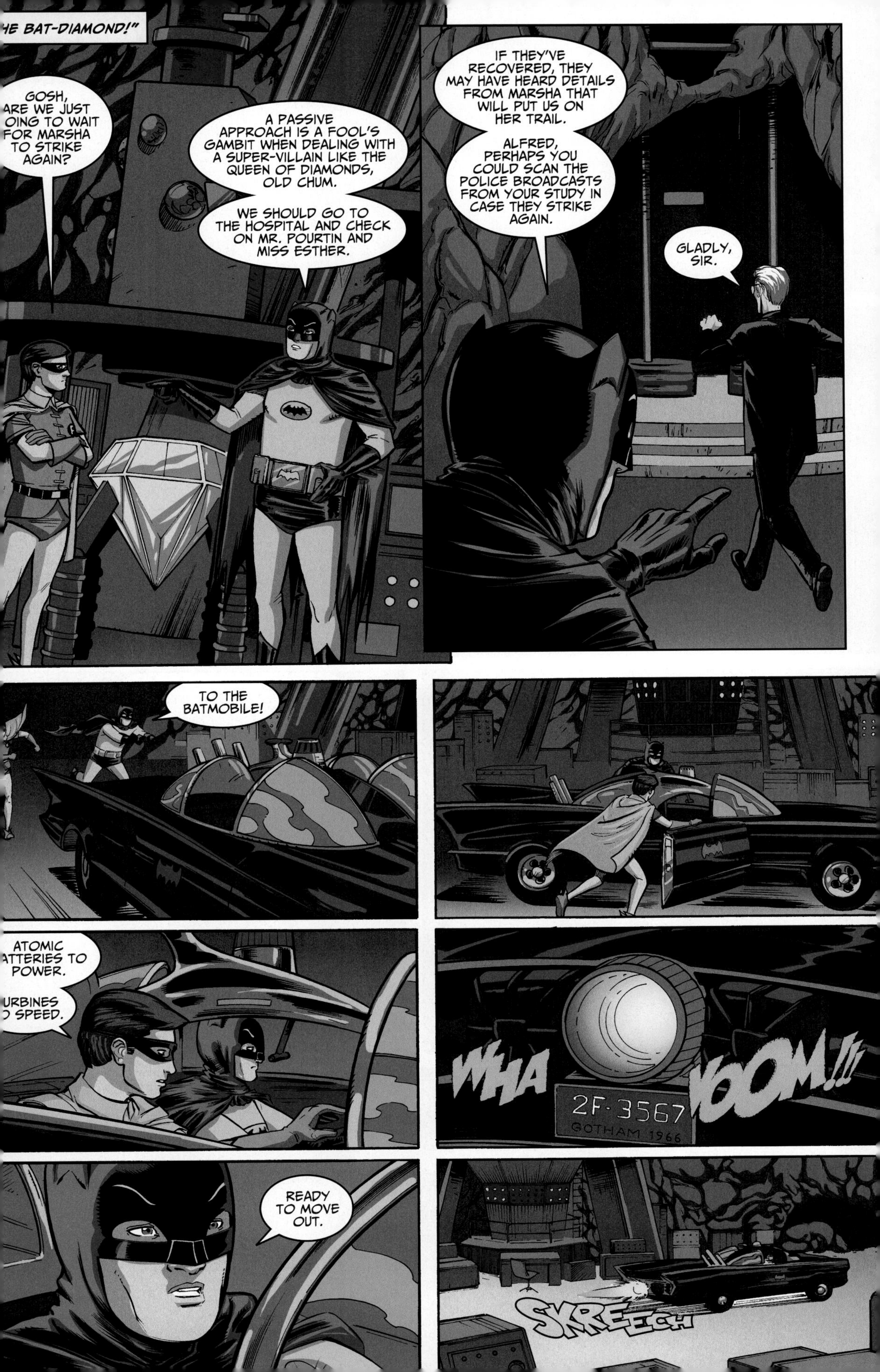
HE BAT-DIAMOND!"
GOSH, ARE WE JUST OING TO WAIT FOR MARSHA TO STRIKE AGAIN?
A PASSIVE APPROACH IS A FOOL'S GAMBIT WHEN DEALING WITH A SUPER-VILLAIN LIKE THE QUEEN OF DIAMONDS, OLD CHUM.
WE SHOULD GO TO THE HOSPITAL AND CHECK ON MR. POURTIN AND MISS ESTHER.
IF THEY'VE RECOVERED, THEY MAY HAVE HEARD DETAILS FROM MARSHA THAT WILL PUT US ON HER TRAIL.
ALFRED, PERHAPS YOU COULD SCAN THE POLICE BROADCASTS FROM YOUR STUDY IN CASE THEY STRIKE AGAIN.
GLADLY, SIR.
TO THE BATMOBILE!
ATOMIC ATTERIES TO POWER.
URBINES O SPEED.
WHA
OOM!!!
2F-3567
GOTHAM 1966
READY TO MOVE OUT.
SKREECH

KRRRNCH

VRNVRNVRNVRN

WE'RE HERE!

WE'RE IN THE BATCAVE!!!

VARUNCH!!!

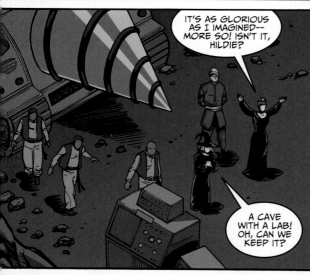

IT'S AS GLORIOUS AS I IMAGINED-- MORE SO! ISN'T IT, HILDIE?

A CAVE WITH A LAB! OH, CAN WE KEEP IT?

THERE IS THAT GORGEOUS MASTERPIECE, BEING GROSSLY MISUSED TO SERVE A MACHINE!

LIBERATE IT, MY LOYAL KNAVES!

YOU BET, MARSHA!

IT'S LIKE WE'VE BROKEN INTO ALADDIN'S CAVE OF WONDERS.

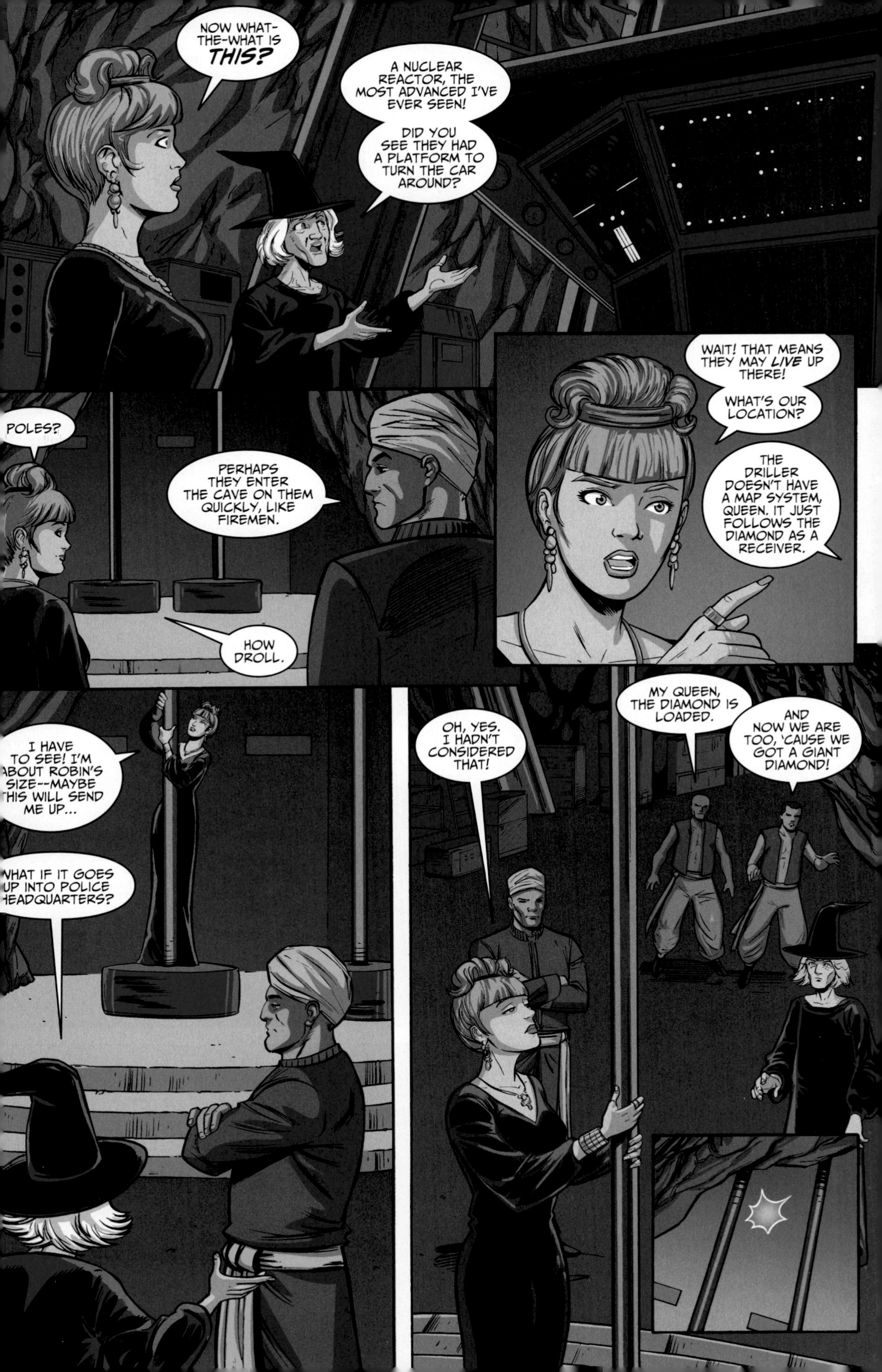
NOW WHAT-THE-WHAT IS THIS?
A NUCLEAR REACTOR, THE MOST ADVANCED I'VE EVER SEEN!
DID YOU SEE THEY HAD A PLATFORM TO TURN THE CAR AROUND?
POLES?
PERHAPS THEY ENTER THE CAVE ON THEM QUICKLY, LIKE FIREMEN.
HOW DROLL.
WAIT! THAT MEANS THEY MAY LIVE UP THERE!
WHAT'S OUR LOCATION?
THE DRILLER DOESN'T HAVE A MAP SYSTEM, QUEEN. IT JUST FOLLOWS THE DIAMOND AS A RECEIVER.
I HAVE TO SEE! I'M ABOUT ROBIN'S SIZE--MAYBE THIS WILL SEND ME UP...
WHAT IF IT GOES UP INTO POLICE HEADQUARTERS?
OH, YES. I HADN'T CONSIDERED THAT!
MY QUEEN, THE DIAMOND IS LOADED.
AND NOW WE ARE TOO, 'CAUSE WE GOT A GIANT DIAMOND!

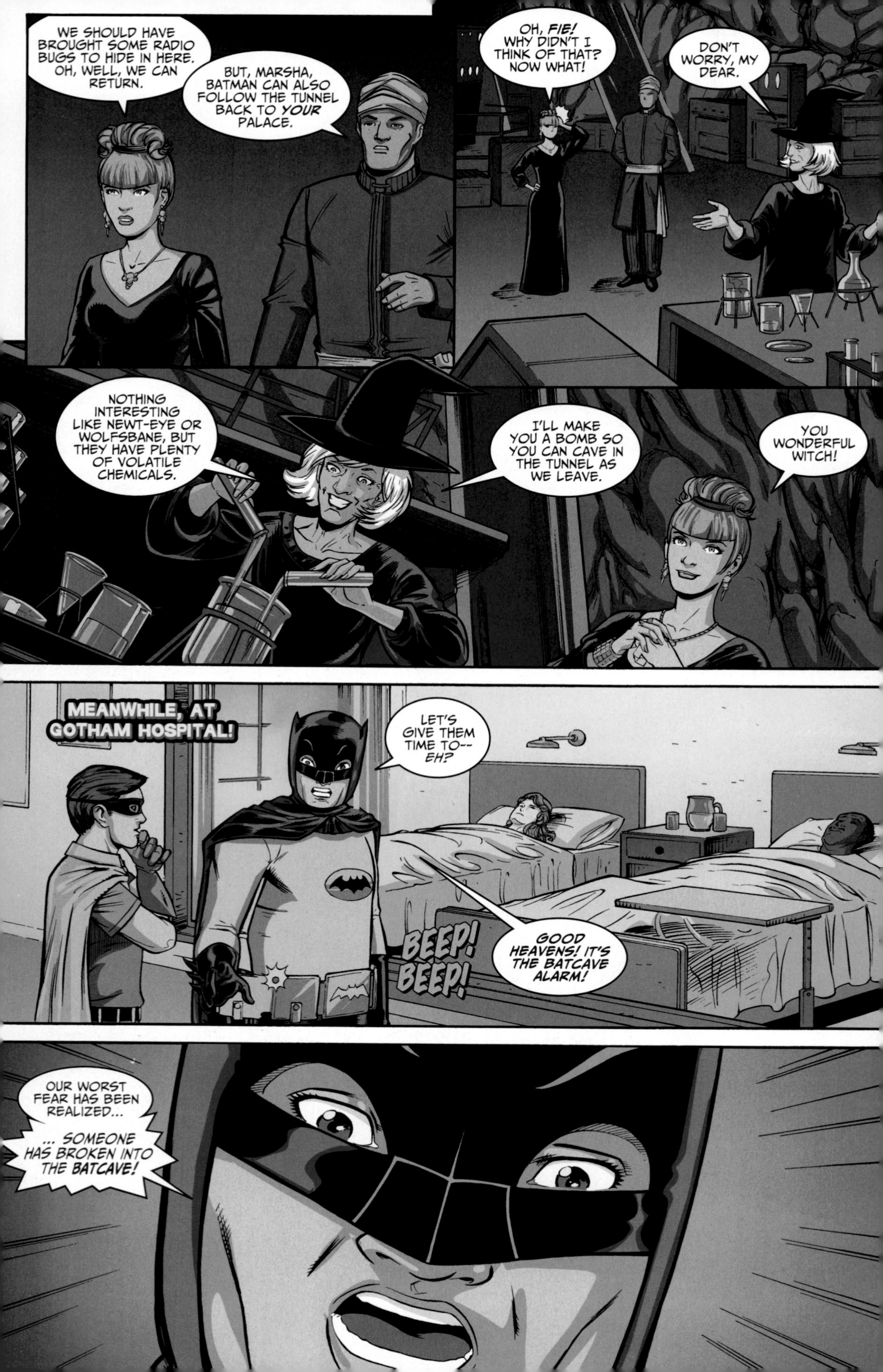
WE SHOULD HAVE BROUGHT SOME RADIO BUGS TO HIDE IN HERE. OH, WELL, WE CAN RETURN.
BUT, MARSHA, BATMAN CAN ALSO FOLLOW THE TUNNEL BACK TO YOUR PALACE.
OH, FIE! WHY DIDN'T I THINK OF THAT? NOW WHAT!
DON'T WORRY, MY DEAR.
NOTHING INTERESTING LIKE NEWT-EYE OR WOLFSBANE, BUT THEY HAVE PLENTY OF VOLATILE CHEMICALS.
I'LL MAKE YOU A BOMB SO YOU CAN CAVE IN THE TUNNEL AS WE LEAVE.
YOU WONDERFUL WITCH!
MEANWHILE, AT GOTHAM HOSPITAL!
LET'S GIVE THEM TIME TO-- EH?
BEEP! BEEP!
GOOD HEAVENS! IT'S THE BATCAVE ALARM!
OUR WORST FEAR HAS BEEN REALIZED...
... SOMEONE HAS BROKEN INTO THE BATCAVE!

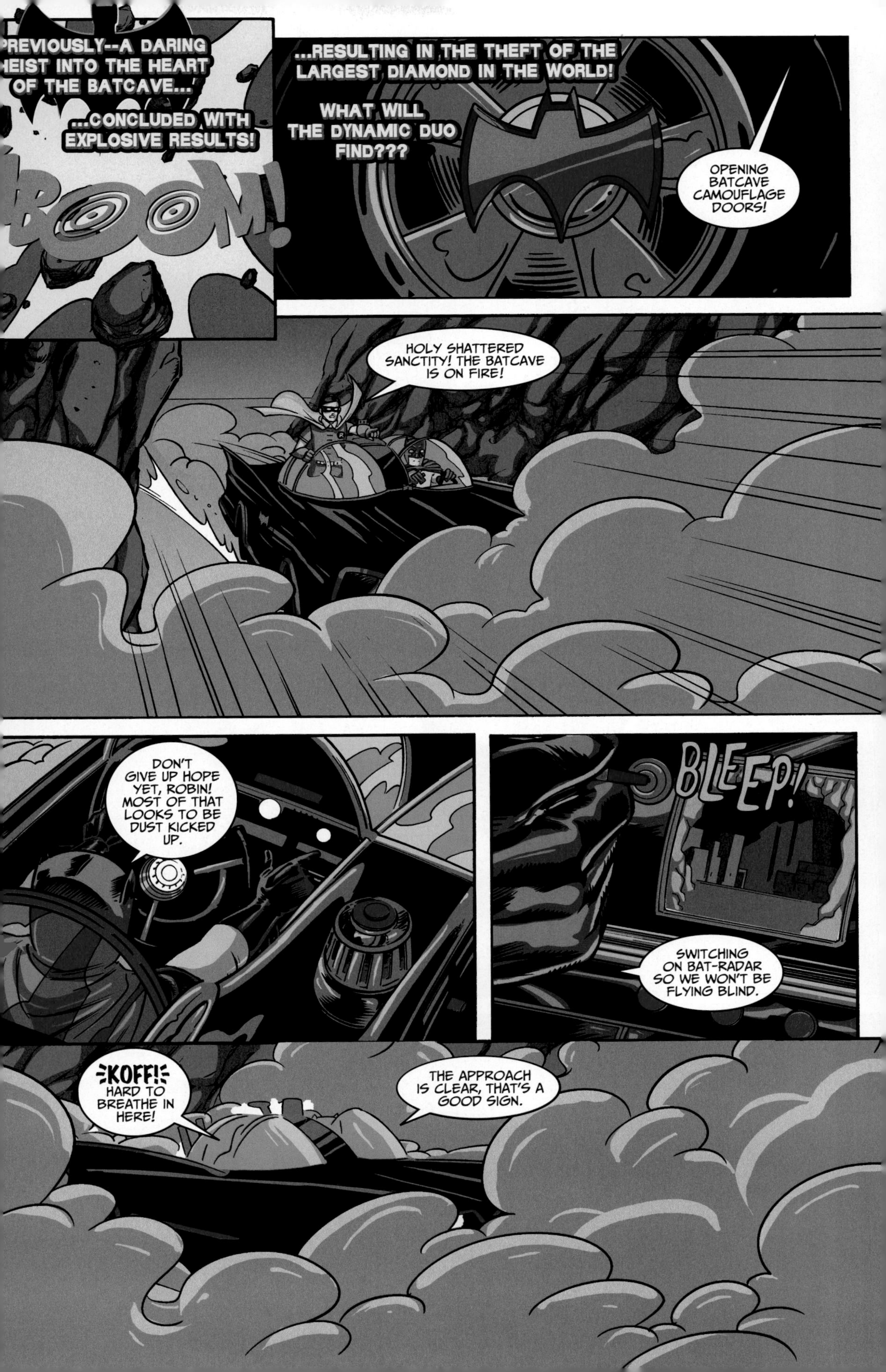
PREVIOUSLY--A DARING HEIST INTO THE HEART OF THE BATCAVE...
...CONCLUDED WITH EXPLOSIVE RESULTS!
BOOM!
...RESULTING IN THE THEFT OF THE LARGEST DIAMOND IN THE WORLD!
WHAT WILL THE DYNAMIC DUO FIND???
OPENING BATCAVE CAMOUFLAGE DOORS!
HOLY SHATTERED SANCTITY! THE BATCAVE IS ON FIRE!
DON'T GIVE UP HOPE YET, ROBIN! MOST OF THAT LOOKS TO BE DUST KICKED UP.
BLEEP!
SWITCHING ON BAT-RADAR SO WE WON'T BE FLYING BLIND.
KOFF! HARD TO BREATHE IN HERE!
THE APPROACH IS CLEAR, THAT'S A GOOD SIGN.

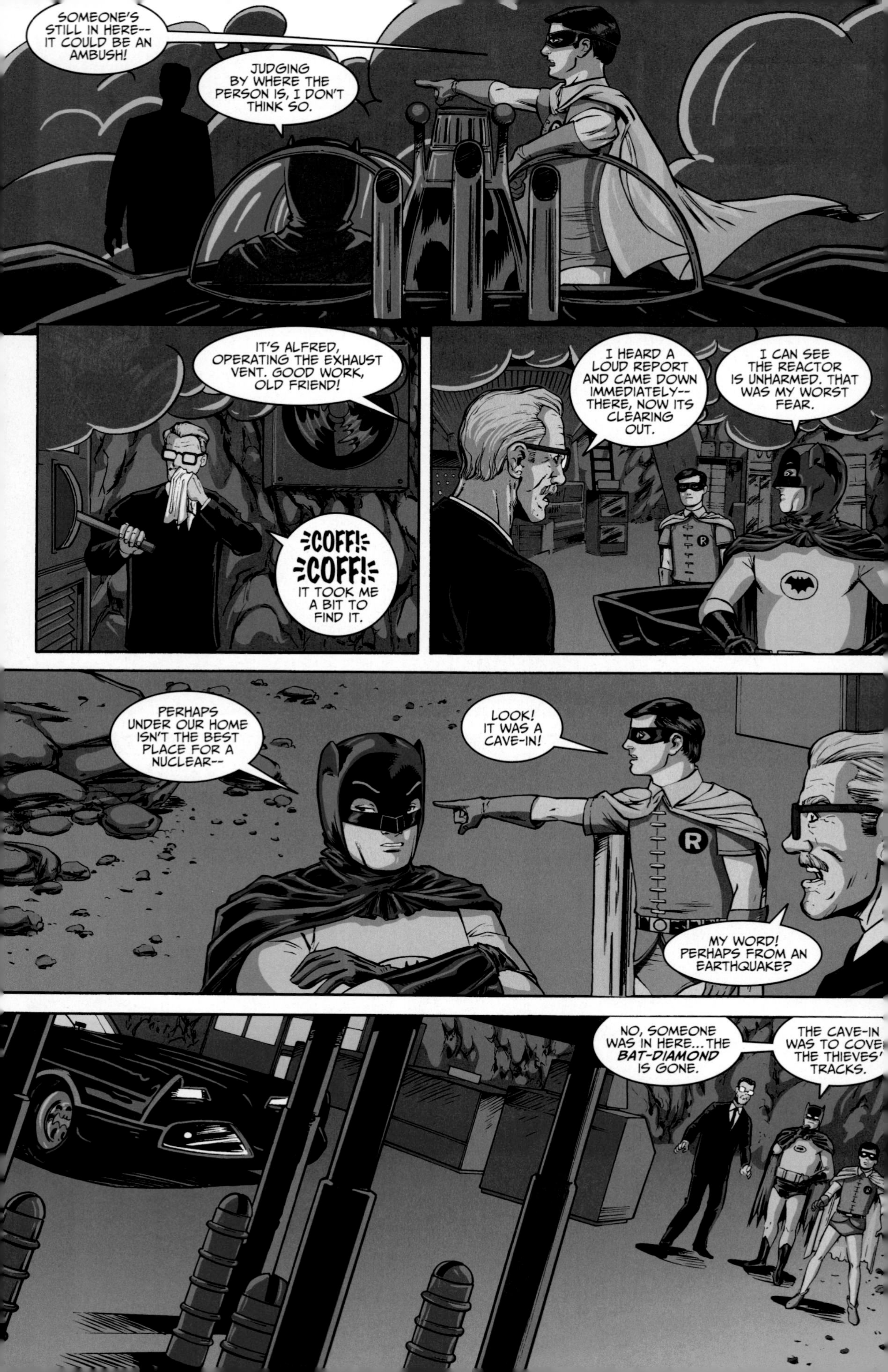

SOMEONE'S STILL IN HERE-- IT COULD BE AN AMBUSH!
JUDGING BY WHERE THE PERSON IS, I DON'T THINK SO.
IT'S ALFRED, OPERATING THE EXHAUST VENT. GOOD WORK, OLD FRIEND!
COFF! COFF! IT TOOK ME A BIT TO FIND IT.
I HEARD A LOUD REPORT AND CAME DOWN IMMEDIATELY-- THERE, NOW ITS CLEARING OUT.
I CAN SEE THE REACTOR IS UNHARMED. THAT WAS MY WORST FEAR.
PERHAPS UNDER OUR HOME ISN'T THE BEST PLACE FOR A NUCLEAR--
LOOK! IT WAS A CAVE-IN!
MY WORD! PERHAPS FROM AN EARTHQUAKE?
NO, SOMEONE WAS IN HERE... THE *BAT-DIAMOND* IS GONE.
THE CAVE-IN WAS TO COVE THE THIEVES' TRACKS.

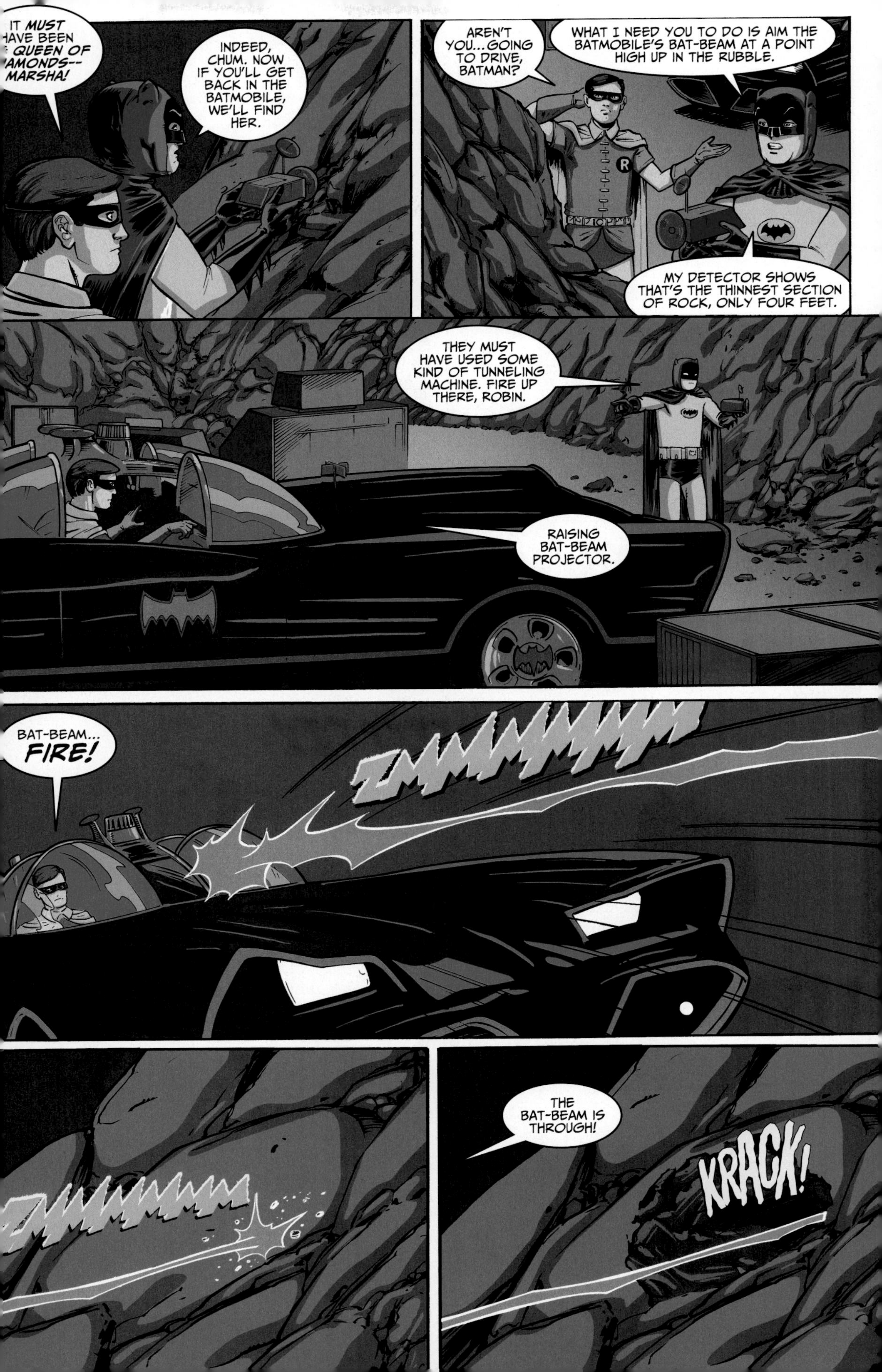
IT MUST HAVE BEEN THE QUEEN OF DIAMONDS-- MARSHA!
INDEED, CHUM. NOW IF YOU'LL GET BACK IN THE BATMOBILE, WE'LL FIND HER.
AREN'T YOU...GOING TO DRIVE, BATMAN?
WHAT I NEED YOU TO DO IS AIM THE BATMOBILE'S BAT-BEAM AT A POINT HIGH UP IN THE RUBBLE.
MY DETECTOR SHOWS THAT'S THE THINNEST SECTION OF ROCK, ONLY FOUR FEET.
THEY MUST HAVE USED SOME KIND OF TUNNELING MACHINE. FIRE UP THERE, ROBIN.
RAISING BAT-BEAM PROJECTOR.
BAT-BEAM... FIRE!
ZMMMMMMM
ZMMMMMMM
THE BAT-BEAM IS THROUGH!
KRACK!

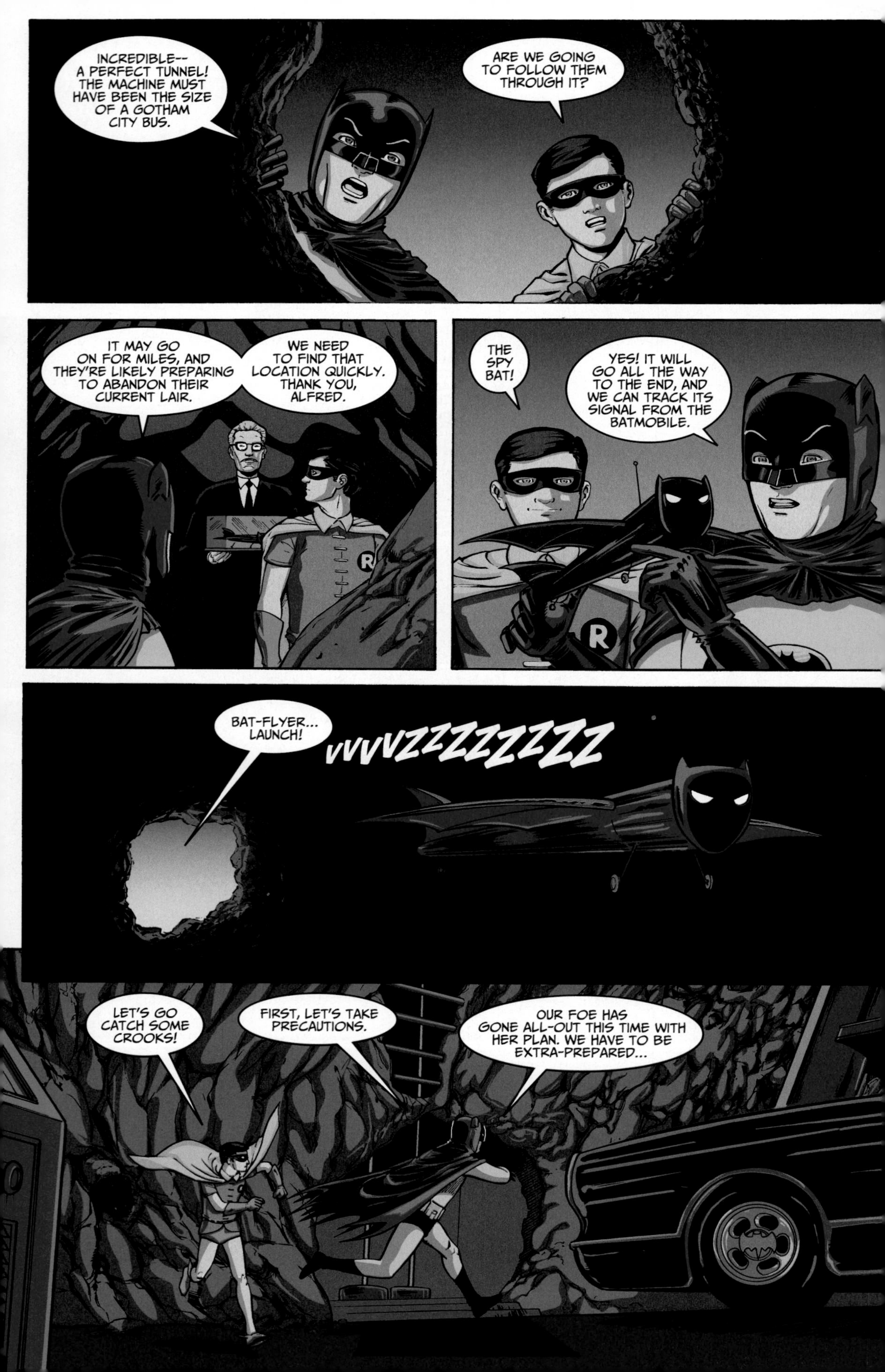

INCREDIBLE-- A PERFECT TUNNEL! THE MACHINE MUST HAVE BEEN THE SIZE OF A GOTHAM CITY BUS.
ARE WE GOING TO FOLLOW THEM THROUGH IT?
IT MAY GO ON FOR MILES, AND THEY'RE LIKELY PREPARING TO ABANDON THEIR CURRENT LAIR.
WE NEED TO FIND THAT LOCATION QUICKLY. THANK YOU, ALFRED.
THE SPY BAT!
YES! IT WILL GO ALL THE WAY TO THE END, AND WE CAN TRACK ITS SIGNAL FROM THE BATMOBILE.
BAT-FLYER... LAUNCH!
VVVVZZZZZZZZ
LET'S GO CATCH SOME CROOKS!
FIRST, LET'S TAKE PRECAUTIONS.
OUR FOE HAS GONE ALL-OUT THIS TIME WITH HER PLAN. WE HAVE TO BE EXTRA-PREPARED...

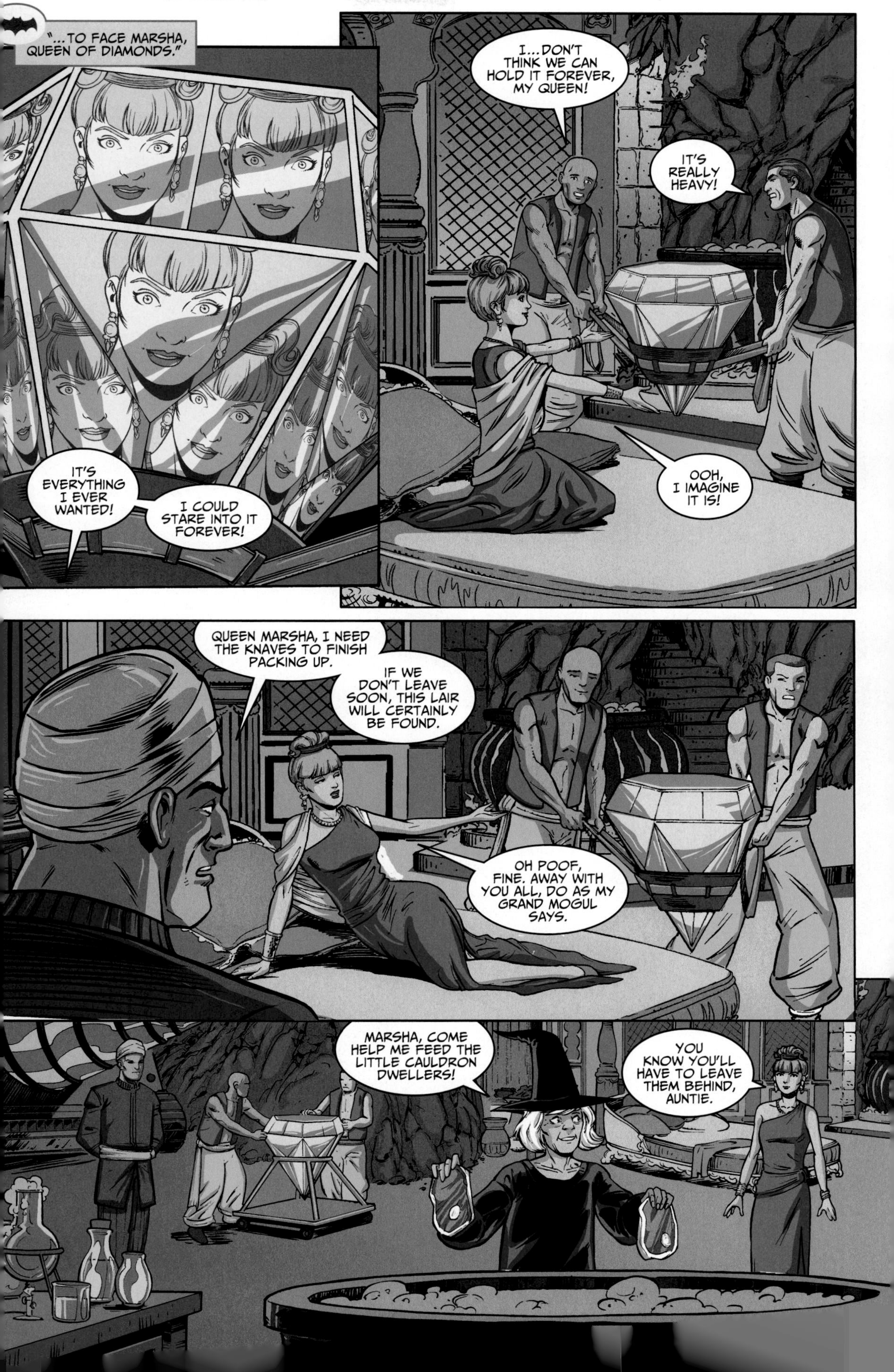
"...TO FACE MARSHA, QUEEN OF DIAMONDS."
IT'S EVERYTHING I EVER WANTED!
I COULD STARE INTO IT FOREVER!
I...DON'T THINK WE CAN HOLD IT FOREVER, MY QUEEN!
IT'S REALLY HEAVY!
OOH, I IMAGINE IT IS!
QUEEN MARSHA, I NEED THE KNAVES TO FINISH PACKING UP.
IF WE DON'T LEAVE SOON, THIS LAIR WILL CERTAINLY BE FOUND.
OH POOF, FINE. AWAY WITH YOU ALL, DO AS MY GRAND MOGUL SAYS.
MARSHA, COME HELP ME FEED THE LITTLE CAULDRON DWELLERS!
YOU KNOW YOU'LL HAVE TO LEAVE THEM BEHIND, AUNTIE.

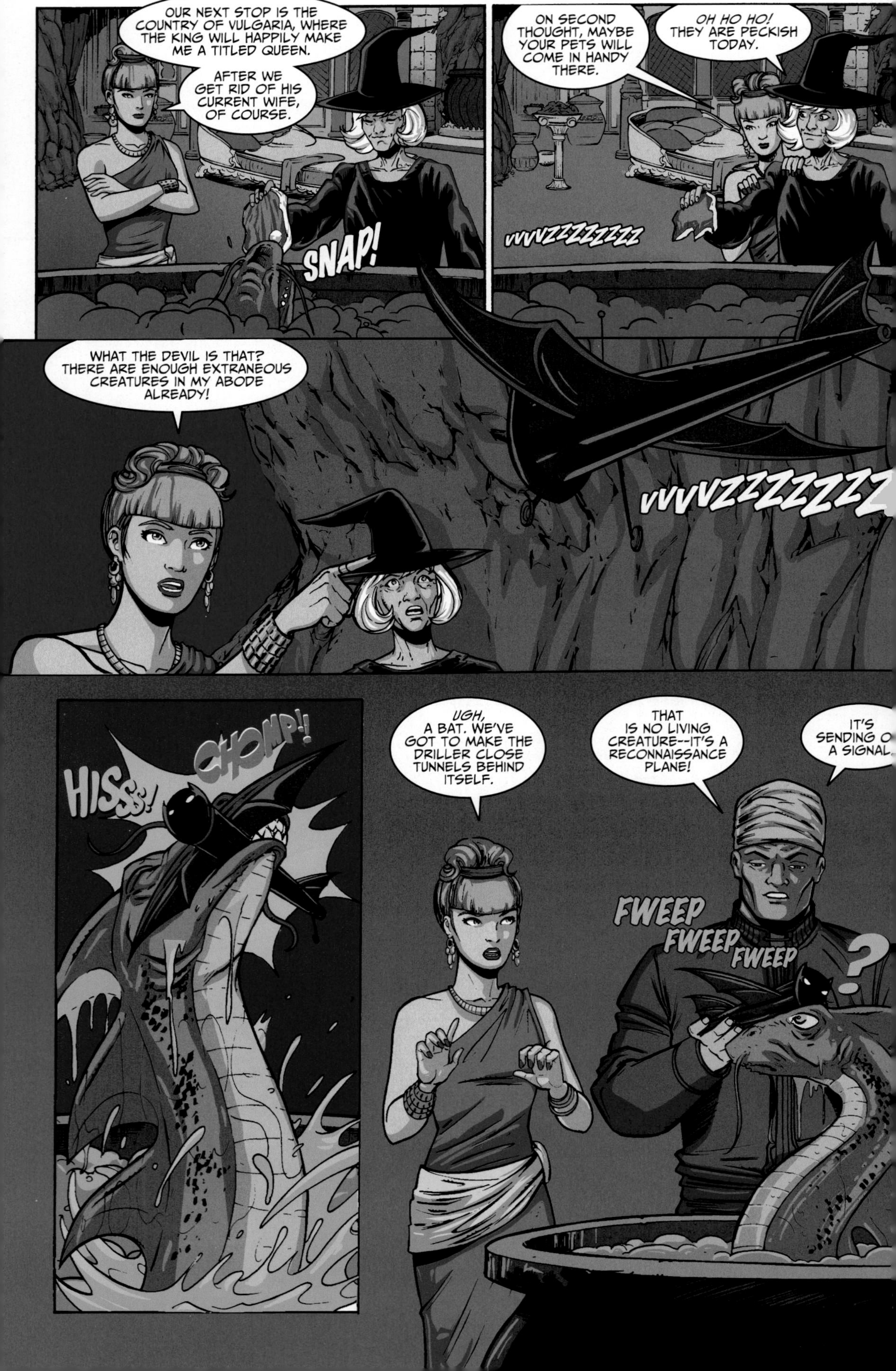

OUR NEXT STOP IS THE COUNTRY OF VULGARIA, WHERE THE KING WILL HAPPILY MAKE ME A TITLED QUEEN.
AFTER WE GET RID OF HIS CURRENT WIFE, OF COURSE.
SNAP!
ON SECOND THOUGHT, MAYBE YOUR PETS WILL COME IN HANDY THERE.
OH HO HO! THEY ARE PECKISH TODAY.
VVVVZZZZZZZZ
WHAT THE DEVIL IS THAT? THERE ARE ENOUGH EXTRANEOUS CREATURES IN MY ABODE ALREADY!
VVVVZZZZZZZZ
HISSS!
CHOMP!!
UGH, A BAT. WE'VE GOT TO MAKE THE DRILLER CLOSE TUNNELS BEHIND ITSELF.
THAT IS NO LIVING CREATURE--IT'S A RECONNAISSANCE PLANE!
IT'S SENDING O A SIGNAL
FWEEP
FWEEP
FWEEP
?

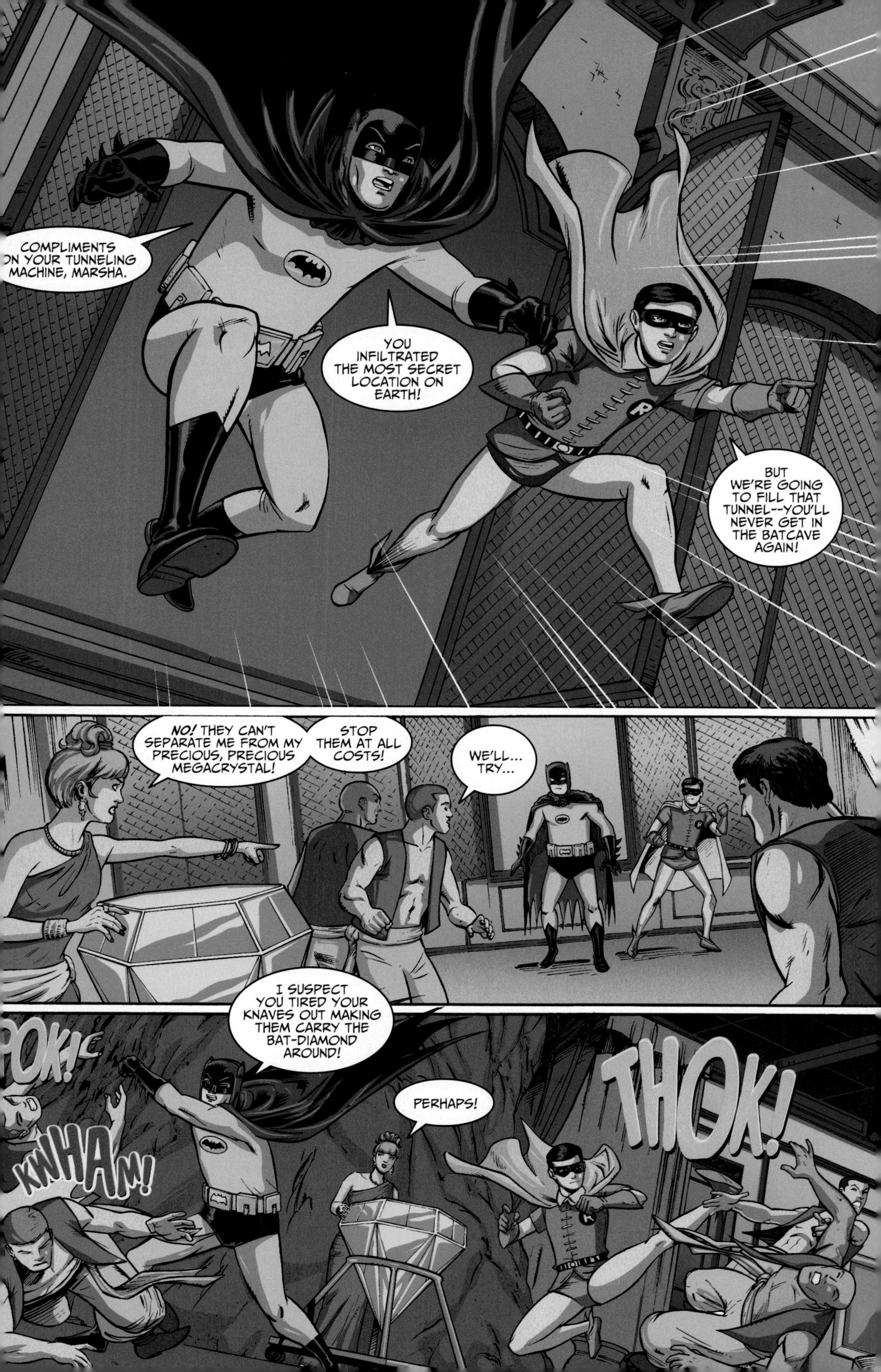
COMPLIMENTS ON YOUR TUNNELING MACHINE, MARSHA.
YOU INFILTRATED THE MOST SECRET LOCATION ON EARTH!
BUT WE'RE GOING TO FILL THAT TUNNEL--YOU'LL NEVER GET IN THE BATCAVE AGAIN!
NO! THEY CAN'T SEPARATE ME FROM MY PRECIOUS, PRECIOUS MEGACRYSTAL!
STOP THEM AT ALL COSTS!
WE'LL... TRY...
I SUSPECT YOU TIRED YOUR KNAVES OUT MAKING THEM CARRY THE BAT-DIAMOND AROUND!
PERHAPS!
KNHAM!
THOK!

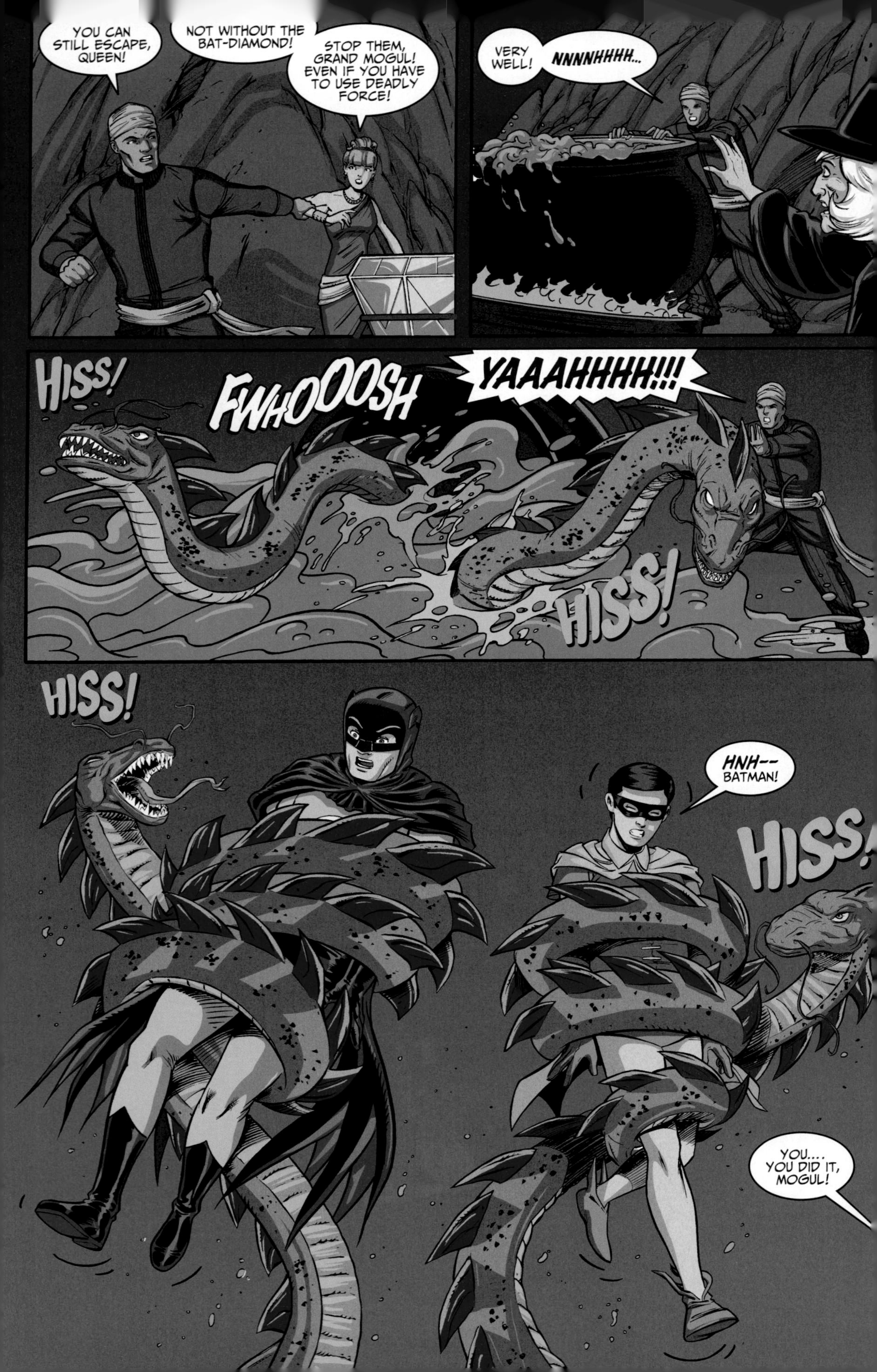

YOU CAN STILL ESCAPE, QUEEN!
NOT WITHOUT THE BAT-DIAMOND!
STOP THEM, GRAND MOGUL! EVEN IF YOU HAVE TO USE DEADLY FORCE!
VERY WELL!
NNNNHHHH...
HISS!
FWHOOOSH
YAAAHHHH!!!
HISS!
HISS!
HNH-- BATMAN!
HISS!
YOU.... YOU DID IT, MOGUL!

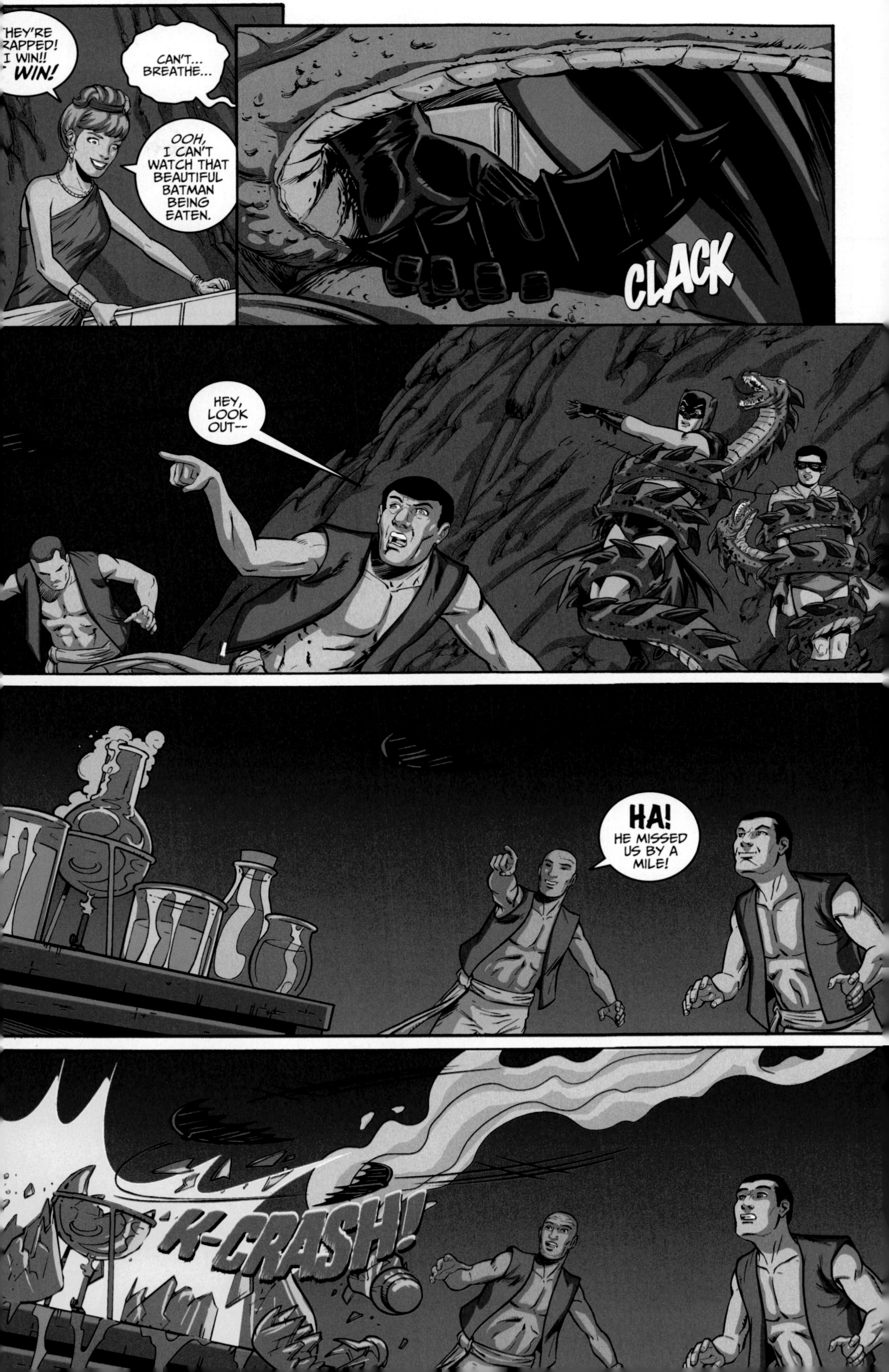

HEY'RE
RAPPED!
I WIN!!
WIN!
CAN'T...
BREATHE...
OOH, I CAN'T WATCH THAT BEAUTIFUL BATMAN BEING EATEN.
CLACK
HEY, LOOK OUT--
HA!
HE MISSED US BY A MILE!
K-CRASH!

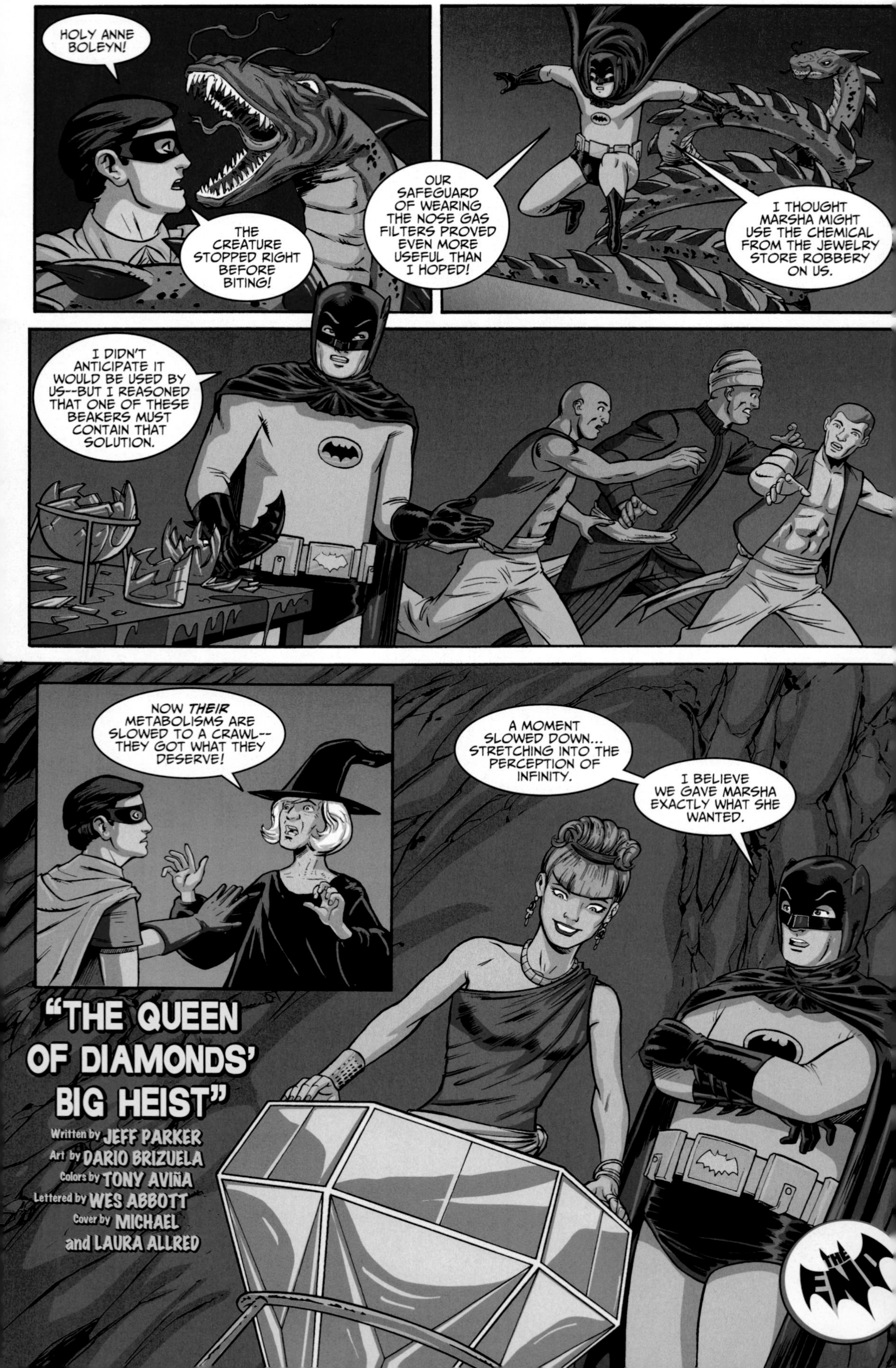

HOLY ANNE BOLEYN!
THE CREATURE STOPPED RIGHT BEFORE BITING!
OUR SAFEGUARD OF WEARING THE NOSE GAS FILTERS PROVED EVEN MORE USEFUL THAN I HOPED!
I THOUGHT MARSHA MIGHT USE THE CHEMICAL FROM THE JEWELRY STORE ROBBERY ON US.
I DIDN'T ANTICIPATE IT WOULD BE USED BY US--BUT I REASONED THAT ONE OF THESE BEAKERS MUST CONTAIN THAT SOLUTION.
NOW THEIR METABOLISMS ARE SLOWED TO A CRAWL--THEY GOT WHAT THEY DESERVE!
A MOMENT SLOWED DOWN... STRETCHING INTO THE PERCEPTION OF INFINITY.
I BELIEVE WE GAVE MARSHA EXACTLY WHAT SHE WANTED.
"THE QUEEN OF DIAMONDS' BIG HEIST"
Written by JEFF PARKER
Art by DARIO BRIZUELA
Colors by TONY AVIÑA
Lettered by WES ABBOTT
Cover by MICHAEL and LAURA ALLRED
THE END

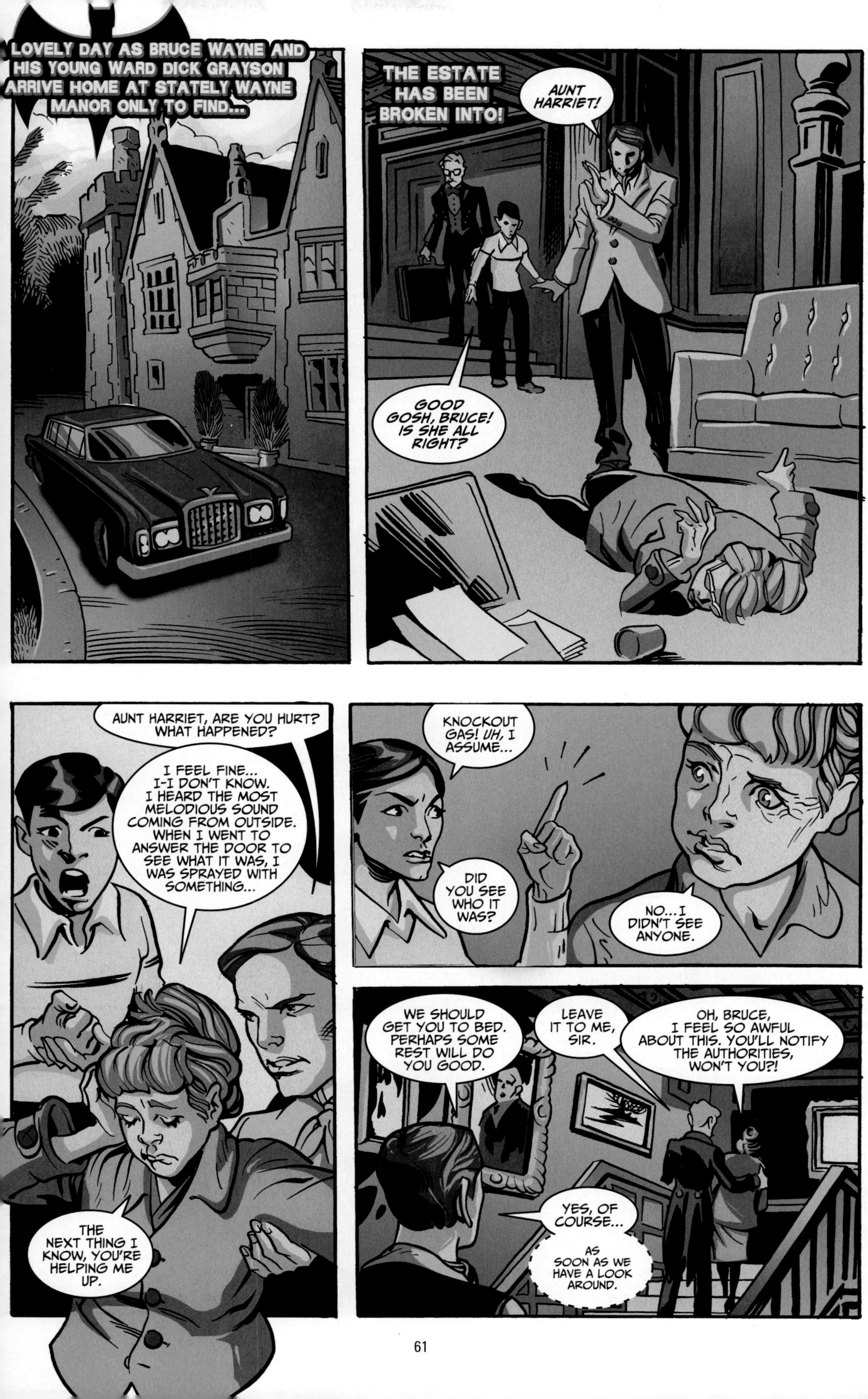
LOVELY DAY AS BRUCE WAYNE AND HIS YOUNG WARD DICK GRAYSON ARRIVE HOME AT STATELY WAYNE MANOR ONLY TO FIND...
THE ESTATE HAS BEEN BROKEN INTO!
AUNT HARRIET!
GOOD GOSH, BRUCE! IS SHE ALL RIGHT?
AUNT HARRIET, ARE YOU HURT? WHAT HAPPENED?
I FEEL FINE... I-I DON'T KNOW. I HEARD THE MOST MELODIOUS SOUND COMING FROM OUTSIDE. WHEN I WENT TO ANSWER THE DOOR TO SEE WHAT IT WAS, I WAS SPRAYED WITH SOMETHING...
THE NEXT THING I KNOW, YOU'RE HELPING ME UP.
KNOCKOUT GAS! UH, I ASSUME...
DID YOU SEE WHO IT WAS?
NO... I DIDN'T SEE ANYONE.
WE SHOULD GET YOU TO BED. PERHAPS SOME REST WILL DO YOU GOOD.
LEAVE IT TO ME, SIR.
OH, BRUCE, I FEEL SO AWFUL ABOUT THIS. YOU'LL NOTIFY THE AUTHORITIES, WON'T YOU?!
YES, OF COURSE...
AS SOON AS WE HAVE A LOOK AROUND.

I'VE LOOKED EVERYWHERE, BRUCE. NOTHING SEEMS TO HAVE BEEN TAKEN.

TO THE UNTRAINED EYE IT MAY SEEM SO, DICK.

BUT ONE THING AND ONE THING ONLY WAS TAKEN.

THE SHAKESPEARE BUST IS NOTICEABLY ABSENT FROM THE DESK.

HOLY PLAYWRIGHT! THE SHAKESPEARE BUST IS MISSING! THAT'S THE KEY TO THE BAT-POLE ENTRANCE! HOW ARE WE SUPPOSED TO GET IN THE BATCAVE WITHOUT IT?

MY WORD! COULD THE DELINQUENTS BE IN THE BATCAVE NOW, SIR?

NO.

HOW CAN YOU TELL?

ALFRED DOES AN IMPECCABLE JOB OF KEEPING ALL OF WAYNE MANOR AT THE PEAK OF CLEANLINESS.

HE WOULD NEVER BE SO CARELESS AS TO LEAVE SCUFFMARKS ON THE FLOOR.

JUDGING BY THE ONES LEFT HERE, I WOULD SAY THERE WERE FOUR PERPETRATORS, THREE MEN AND A WOMAN.

THE SCUFFMARKS LEAD HERE TO THE DESK AND THEN BACK OUT THE FRONT DOOR. THEY NEVER GO ANYWHERE NEAR THE BOOKCASE ENTRANCE TO THE BATPOLES.

HOW ARE WE SUPPOSED TO GET TO THE BATCAVE? WE CAN'T GET IN THE USUAL WAY WITHOUT THAT BUTTON...

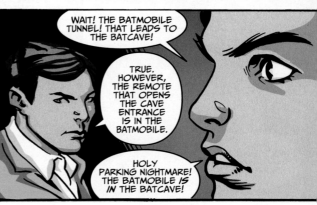

WAIT! THE BATMOBILE TUNNEL! THAT LEADS TO THE BATCAVE!

TRUE. HOWEVER, THE REMOTE THAT OPENS THE CAVE ENTRANCE IS IN THE BATMOBILE.

HOLY PARKING NIGHTMARE! THE BATMOBILE IS IN THE BATCAVE!

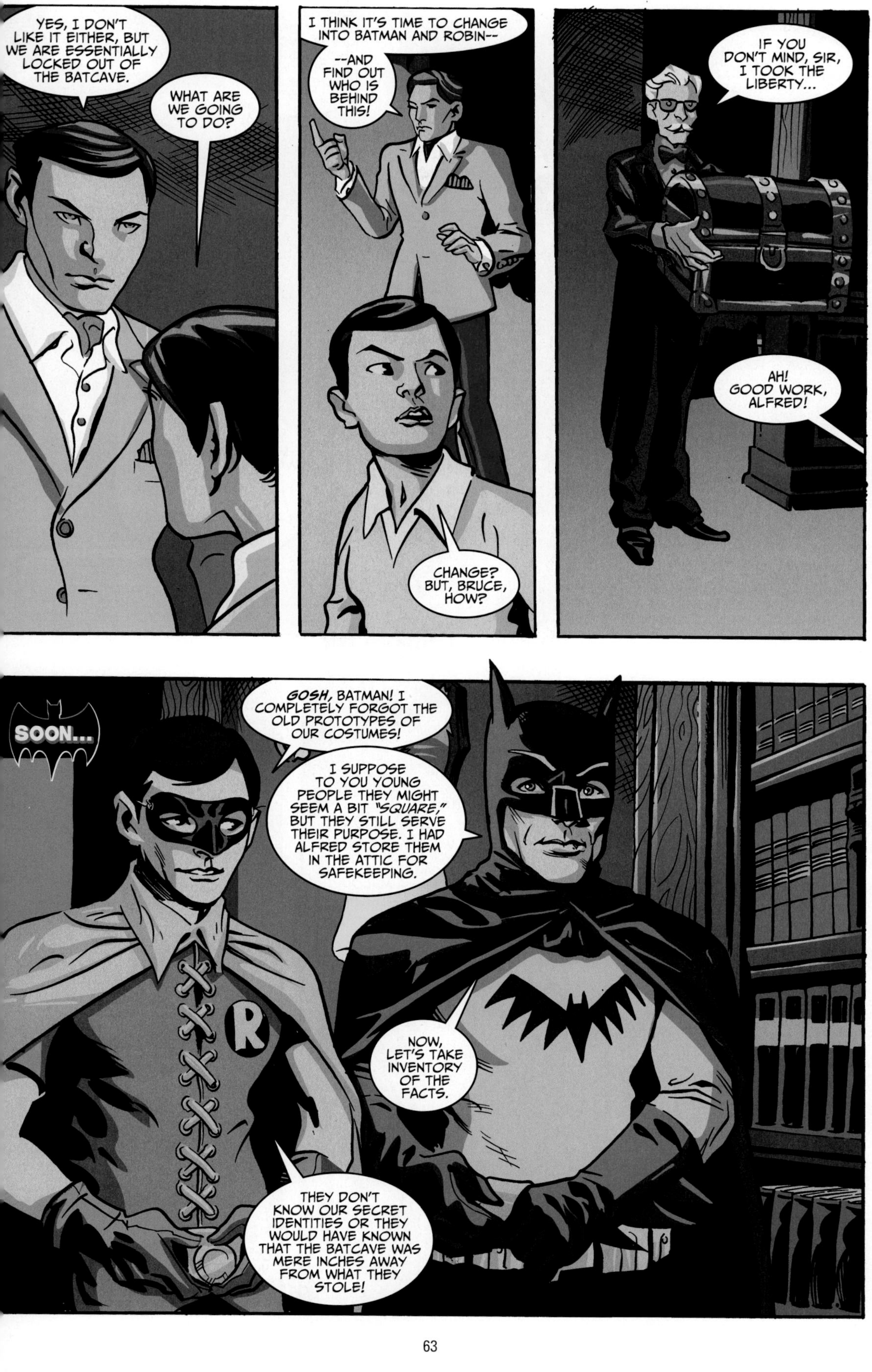
YES, I DON'T LIKE IT EITHER, BUT WE ARE ESSENTIALLY LOCKED OUT OF THE BATCAVE.
WHAT ARE WE GOING TO DO?
I THINK IT'S TIME TO CHANGE INTO BATMAN AND ROBIN--
--AND FIND OUT WHO IS BEHIND THIS!
CHANGE? BUT, BRUCE, HOW?
IF YOU DON'T MIND, SIR, I TOOK THE LIBERTY...
AH! GOOD WORK, ALFRED!
SOON...
GOSH, BATMAN! I COMPLETELY FORGOT THE OLD PROTOTYPES OF OUR COSTUMES!
I SUPPOSE TO YOU YOUNG PEOPLE THEY MIGHT SEEM A BIT *"SQUARE,"* BUT THEY STILL SERVE THEIR PURPOSE. I HAD ALFRED STORE THEM IN THE ATTIC FOR SAFEKEEPING.
NOW, LET'S TAKE INVENTORY OF THE FACTS.
THEY DON'T KNOW OUR SECRET IDENTITIES OR THEY WOULD HAVE KNOWN THAT THE BATCAVE WAS MERE INCHES AWAY FROM WHAT THEY STOLE!

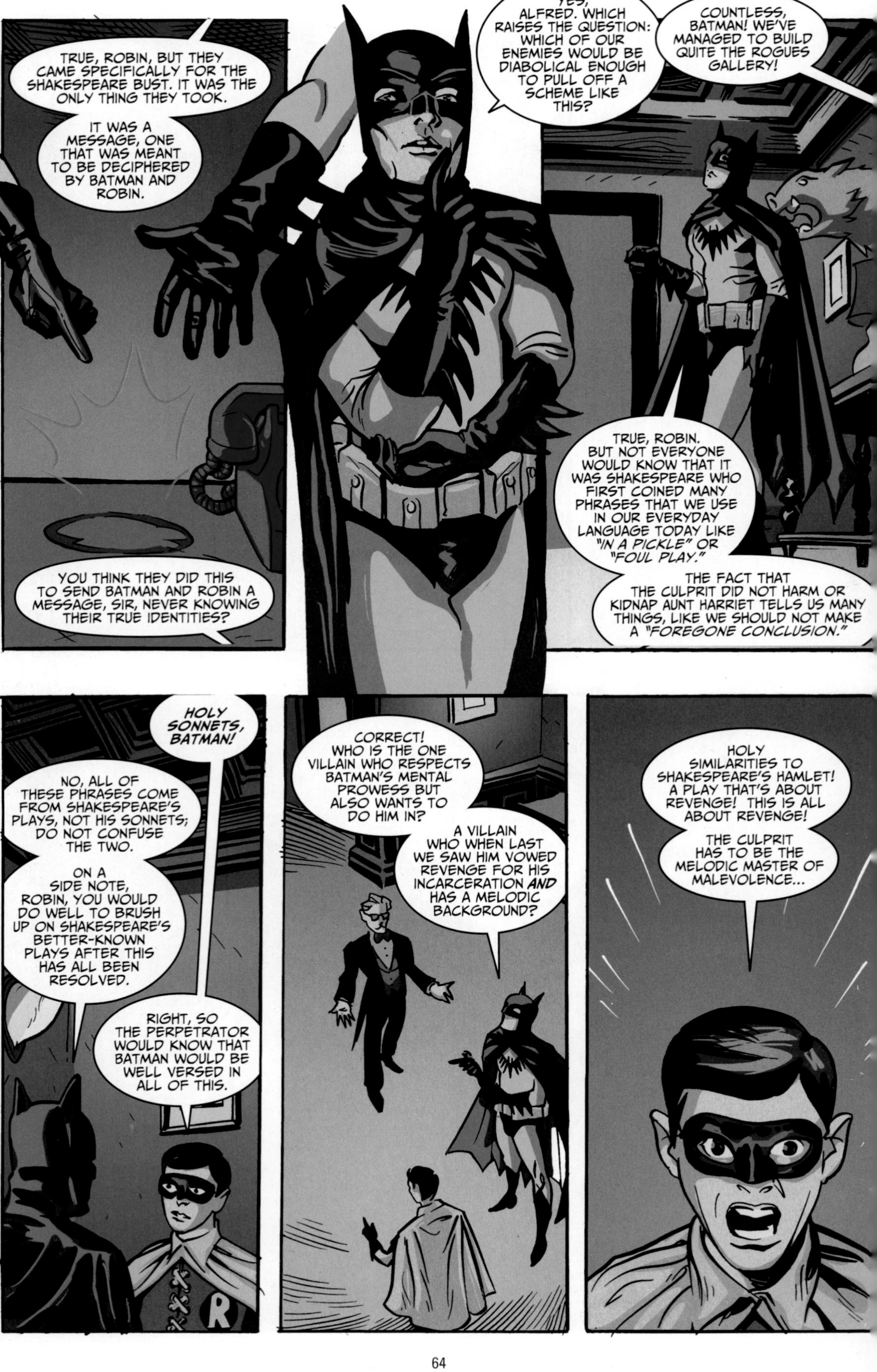
TRUE, ROBIN, BUT THEY CAME SPECIFICALLY FOR THE SHAKESPEARE BUST. IT WAS THE ONLY THING THEY TOOK.
IT WAS A MESSAGE, ONE THAT WAS MEANT TO BE DECIPHERED BY BATMAN AND ROBIN.
YOU THINK THEY DID THIS TO SEND BATMAN AND ROBIN A MESSAGE, SIR, NEVER KNOWING THEIR TRUE IDENTITIES?
YES, ALFRED. WHICH RAISES THE QUESTION: WHICH OF OUR ENEMIES WOULD BE DIABOLICAL ENOUGH TO PULL OFF A SCHEME LIKE THIS?
COUNTLESS, BATMAN! WE'VE MANAGED TO BUILD QUITE THE ROGUES GALLERY!
TRUE, ROBIN. BUT NOT EVERYONE WOULD KNOW THAT IT WAS SHAKESPEARE WHO FIRST COINED MANY PHRASES THAT WE USE IN OUR EVERYDAY LANGUAGE TODAY LIKE *"IN A PICKLE"* OR *"FOUL PLAY."*
THE FACT THAT THE CULPRIT DID NOT HARM OR KIDNAP AUNT HARRIET TELLS US MANY THINGS, LIKE WE SHOULD NOT MAKE A *"FOREGONE CONCLUSION."*
HOLY SONNETS, BATMAN!
NO, ALL OF THESE PHRASES COME FROM SHAKESPEARE'S PLAYS, NOT HIS SONNETS; DO NOT CONFUSE THE TWO.
ON A SIDE NOTE, ROBIN, YOU WOULD DO WELL TO BRUSH UP ON SHAKESPEARE'S BETTER-KNOWN PLAYS AFTER THIS HAS ALL BEEN RESOLVED.
RIGHT, SO THE PERPETRATOR WOULD KNOW THAT BATMAN WOULD BE WELL VERSED IN ALL OF THIS.
CORRECT! WHO IS THE ONE VILLAIN WHO RESPECTS BATMAN'S MENTAL PROWESS BUT ALSO WANTS TO DO HIM IN?
A VILLAIN WHO WHEN LAST WE SAW HIM VOWED REVENGE FOR HIS INCARCERATION ***AND*** HAS A MELODIC BACKGROUND?
HOLY SIMILARITIES TO SHAKESPEARE'S HAMLET! A PLAY THAT'S ABOUT REVENGE! THIS IS ALL ABOUT REVENGE!
THE CULPRIT HAS TO BE THE MELODIC MASTER OF MALEVOLENCE...
R

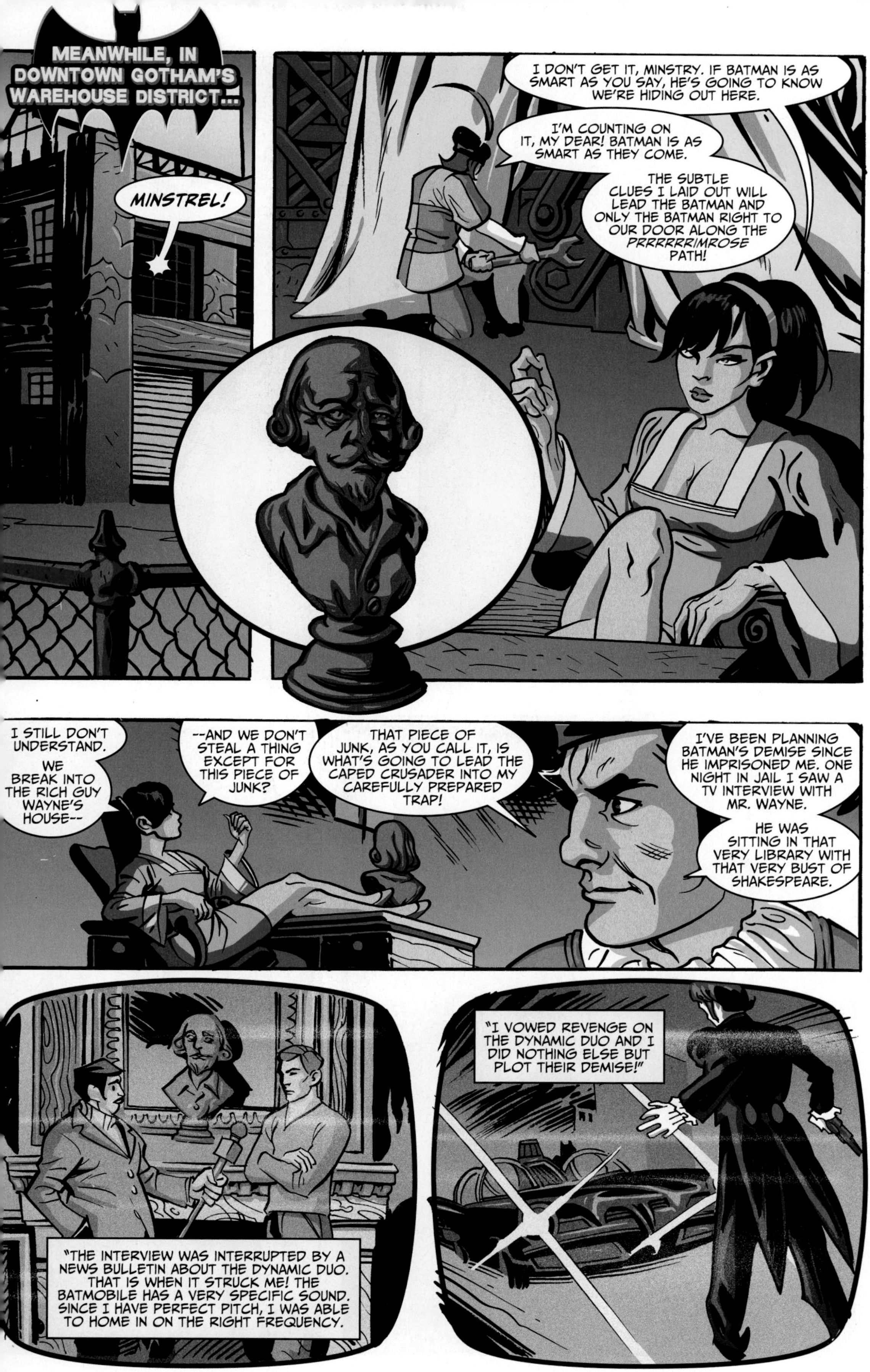
MEANWHILE, IN DOWNTOWN GOTHAM'S WAREHOUSE DISTRICT...
MINSTREL!
I DON'T GET IT, MINSTRY. IF BATMAN IS AS SMART AS YOU SAY, HE'S GOING TO KNOW WE'RE HIDING OUT HERE.
I'M COUNTING ON IT, MY DEAR! BATMAN IS AS SMART AS THEY COME.
THE SUBTLE CLUES I LAID OUT WILL LEAD THE BATMAN AND ONLY THE BATMAN RIGHT TO OUR DOOR ALONG THE *PRRRRRRIMROSE* PATH!
I STILL DON'T UNDERSTAND.
WE BREAK INTO THE RICH GUY WAYNE'S HOUSE--
--AND WE DON'T STEAL A THING EXCEPT FOR THIS PIECE OF JUNK?
THAT PIECE OF JUNK, AS YOU CALL IT, IS WHAT'S GOING TO LEAD THE CAPED CRUSADER INTO MY CAREFULLY PREPARED TRAP!
I'VE BEEN PLANNING BATMAN'S DEMISE SINCE HE IMPRISONED ME. ONE NIGHT IN JAIL I SAW A TV INTERVIEW WITH MR. WAYNE.
HE WAS SITTING IN THAT VERY LIBRARY WITH THAT VERY BUST OF SHAKESPEARE.
"THE INTERVIEW WAS INTERRUPTED BY A NEWS BULLETIN ABOUT THE DYNAMIC DUO. THAT IS WHEN IT STRUCK ME! THE BATMOBILE HAS A VERY SPECIFIC SOUND. SINCE I HAVE PERFECT PITCH, I WAS ABLE TO HOME IN ON THE RIGHT FREQUENCY.
"I VOWED REVENGE ON THE DYNAMIC DUO AND I DID NOTHING ELSE BUT PLOT THEIR DEMISE!"

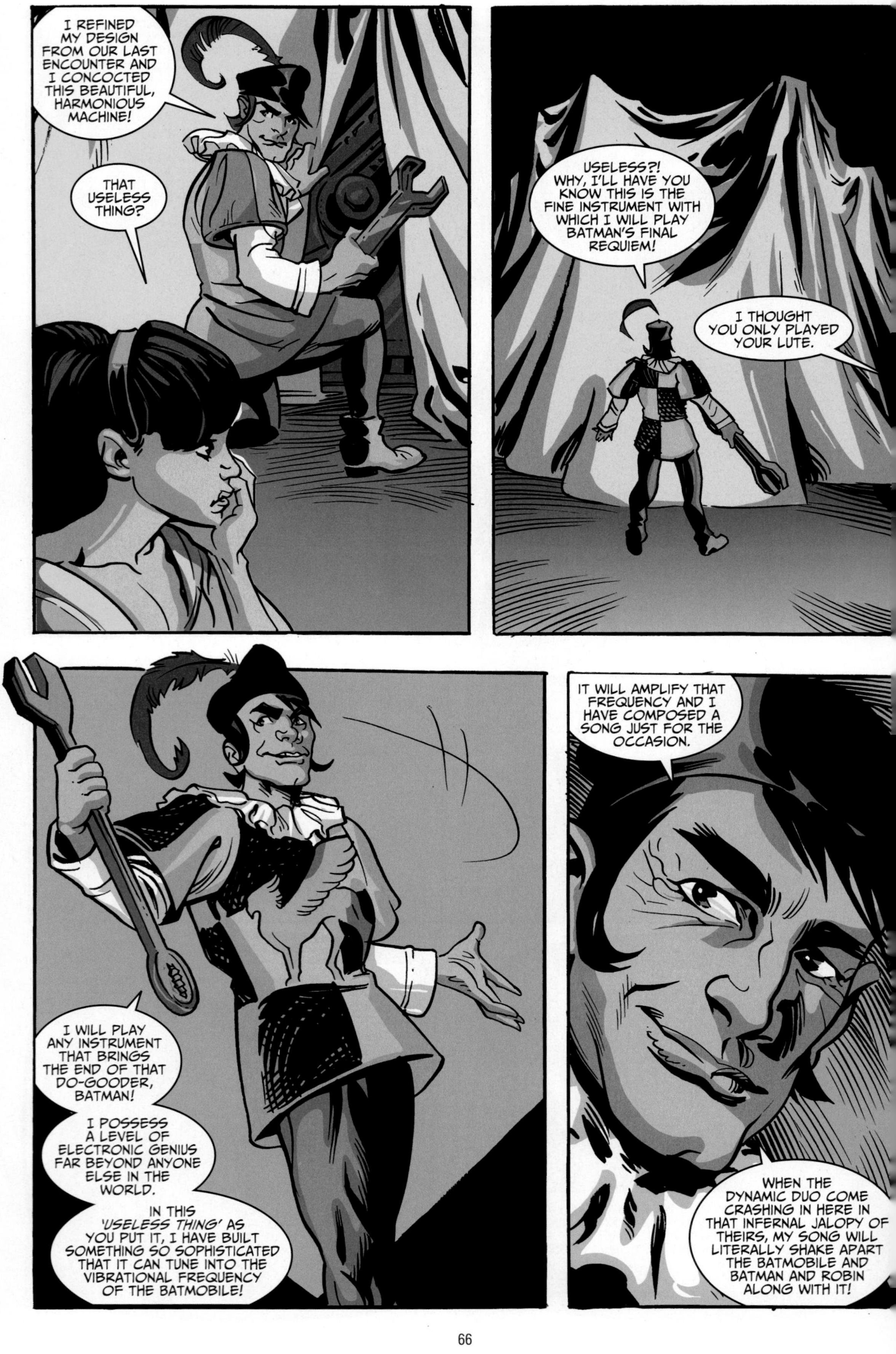
I REFINED MY DESIGN FROM OUR LAST ENCOUNTER AND I CONCOCTED THIS BEAUTIFUL, HARMONIOUS MACHINE!
THAT USELESS THING?
USELESS?! WHY, I'LL HAVE YOU KNOW THIS IS THE FINE INSTRUMENT WITH WHICH I WILL PLAY BATMAN'S FINAL REQUIEM!
I THOUGHT YOU ONLY PLAYED YOUR LUTE.
I WILL PLAY ANY INSTRUMENT THAT BRINGS THE END OF THAT DO-GOODER, BATMAN!
I POSSESS A LEVEL OF ELECTRONIC GENIUS FAR BEYOND ANYONE ELSE IN THE WORLD.
IN THIS *'USELESS THING'* AS YOU PUT IT, I HAVE BUILT SOMETHING SO SOPHISTICATED THAT IT CAN TUNE INTO THE VIBRATIONAL FREQUENCY OF THE BATMOBILE!
IT WILL AMPLIFY THAT FREQUENCY AND I HAVE COMPOSED A SONG JUST FOR THE OCCASION.
WHEN THE DYNAMIC DUO COME CRASHING IN HERE IN THAT INFERNAL JALOPY OF THEIRS, MY SONG WILL LITERALLY SHAKE APART THE BATMOBILE AND BATMAN AND ROBIN ALONG WITH IT!

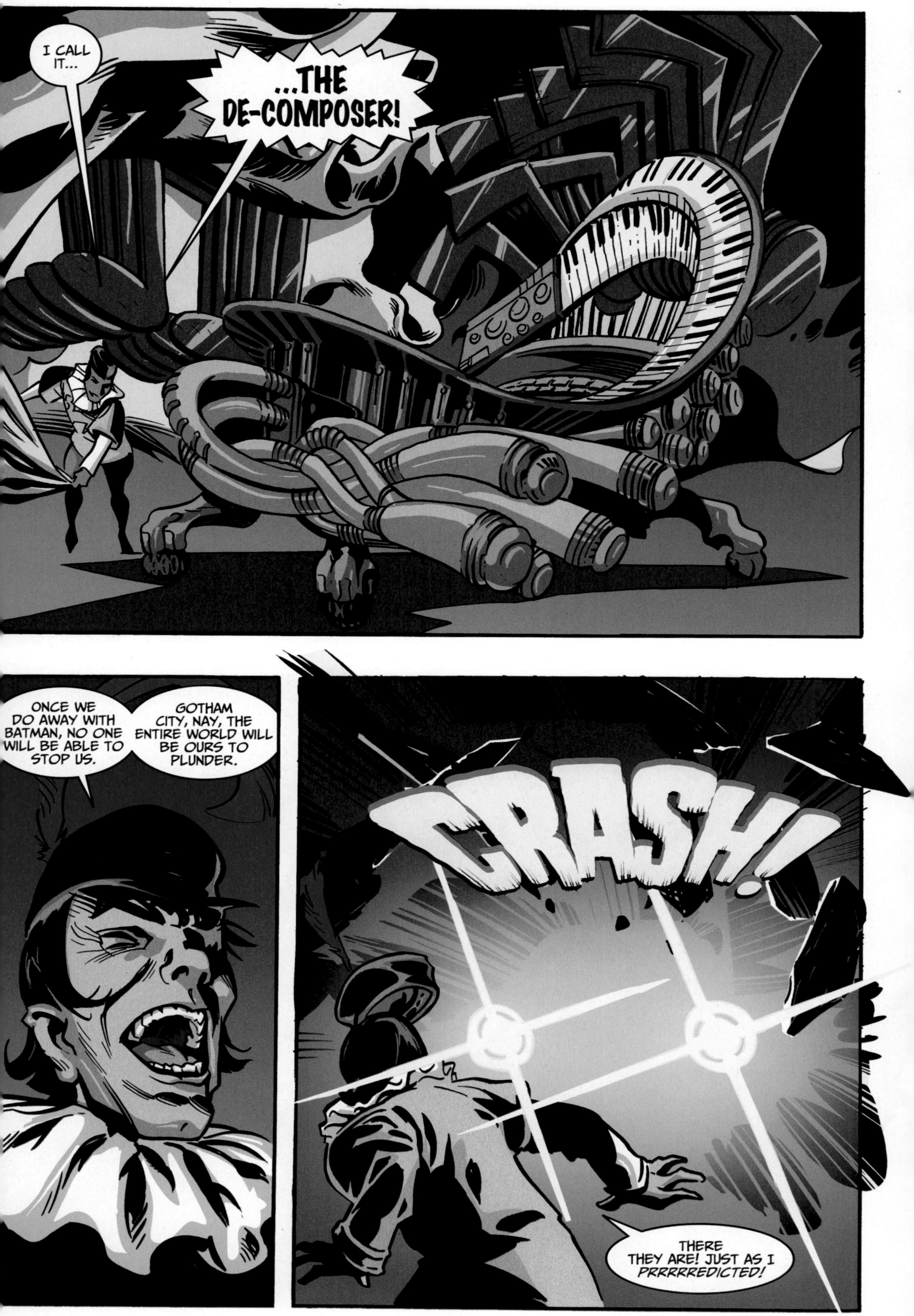
I CALL IT...
...THE DE-COMPOSER!
ONCE WE DO AWAY WITH BATMAN, NO ONE WILL BE ABLE TO STOP US.
GOTHAM CITY, NAY, THE ENTIRE WORLD WILL BE OURS TO PLUNDER.
CRASH!
THERE THEY ARE! JUST AS I *PRRRRREDICTED!*

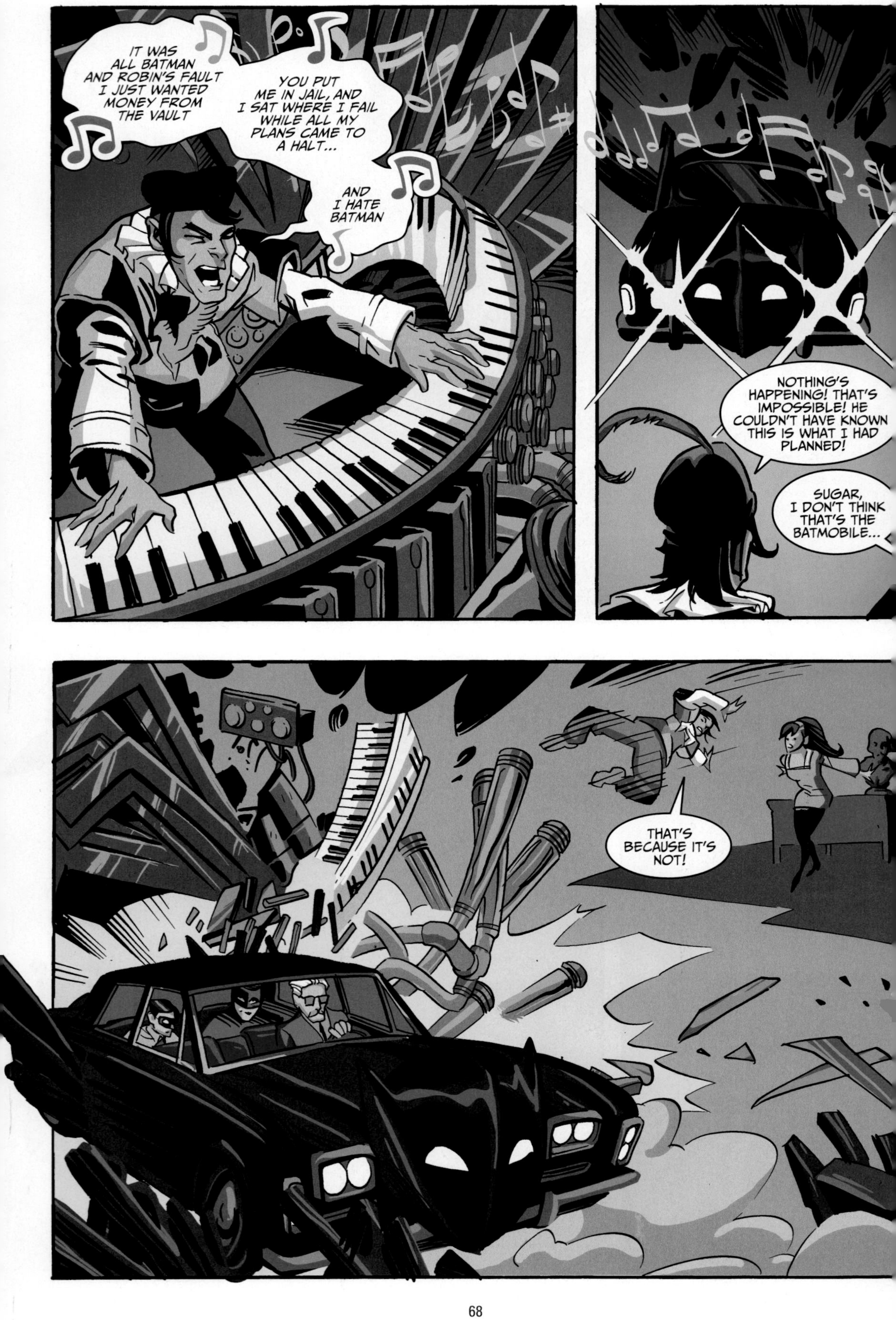
IT WAS ALL BATMAN AND ROBIN'S FAULT I JUST WANTED MONEY FROM THE VAULT
YOU PUT ME IN JAIL, AND I SAT WHERE I FAIL WHILE ALL MY PLANS CAME TO A HALT...
AND I HATE BATMAN
NOTHING'S HAPPENING! THAT'S IMPOSSIBLE! HE COULDN'T HAVE KNOWN THIS IS WHAT I HAD PLANNED!
SUGAR, I DON'T THINK THAT'S THE BATMOBILE...
THAT'S BECAUSE IT'S NOT!

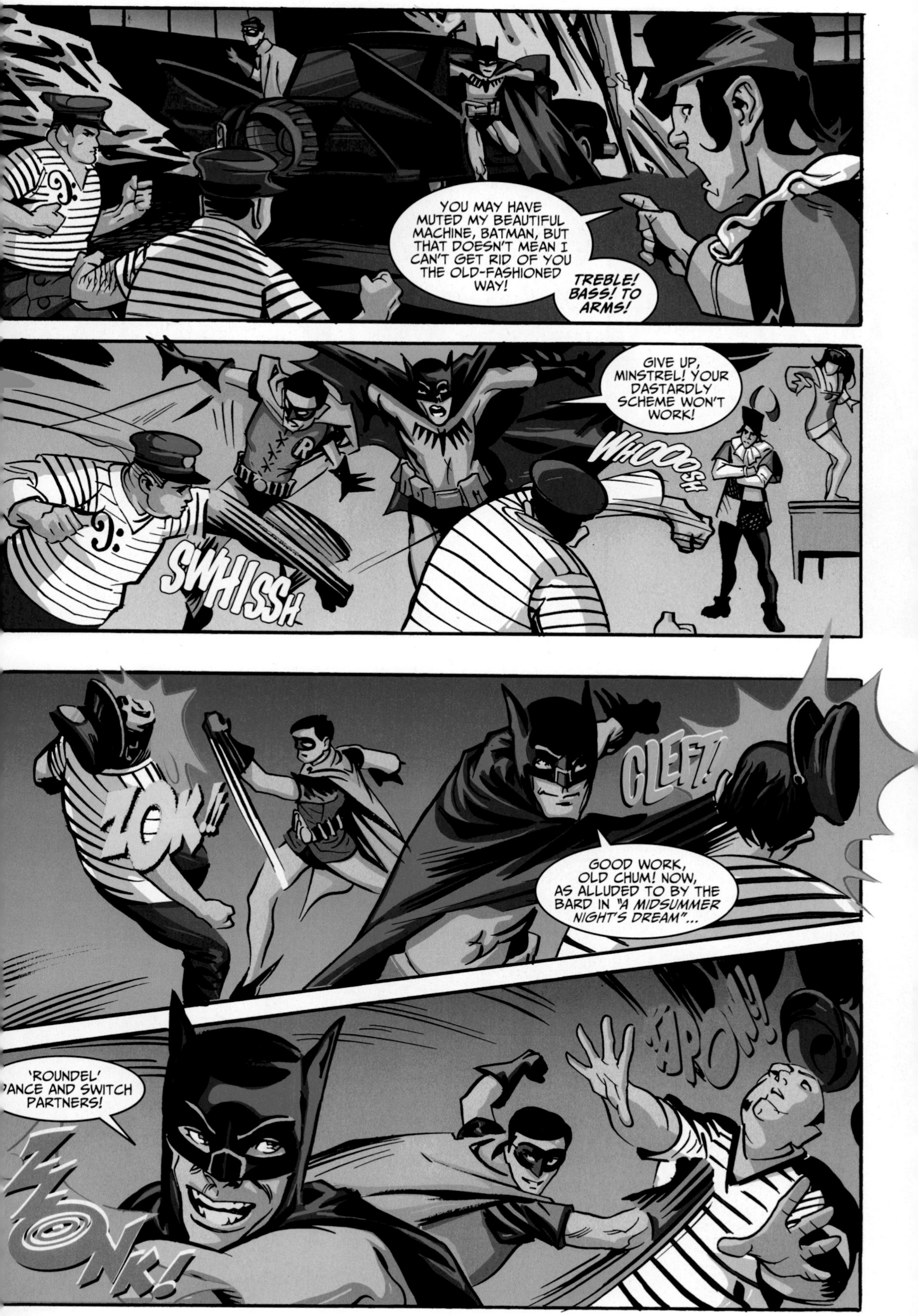
YOU MAY HAVE MUTED MY BEAUTIFUL MACHINE, BATMAN, BUT THAT DOESN'T MEAN I CAN'T GET RID OF YOU THE OLD-FASHIONED WAY!
TREBLE! BASS! TO ARMS!
GIVE UP, MINSTREL! YOUR DASTARDLY SCHEME WON'T WORK!
WHOOOOSH
SWHISSH
ZOK!
CLEFT!
GOOD WORK, OLD CHUM! NOW, AS ALLUDED TO BY THE BARD IN "A MIDSUMMER NIGHT'S DREAM"...
'ROUNDEL' DANCE AND SWITCH PARTNERS!
THWOK!
ZZONK!

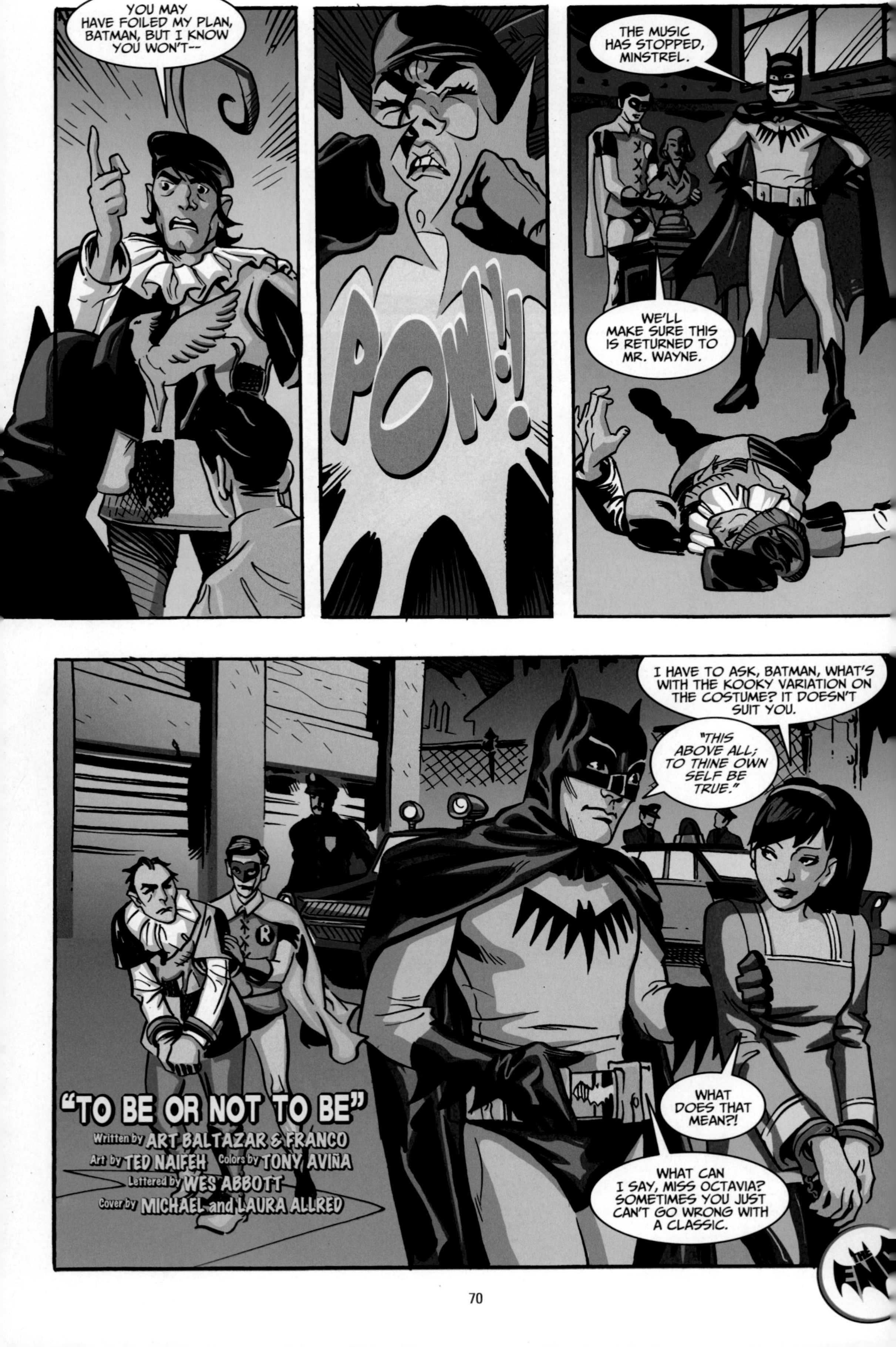
YOU MAY HAVE FOILED MY PLAN, BATMAN, BUT I KNOW YOU WON'T--
POW!!
THE MUSIC HAS STOPPED, MINSTREL.
WE'LL MAKE SURE THIS IS RETURNED TO MR. WAYNE.
I HAVE TO ASK, BATMAN, WHAT'S WITH THE KOOKY VARIATION ON THE COSTUME? IT DOESN'T SUIT YOU.
"THIS ABOVE ALL; TO THINE OWN SELF BE TRUE."
WHAT DOES THAT MEAN?!
WHAT CAN I SAY, MISS OCTAVIA? SOMETIMES YOU JUST CAN'T GO WRONG WITH A CLASSIC.
"TO BE OR NOT TO BE"
Written by ART BALTAZAR & FRANCO
Art by TED NAIFEH Colors by TONY AVIÑA
Lettered by WES ABBOTT
Cover by MICHAEL and LAURA ALLRED

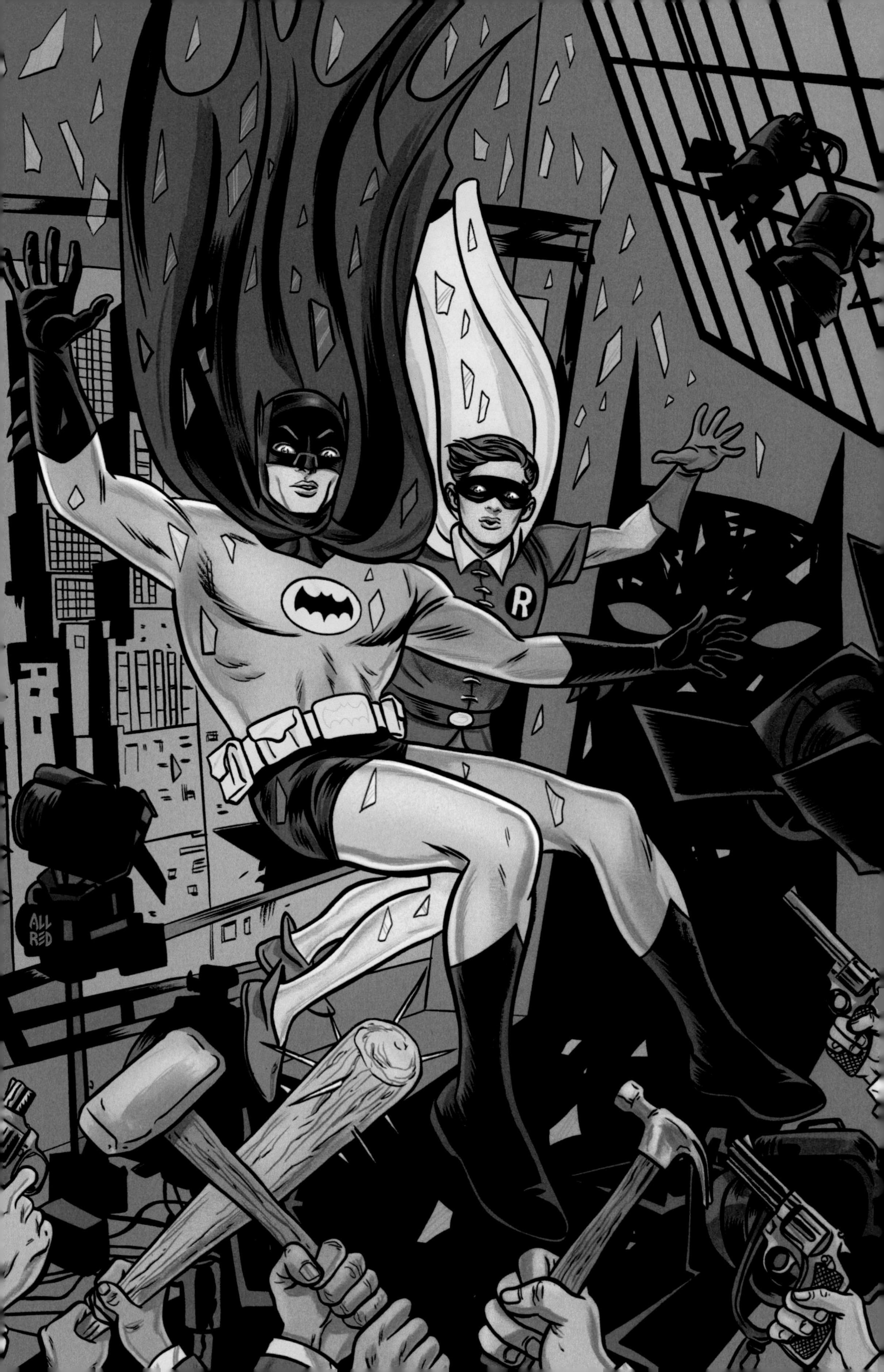
ALL
RED

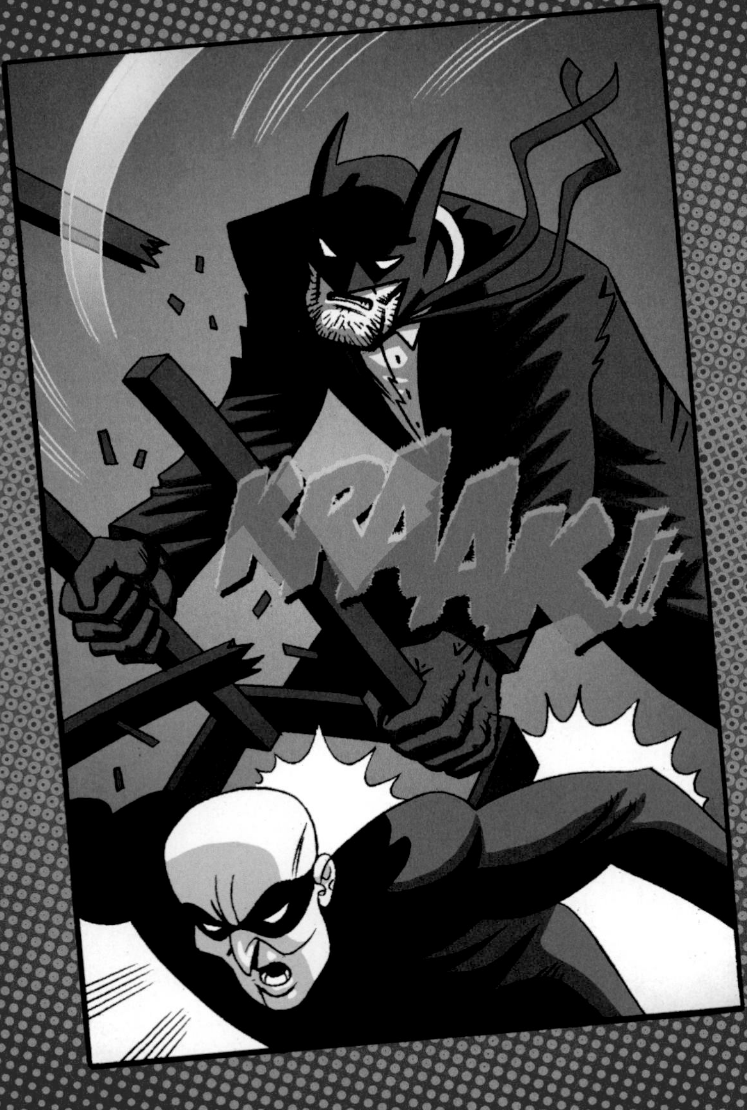
KRAAK!!

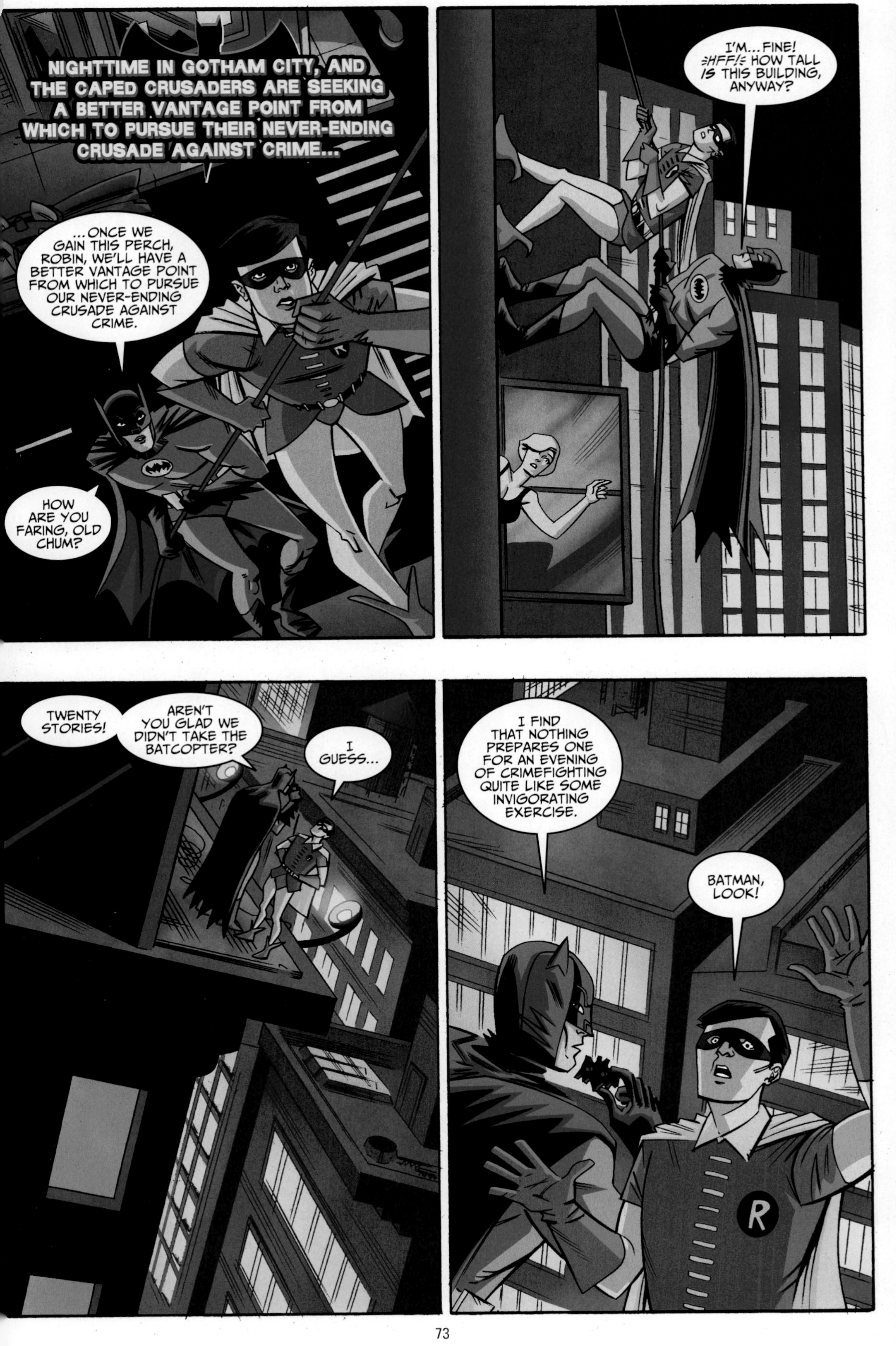
NIGHTTIME IN GOTHAM CITY, AND THE CAPED CRUSADERS ARE SEEKING A BETTER VANTAGE POINT FROM WHICH TO PURSUE THEIR NEVER-ENDING CRUSADE AGAINST CRIME...
...ONCE WE GAIN THIS PERCH, ROBIN, WE'LL HAVE A BETTER VANTAGE POINT FROM WHICH TO PURSUE OUR NEVER-ENDING CRUSADE AGAINST CRIME.
HOW ARE YOU FARING, OLD CHUM?
I'M...FINE! =HFF!= HOW TALL IS THIS BUILDING, ANYWAY?
TWENTY STORIES!
AREN'T YOU GLAD WE DIDN'T TAKE THE BATCOPTER?
I GUESS...
I FIND THAT NOTHING PREPARES ONE FOR AN EVENING OF CRIMEFIGHTING QUITE LIKE SOME INVIGORATING EXERCISE.
BATMAN, LOOK!

THE DARK KNIGHT DETECTIVE

A FRED FILLIPS PRODUCTION

...ader ...EVER ...fore... ...' Show! ...AT-urday ...LY on Gotham 8!

HOLY PRIME TIME!

LIKE YOU'D EVER AGREE TO SOMETHING LIKE THAT! YOU SHOULD *SUE.*

HMM...

WHILE THIS SORT OF...EXPOSURE IS NOT SOMETHING I WOULD NORMALLY SEEK, WE MUST REALIZE THAT OUR HEROIC EXPLOITS HAVE INSPIRED THE CITIZENS OF GOTHAM.

AS SUCH, DEPICTING US IN FORMS OF MASS COMMUNICATION IS TO BE EXPECTED. EVEN TAKEN AS A COMPLIMENT.

I DON'T KNO--*HEY!* A JEWELRY STORE ROBBERY!

WELL SPOTTED, ROBIN. DUTY CALLS!

A BATMAN TELEVISION SHOW? FIND OUT IF THE DYNAMIC DUO IS READY FOR THEIR CLOSE-UP IN...

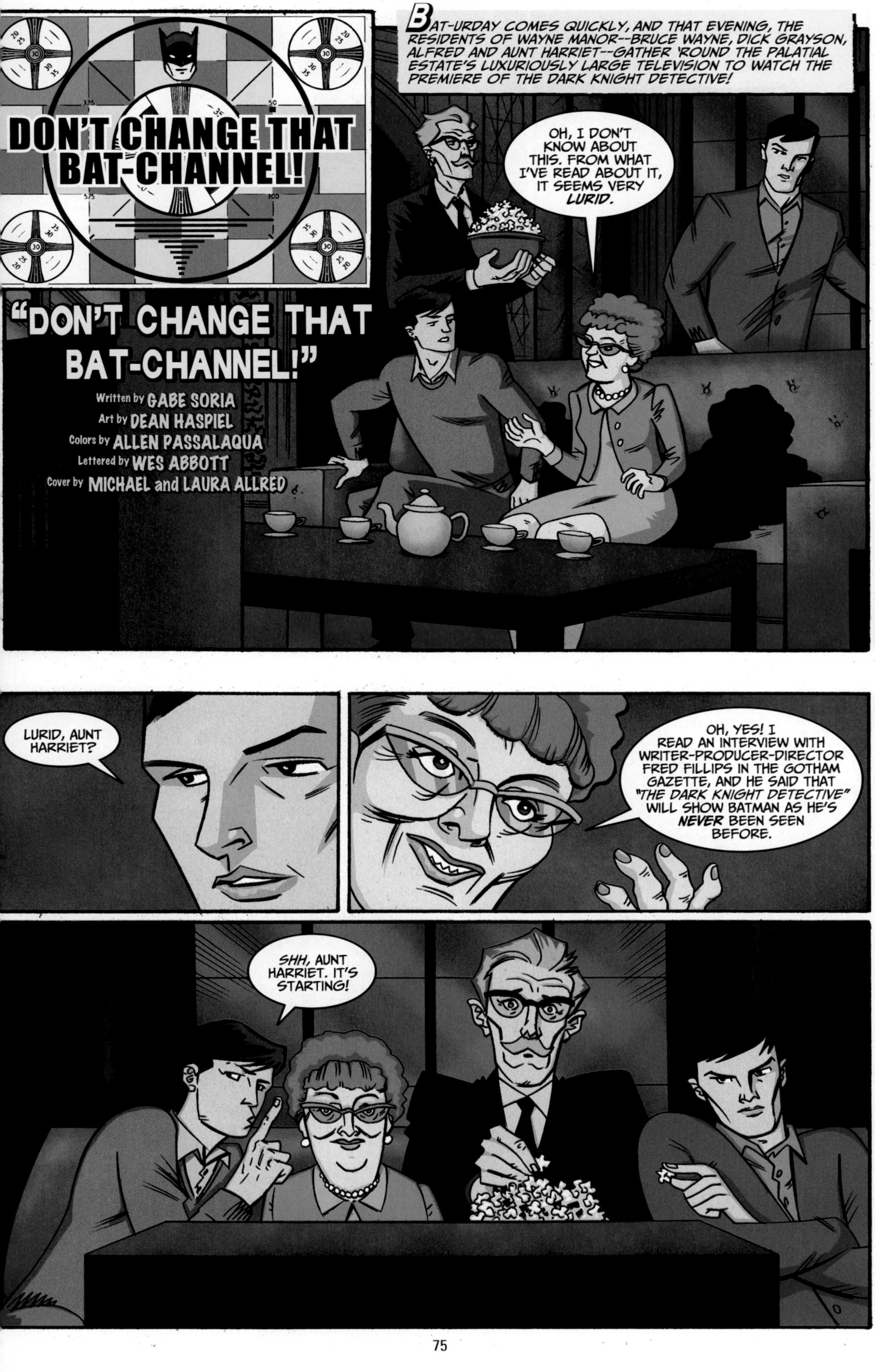
DON'T CHANGE THAT BAT-CHANNEL!
"DON'T CHANGE THAT BAT-CHANNEL!"
Written by GABE SORIA
Art by DEAN HASPIEL
Colors by ALLEN PASSALAQUA
Lettered by WES ABBOTT
Cover by MICHAEL and LAURA ALLRED
BAT-URDAY COMES QUICKLY, AND THAT EVENING, THE RESIDENTS OF WAYNE MANOR--BRUCE WAYNE, DICK GRAYSON, ALFRED AND AUNT HARRIET--GATHER 'ROUND THE PALATIAL ESTATE'S LUXURIOUSLY LARGE TELEVISION TO WATCH THE PREMIERE OF THE DARK KNIGHT DETECTIVE!
OH, I DON'T KNOW ABOUT THIS. FROM WHAT I'VE READ ABOUT IT, IT SEEMS VERY LURID.
LURID, AUNT HARRIET?
OH, YES! I READ AN INTERVIEW WITH WRITER-PRODUCER-DIRECTOR FRED FILLIPS IN THE GOTHAM GAZETTE, AND HE SAID THAT "THE DARK KNIGHT DETECTIVE" WILL SHOW BATMAN AS HE'S NEVER BEEN SEEN BEFORE.
SHH, AUNT HARRIET. IT'S STARTING!

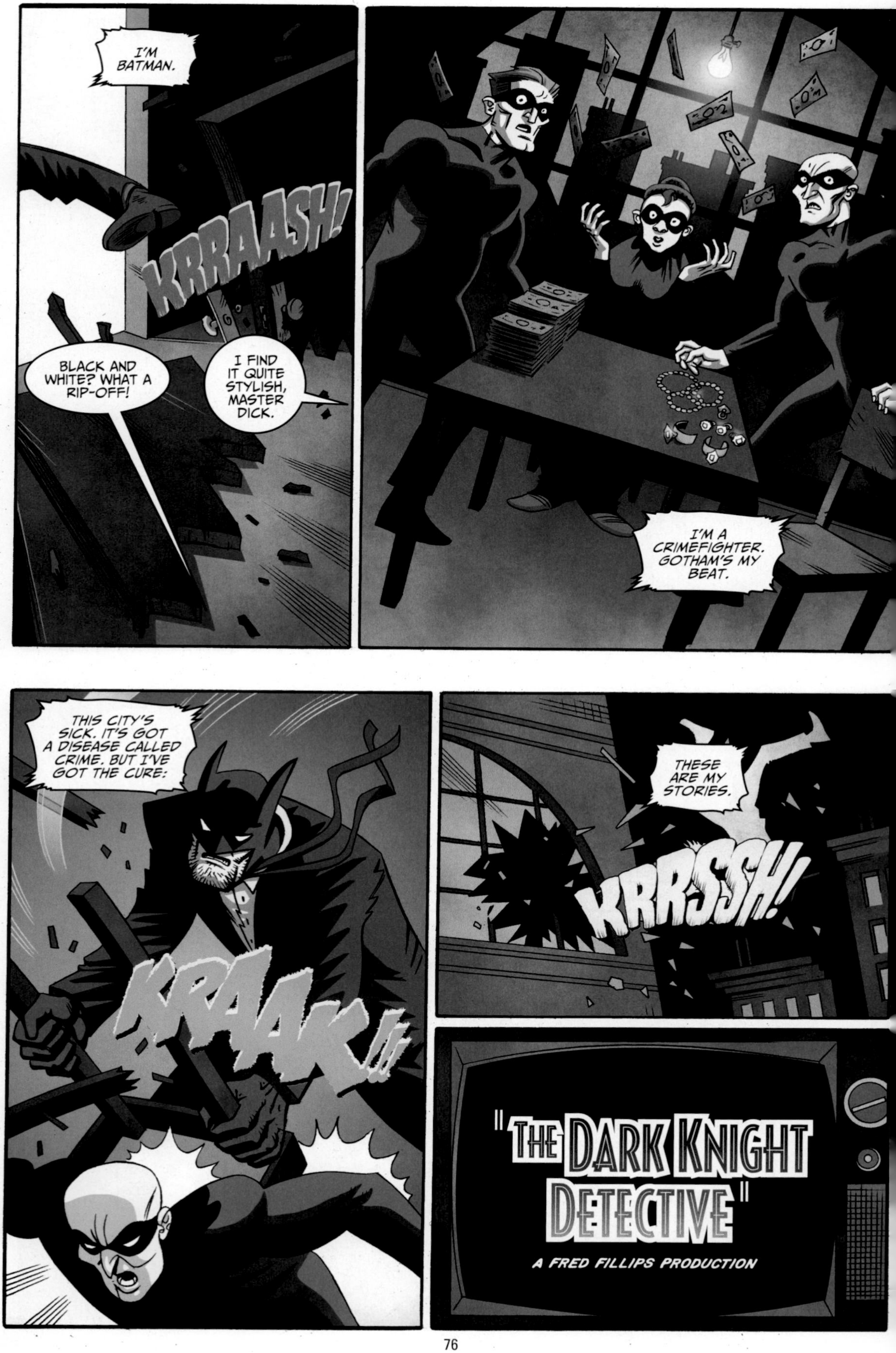
I'M BATMAN.
KRRAASH!
BLACK AND WHITE? WHAT A RIP-OFF!
I FIND IT QUITE STYLISH, MASTER DICK.
I'M A CRIMEFIGHTER. GOTHAM'S MY BEAT.
THIS CITY'S SICK. IT'S GOT A DISEASE CALLED CRIME. BUT I'VE GOT THE CURE:
KRAAK!!!
THESE ARE MY STORIES.
KRRSSH!
"THE DARK KNIGHT DETECTIVE"
A FRED FILLIPS PRODUCTION

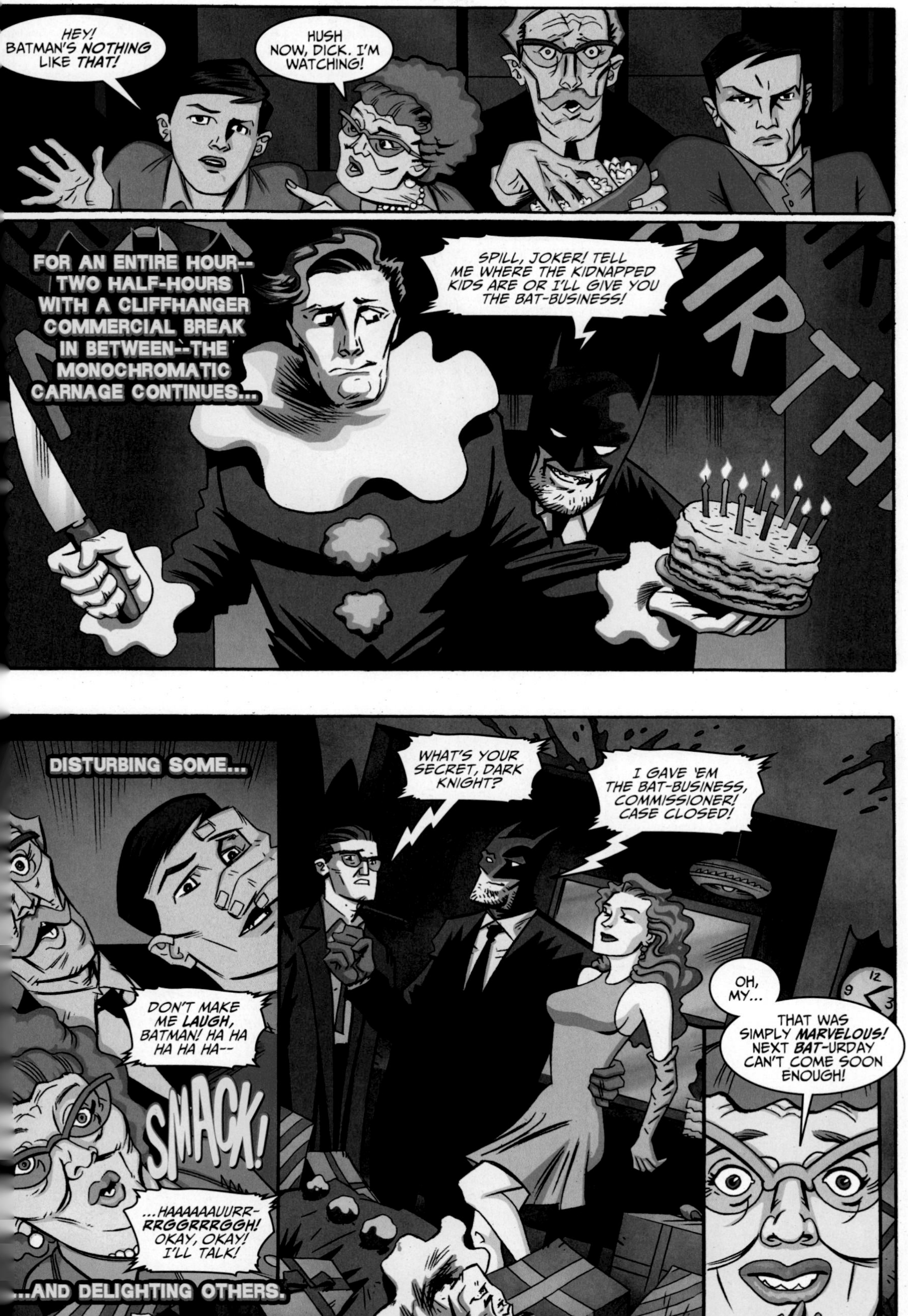

HEY! BATMAN'S NOTHING LIKE THAT!
HUSH NOW, DICK. I'M WATCHING!
FOR AN ENTIRE HOUR--TWO HALF-HOURS WITH A CLIFFHANGER COMMERCIAL BREAK IN BETWEEN--THE MONOCHROMATIC CARNAGE CONTINUES...
SPILL, JOKER! TELL ME WHERE THE KIDNAPPED KIDS ARE OR I'LL GIVE YOU THE BAT-BUSINESS!
DISTURBING SOME...
DON'T MAKE ME LAUGH, BATMAN! HA HA HA HA HA--
SMACK!
...HAAAAAAUURR-RRGGRRRGGH! OKAY, OKAY! I'LL TALK!
...AND DELIGHTING OTHERS.
WHAT'S YOUR SECRET, DARK KNIGHT?
I GAVE 'EM THE BAT-BUSINESS, COMMISSIONER! CASE CLOSED!
OH, MY...
THAT WAS SIMPLY MARVELOUS! NEXT BAT-URDAY CAN'T COME SOON ENOUGH!

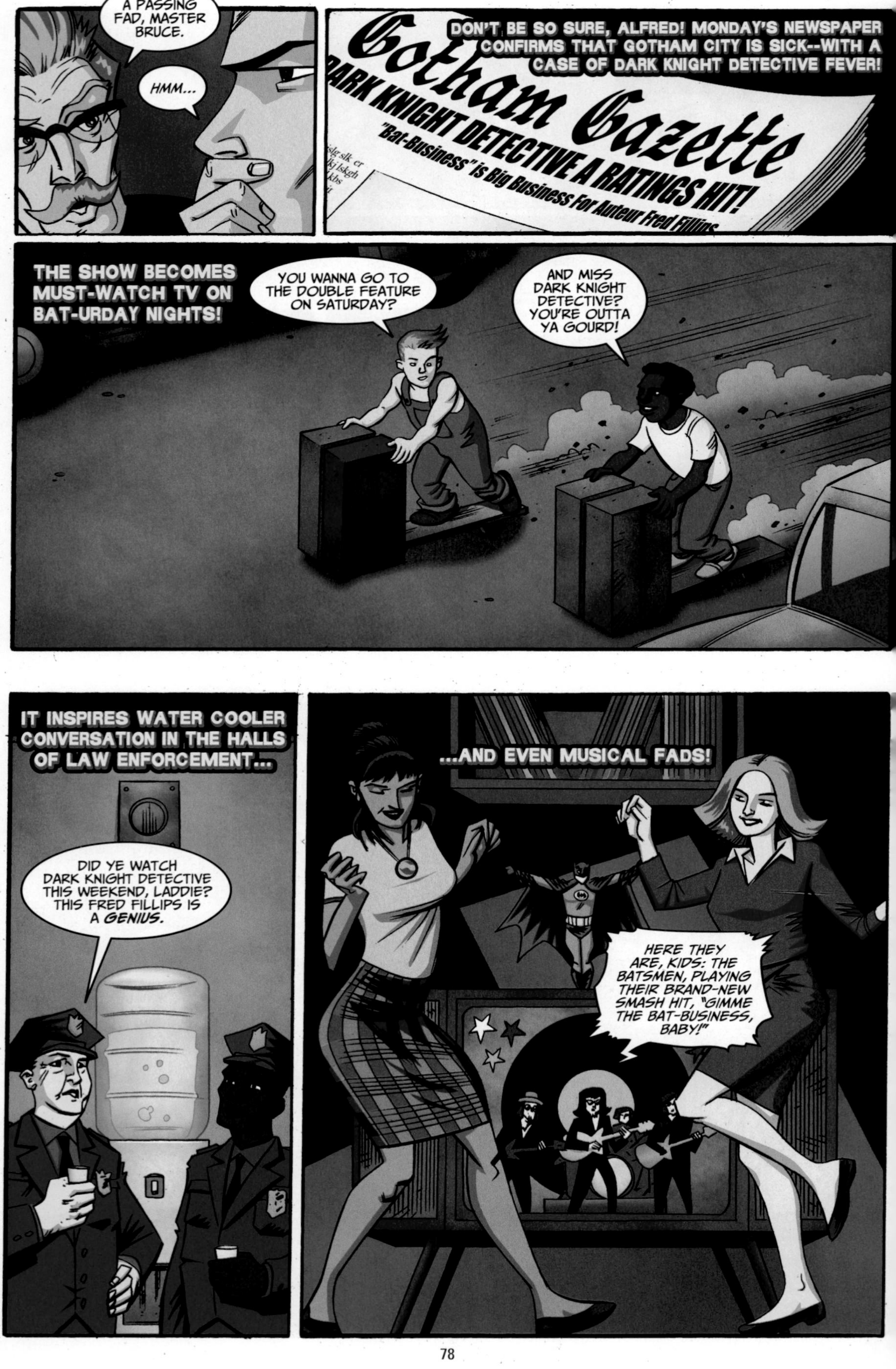

A PASSING FAD, MASTER BRUCE.
HMM...
DON'T BE SO SURE, ALFRED! MONDAY'S NEWSPAPER CONFIRMS THAT GOTHAM CITY IS SICK--WITH A CASE OF DARK KNIGHT DETECTIVE FEVER!
Gotham Gazette
DARK KNIGHT DETECTIVE A RATINGS HIT!
"Bat-Business" is Big Business For Auteur Fred
THE SHOW BECOMES MUST-WATCH TV ON BAT-URDAY NIGHTS!
YOU WANNA GO TO THE DOUBLE FEATURE ON SATURDAY?
AND MISS DARK KNIGHT DETECTIVE? YOU'RE OUTTA YA GOURD!
IT INSPIRES WATER COOLER CONVERSATION IN THE HALLS OF LAW ENFORCEMENT...
DID YE WATCH DARK KNIGHT DETECTIVE THIS WEEKEND, LADDIE? THIS FRED FILLIPS IS A GENIUS.
...AND EVEN MUSICAL FADS!
HERE THEY ARE, KIDS: THE BATSMEN, PLAYING THEIR BRAND-NEW SMASH HIT, "GIMME THE BAT-BUSINESS, BABY!"

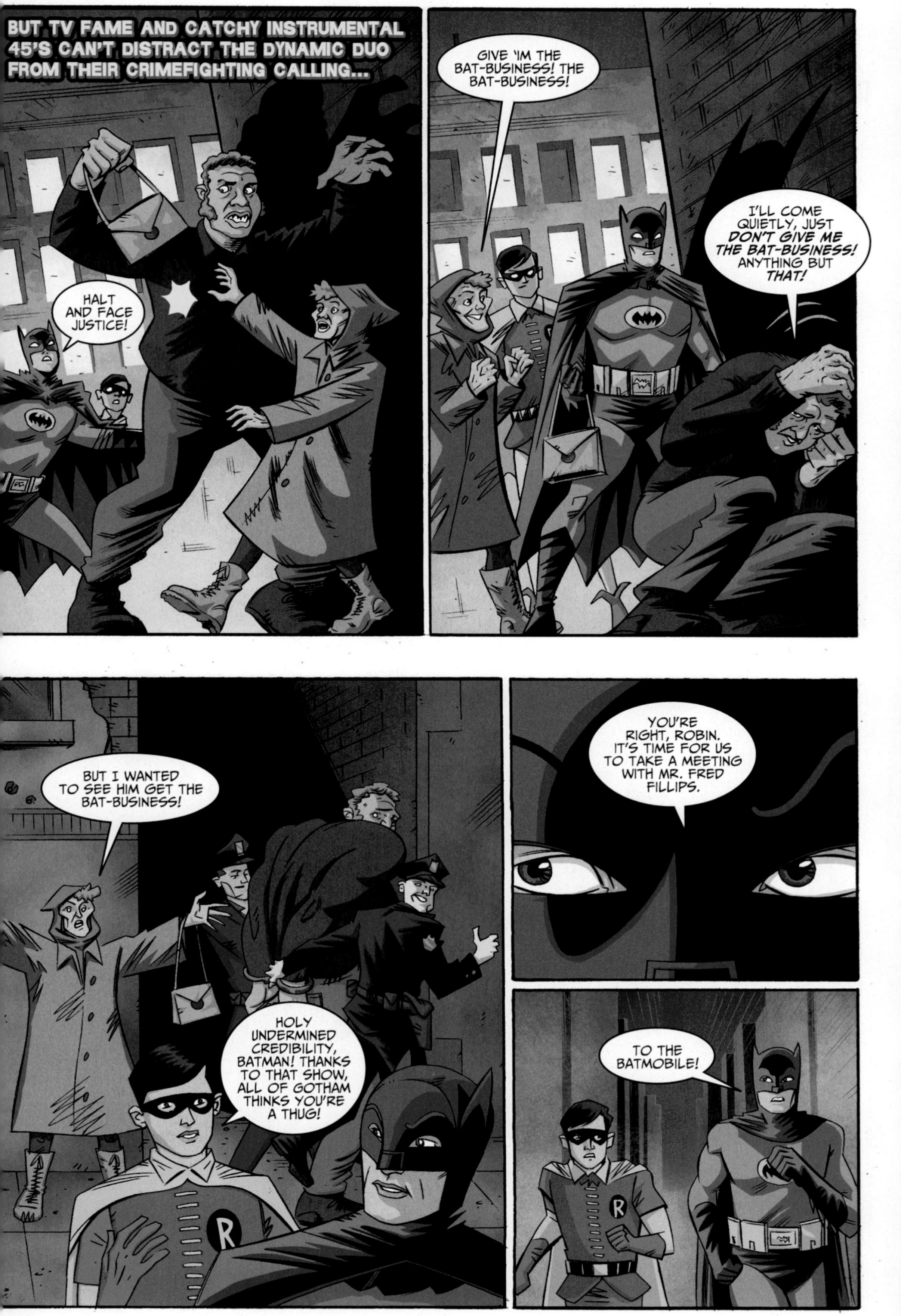
BUT TV FAME AND CATCHY INSTRUMENTAL 45'S CAN'T DISTRACT THE DYNAMIC DUO FROM THEIR CRIMEFIGHTING CALLING...
HALT AND FACE JUSTICE!
GIVE 'IM THE BAT-BUSINESS! THE BAT-BUSINESS!
I'LL COME QUIETLY, JUST *DON'T GIVE ME THE BAT-BUSINESS!* ANYTHING BUT *THAT!*
BUT I WANTED TO SEE HIM GET THE BAT-BUSINESS!
HOLY UNDERMINED CREDIBILITY, BATMAN! THANKS TO THAT SHOW, ALL OF GOTHAM THINKS YOU'RE A THUG!
YOU'RE RIGHT, ROBIN. IT'S TIME FOR US TO TAKE A MEETING WITH MR. FRED FILLIPS.
TO THE BATMOBILE!

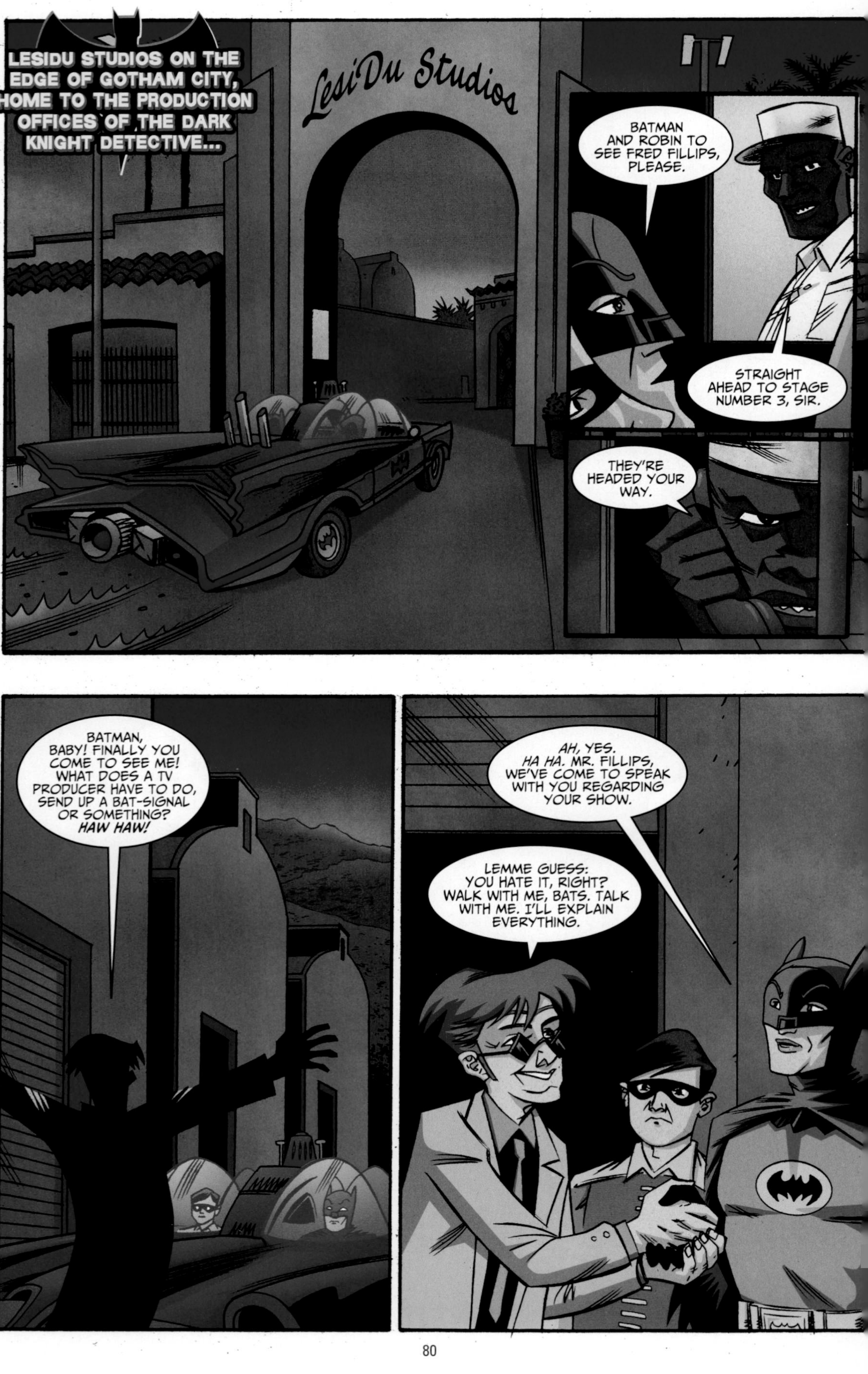
LESIDU STUDIOS ON THE EDGE OF GOTHAM CITY, HOME TO THE PRODUCTION OFFICES OF THE DARK KNIGHT DETECTIVE...
LesiDu Studios
BATMAN AND ROBIN TO SEE FRED FILLIPS, PLEASE.
STRAIGHT AHEAD TO STAGE NUMBER 3, SIR.
THEY'RE HEADED YOUR WAY.
BATMAN, BABY! FINALLY YOU COME TO SEE ME! WHAT DOES A TV PRODUCER HAVE TO DO, SEND UP A BAT-SIGNAL OR SOMETHING? HAW HAW!
AH, YES. HA HA. MR. FILLIPS, WE'VE COME TO SPEAK WITH YOU REGARDING YOUR SHOW.
LEMME GUESS: YOU HATE IT, RIGHT? WALK WITH ME, BATS. TALK WITH ME. I'LL EXPLAIN EVERYTHING.

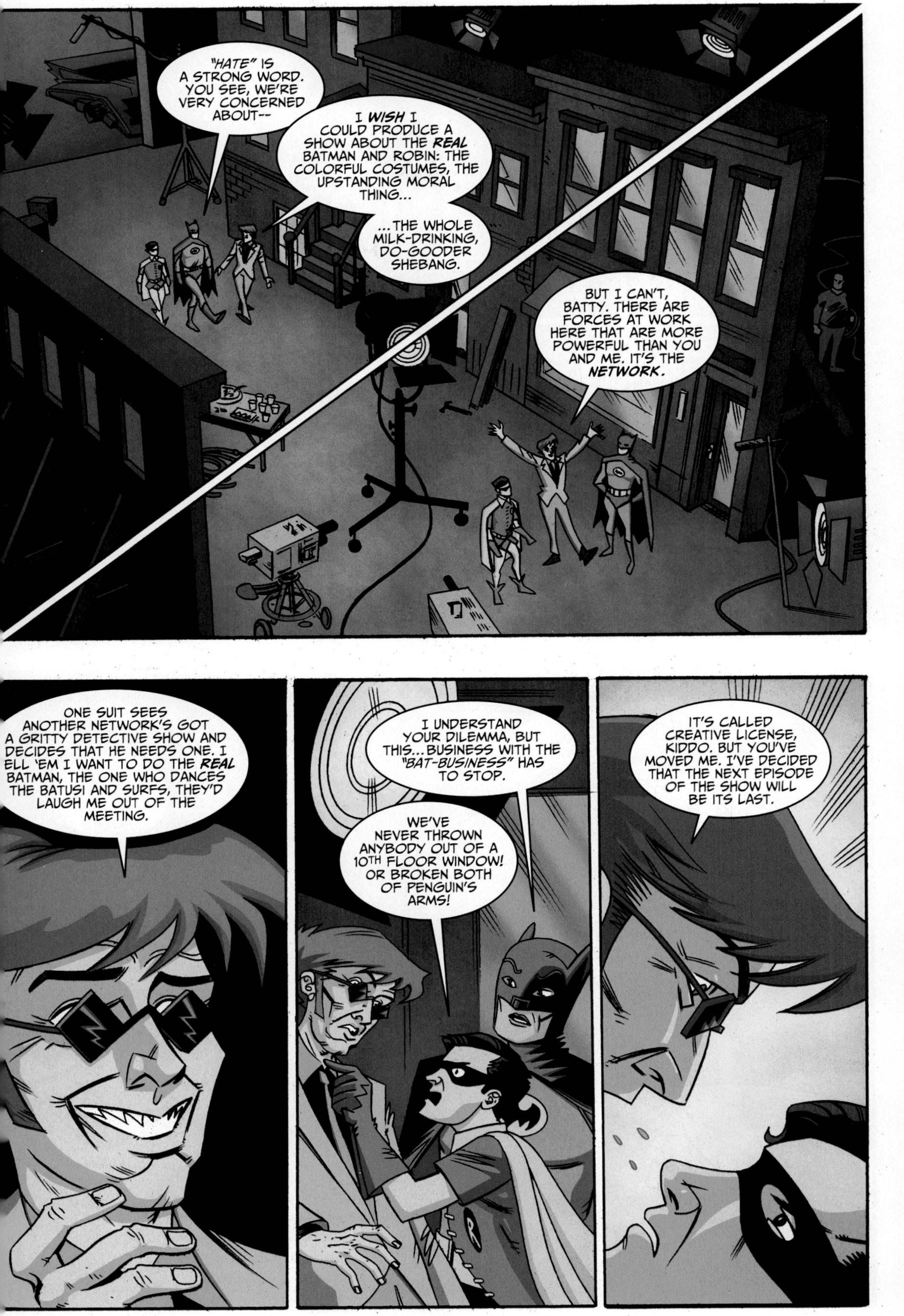
"HATE" IS A STRONG WORD. YOU SEE, WE'RE VERY CONCERNED ABOUT--
I *WISH* I COULD PRODUCE A SHOW ABOUT THE *REAL* BATMAN AND ROBIN: THE COLORFUL COSTUMES, THE UPSTANDING MORAL THING...
...THE WHOLE MILK-DRINKING, DO-GOODER SHEBANG.
BUT I CAN'T, BATTY. THERE ARE FORCES AT WORK HERE THAT ARE MORE POWERFUL THAN YOU AND ME. IT'S THE *NETWORK.*
ONE SUIT SEES ANOTHER NETWORK'S GOT A GRITTY DETECTIVE SHOW AND DECIDES THAT HE NEEDS ONE. I ELL 'EM I WANT TO DO THE *REAL* BATMAN, THE ONE WHO DANCES THE BATUSI AND SURFS, THEY'D LAUGH ME OUT OF THE MEETING.
I UNDERSTAND YOUR DILEMMA, BUT THIS...BUSINESS WITH THE *"BAT-BUSINESS"* HAS TO STOP.
WE'VE NEVER THROWN ANYBODY OUT OF A 10TH FLOOR WINDOW! OR BROKEN BOTH OF PENGUIN'S ARMS!
IT'S CALLED CREATIVE LICENSE, KIDDO. BUT YOU'VE MOVED ME. I'VE DECIDED THAT THE NEXT EPISODE OF THE SHOW WILL BE ITS LAST.

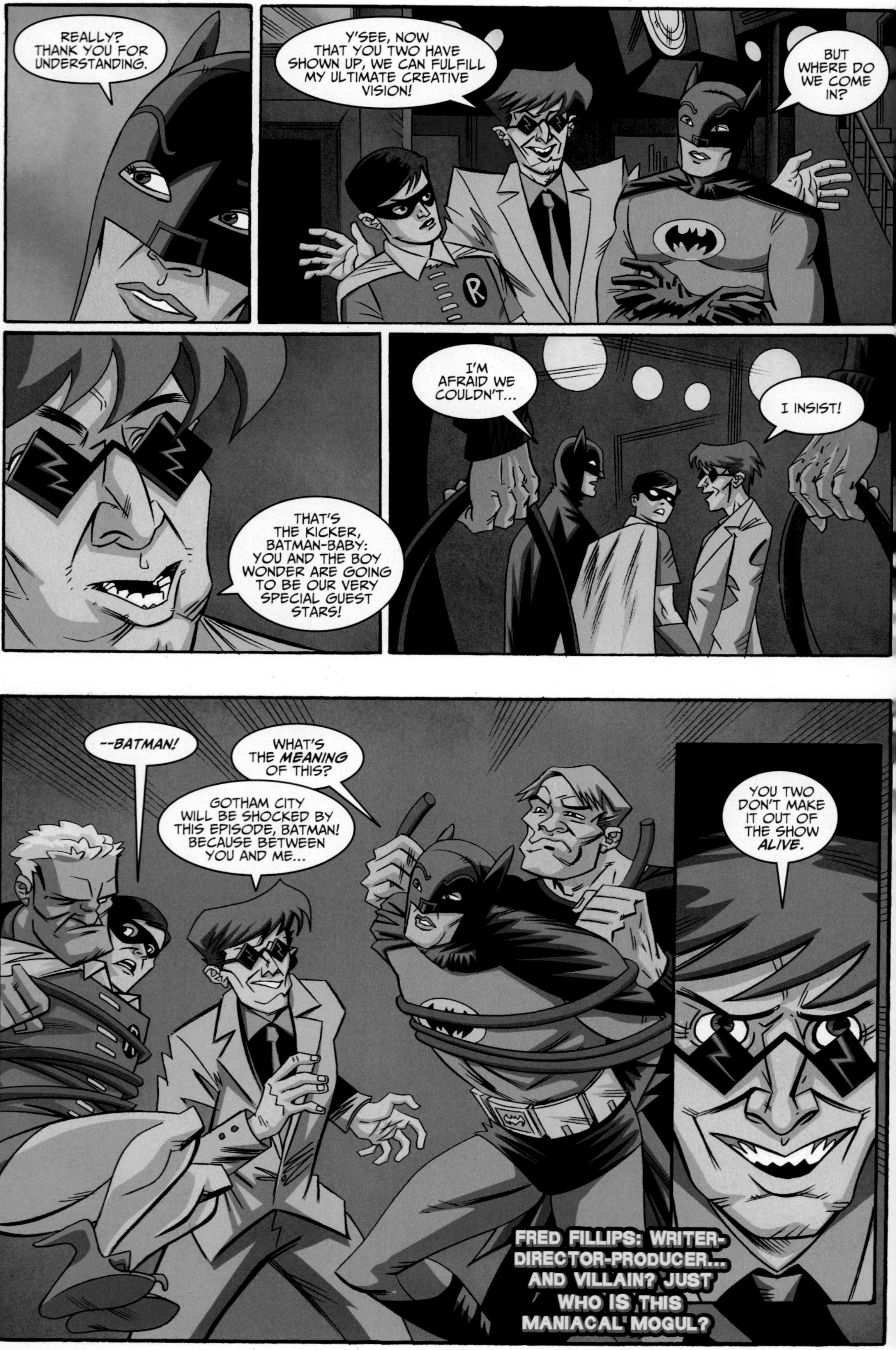
REALLY? THANK YOU FOR UNDERSTANDING.
Y'SEE, NOW THAT YOU TWO HAVE SHOWN UP, WE CAN FULFILL MY ULTIMATE CREATIVE VISION!
BUT WHERE DO WE COME IN?
THAT'S THE KICKER, BATMAN-BABY: YOU AND THE BOY WONDER ARE GOING TO BE OUR VERY SPECIAL GUEST STARS!
I'M AFRAID WE COULDN'T...
I INSIST!
--BATMAN!
WHAT'S THE *MEANING* OF THIS?
GOTHAM CITY WILL BE SHOCKED BY THIS EPISODE, BATMAN! BECAUSE BETWEEN YOU AND ME...
YOU TWO DON'T MAKE IT OUT OF THE SHOW *ALIVE.*
FRED FILLIPS: WRITER-DIRECTOR-PRODUCER... AND VILLAIN? JUST WHO IS THIS MANIACAL MOGUL?

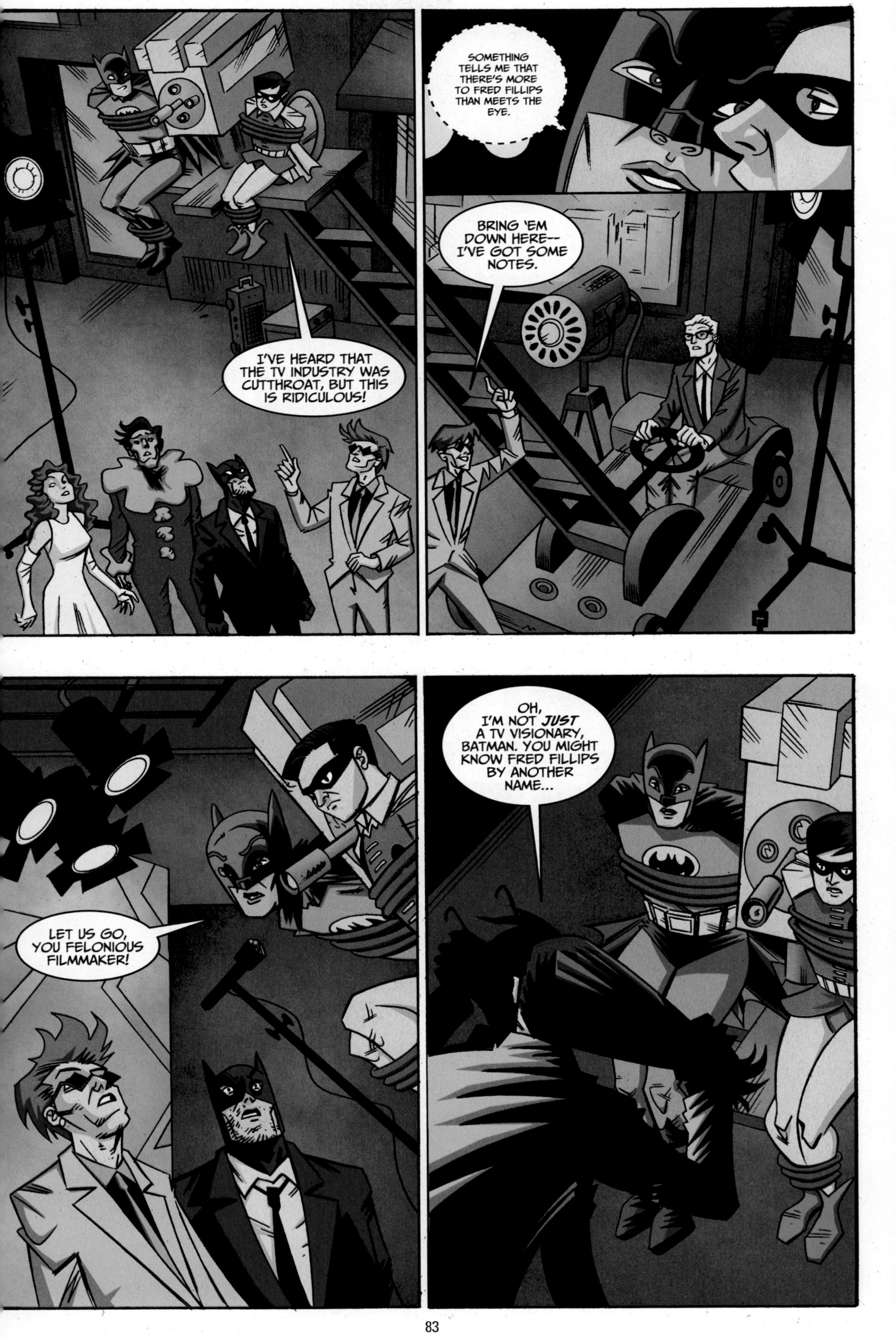
I'VE HEARD THAT THE TV INDUSTRY WAS CUTTHROAT, BUT THIS IS RIDICULOUS!
SOMETHING TELLS ME THAT THERE'S MORE TO FRED FILLIPS THAN MEETS THE EYE.
BRING 'EM DOWN HERE-- I'VE GOT SOME NOTES.
LET US GO, YOU FELONIOUS FILMMAKER!
OH, I'M NOT *JUST* A TV VISIONARY, BATMAN. YOU MIGHT KNOW FRED FILLIPS BY ANOTHER NAME...

FALSE FACE!

YOU DASTARDLY DECEIVER!

"ORIGINALLY, I WANTED TO WORK IN A FIELD WHERE I COULD PURSUE MY CRIMINAL INCLINATIONS IN A QUASI-LEGAL WAY.

FRED FILLIPS PRODUCTIONS

"BUT WHEN I CAME UP WITH THIS IDEA, I KNEW IT WAS THE ULTIMATE CAPER.

FRED FILLIPS PRODUCTIONS

"WHY NOT RUIN THE REPUTATION OF THE REAL BATMAN AND ROBIN *AND* LURE YOU TO YOUR DOOM WHILE MAKING A PILE OF DOUGH?"

The Dark Knight Detective "Pilot Episode" Written By Fred Fillips

GREENLIGHT

A TV PRODUCER *AND* A MASTER CRIMINAL? *TWICE* AS EVIL!

YOU'LL NEVER GET AWAY WITH THIS.

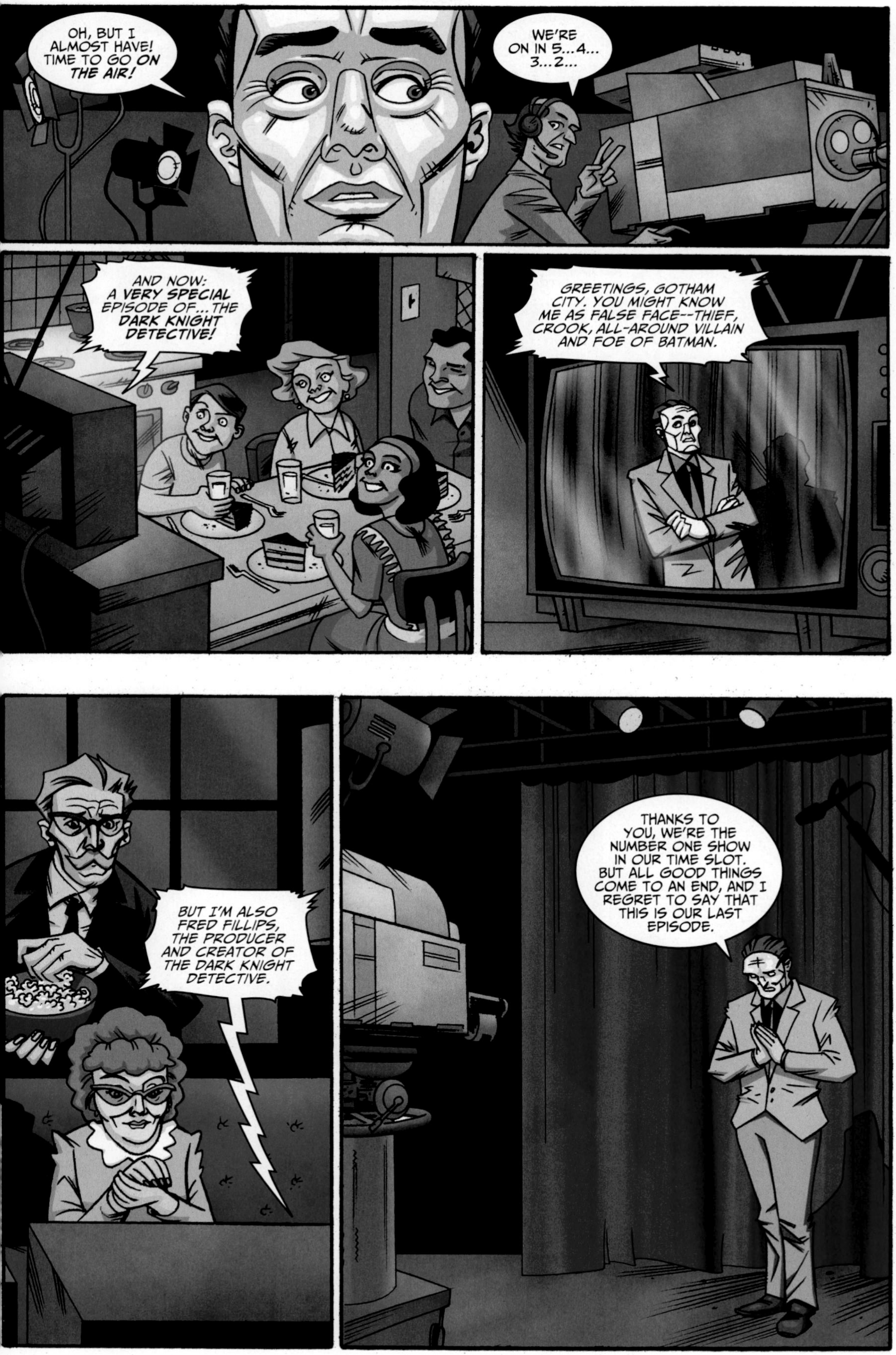
OH, BUT I ALMOST HAVE! TIME TO GO ON THE AIR!
WE'RE ON IN 5...4... 3...2...
AND NOW: A VERY SPECIAL EPISODE OF... THE DARK KNIGHT DETECTIVE!
GREETINGS, GOTHAM CITY. YOU MIGHT KNOW ME AS FALSE FACE--THIEF, CROOK, ALL-AROUND VILLAIN AND FOE OF BATMAN.
BUT I'M ALSO FRED FILLIPS, THE PRODUCER AND CREATOR OF THE DARK KNIGHT DETECTIVE.
THANKS TO YOU, WE'RE THE NUMBER ONE SHOW IN OUR TIME SLOT. BUT ALL GOOD THINGS COME TO AN END, AND I REGRET TO SAY THAT THIS IS OUR LAST EPISODE.

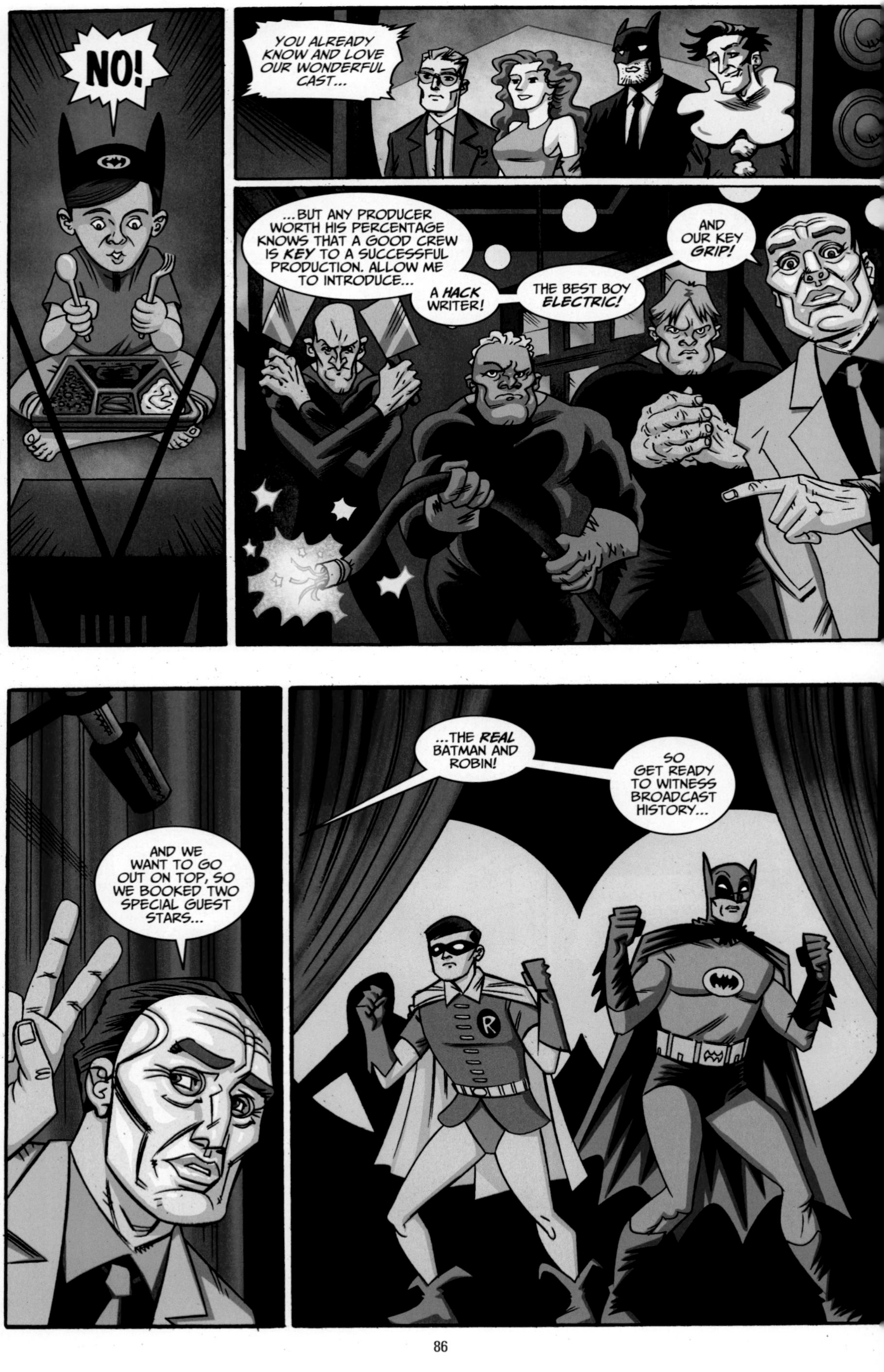
NO!
YOU ALREADY KNOW AND LOVE OUR WONDERFUL CAST...
...BUT ANY PRODUCER WORTH HIS PERCENTAGE KNOWS THAT A GOOD CREW IS KEY TO A SUCCESSFUL PRODUCTION. ALLOW ME TO INTRODUCE...
A HACK WRITER!
THE BEST BOY ELECTRIC!
AND OUR KEY GRIP!
AND WE WANT TO GO OUT ON TOP, SO WE BOOKED TWO SPECIAL GUEST STARS...
...THE REAL BATMAN AND ROBIN!
SO GET READY TO WITNESS BROADCAST HISTORY...

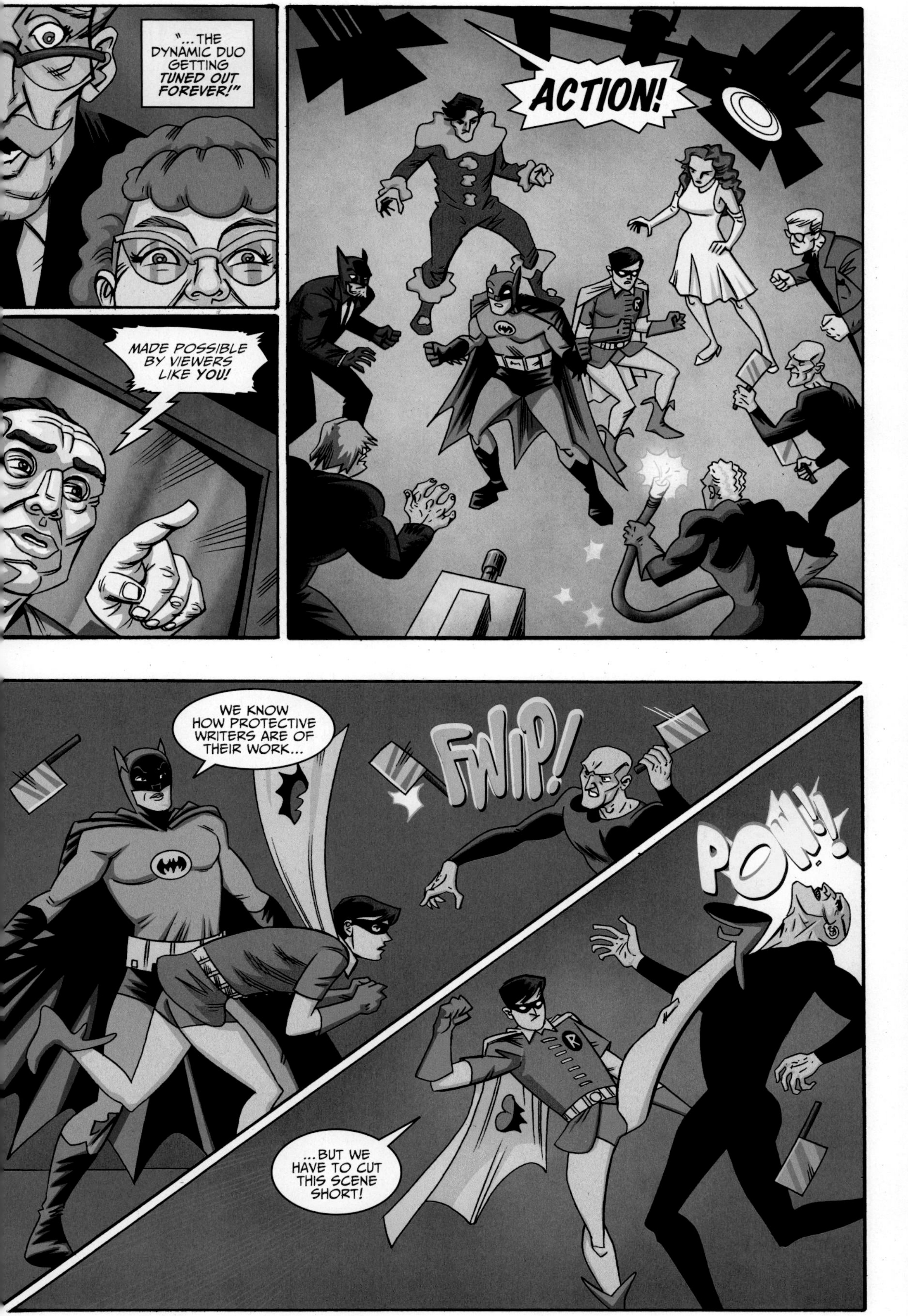
"...THE DYNAMIC DUO GETTING TUNED OUT FOREVER!"
ACTION!
MADE POSSIBLE BY VIEWERS LIKE YOU!
WE KNOW HOW PROTECTIVE WRITERS ARE OF THEIR WORK...
FWIP!
POW!!
...BUT WE HAVE TO CUT THIS SCENE SHORT!

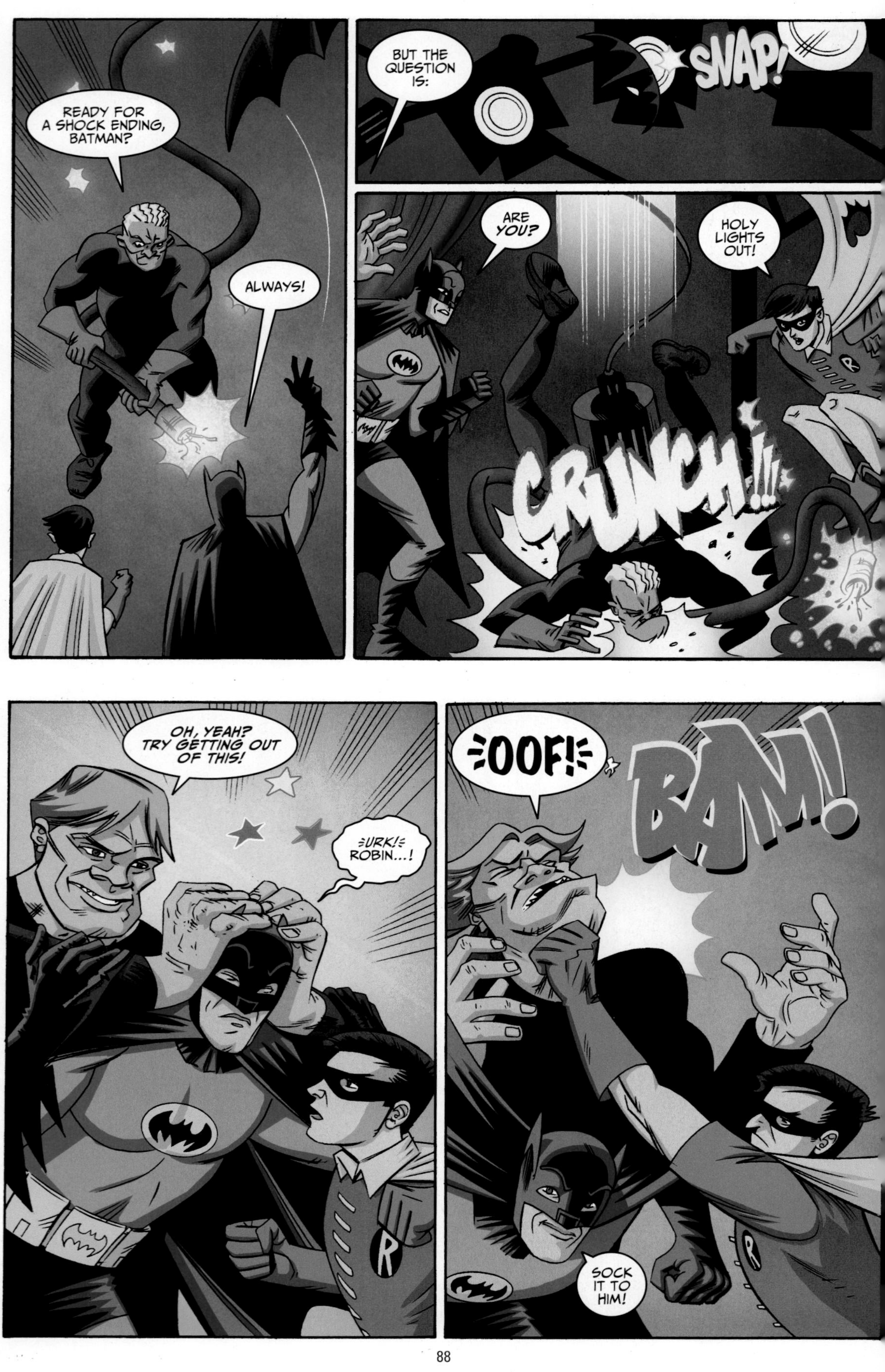
READY FOR A SHOCK ENDING, BATMAN?
ALWAYS!
BUT THE QUESTION IS:
SNAP!
ARE YOU?
HOLY LIGHTS OUT!
CRUNCH!!!
OH, YEAH? TRY GETTING OUT OF THIS!
URK! ROBIN...!
OOF!
BAM!
SOCK IT TO HIM!

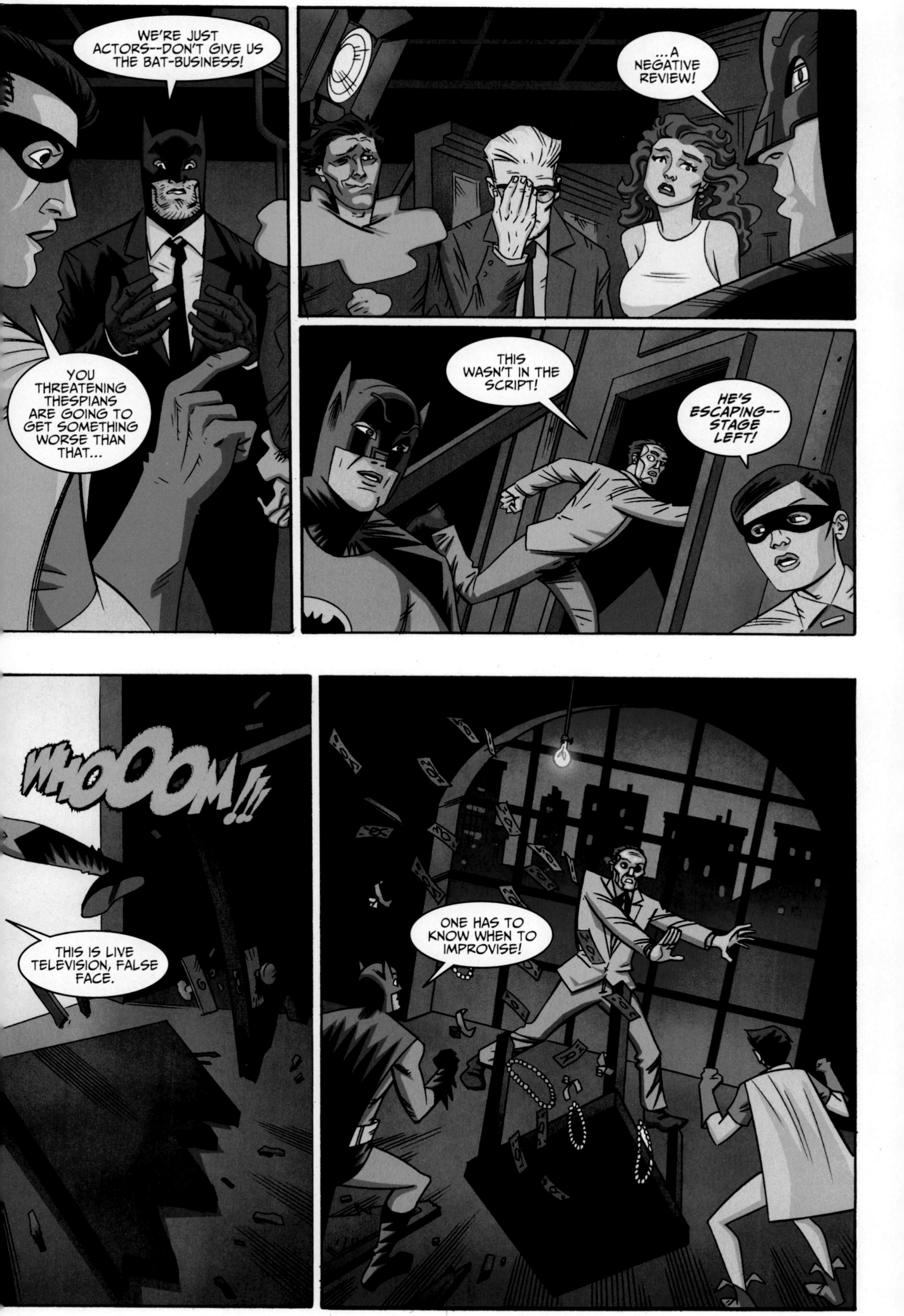
WE'RE JUST ACTORS--DON'T GIVE US THE BAT-BUSINESS!
YOU THREATENING THESPIANS ARE GOING TO GET SOMETHING WORSE THAN THAT...
...A NEGATIVE REVIEW!
THIS WASN'T IN THE SCRIPT!
HE'S ESCAPING-- STAGE LEFT!
WHOOOM!!!
THIS IS LIVE TELEVISION, FALSE FACE.
ONE HAS TO KNOW WHEN TO IMPROVISE!

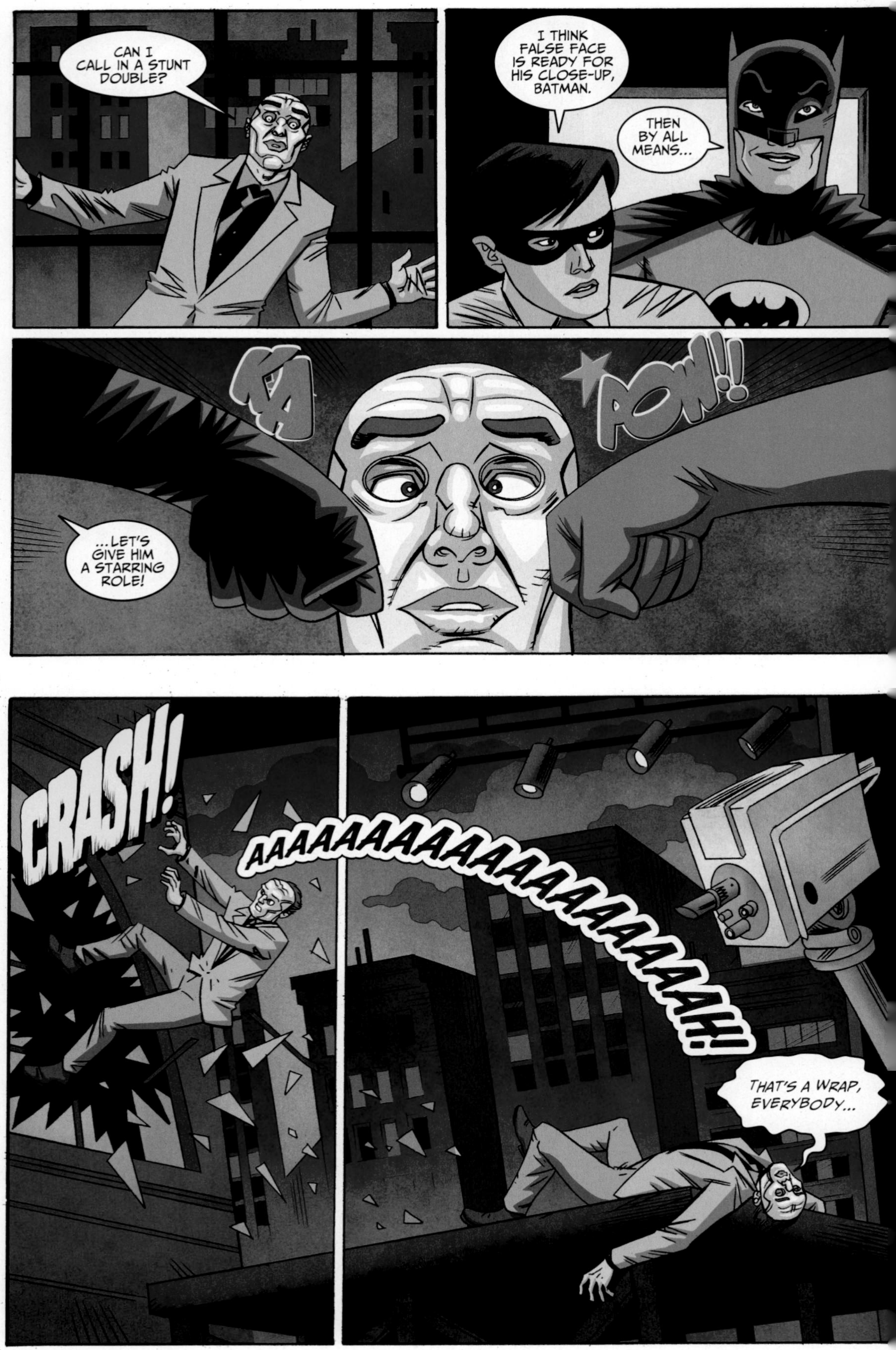
CAN I CALL IN A STUNT DOUBLE?
I THINK FALSE FACE IS READY FOR HIS CLOSE-UP, BATMAN.
THEN BY ALL MEANS...
KA
POW!!
...LET'S GIVE HIM A STARRING ROLE!
CRASH!
AAAAAAAAAAAAAAAAAAAAAAAAH!!
THAT'S A WRAP, EVERYBODY...

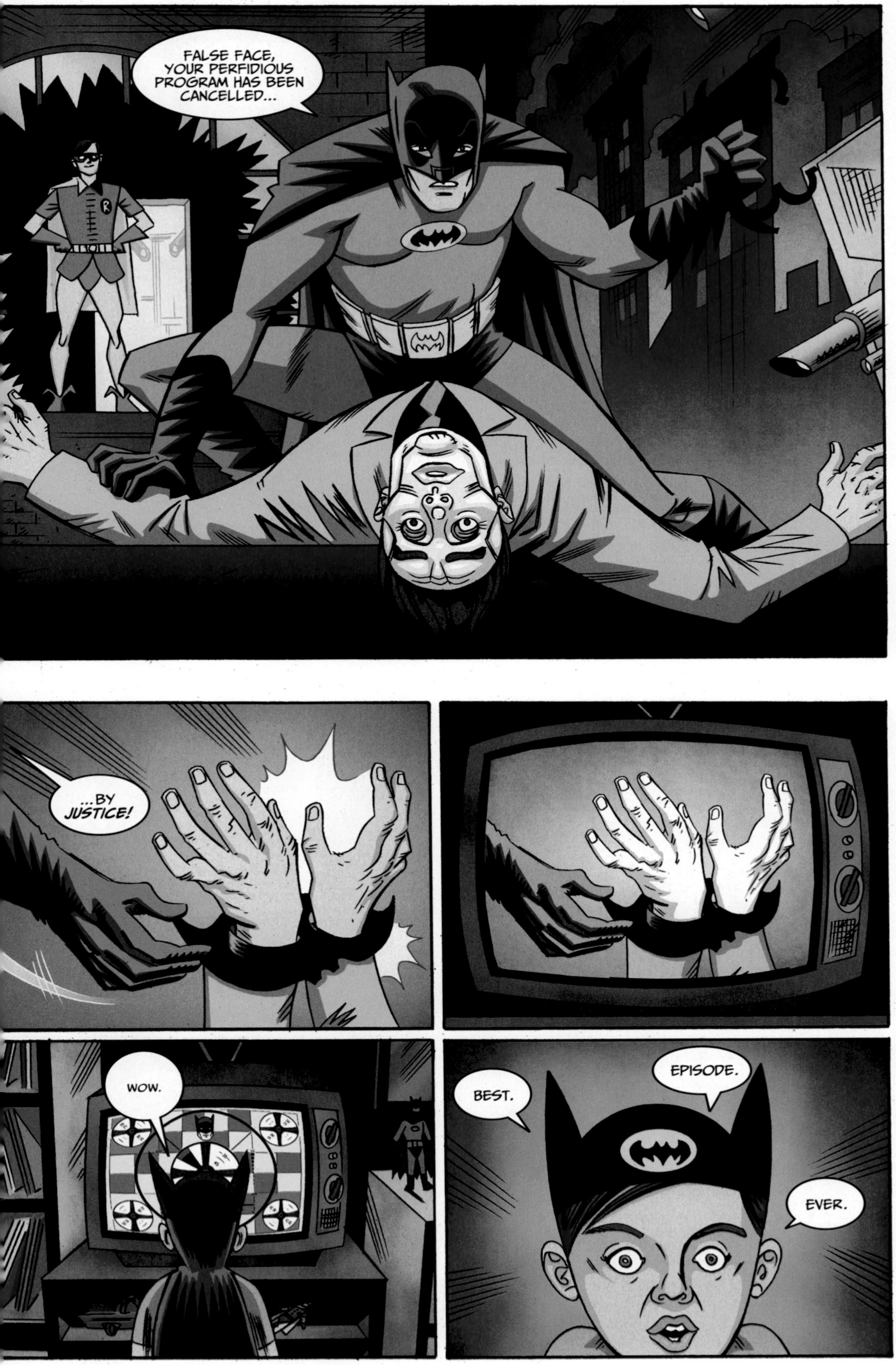
FALSE FACE, YOUR PERFIDIOUS PROGRAM HAS BEEN CANCELLED...
...BY JUSTICE!
WOW.
BEST.
EPISODE.
EVER.

MONTHS LATER, BRUCE WAYNE AND DICK GRAYSON ARE ONCE AGAIN UNWINDING IN FRONT OF THE TELEVISION, BUT THIS TIME, THEY'RE TUNED IN TO THE ANNUAL BIG TV AWARDS SHOW...

IF "THE WACKY WORLD OF GOOGY DILLS" DOESN'T WIN BEST COMEDY, THAT'LL BE A *REAL* CRIME.

A MOMENT, CHUM. I'D LIKE TO HEAR THIS.

EVERY YEAR, THE BIG TV AWARDS CHOOSES TO IDENTIFY ONE PROGRAM THAT HAS ADVANCED TELEVISION AS AN ART FORM.

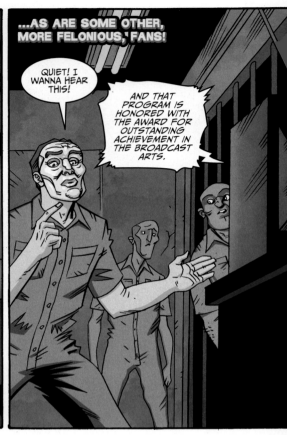

...AS ARE SOME OTHER, MORE FELONIOUS, FANS!

QUIET! I WANNA HEAR THIS!

AND THAT PROGRAM IS HONORED WITH THE AWARD FOR OUTSTANDING ACHIEVEMENT IN THE BROADCAST ARTS.

THIS YEAR, THE PRIZE GOES TO...

...THE FINAL EPISODE OF "THE DARK KNIGHT DETECTIVE"! FALSE FACE AND BATMAN, PRODUCERS!

ACCEPTING THE AWARD ON THEIR BEHALF IS CORSON BELLES, STAR OF THE HIT SHOW "THE DOOM PATROL"!

VICTORY!

I CAN'T BELIEVE IT-- FALSE FACE TRIES TO GIVE US THE FINAL CUT AND HE GETS A TROPHY FOR IT!

IT JUST GOES TO SHOW YOU, DICK...

THEY LIKED ME! THEY REALLY LIKED ME!

"...CRIME DOESN'T PAY...

"...BUT IT *CAN* BE CREATIVELY REWARDING."

THE END

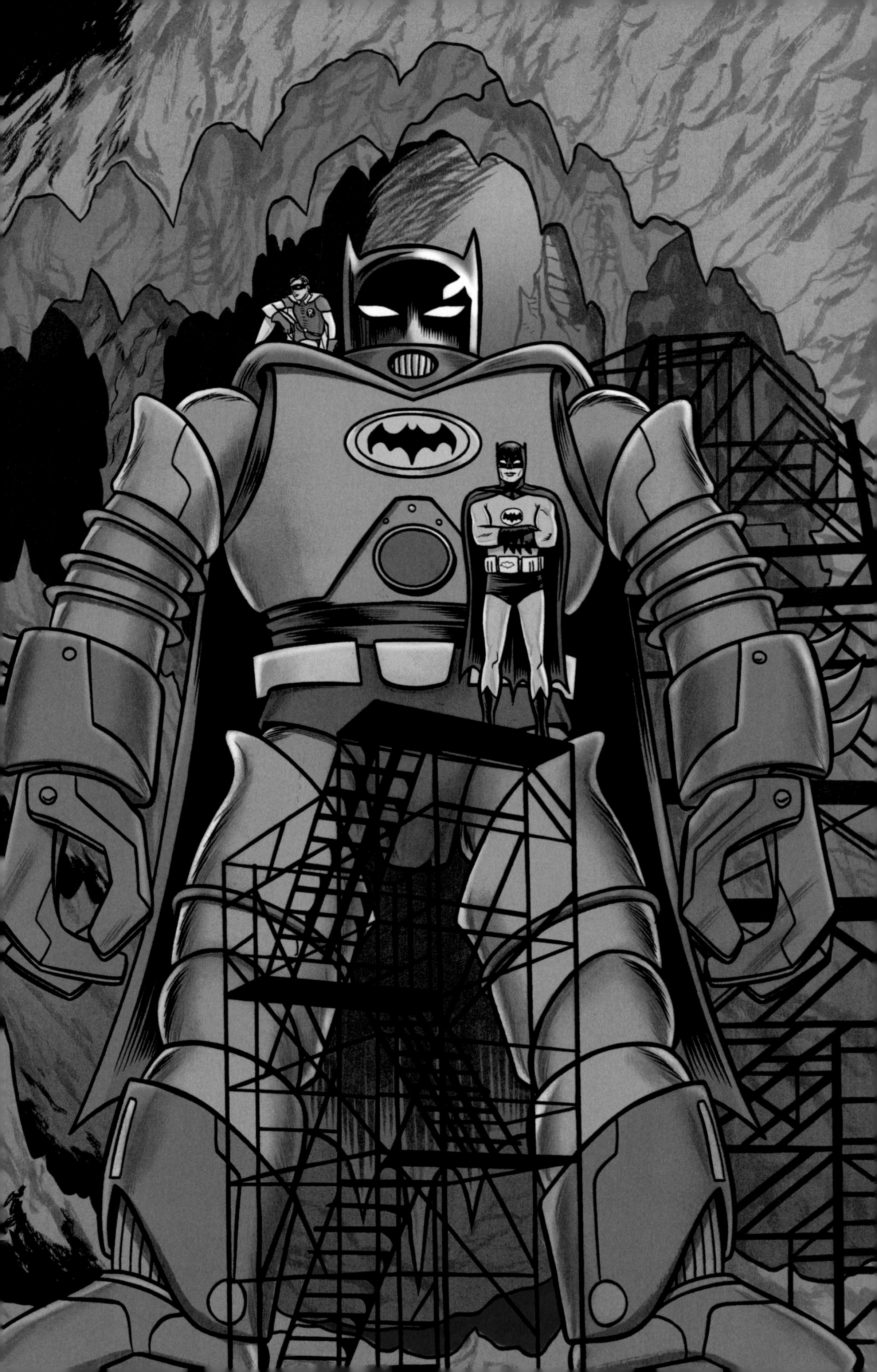

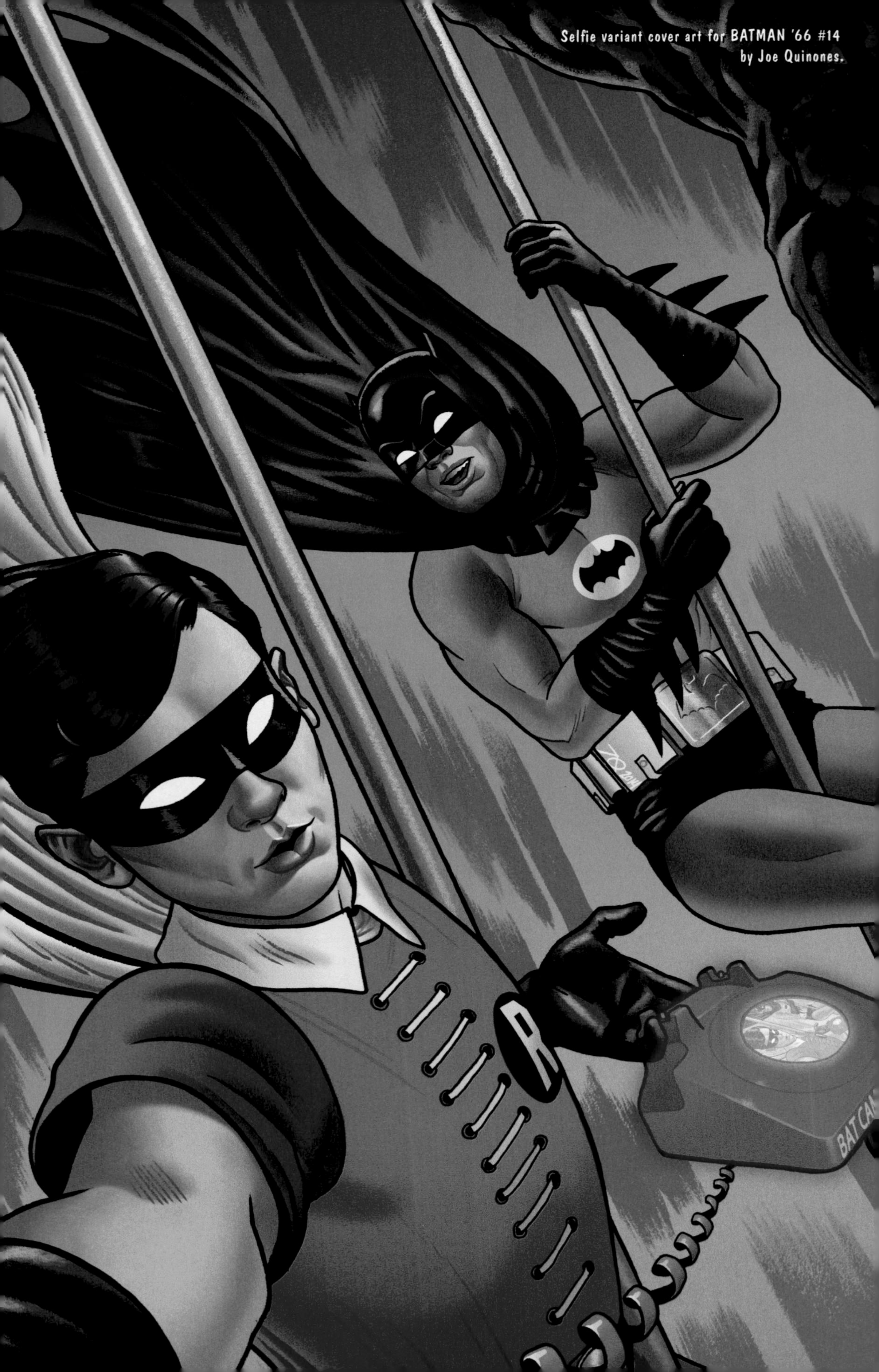

Selfie variant cover art for BATMAN '66 #14
by Joe Quinones.

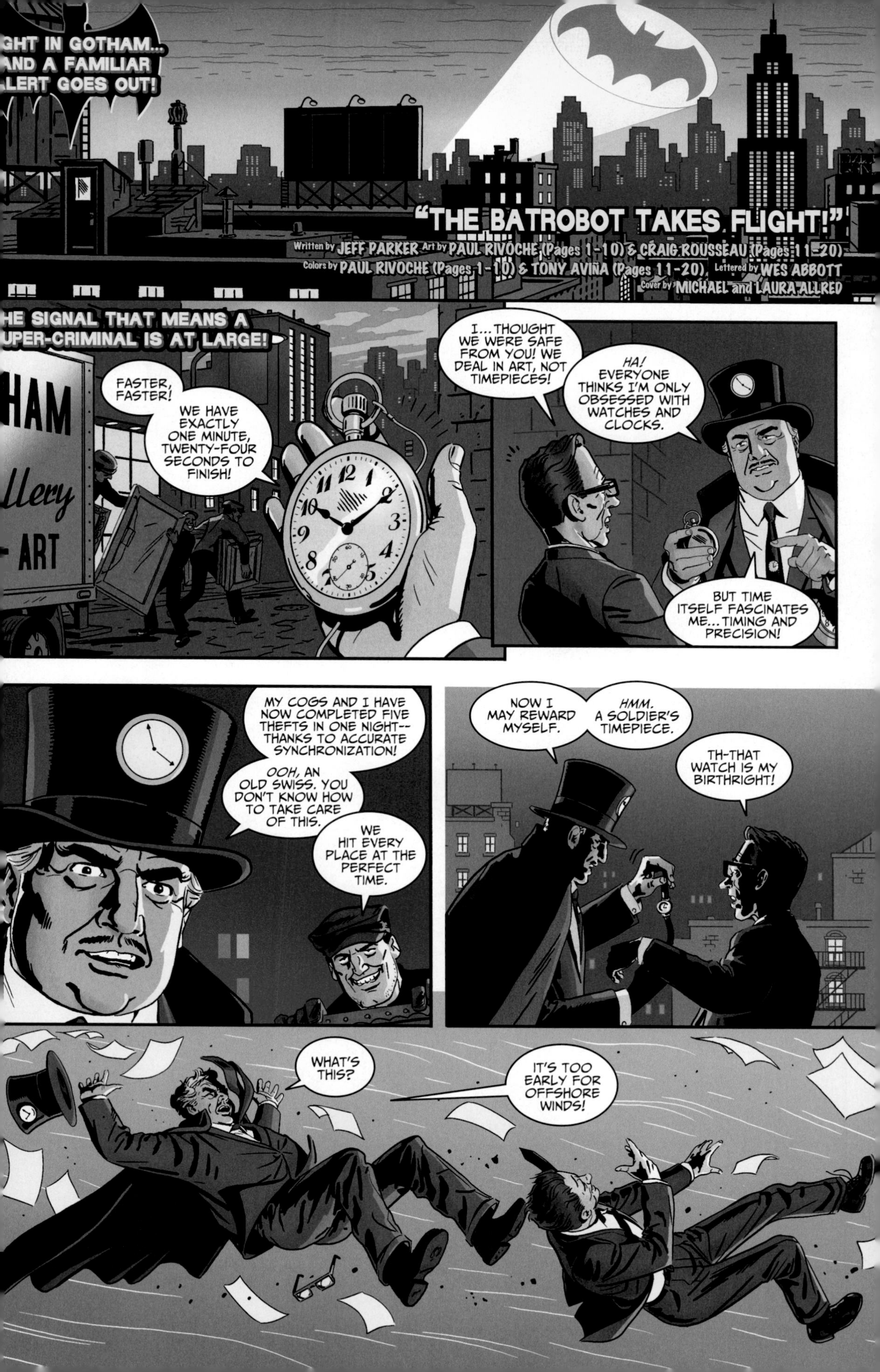

GHT IN GOTHAM... AND A FAMILIAR LERT GOES OUT!
"THE BATROBOT TAKES FLIGHT!"
Written by JEFF PARKER Art by PAUL RIVOCHE (Pages 1-10) & CRAIG ROUSSEAU (Pages 11-20)
Colors by PAUL RIVOCHE (Pages 1-10) & TONY AVIÑA (Pages 11-20) Lettered by WES ABBOTT
Cover by MICHAEL and LAURA ALLRED
HE SIGNAL THAT MEANS A UPER-CRIMINAL IS AT LARGE!
HAM
llery
ART
FASTER, FASTER!
WE HAVE EXACTLY ONE MINUTE, TWENTY-FOUR SECONDS TO FINISH!
I... THOUGHT WE WERE SAFE FROM YOU! WE DEAL IN ART, NOT TIMEPIECES!
HA! EVERYONE THINKS I'M ONLY OBSESSED WITH WATCHES AND CLOCKS.
BUT TIME ITSELF FASCINATES ME... TIMING AND PRECISION!
MY COGS AND I HAVE NOW COMPLETED FIVE THEFTS IN ONE NIGHT-- THANKS TO ACCURATE SYNCHRONIZATION!
OOH, AN OLD SWISS. YOU DON'T KNOW HOW TO TAKE CARE OF THIS.
WE HIT EVERY PLACE AT THE PERFECT TIME.
NOW I MAY REWARD MYSELF.
HMM. A SOLDIER'S TIMEPIECE.
TH-THAT WATCH IS MY BIRTHRIGHT!
WHAT'S THIS?
IT'S TOO EARLY FOR OFFSHORE WINDS!

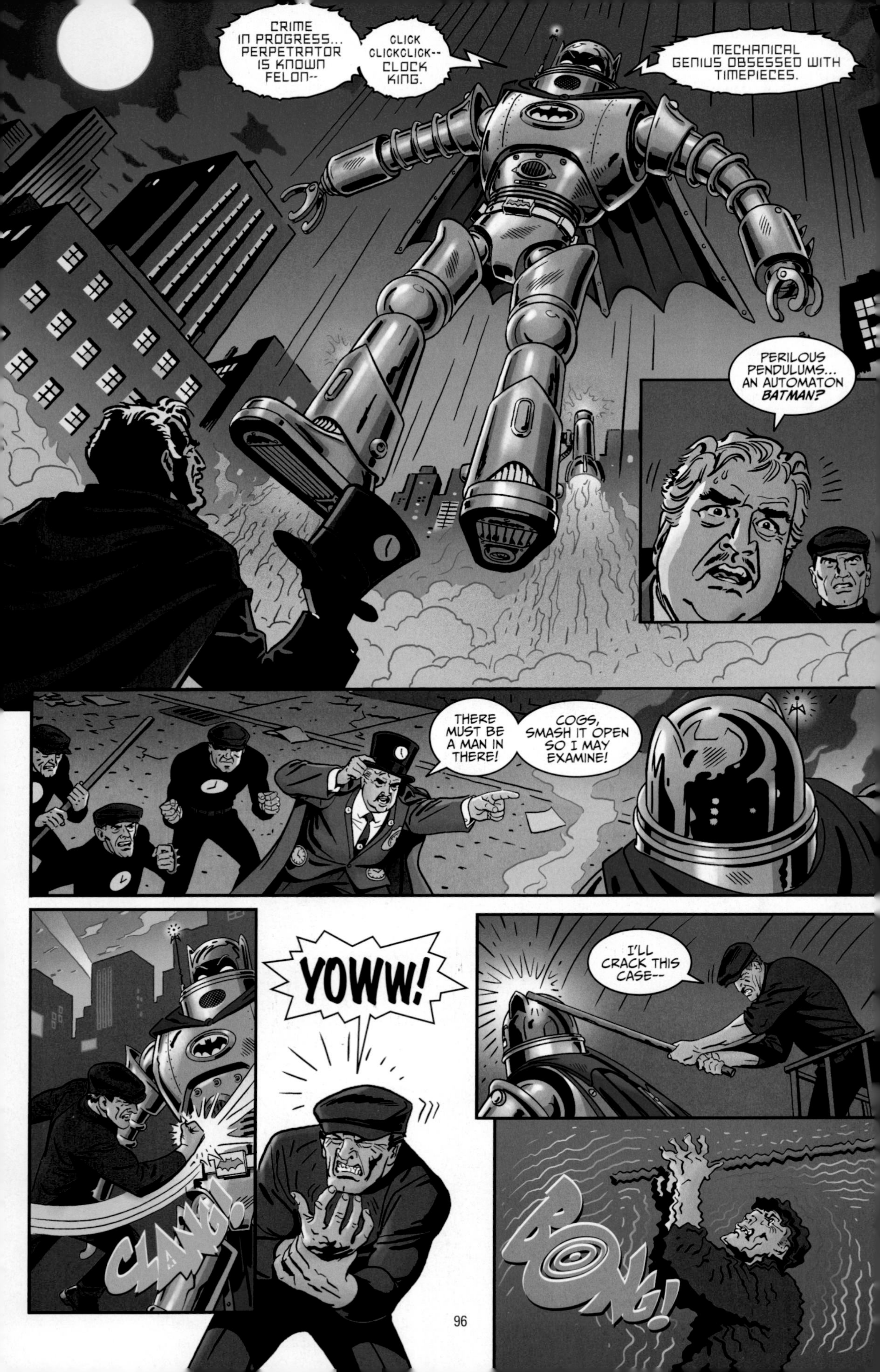
CRIME IN PROGRESS... PERPETRATOR IS KNOWN FELON--
CLICK CLICKCLICK-- CLOCK KING.
MECHANICAL GENIUS OBSESSED WITH TIMEPIECES.
PERILOUS PENDULUMS... AN AUTOMATON *BATMAN?*
THERE MUST BE A MAN IN THERE!
COGS, SMASH IT OPEN SO I MAY EXAMINE!
CLANG!
YOWW!
I'LL CRACK THIS CASE--
BONG!

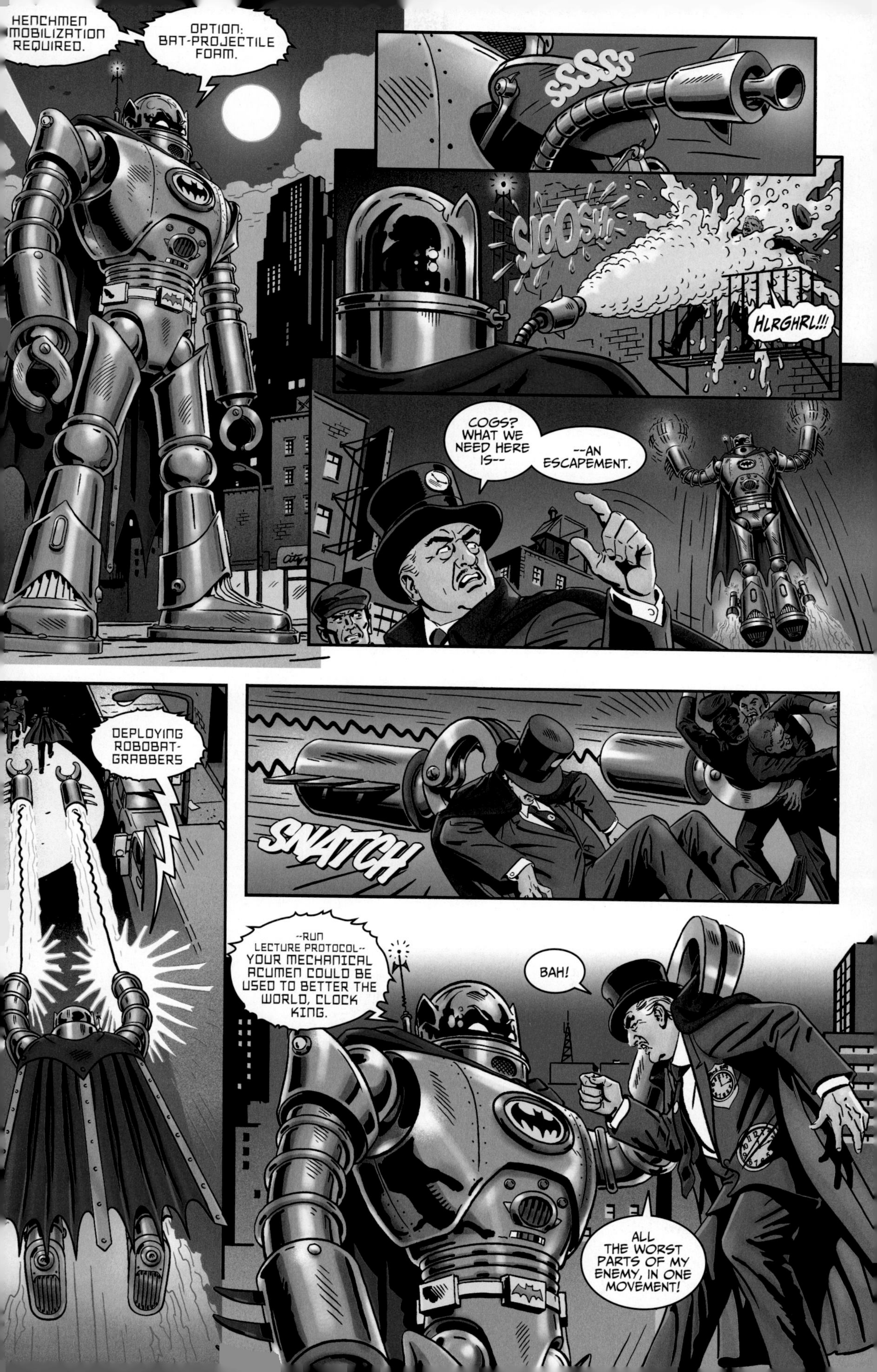
HENCHMEN MOBILIZATION REQUIRED.
OPTION: BAT-PROJECTILE FOAM.
sSSSSS
SLOOSH!
HLRGHRL!!!
COGS? WHAT WE NEED HERE IS--
--AN ESCAPEMENT.
DEPLOYING ROBOBAT-GRABBERS
SNATCH
--RUN LECTURE PROTOCOL-- YOUR MECHANICAL ACUMEN COULD BE USED TO BETTER THE WORLD, CLOCK KING.
BAH!
ALL THE WORST PARTS OF MY ENEMY, IN ONE MOVEMENT!

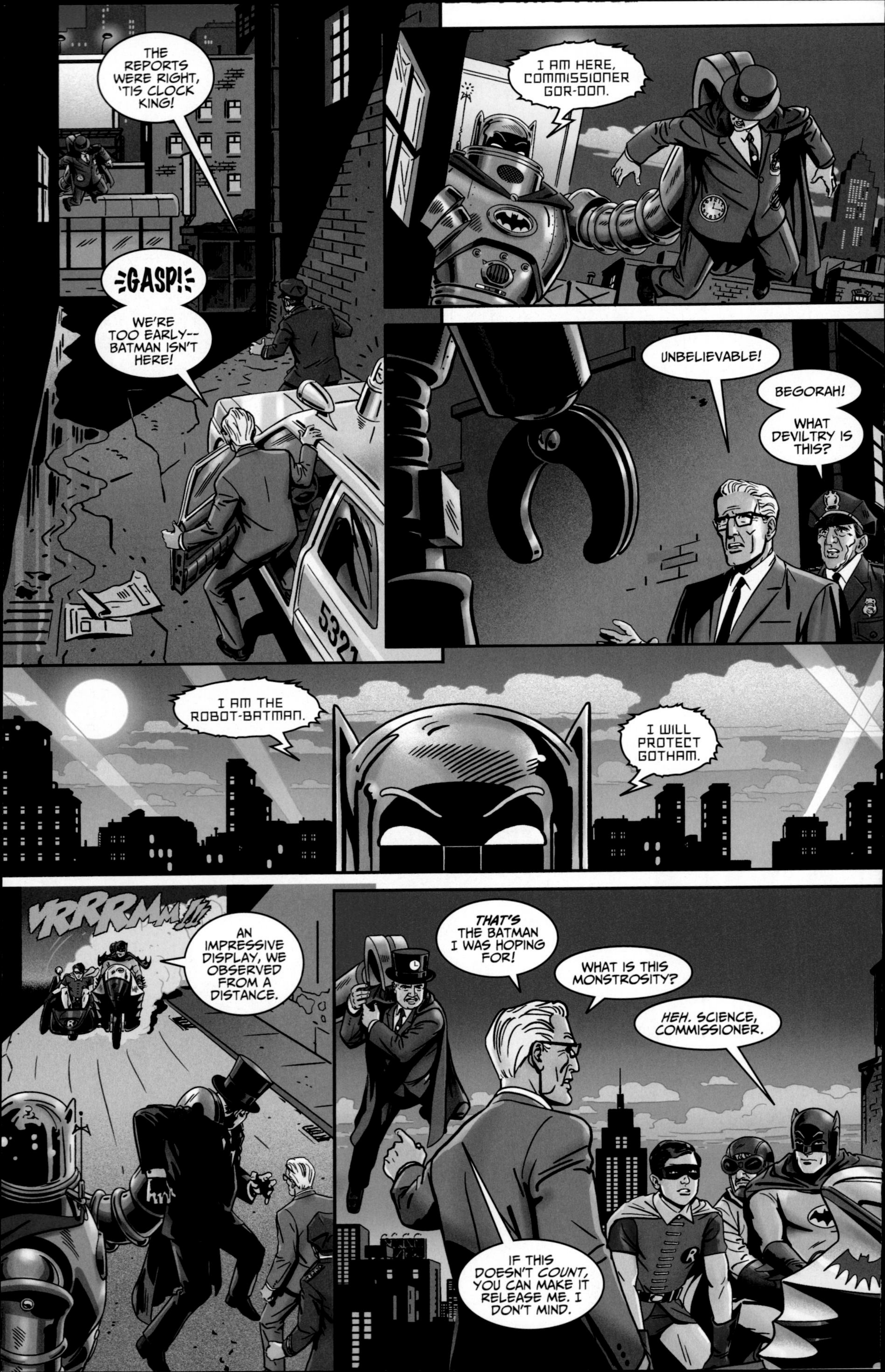
THE REPORTS WERE RIGHT, 'TIS CLOCK KING!
GASP!
WE'RE TOO EARLY-- BATMAN ISN'T HERE!
5321
I AM HERE, COMMISSIONER GOR-DON.
UNBELIEVABLE!
BEGORAH!
WHAT DEVILTRY IS THIS?
I AM THE ROBOT-BATMAN.
I WILL PROTECT GOTHAM.
VRRRMM!!
AN IMPRESSIVE DISPLAY, WE OBSERVED FROM A DISTANCE.
THAT'S THE BATMAN I WAS HOPING FOR!
WHAT IS THIS MONSTROSITY?
HEH. SCIENCE, COMMISSIONER.
IF THIS DOESN'T COUNT, YOU CAN MAKE IT RELEASE ME. I DON'T MIND.

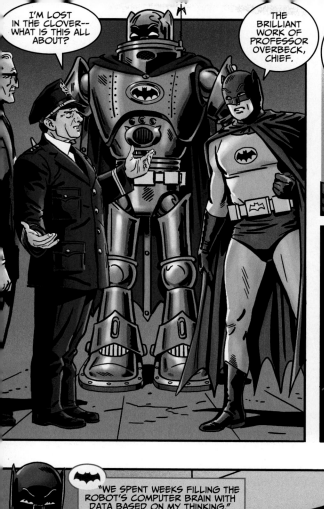

I'M LOST IN THE CLOVER-- WHAT IS THIS ALL ABOUT?

THE BRILLIANT WORK OF PROFESSOR OVERBECK, CHIEF.

SADLY, HIS INVENTIONS HAVE BEEN TWISTED TO EVIL ENDS BY CRIMINAL FORCES IN THE PAST. HE WANTED TO MAKE AMENDS TO THE CITY OF GOTHAM.

JA, VERY MUCH.

THAT'S WHEN HE APPROACHED ME WITH THE IDEA OF BUILDING AN *ANDROID GUARDIAN* TO PROTECT GOTHAM WHEN I AM CALLED AWAY.

THE SCHEMATICS HE SHOWED ME WERE IMPRESSIVE, SO I AGREED TO PARTICIPATE IN THE CREATION.

"WE SPENT WEEKS FILLING THE ROBOT'S COMPUTER BRAIN WITH DATA BASED ON MY THINKING."

NOW, HOW VOULD YOU DEAL VITH THAT SCENARIO?

RIDDLER AND PENGUIN WITH GAS GRENADES?

FIRST, I WOULD THROW A BATARANG TO BRING DOWN RIDDLER, AS HE'S THE MORE AGILE OPPONENT...

"WE IMPLEMENTED SOME OF MY OWN CRIMEFIGHTING INVENTIONS THAT WERE TOO BIG FOR UTILITY BELT STORAGE.

"THE BATMAN ROBOT IS INCREDIBLY VERSATILE AND HAS ITS OWN INTERNAL BAT-COMPUTER."

ZZZZ!!!

99

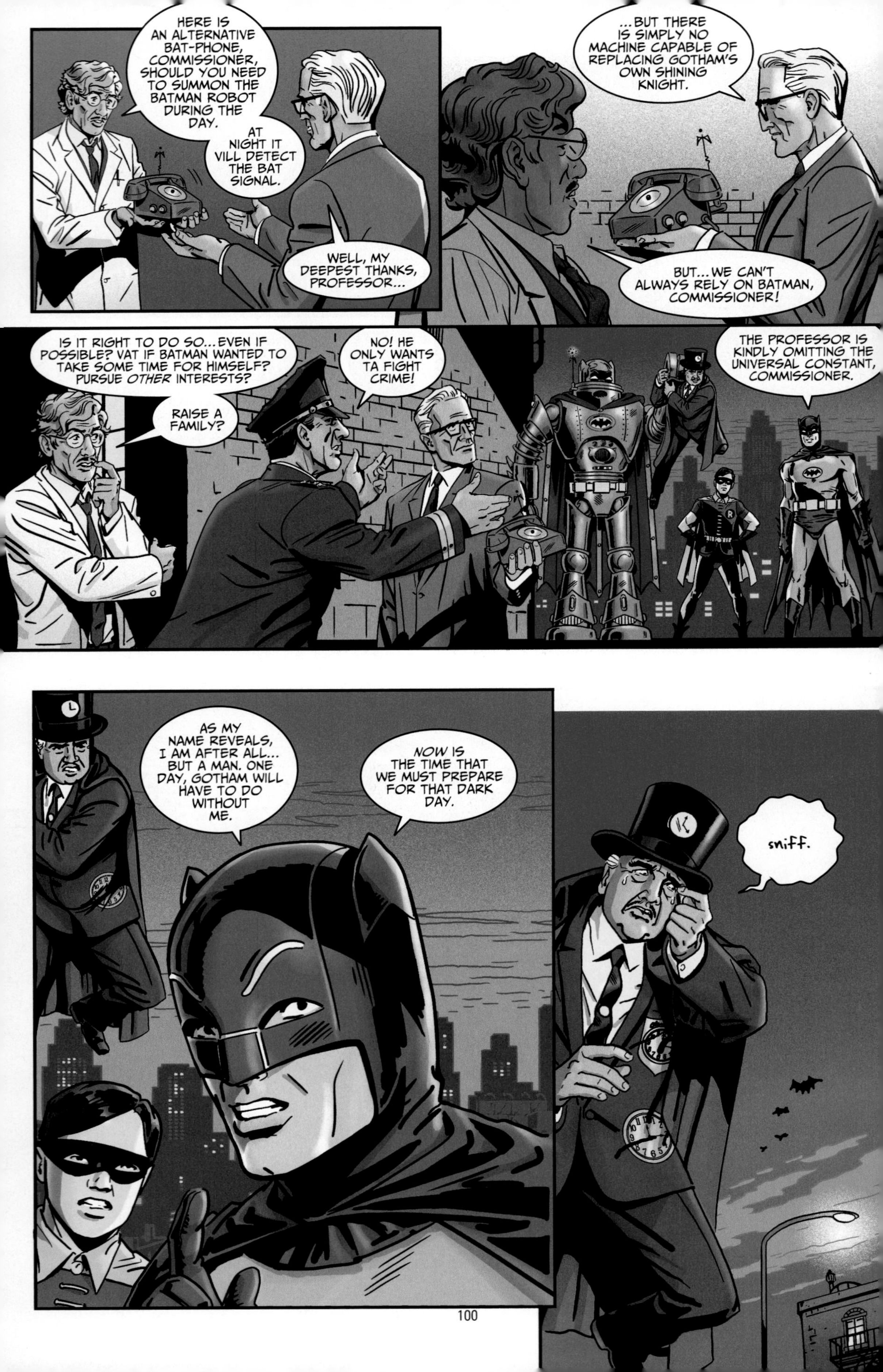
HERE IS AN ALTERNATIVE BAT-PHONE, COMMISSIONER, SHOULD YOU NEED TO SUMMON THE BATMAN ROBOT DURING THE DAY.
AT NIGHT IT VILL DETECT THE BAT SIGNAL.
WELL, MY DEEPEST THANKS, PROFESSOR...
...BUT THERE IS SIMPLY NO MACHINE CAPABLE OF REPLACING GOTHAM'S OWN SHINING KNIGHT.
BUT... WE CAN'T ALWAYS RELY ON BATMAN, COMMISSIONER!
IS IT RIGHT TO DO SO...EVEN IF POSSIBLE? VAT IF BATMAN WANTED TO TAKE SOME TIME FOR HIMSELF? PURSUE *OTHER* INTERESTS?
RAISE A FAMILY?
NO! HE ONLY WANTS TA FIGHT CRIME!
THE PROFESSOR IS KINDLY OMITTING THE UNIVERSAL CONSTANT, COMMISSIONER.
AS MY NAME REVEALS, I AM AFTER ALL... BUT A MAN. ONE DAY, GOTHAM WILL HAVE TO DO WITHOUT ME.
NOW IS THE TIME THAT WE MUST PREPARE FOR THAT DARK DAY.
sniff.

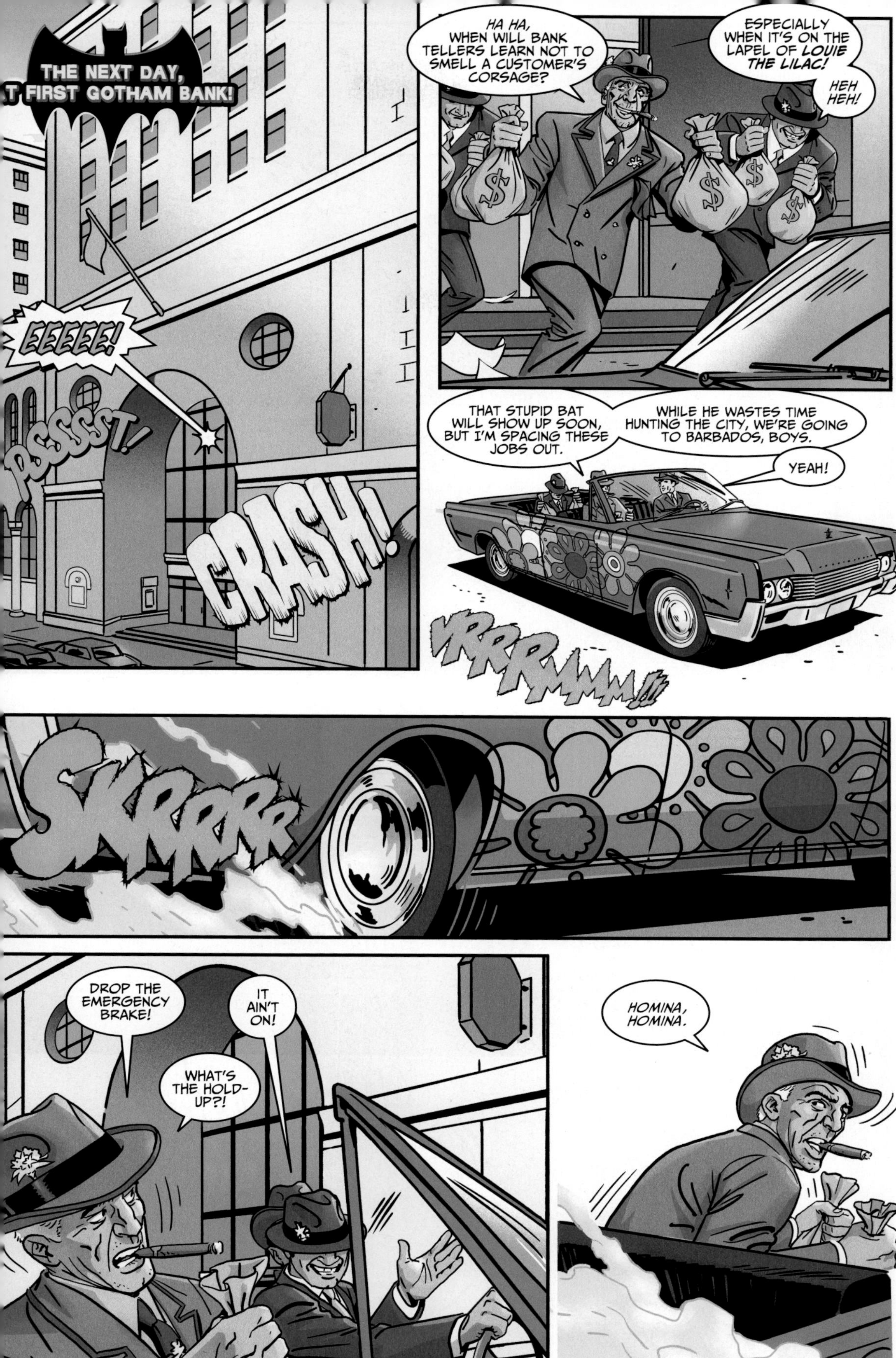
THE NEXT DAY, AT FIRST GOTHAM BANK!
EEEEEE!
PSSSSST!
CRASH!
HA HA, WHEN WILL BANK TELLERS LEARN NOT TO SMELL A CUSTOMER'S CORSAGE?
ESPECIALLY WHEN IT'S ON THE LAPEL OF LOUIE THE LILAC!
HEH HEH!
THAT STUPID BAT WILL SHOW UP SOON, BUT I'M SPACING THESE JOBS OUT.
WHILE HE WASTES TIME HUNTING THE CITY, WE'RE GOING TO BARBADOS, BOYS.
YEAH!
VRRRMMM!!
SKRRRR
DROP THE EMERGENCY BRAKE!
IT AIN'T ON!
WHAT'S THE HOLD-UP?!
HOMINA, HOMINA.

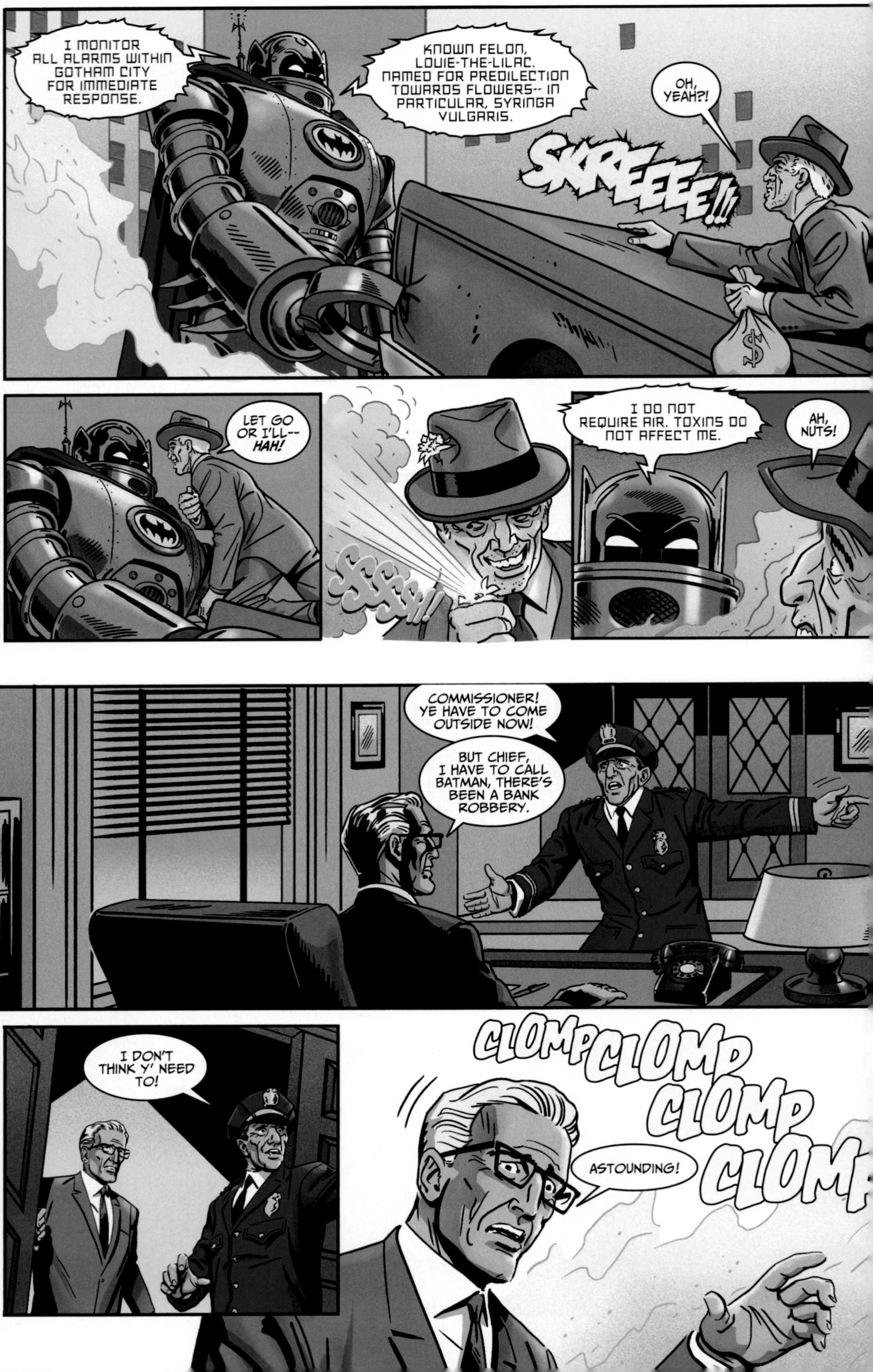
I MONITOR ALL ALARMS WITHIN GOTHAM CITY FOR IMMEDIATE RESPONSE.
KNOWN FELON, LOUIE-THE-LILAC. NAMED FOR PREDILECTION TOWARDS FLOWERS-- IN PARTICULAR, SYRINGA VULGARIS.
OH, YEAH?!
SKREEEEE!!
LET GO OR I'LL-- HAH!
SSSSH!
I DO NOT REQUIRE AIR. TOXINS DO NOT AFFECT ME.
AH, NUTS!
COMMISSIONER! YE HAVE TO COME OUTSIDE NOW!
BUT CHIEF, I HAVE TO CALL BATMAN, THERE'S BEEN A BANK ROBBERY.
I DON'T THINK Y' NEED TO!
CLOMP CLOMP CLOMP CLOMP
ASTOUNDING!

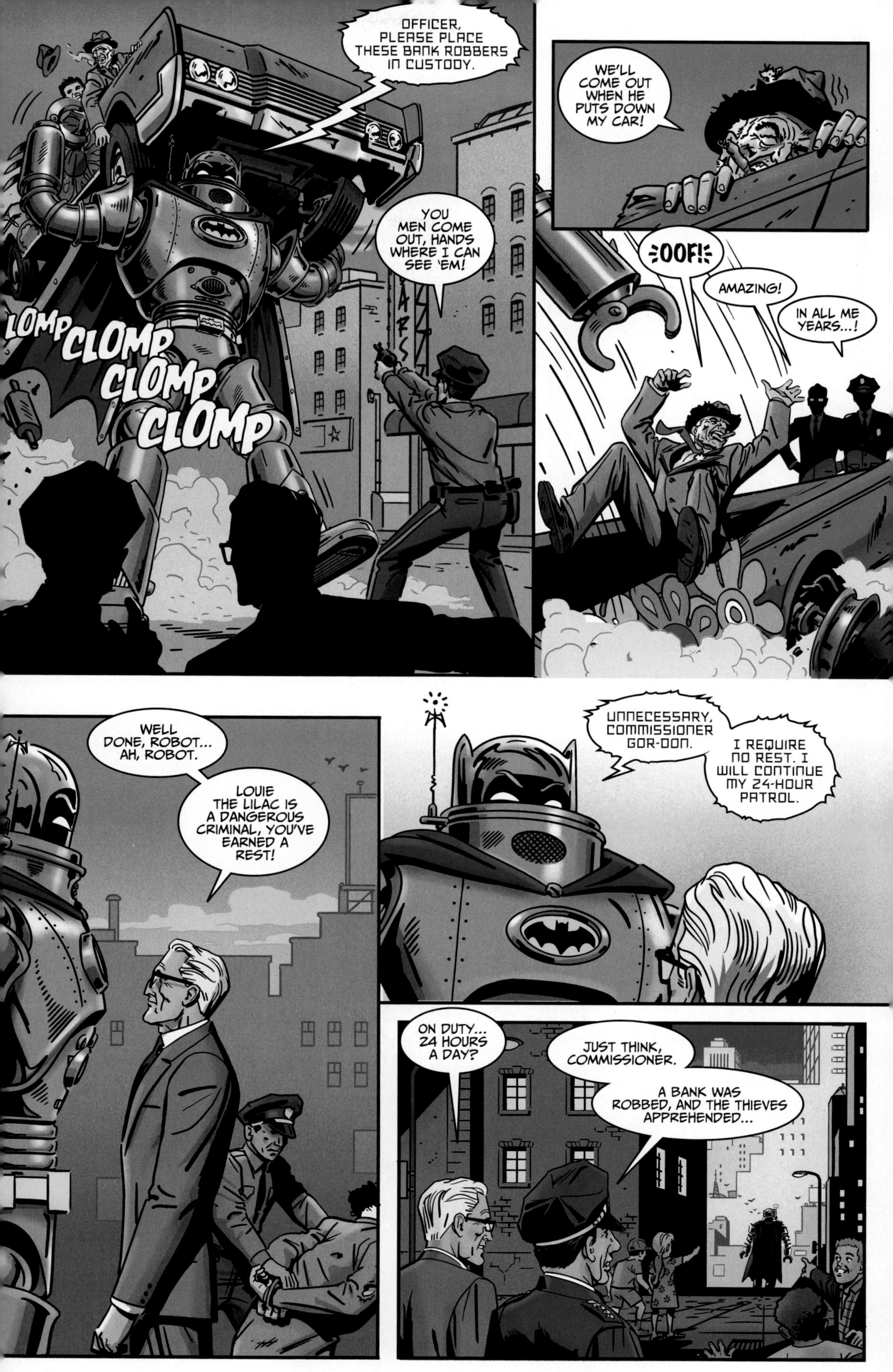
OFFICER, PLEASE PLACE THESE BANK ROBBERS IN CUSTODY.
YOU MEN COME OUT, HANDS WHERE I CAN SEE 'EM!
LOMP CLOMP CLOMP CLOMP
WE'LL COME OUT WHEN HE PUTS DOWN MY CAR!
OOF!
AMAZING!
IN ALL ME YEARS...!
WELL DONE, ROBOT... AH, ROBOT.
LOUIE THE LILAC IS A DANGEROUS CRIMINAL, YOU'VE EARNED A REST!
UNNECESSARY, COMMISSIONER GOR-DON.
I REQUIRE NO REST. I WILL CONTINUE MY 24-HOUR PATROL.
ON DUTY... 24 HOURS A DAY?
JUST THINK, COMMISSIONER.
A BANK WAS ROBBED, AND THE THIEVES APPREHENDED...

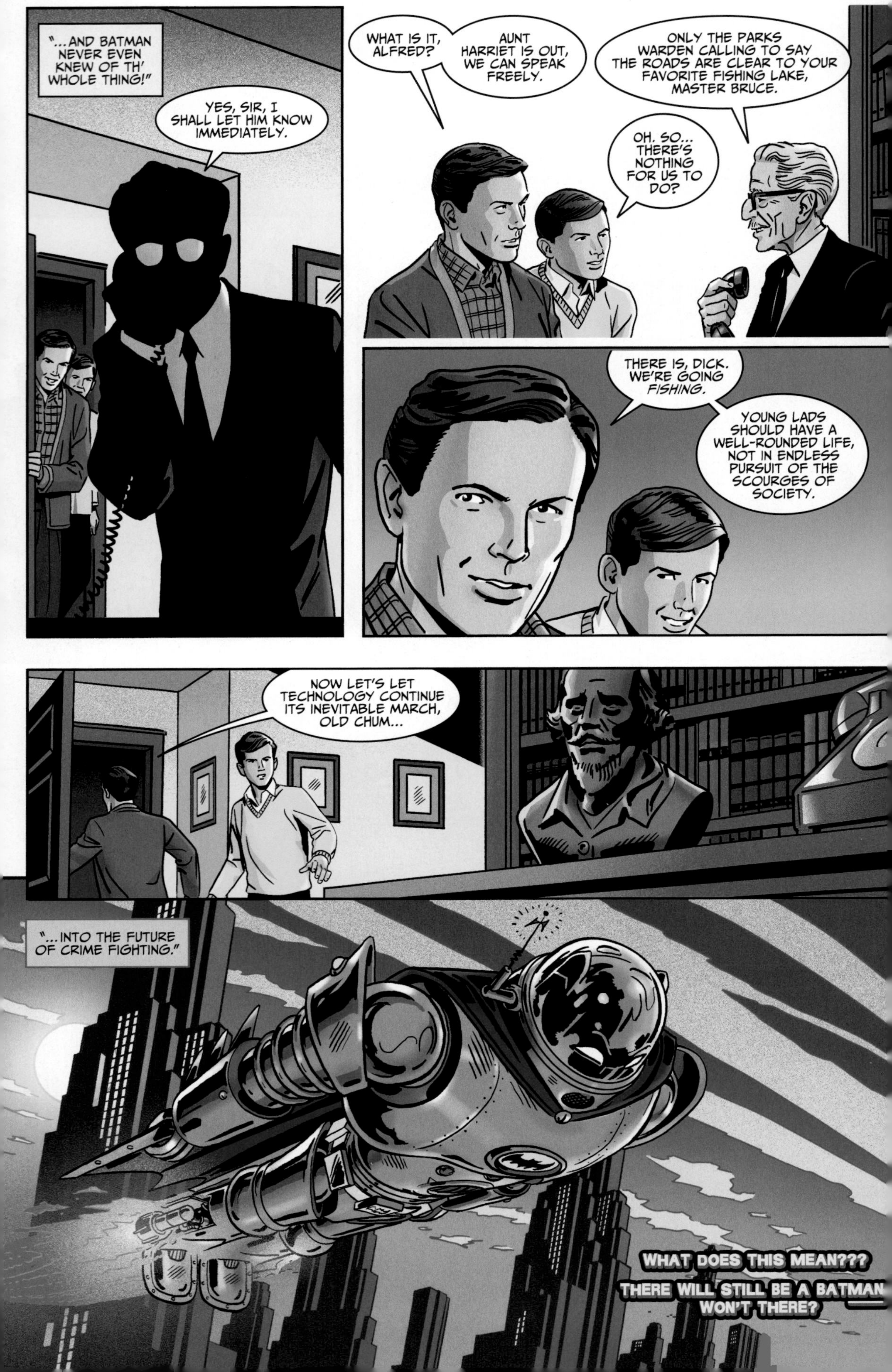
"...AND BATMAN NEVER EVEN KNEW OF TH' WHOLE THING!"
YES, SIR, I SHALL LET HIM KNOW IMMEDIATELY.
WHAT IS IT, ALFRED?
AUNT HARRIET IS OUT, WE CAN SPEAK FREELY.
ONLY THE PARKS WARDEN CALLING TO SAY THE ROADS ARE CLEAR TO YOUR FAVORITE FISHING LAKE, MASTER BRUCE.
OH. SO... THERE'S NOTHING FOR US TO DO?
THERE IS, DICK. WE'RE GOING *FISHING.*
YOUNG LADS SHOULD HAVE A WELL-ROUNDED LIFE, NOT IN ENDLESS PURSUIT OF THE SCOURGES OF SOCIETY.
NOW LET'S LET TECHNOLOGY CONTINUE ITS INEVITABLE MARCH, OLD CHUM...
"...INTO THE FUTURE OF CRIME FIGHTING."
WHAT DOES THIS MEAN???
THERE WILL STILL BE A BATMAN WON'T THERE?

BEEN EVEN MORE OF THE INCREDIBLE -STOPPING MACHINE TED BY PROFESSOR OVERBECK...

...THE ROBOT BATMAN!

WHAM 91.5

ROBOT BATMAN HAS WORKED TIRELESSLY AROUND THE CLOCK, ROUNDING UP THE MOST DANGEROUS CRIMINALS OF GOTHAM.

p-Ping!
Ping!
Ping!

CONFOUND IT, I'M ALMOST OUT OF ARROWS!

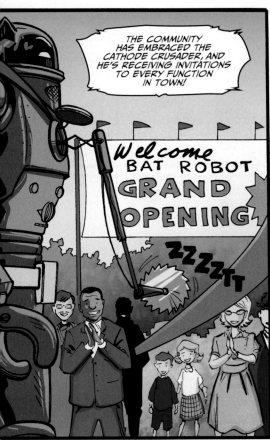

THE COMMUNITY HAS EMBRACED THE CATHODE CRUSADER, AND HE'S RECEIVING INVITATIONS TO EVERY FUNCTION IN TOWN!

Welcome BAT ROBOT GRAND OPENING

ZZZZTT

TODAY THE "SPARK KNIGHT" ARRIVED TO INVESTIGATE A CRIMINAL PRANK AT THE GREENWOOD PARK FOUNTAIN.

WE NOW KNOW WHERE THE MISSING MASCOT FROM THE DUNBAR DRIVE-IN IS, AND ATTACHED TO THE DUNBAR'S LARGE LAD...

--WAS A RIDDLE WRITTEN ON A PLAYING CARD! MORE ON THIS AT THE TOP OF THE HOUR.

GOSH!

RUSH

DUNBAR'S IS THE HOME OF THE BAT-BURGER, AND A RIDDLE WAS LEFT!

SURE SOUNDS LIKE SOMEONE FAMILIAR IS SENDING BATMAN A MESSAGE.

THAT MESSAGE, DICK, IS FOR THE BATMAN ROBOT.

WE ARE SEEING THE OTHER PURSUITS LIFE OFFERS.

OLD CHUM

SURE, BRUCE. I GUESS... I NEVER THOUGHT IT WOULD BE POSSIBLE TO REPLACE BATMAN.

CHANGE IS A UNIVERSAL CONSTANT.

EVEN COMMISSIONER GORDON HAS WARMED TO THE IDEA OF THE ROBOT PROTECTING GOTHAM.

I SHOULD SAY I HAVE!

COMMISSIONER GORDON! CHIEF O'HARA!

MOONEY, DID YE COPY DOWN THE RIDDLE THE ROBOT FOUND?

EVERYTHIN'S WELL IN HAND AT HOME.

ME MEN ARE SENDIN' US UPDATES BY RADIO.

AYE, CHIEF IT'S A SHOR ONE, A BOA FROM THE RIDDLER...

OLD CHUM

106

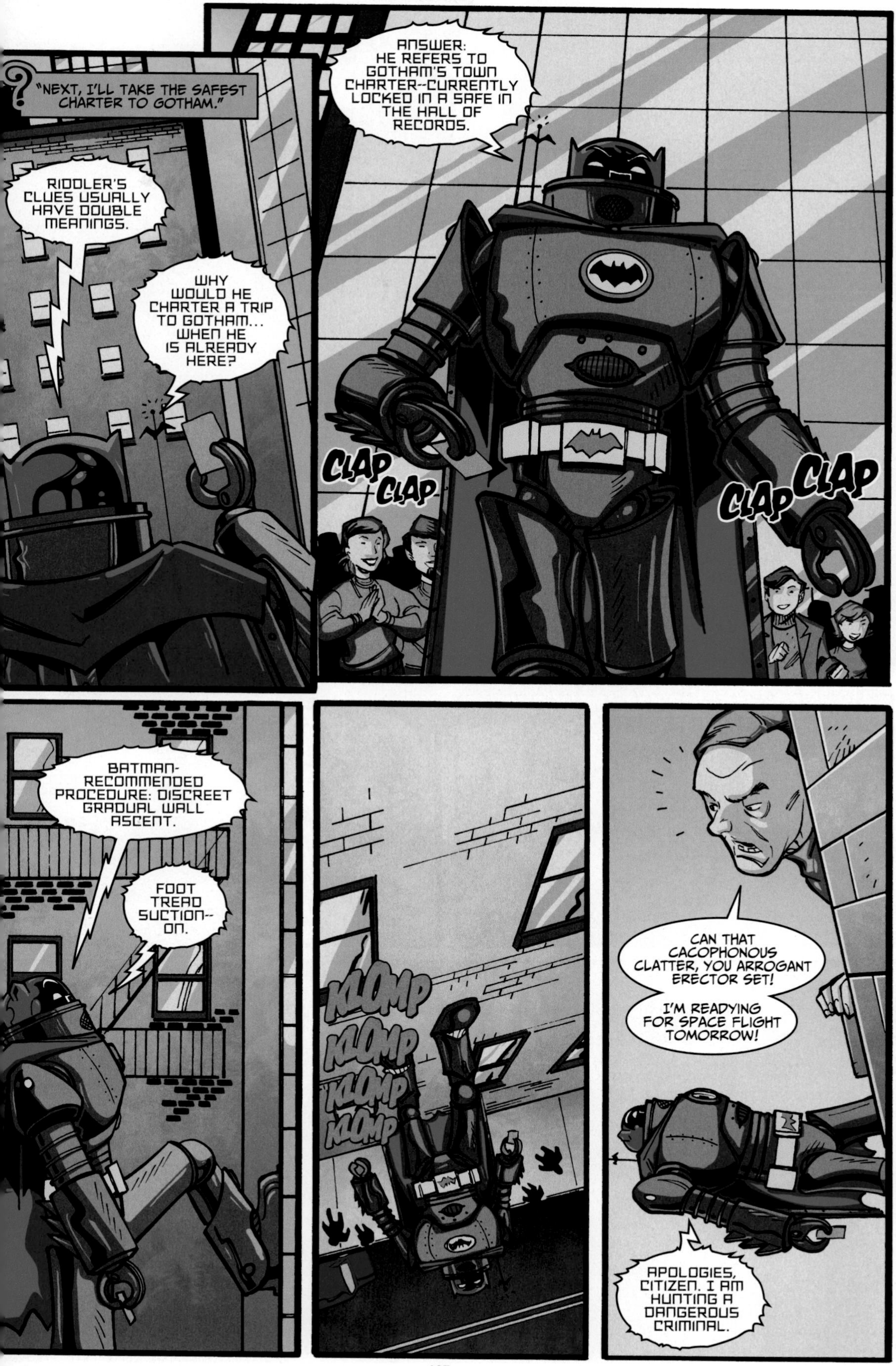
"NEXT, I'LL TAKE THE SAFEST CHARTER TO GOTHAM."
RIDDLER'S CLUES USUALLY HAVE DOUBLE MEANINGS.
WHY WOULD HE CHARTER A TRIP TO GOTHAM... WHEN HE IS ALREADY HERE?
ANSWER: HE REFERS TO GOTHAM'S TOWN CHARTER--CURRENTLY LOCKED IN A SAFE IN THE HALL OF RECORDS.
CLAP CLAP
CLAP CLAP
BATMAN-RECOMMENDED PROCEDURE: DISCREET GRADUAL WALL ASCENT.
FOOT TREAD SUCTION--ON.
KLOMP KLOMP KLOMP KLOMP
CAN THAT CACOPHONOUS CLATTER, YOU ARROGANT ERECTOR SET!
I'M READYING FOR SPACE FLIGHT TOMORROW!
APOLOGIES, CITIZEN. I AM HUNTING A DANGEROUS CRIMINAL.

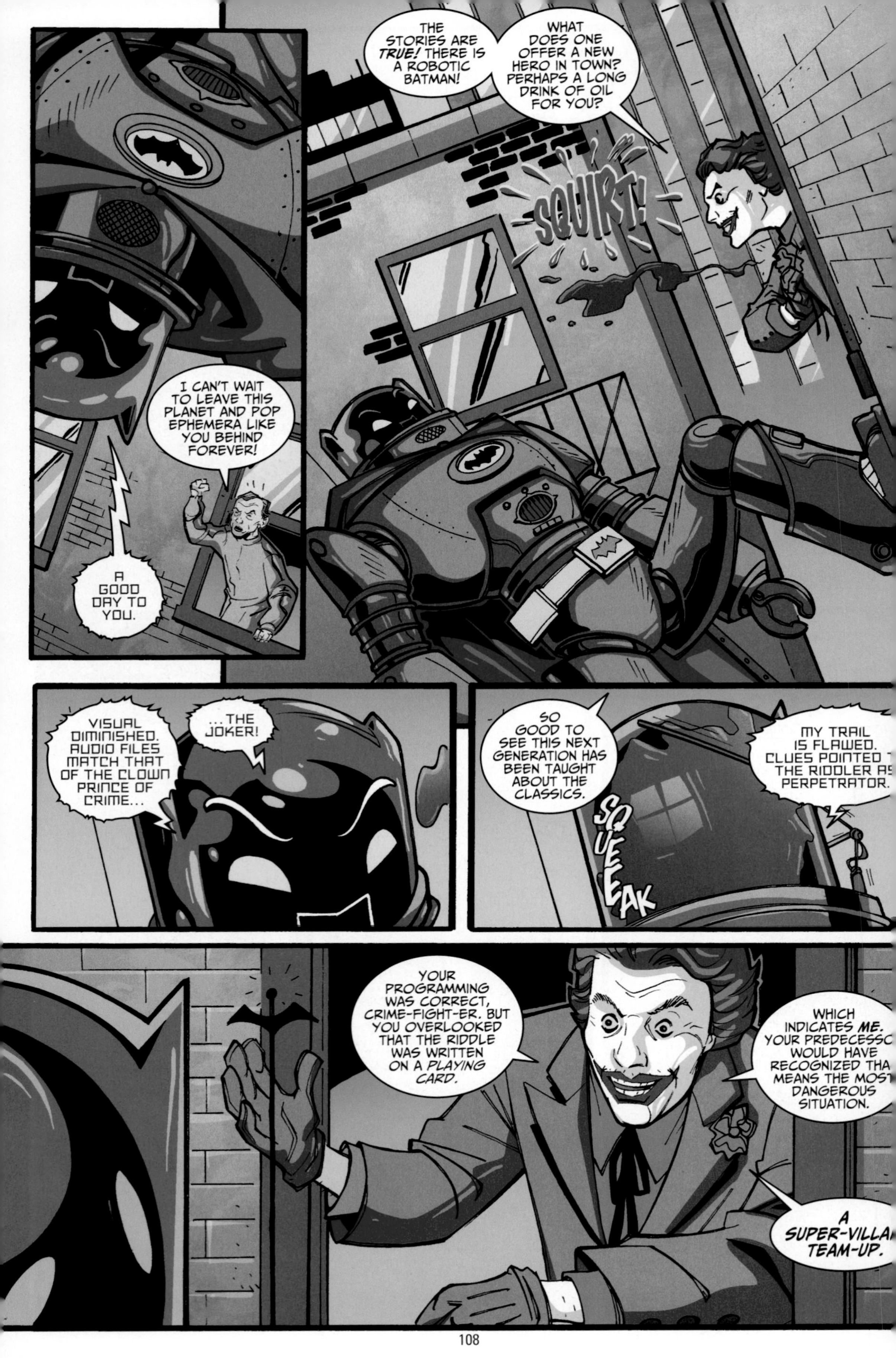
THE STORIES ARE TRUE! THERE IS A ROBOTIC BATMAN!
WHAT DOES ONE OFFER A NEW HERO IN TOWN? PERHAPS A LONG DRINK OF OIL FOR YOU?
SQUIRT!
I CAN'T WAIT TO LEAVE THIS PLANET AND POP EPHEMERA LIKE YOU BEHIND FOREVER!
A GOOD DAY TO YOU.
VISUAL DIMINISHED. AUDIO FILES MATCH THAT OF THE CLOWN PRINCE OF CRIME...
...THE JOKER!
SO GOOD TO SEE THIS NEXT GENERATION HAS BEEN TAUGHT ABOUT THE CLASSICS.
SQUEEEAK
MY TRAIL IS FLAWED. CLUES POINTED T THE RIDDLER AS PERPETRATOR.
YOUR PROGRAMMING WAS CORRECT, CRIME-FIGHT-ER. BUT YOU OVERLOOKED THAT THE RIDDLE WAS WRITTEN ON A PLAYING CARD.
WHICH INDICATES ME. YOUR PREDECESSC WOULD HAVE RECOGNIZED THA MEANS THE MOST DANGEROUS SITUATION.
A SUPER-VILLA TEAM-UP.

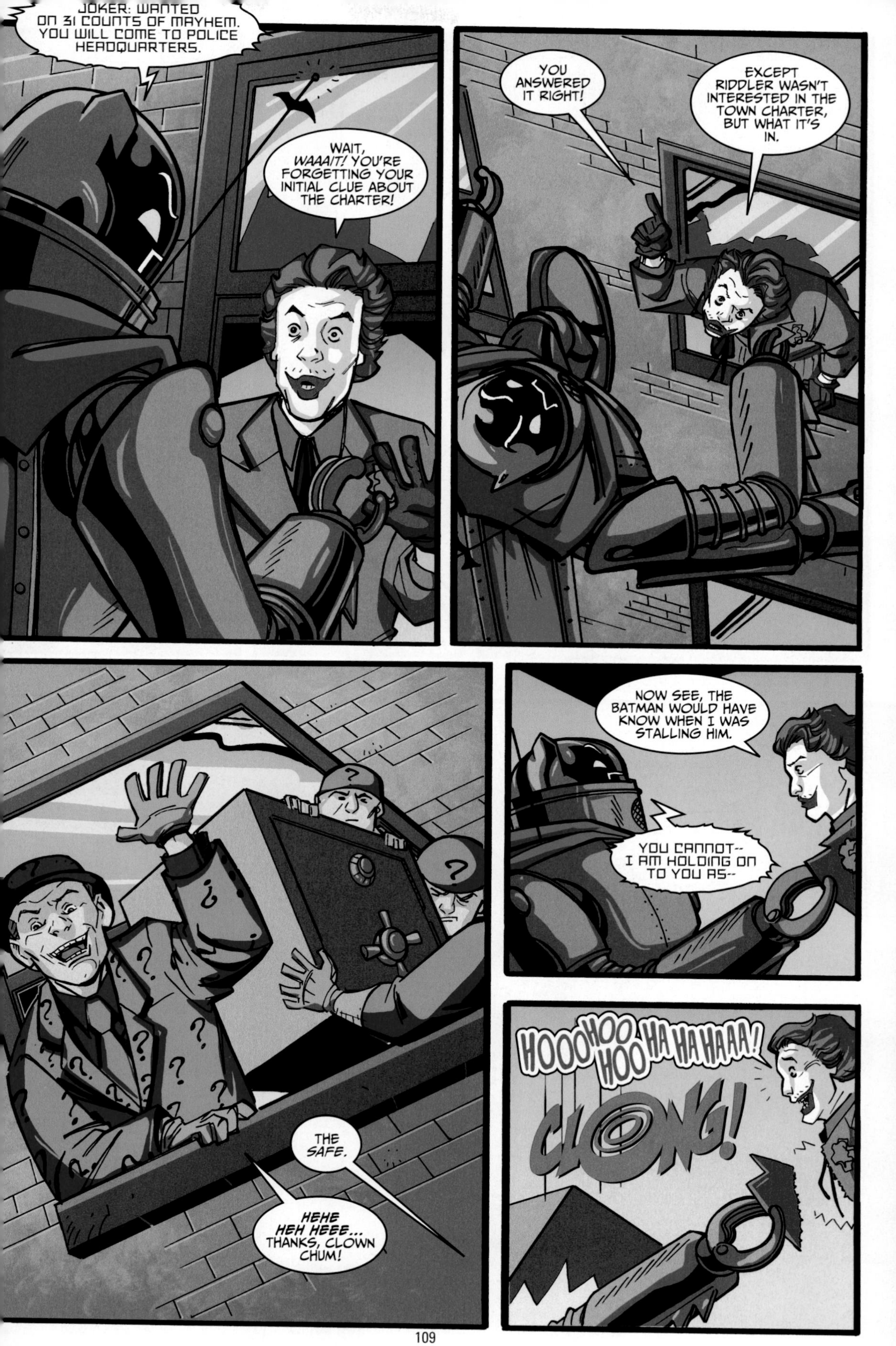
JOKER: WANTED ON 31 COUNTS OF MAYHEM. YOU WILL COME TO POLICE HEADQUARTERS.
WAIT, WAAAIT! YOU'RE FORGETTING YOUR INITIAL CLUE ABOUT THE CHARTER!
YOU ANSWERED IT RIGHT!
EXCEPT RIDDLER WASN'T INTERESTED IN THE TOWN CHARTER, BUT WHAT IT'S IN.
THE SAFE.
HEHE HEH HEEE... THANKS, CLOWN CHUM!
NOW SEE, THE BATMAN WOULD HAVE KNOW WHEN I WAS STALLING HIM.
YOU CANNOT-- I AM HOLDING ON TO YOU AS--
HOOOHOO HOO HA HA HAAA!
CLONG!

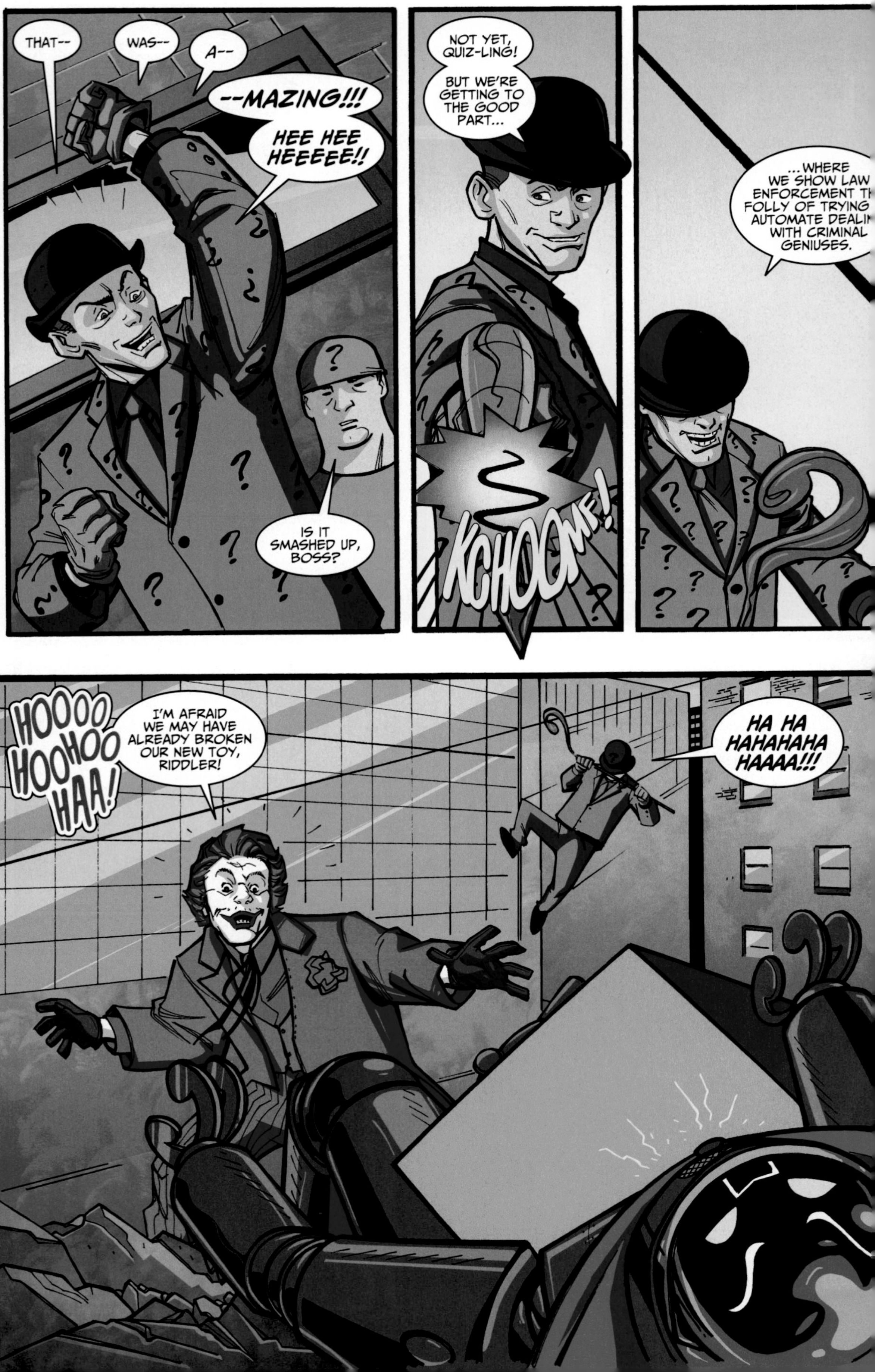
THAT--
WAS--
A--
--MAZING!!!
HEE HEE HEEEEEE!!
IS IT SMASHED UP, BOSS?
NOT YET, QUIZ-LING!
BUT WE'RE GETTING TO THE GOOD PART...
KCHOOMF!
...WHERE WE SHOW LAW ENFORCEMENT TH FOLLY OF TRYING AUTOMATE DEALIN WITH CRIMINAL GENIUSES.
HOOOO HOOHOO HAA!
I'M AFRAID WE MAY HAVE ALREADY BROKEN OUR NEW TOY, RIDDLER!
HA HA HAHAHAHA HAAAA!!!

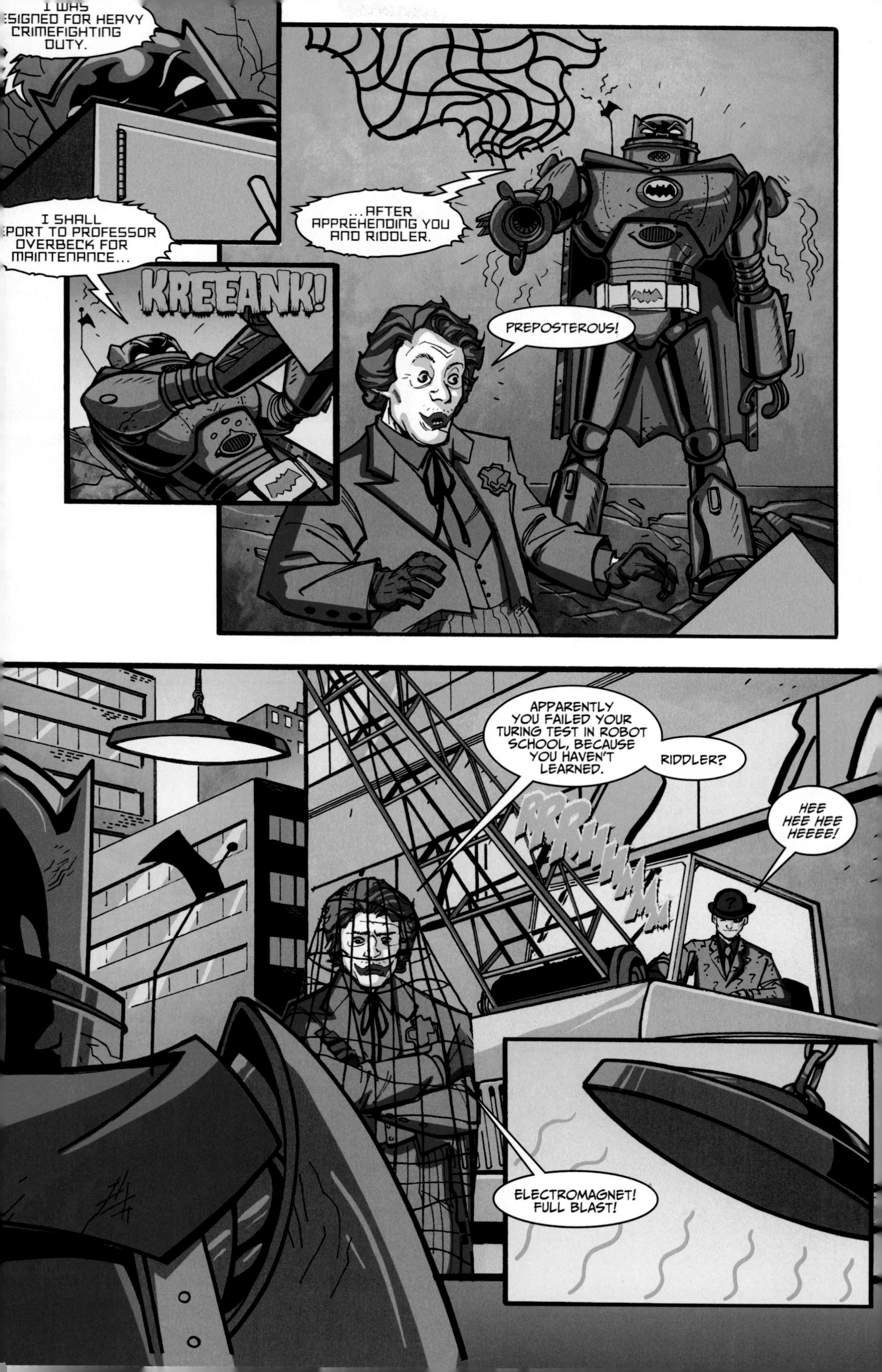

I WAS
ESIGNED FOR HEAVY
CRIMEFIGHTING
DUTY.
I SHALL
EPORT TO PROFESSOR
OVERBECK FOR
MAINTENANCE...
KREEANK!
...AFTER
APPREHENDING YOU
AND RIDDLER.
PREPOSTEROUS!
APPARENTLY
YOU FAILED YOUR
TURING TEST IN ROBOT
SCHOOL, BECAUSE
YOU HAVEN'T
LEARNED.
RIDDLER?
HEE
HEE HEE
HEEEE!
ELECTROMAGNET!
FULL BLAST!

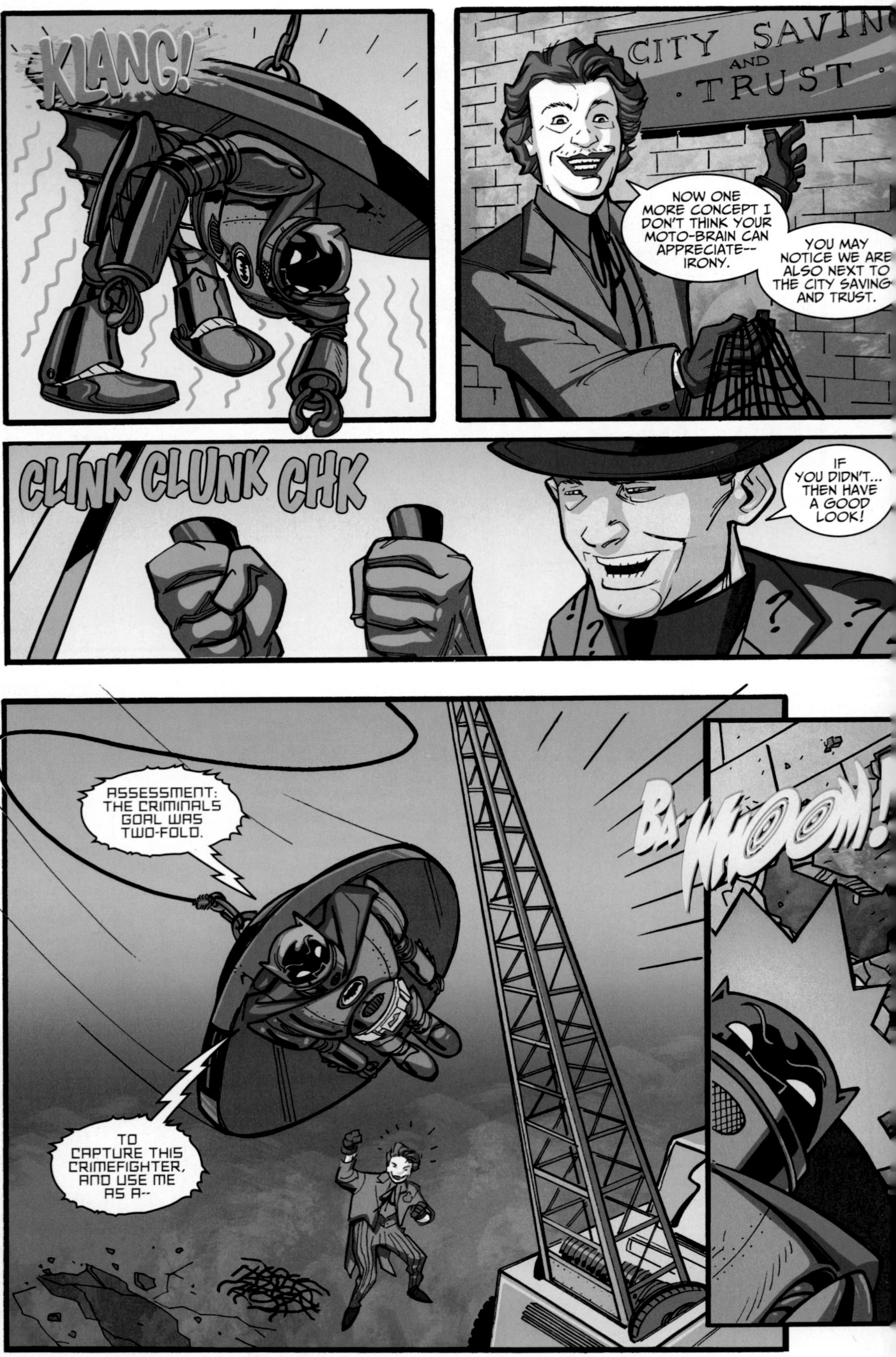
KLANG!
CITY SAVIN
AND
TRUST
NOW ONE MORE CONCEPT I DON'T THINK YOUR MOTO-BRAIN CAN APPRECIATE-- IRONY.
YOU MAY NOTICE WE ARE ALSO NEXT TO THE CITY SAVING AND TRUST.
CLINK CLUNK CHK
IF YOU DIDN'T... THEN HAVE A GOOD LOOK!
ASSESSMENT: THE CRIMINALS GOAL WAS TWO-FOLD.
TO CAPTURE THIS CRIMEFIGHTER, AND USE ME AS A--
BA-WHOOOM!

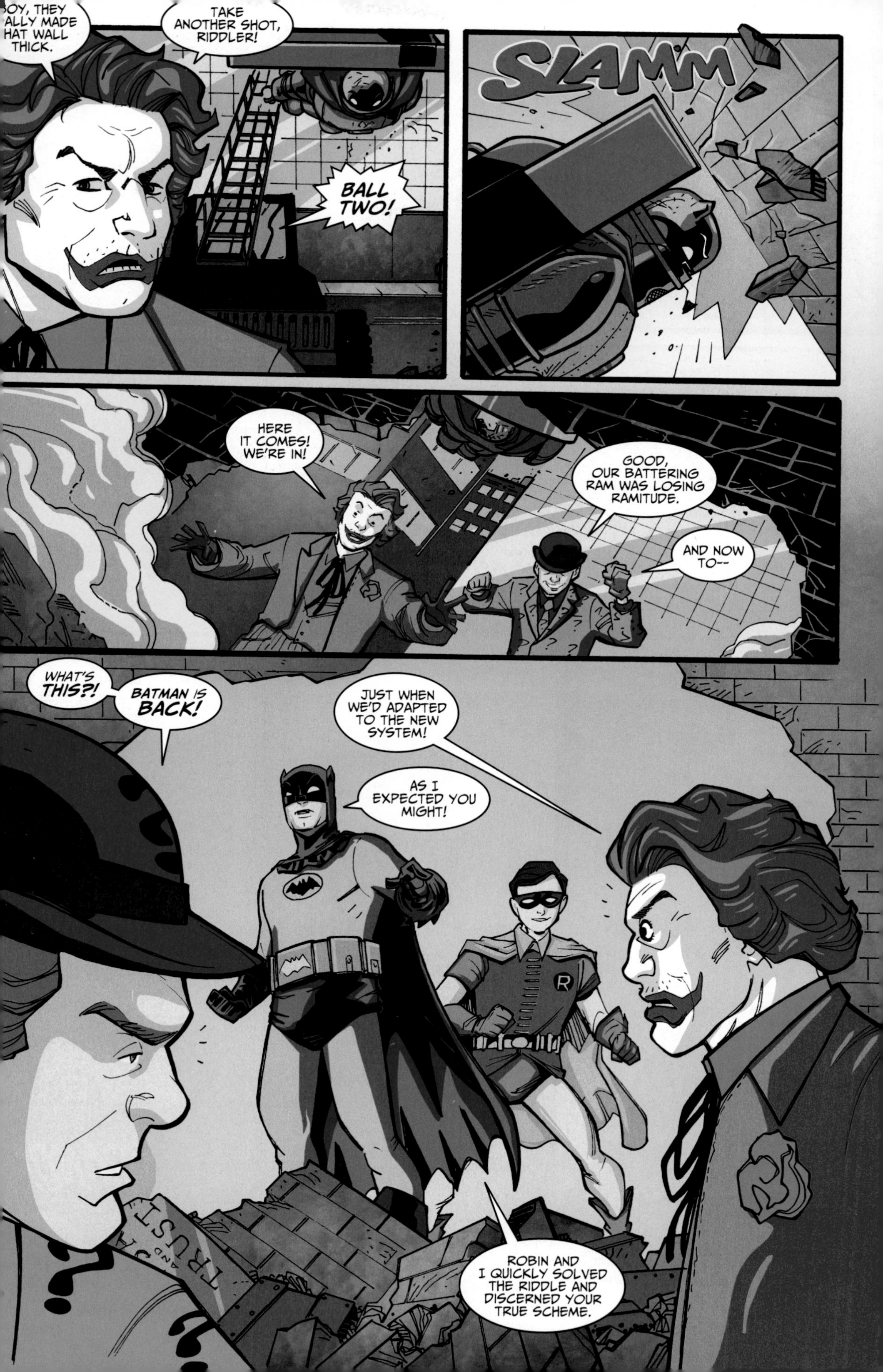
BOY, THEY REALLY MADE THAT WALL THICK.
TAKE ANOTHER SHOT, RIDDLER!
BALL TWO!
SLAMM
HERE IT COMES! WE'RE IN!
GOOD, OUR BATTERING RAM WAS LOSING RAMITUDE.
AND NOW TO--
WHAT'S THIS?!
BATMAN IS BACK!
JUST WHEN WE'D ADAPTED TO THE NEW SYSTEM!
AS I EXPECTED YOU MIGHT!
ROBIN AND I QUICKLY SOLVED THE RIDDLE AND DISCERNED YOUR TRUE SCHEME.

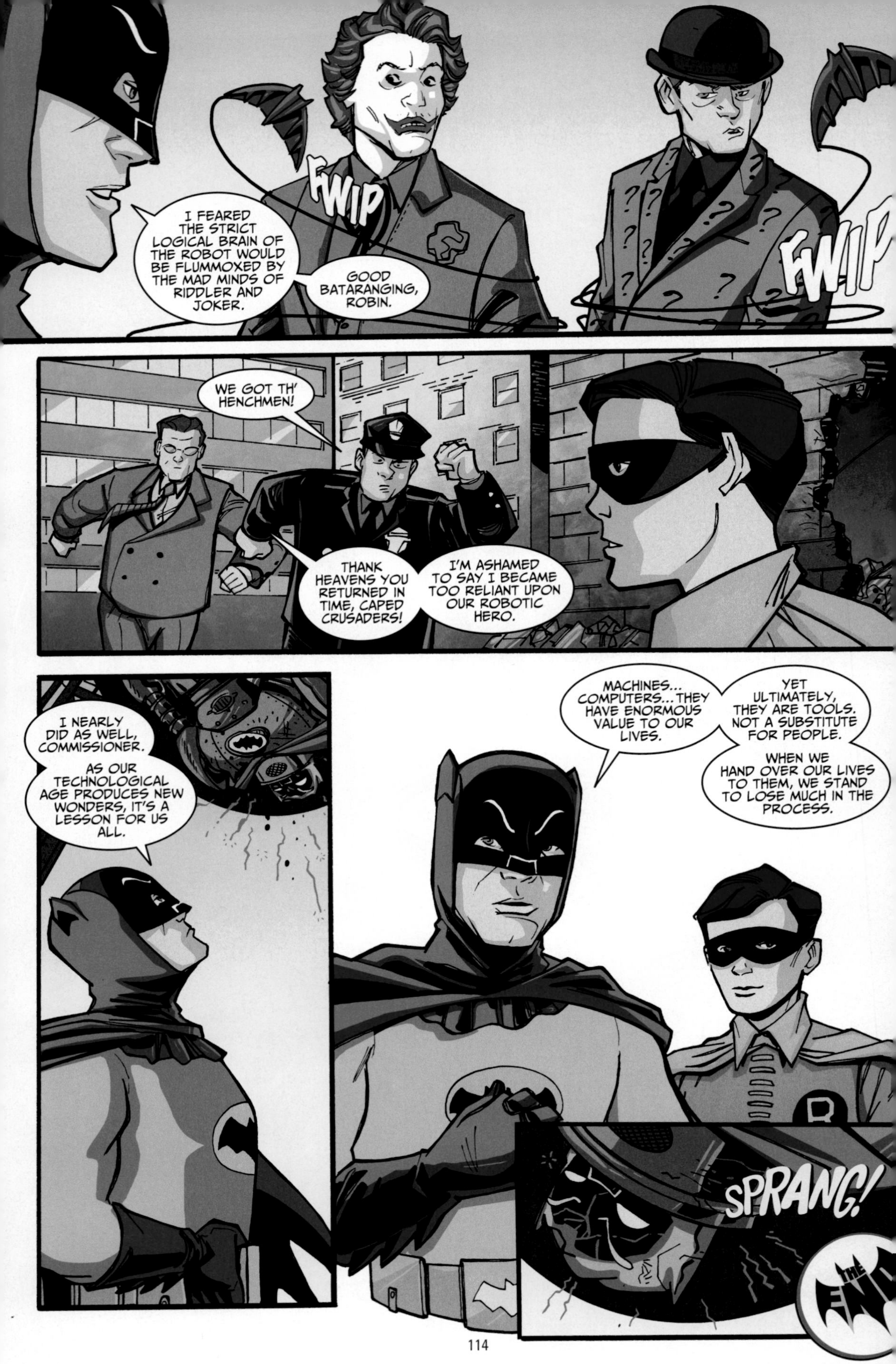
I FEARED THE STRICT LOGICAL BRAIN OF THE ROBOT WOULD BE FLUMMOXED BY THE MAD MINDS OF RIDDLER AND JOKER.
GOOD BATARANGING, ROBIN.
FWIP
FWIP
WE GOT TH' HENCHMEN!
THANK HEAVENS YOU RETURNED IN TIME, CAPED CRUSADERS!
I'M ASHAMED TO SAY I BECAME TOO RELIANT UPON OUR ROBOTIC HERO.
I NEARLY DID AS WELL, COMMISSIONER.
AS OUR TECHNOLOGICAL AGE PRODUCES NEW WONDERS, IT'S A LESSON FOR US ALL.
MACHINES... COMPUTERS... THEY HAVE ENORMOUS VALUE TO OUR LIVES.
YET ULTIMATELY, THEY ARE TOOLS. NOT A SUBSTITUTE FOR PEOPLE.
WHEN WE HAND OVER OUR LIVES TO THEM, WE STAND TO LOSE MUCH IN THE PROCESS.
SPRANG!
THE END

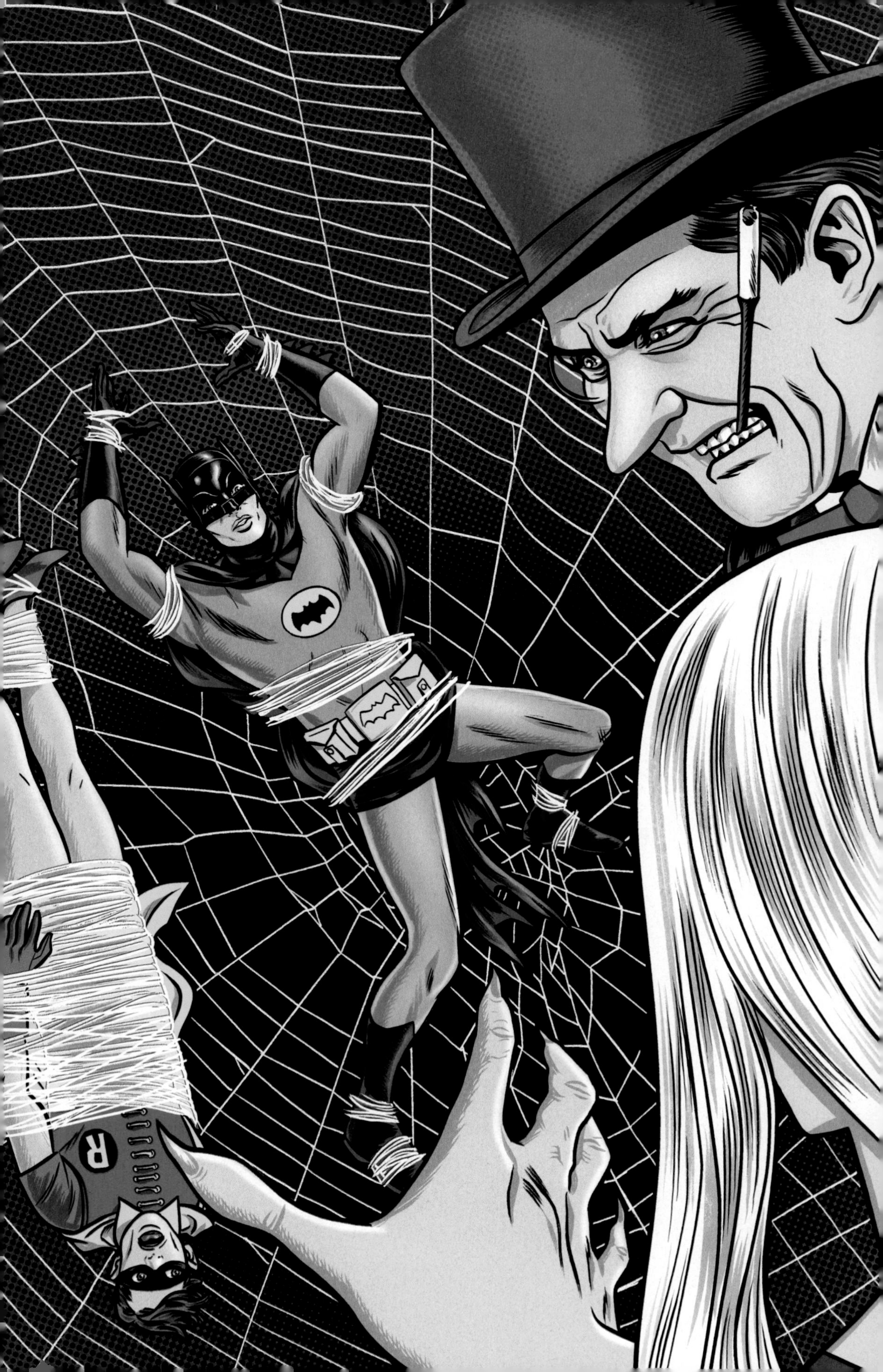

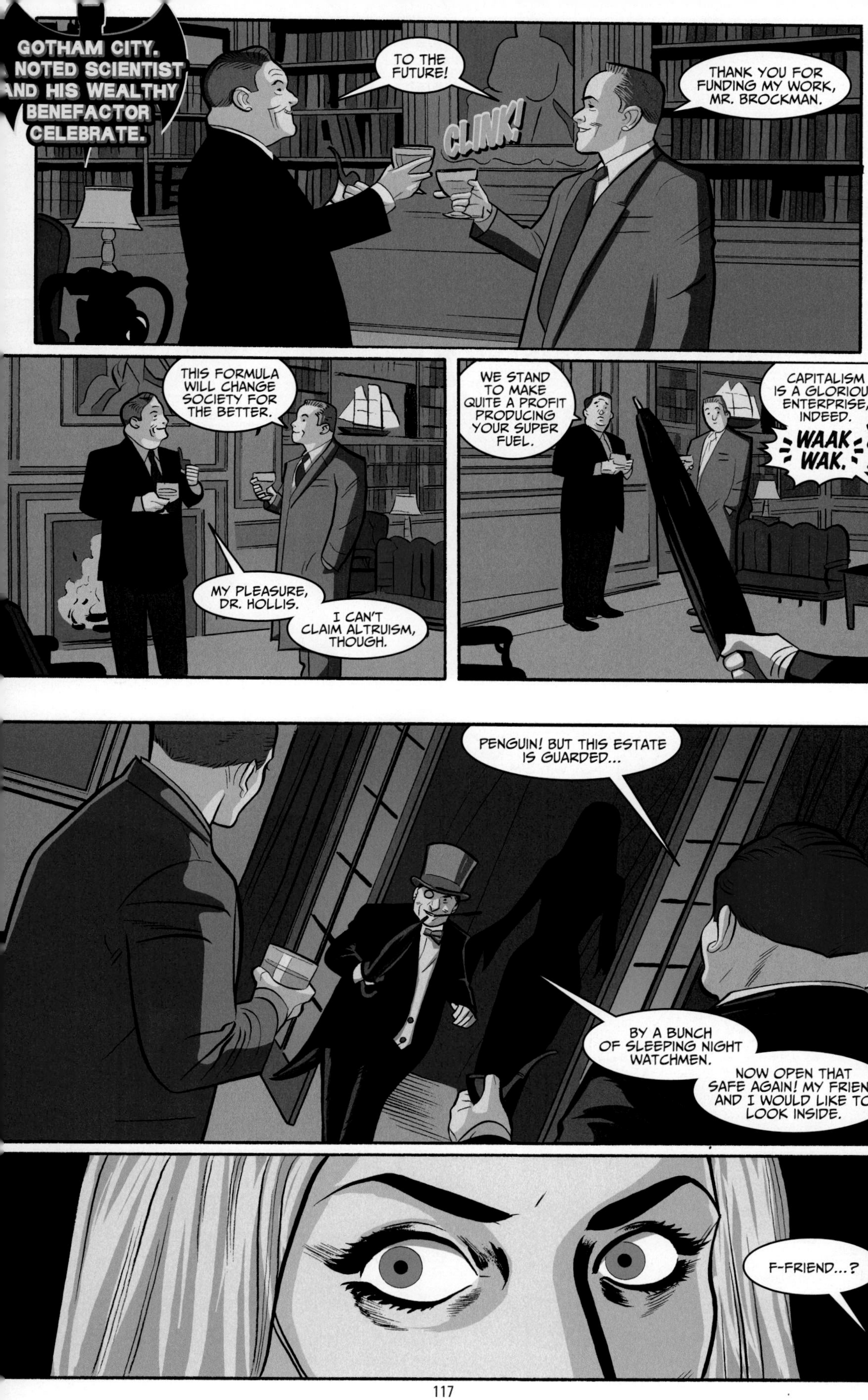
GOTHAM CITY. NOTED SCIENTIST AND HIS WEALTHY BENEFACTOR CELEBRATE.
TO THE FUTURE!
CLINK!
THANK YOU FOR FUNDING MY WORK, MR. BROCKMAN.
THIS FORMULA WILL CHANGE SOCIETY FOR THE BETTER.
MY PLEASURE, DR. HOLLIS.
I CAN'T CLAIM ALTRUISM, THOUGH.
WE STAND TO MAKE QUITE A PROFIT PRODUCING YOUR SUPER FUEL.
CAPITALISM IS A GLORIOUS ENTERPRISE, INDEED.
WAAK WAK.
PENGUIN! BUT THIS ESTATE IS GUARDED...
BY A BUNCH OF SLEEPING NIGHT WATCHMEN.
NOW OPEN THAT SAFE AGAIN! MY FRIEND AND I WOULD LIKE TO LOOK INSIDE.
F-FRIEND...?

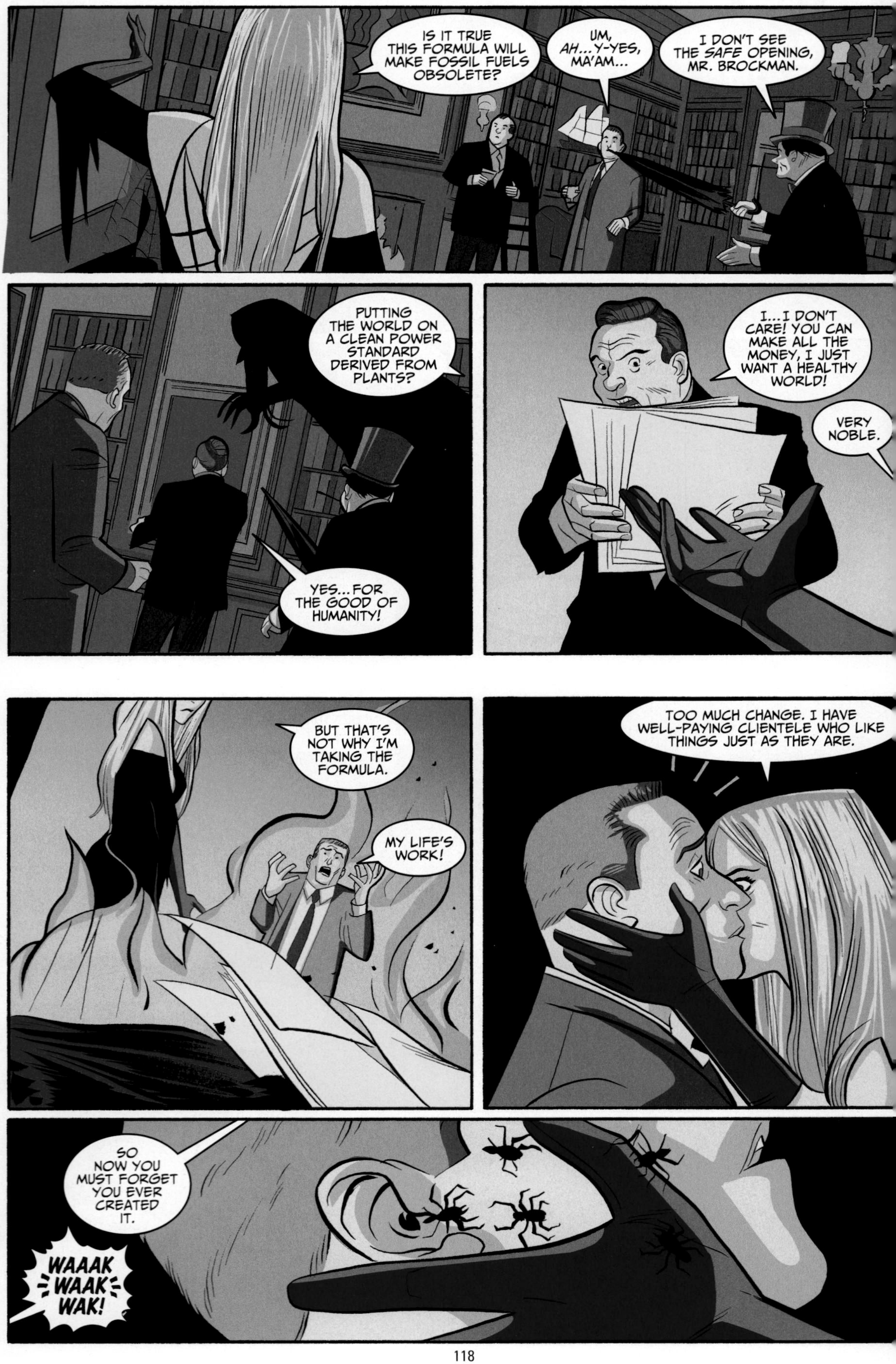
IS IT TRUE THIS FORMULA WILL MAKE FOSSIL FUELS OBSOLETE?
UM, AH...Y-YES, MA'AM...
I DON'T SEE THE SAFE OPENING, MR. BROCKMAN.
PUTTING THE WORLD ON A CLEAN POWER STANDARD DERIVED FROM PLANTS?
YES...FOR THE GOOD OF HUMANITY!
I...I DON'T CARE! YOU CAN MAKE ALL THE MONEY, I JUST WANT A HEALTHY WORLD!
VERY NOBLE.
BUT THAT'S NOT WHY I'M TAKING THE FORMULA.
MY LIFE'S WORK!
TOO MUCH CHANGE. I HAVE WELL-PAYING CLIENTELE WHO LIKE THINGS JUST AS THEY ARE.
SO NOW YOU MUST FORGET YOU EVER CREATED IT.
WAAAK WAAK WAK!

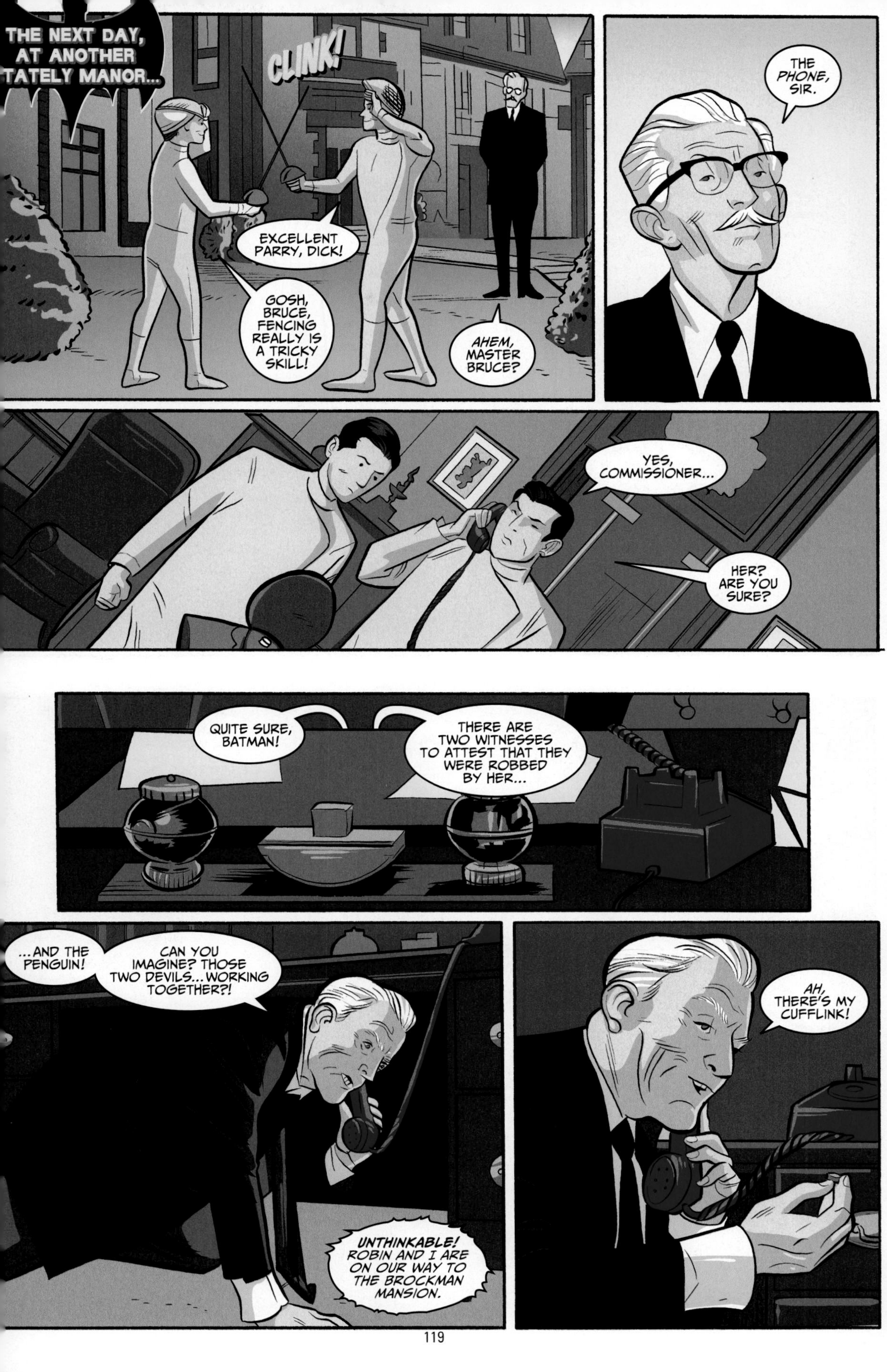

THE NEXT DAY, AT ANOTHER TATELY MANOR...
CLINK!
EXCELLENT PARRY, DICK!
GOSH, BRUCE, FENCING REALLY IS A TRICKY SKILL!
AHEM, MASTER BRUCE?
THE PHONE, SIR.
YES, COMMISSIONER...
HER? ARE YOU SURE?
QUITE SURE, BATMAN!
THERE ARE TWO WITNESSES TO ATTEST THAT THEY WERE ROBBED BY HER...
...AND THE PENGUIN!
CAN YOU IMAGINE? THOSE TWO DEVILS...WORKING TOGETHER?!
UNTHINKABLE! ROBIN AND I ARE ON OUR WAY TO THE BROCKMAN MANSION.
AH, THERE'S MY CUFFLINK!

SOON, AT GOTHAM HOSPITAL'S MENTAL WARD...

WE FIND NO PUNCTURE WOUNDS OR SIGNS OF HIS HAVING BEEN GIVEN A DRUG BY MOUTH.

YOU WOULDN'T. A TOXIN WAS APPLIED IN A DIFFERENT WAY.

WHAT HAVE YOU FOUND THAT OUR TEAM COULDN'T?

A SPIDER'S EGG SAC IN THE VICTIM'S EAR CANAL.

OHH--

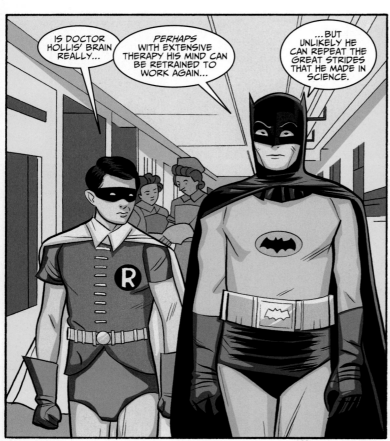

IS DOCTOR HOLLIS' BRAIN REALLY...

PERHAPS WITH EXTENSIVE THERAPY HIS MIND CAN BE RETRAINED TO WORK AGAIN...

...BUT UNLIKELY HE CAN REPEAT THE GREAT STRIDES THAT HE MADE IN SCIENCE.

THE BLACK WIDOW'S CARESS IS EITHER DEBILITATING OR DEADLY.

BATMAN! THERE'S BEEN ANOTHER CRIME!

A HUGE EXPLOSION--

--AT TH' CITY SAVINGS & TRUST!

--WHILE THE PENGUIN HAD US DISTRACTED INSIDE, THIS OTHER WOMAN AND HER MEN BLASTED THE BACK OF THE VAULT'S WALL!

THEY MADE OFF WITH AT LEAST A HUNDRED THOUSAND!

THANKFULLY PEOPLE HAVE BEEN HELPING US GATHER UP THE LOOSE BILLS.

YOU CAN ALWAYS COUNT ON THE DECENCY OF GOTHAM'S CITIZENRY IN TRYING TIMES.

IF THERE WERE ANY CLUES, THAT EXPLOSION ANNIHILATED THEM.

AU CONTRAIRE, ROBIN. LOOK!

AN UNFIRED MORTAR, PROBABLY A FIRST ATTEMPT AT BLOWING THE WALL.

OLD, UNRELIABLE ORDNANCE, PROBABLY STORED FOR SEVERAL YEARS...

... I THINK WE SHOULD INVESTIGATE THE OLD ARMORY OUTSIDE OF TOWN.

TO THE BATMOBILE!

WE'VE COUNTED $163,000!

WAAK WAK WAAAK!

WHO SAYS IT'S BAD LUCK TO OPEN AN UMBRELLA INDOORS! HAH!

WAAHK

I GRABBED ALMOST THAT MUCH MYSELF--

--IF THE @&?$#! CLASP WILL SIMPLY--

THRAASH

WHAT THE BLAZES!

A DISGUSTING FLY WAS HOVERING BY YOUR HAT. I DETEST DROSOPHILA SO.

AH... YES, YES.

STILL, YOU MIGHT TAKE CARE WITH MY CHAPEAU, THIS WAS A GIFT FROM THE MAD HATTER...

PFAH, THERE IS NO LUXURY YOU SHALL NOT HAVE NOW, PENGUIN!

YOU HAVE MADE THE SOUND CHOICE OF THROWING IN YOUR LOT WI' THE CRAFTY CRIMINAL GENIUS OF THE BLAC WIDOW.

GOTHAM'S POLICE FORCE IS STILL A SIMPERING MOCKERY, ONLY USEFUL TO DRIVE AWAY FELONS DEFEATED BY THAT JUSTICE-OBSESSED BAT.

ONCE HE'S GONE, THE CITY WILL ROLL OVER AND LIE DOWN IN TOTAL SUBMISSION.

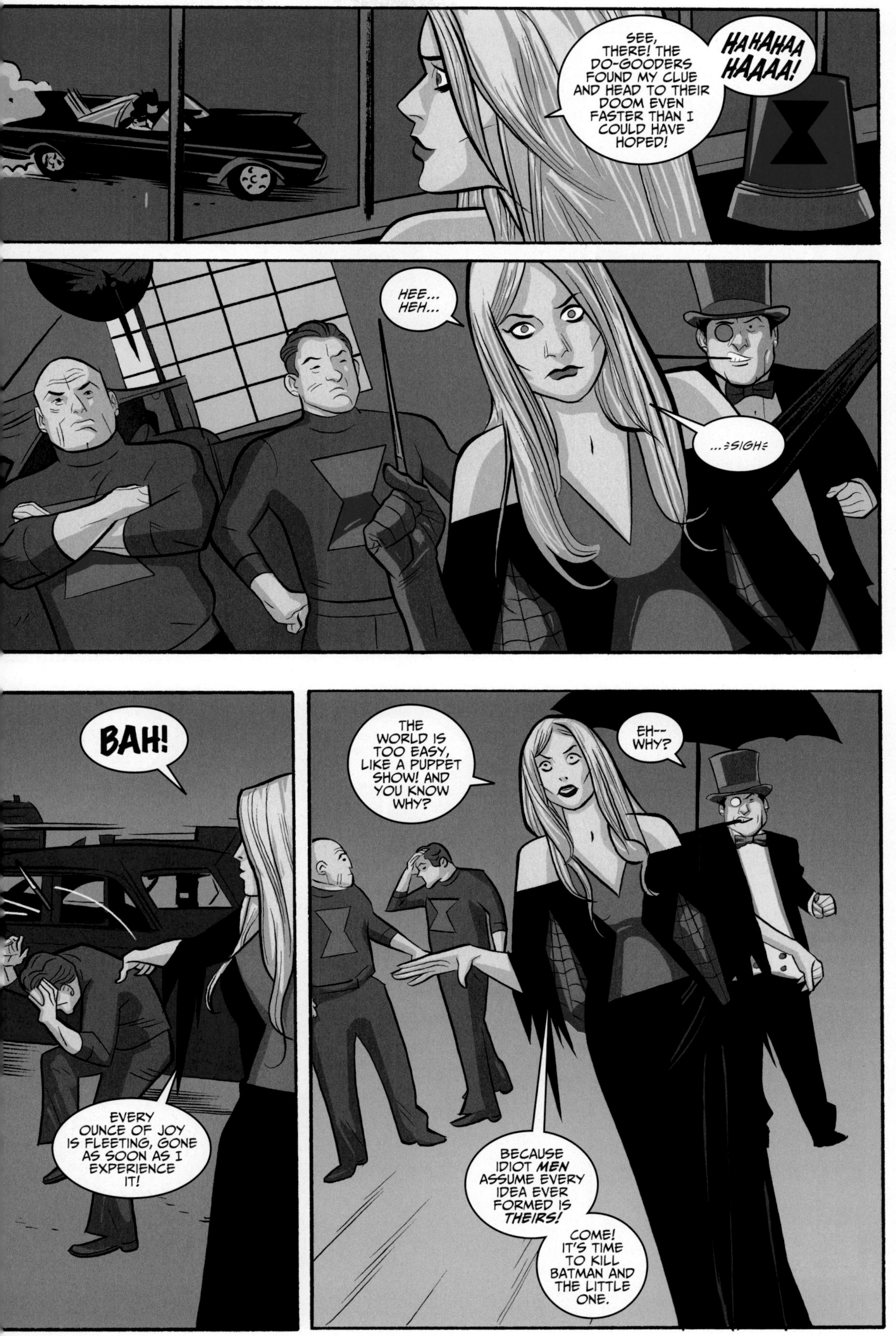
SEE, THERE! THE DO-GOODERS FOUND MY CLUE AND HEAD TO THEIR DOOM EVEN FASTER THAN I COULD HAVE HOPED!
HAHAHAA HAAAA!
HEE... HEH...
...SIGH
BAH!
EVERY OUNCE OF JOY IS FLEETING, GONE AS SOON AS I EXPERIENCE IT!
THE WORLD IS TOO EASY, LIKE A PUPPET SHOW! AND YOU KNOW WHY?
EH-- WHY?
BECAUSE IDIOT MEN ASSUME EVERY IDEA EVER FORMED IS THEIRS!
COME! IT'S TIME TO KILL BATMAN AND THE LITTLE ONE.

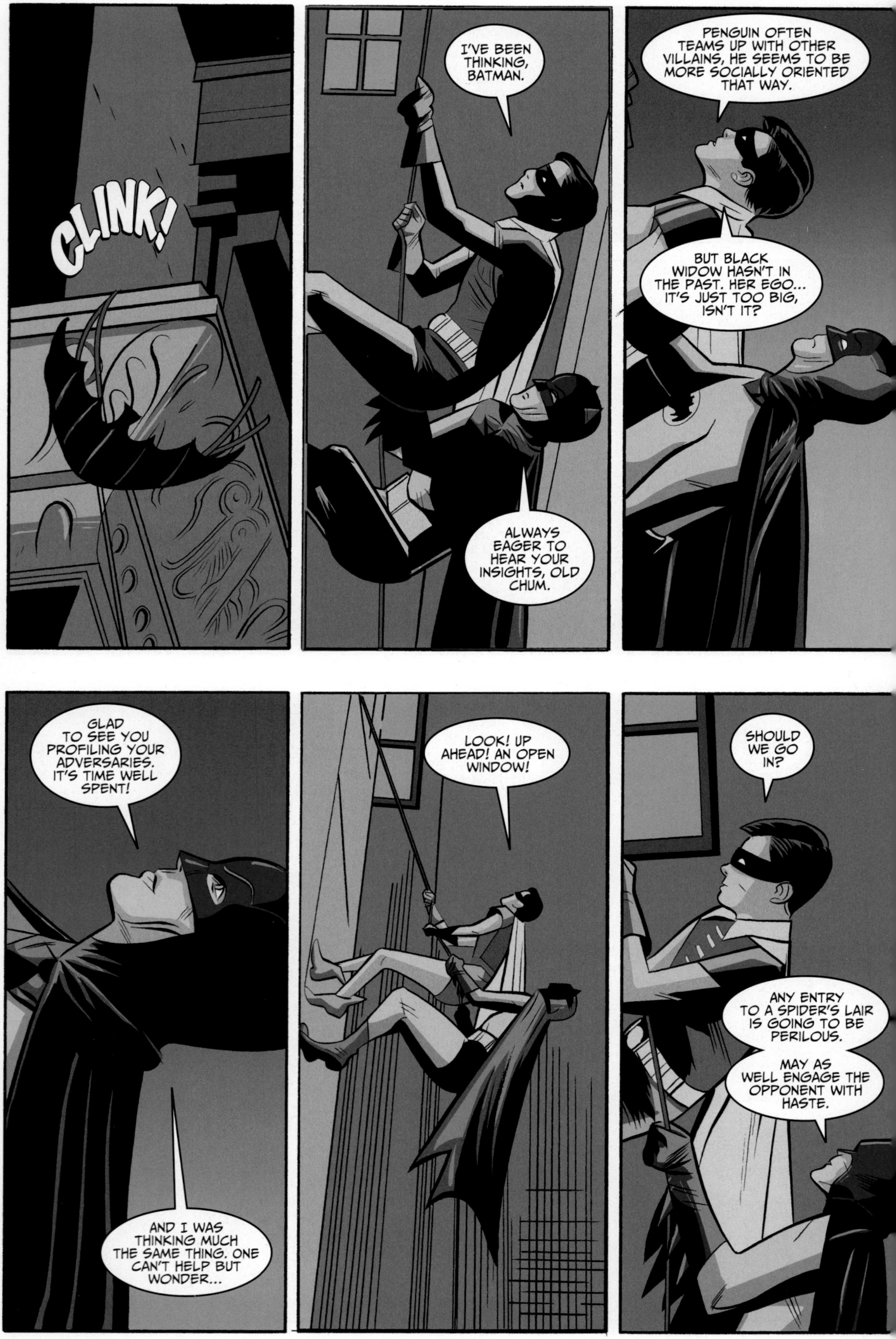
CLINK!
I'VE BEEN THINKING, BATMAN.
ALWAYS EAGER TO HEAR YOUR INSIGHTS, OLD CHUM.
PENGUIN OFTEN TEAMS UP WITH OTHER VILLAINS, HE SEEMS TO BE MORE SOCIALLY ORIENTED THAT WAY.
BUT BLACK WIDOW HASN'T IN THE PAST. HER EGO... IT'S JUST TOO BIG, ISN'T IT?
GLAD TO SEE YOU PROFILING YOUR ADVERSARIES. IT'S TIME WELL SPENT!
AND I WAS THINKING MUCH THE SAME THING. ONE CAN'T HELP BUT WONDER...
LOOK! UP AHEAD! AN OPEN WINDOW!
SHOULD WE GO IN?
ANY ENTRY TO A SPIDER'S LAIR IS GOING TO BE PERILOUS.
MAY AS WELL ENGAGE THE OPPONENT WITH HASTE.

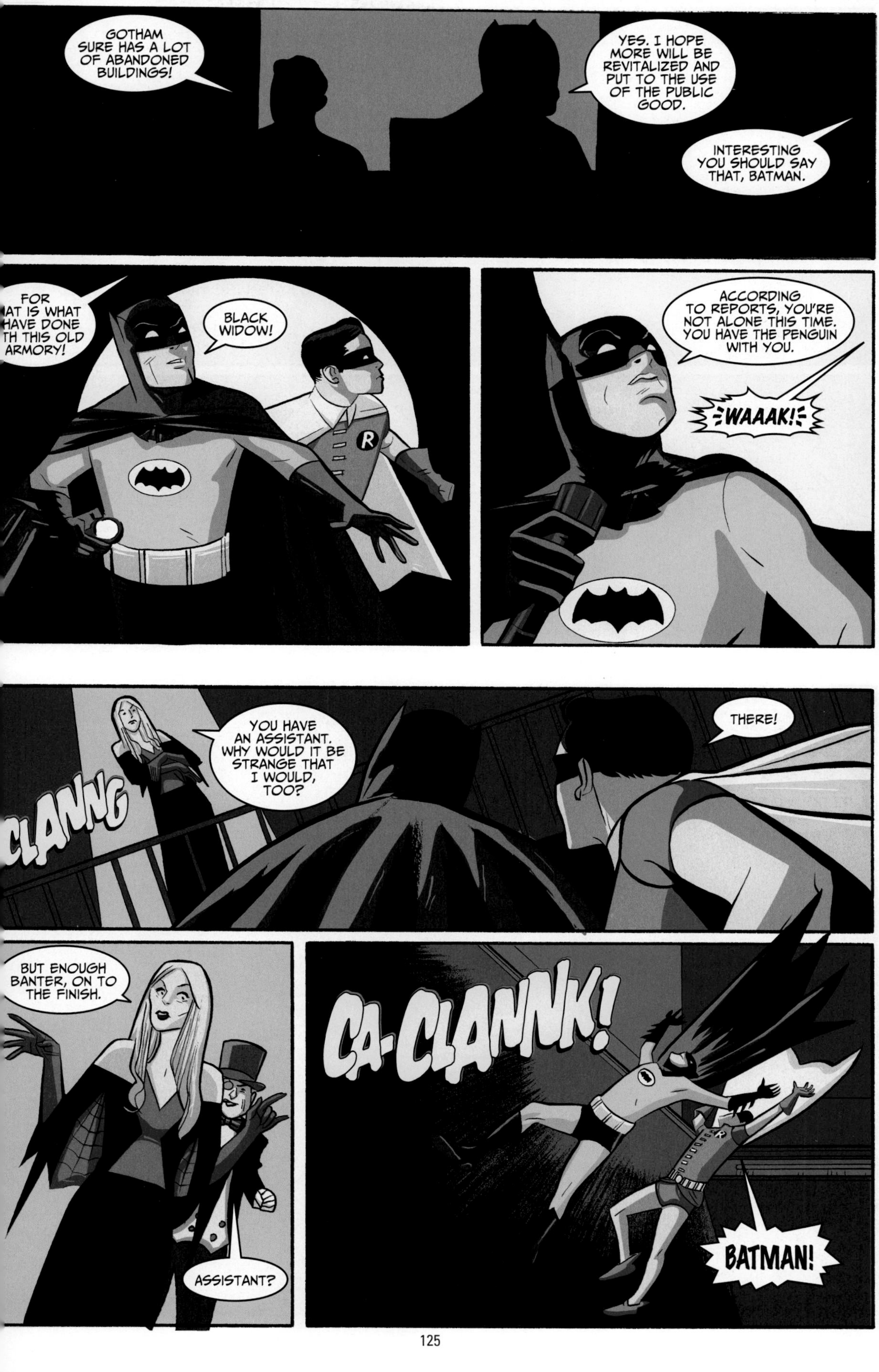
GOTHAM SURE HAS A LOT OF ABANDONED BUILDINGS!
YES. I HOPE MORE WILL BE REVITALIZED AND PUT TO THE USE OF THE PUBLIC GOOD.
INTERESTING YOU SHOULD SAY THAT, BATMAN.
FOR
AT IS WHAT
HAVE DONE
TH THIS OLD
ARMORY!
BLACK WIDOW!
ACCORDING TO REPORTS, YOU'RE NOT ALONE THIS TIME. YOU HAVE THE PENGUIN WITH YOU.
WAAAK!
YOU HAVE AN ASSISTANT. WHY WOULD IT BE STRANGE THAT I WOULD, TOO?
CLANNG
THERE!
BUT ENOUGH BANTER, ON TO THE FINISH.
ASSISTANT?
CA-CLANNK!
BATMAN!

WHAT YOU'RE TRAPPED IN IS ACTUAL SILK MADE BY THE BLACK WIDOW SPIDER.

STRONGER THAN STEEL, COVETED BY INDUSTRY AND THE MILITARY.

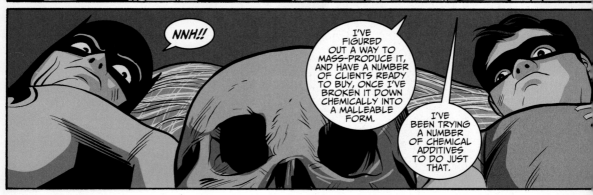

NNH!!

I'VE FIGURED OUT A WAY TO MASS-PRODUCE IT, AND HAVE A NUMBER OF CLIENTS READY TO BUY, ONCE I'VE BROKEN IT DOWN CHEMICALLY INTO A MALLEABLE FORM.

I'VE BEEN TRYING A NUMBER OF CHEMICAL ADDITIVES TO DO JUST THAT.

NONE HAVE WORKED SO FAR...EXCEPT ON OTHER INTRUDERS INVESTIGATING MY OPERATION.

BUT THAT'S SCIENCE, ISN'T IT? TRY AND TRY AGAIN.

POUR THE LIQUID!

WAAK WAK!

HAVE THE DYNAMIC DUO FINALLY MET DEFEAT?

AS SKELETONS IN A SPIDER'S SILK?

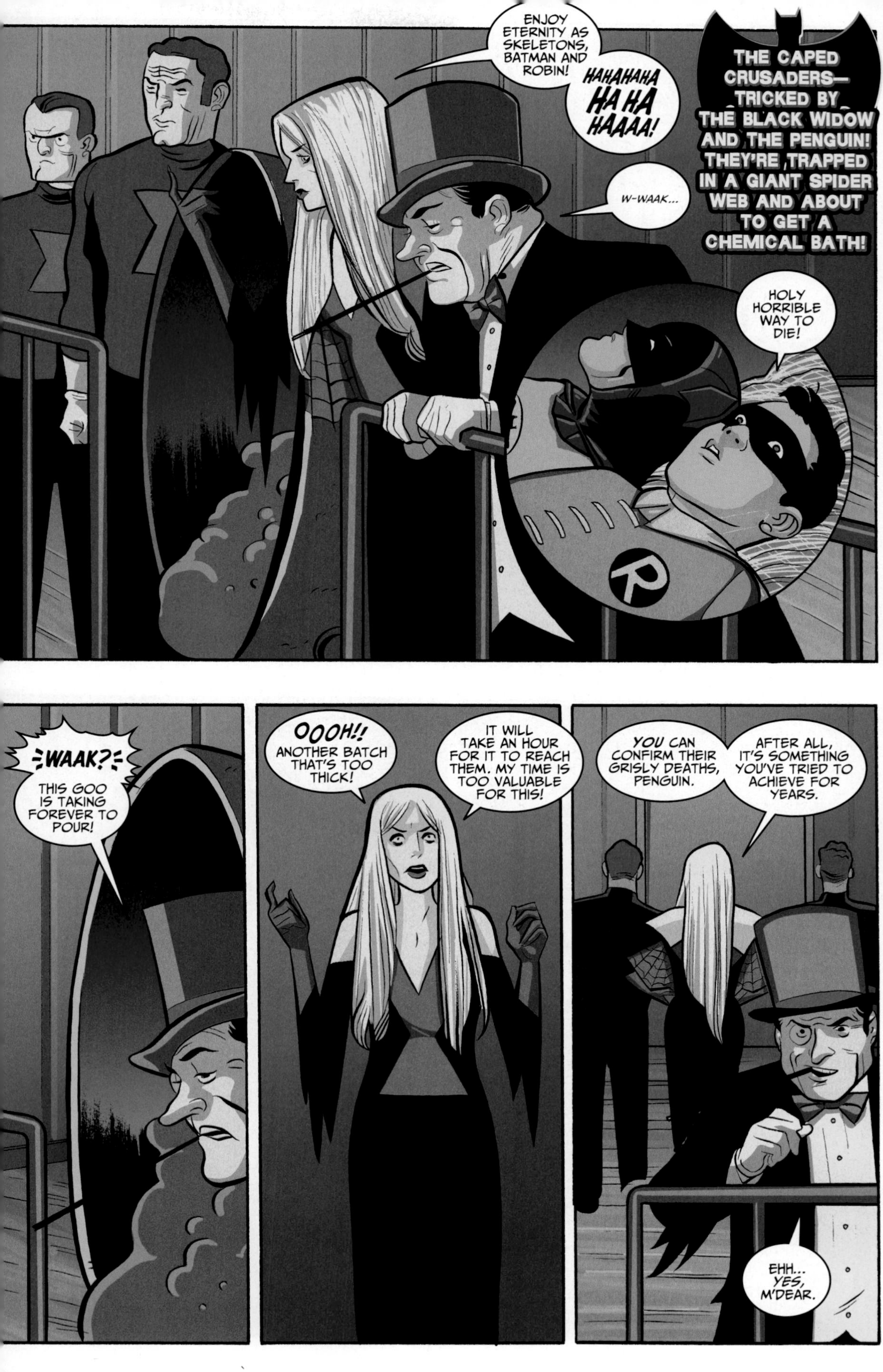
THE CAPED CRUSADERS— TRICKED BY THE BLACK WIDOW AND THE PENGUIN! THEY'RE TRAPPED IN A GIANT SPIDER WEB AND ABOUT TO GET A CHEMICAL BATH!
ENJOY ETERNITY AS SKELETONS, BATMAN AND ROBIN!
HAHAHAHA HA HA HAAAA!
W-WAAK...
HOLY HORRIBLE WAY TO DIE!
WAAK?
THIS GOO IS TAKING FOREVER TO POUR!
OOOH!! ANOTHER BATCH THAT'S TOO THICK!
IT WILL TAKE AN HOUR FOR IT TO REACH THEM. MY TIME IS TOO VALUABLE FOR THIS!
YOU CAN CONFIRM THEIR GRISLY DEATHS, PENGUIN.
AFTER ALL, IT'S SOMETHING YOU'VE TRIED TO ACHIEVE FOR YEARS.
EHH... YES, M'DEAR.

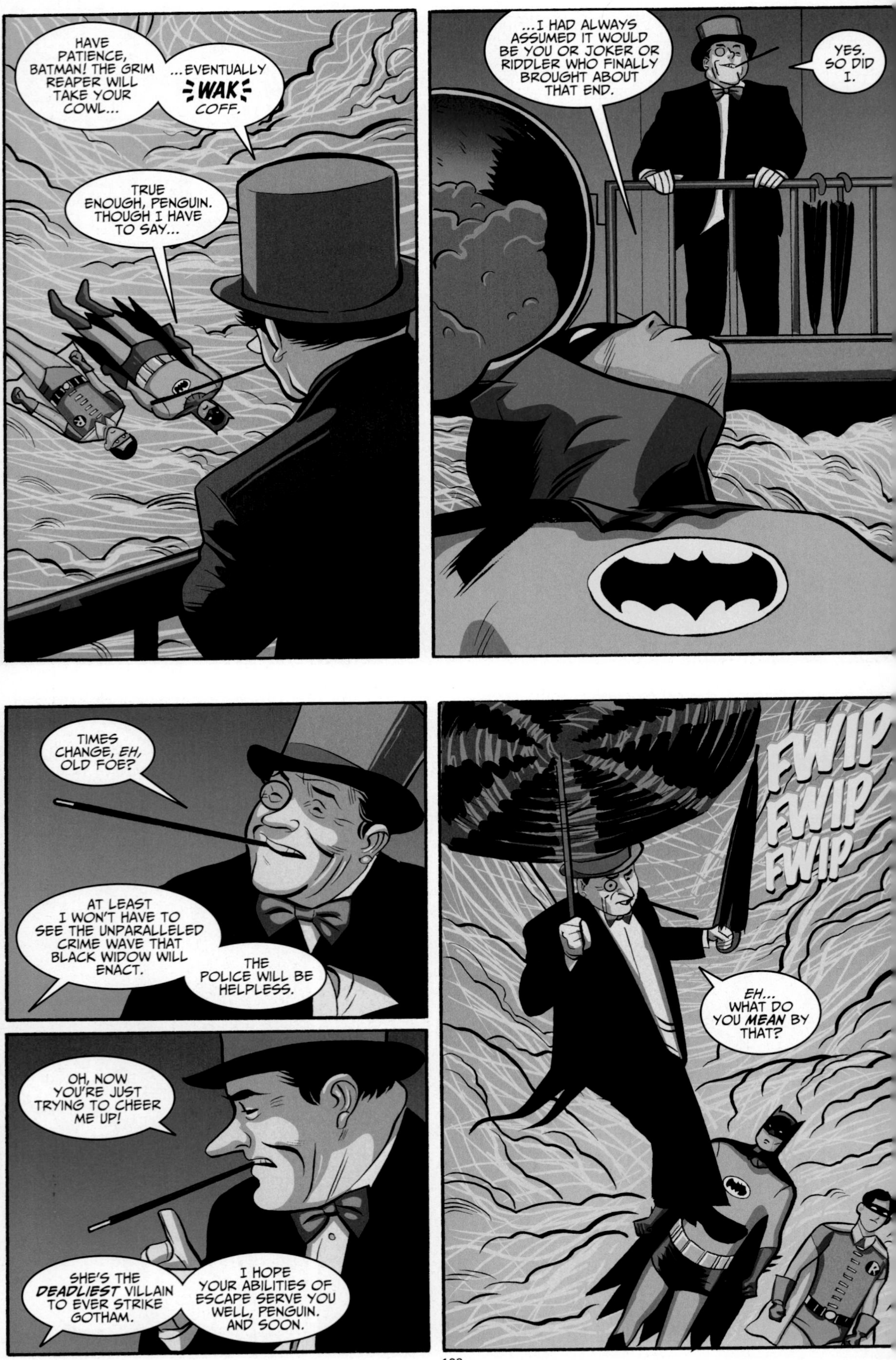
HAVE PATIENCE, BATMAN! THE GRIM REAPER WILL TAKE YOUR COWL...
...EVENTUALLY
WAK
COFF.
TRUE ENOUGH, PENGUIN. THOUGH I HAVE TO SAY...
...I HAD ALWAYS ASSUMED IT WOULD BE YOU OR JOKER OR RIDDLER WHO FINALLY BROUGHT ABOUT THAT END.
YES. SO DID I.
TIMES CHANGE, EH, OLD FOE?
AT LEAST I WON'T HAVE TO SEE THE UNPARALLELED CRIME WAVE THAT BLACK WIDOW WILL ENACT.
THE POLICE WILL BE HELPLESS.
OH, NOW YOU'RE JUST TRYING TO CHEER ME UP!
SHE'S THE DEADLIEST VILLAIN TO EVER STRIKE GOTHAM.
I HOPE YOUR ABILITIES OF ESCAPE SERVE YOU WELL, PENGUIN. AND SOON.
FWIP FWIP FWIP
EH... WHAT DO YOU MEAN BY THAT?

IT'S RIGHT THERE IN HER NAME, AFTER ALL. *BLACK WIDOW.*

THE SPIDER THAT *KILLS* AND *CONSUMES* ITS MATE ONCE HE'S OF NO USE TO HER.

STILL, IF ANYONE CAN ESCAPE HER DEADLY WRATH, IT'S YOU, PENGUIN.

I... YOU DON'T KNOW WHAT KIND OF FORCE SHE HAS PROTECTING THIS ARMORY!

I CAN'T TAKE THE CHANCE TO TRY TO GET AWAY ALONE!

IF I FREE YOU, CAN I COUNT ON YOUR HELP?

GOSH!

PSSSSSHH

DESPERATE SITUATIONS SOMETIMES CALL FOR STRANGE BEDFELLOWS, ROBIN.

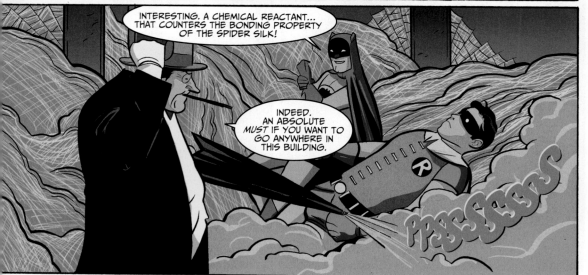

INTERESTING. A CHEMICAL REACTANT... THAT COUNTERS THE BONDING PROPERTY OF THE SPIDER SILK!

INDEED. AN ABSOLUTE *MUST* IF YOU WANT TO GO ANYWHERE IN THIS BUILDING.

PSSSSSS

129

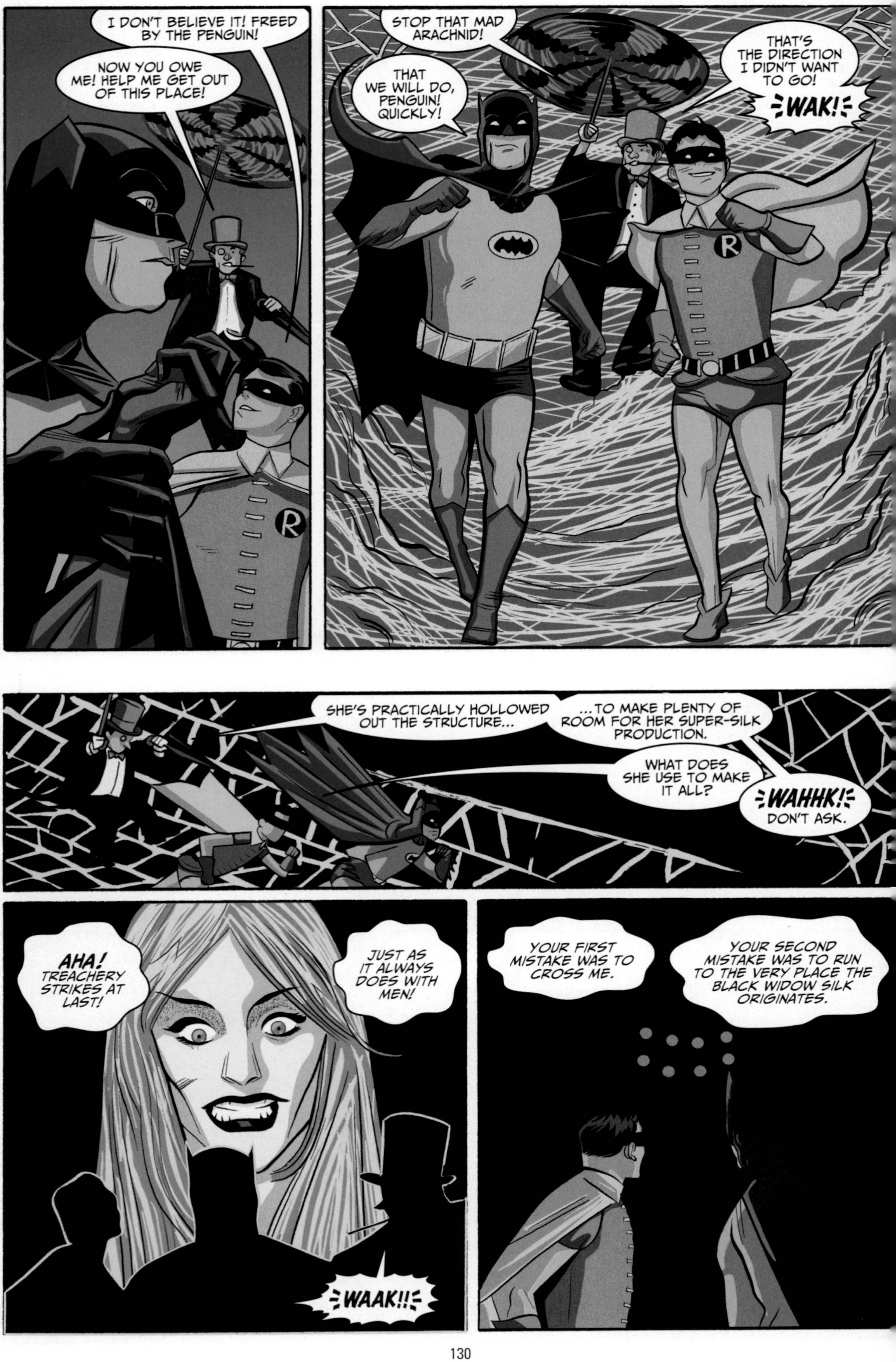
I DON'T BELIEVE IT! FREED BY THE PENGUIN!
NOW YOU OWE ME! HELP ME GET OUT OF THIS PLACE!
STOP THAT MAD ARACHNID!
THAT WE WILL DO, PENGUIN! QUICKLY!
THAT'S THE DIRECTION I DIDN'T WANT TO GO!
WAK!
SHE'S PRACTICALLY HOLLOWED OUT THE STRUCTURE...
...TO MAKE PLENTY OF ROOM FOR HER SUPER-SILK PRODUCTION.
WHAT DOES SHE USE TO MAKE IT ALL?
WAHHK! DON'T ASK.
AHA! TREACHERY STRIKES AT LAST!
JUST AS IT ALWAYS DOES WITH MEN!
WAAK!!
YOUR FIRST MISTAKE WAS TO CROSS ME.
YOUR SECOND MISTAKE WAS TO RUN TO THE VERY PLACE THE BLACK WIDOW SILK ORIGINATES.

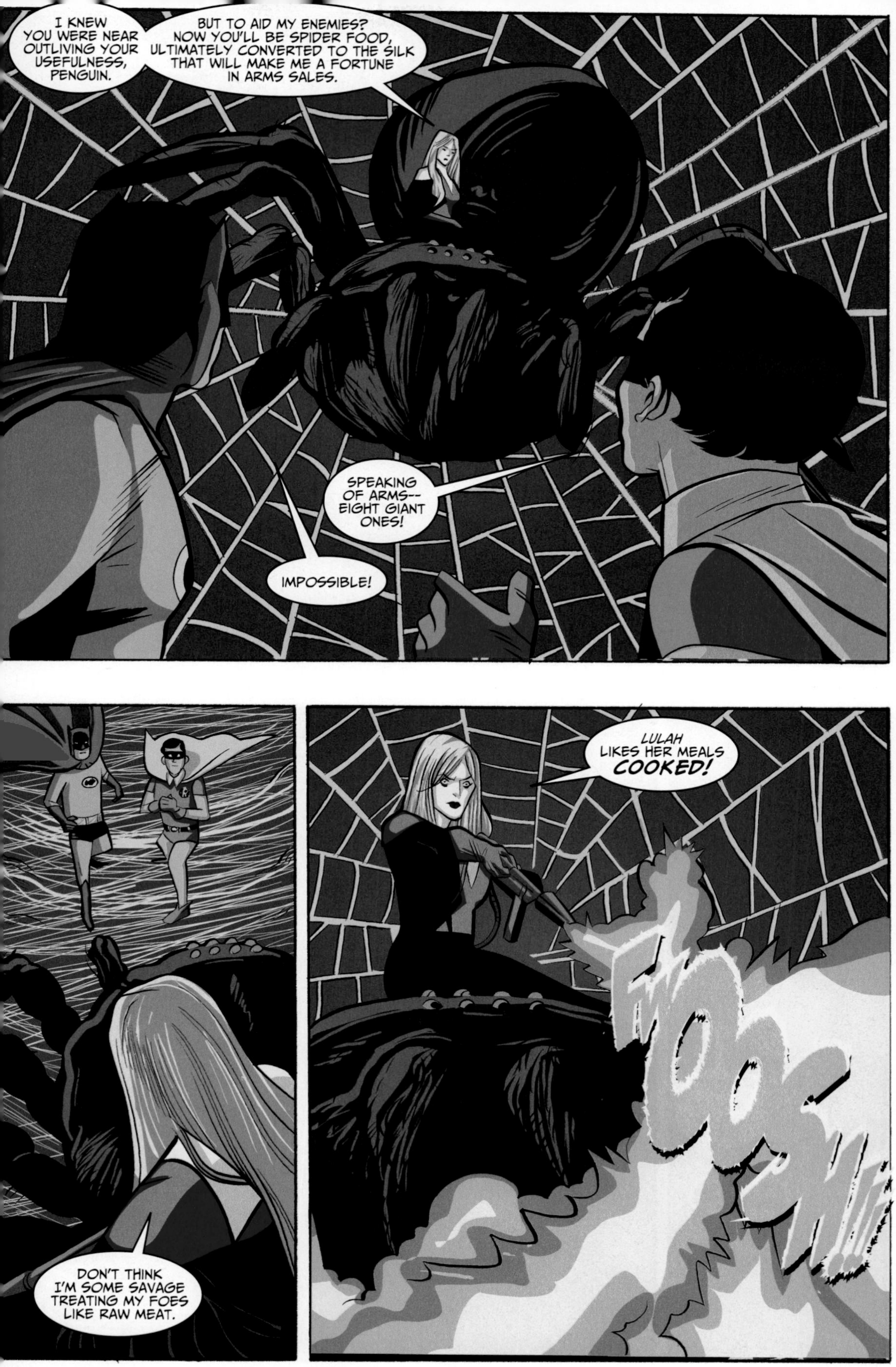
I KNEW YOU WERE NEAR OUTLIVING YOUR USEFULNESS, PENGUIN.
BUT TO AID MY ENEMIES? NOW YOU'LL BE SPIDER FOOD, ULTIMATELY CONVERTED TO THE SILK THAT WILL MAKE ME A FORTUNE IN ARMS SALES.
SPEAKING OF ARMS-- EIGHT GIANT ONES!
IMPOSSIBLE!
DON'T THINK I'M SOME SAVAGE TREATING MY FOES LIKE RAW MEAT.
LULAH LIKES HER MEALS COOKED!
FWOOSH!!!

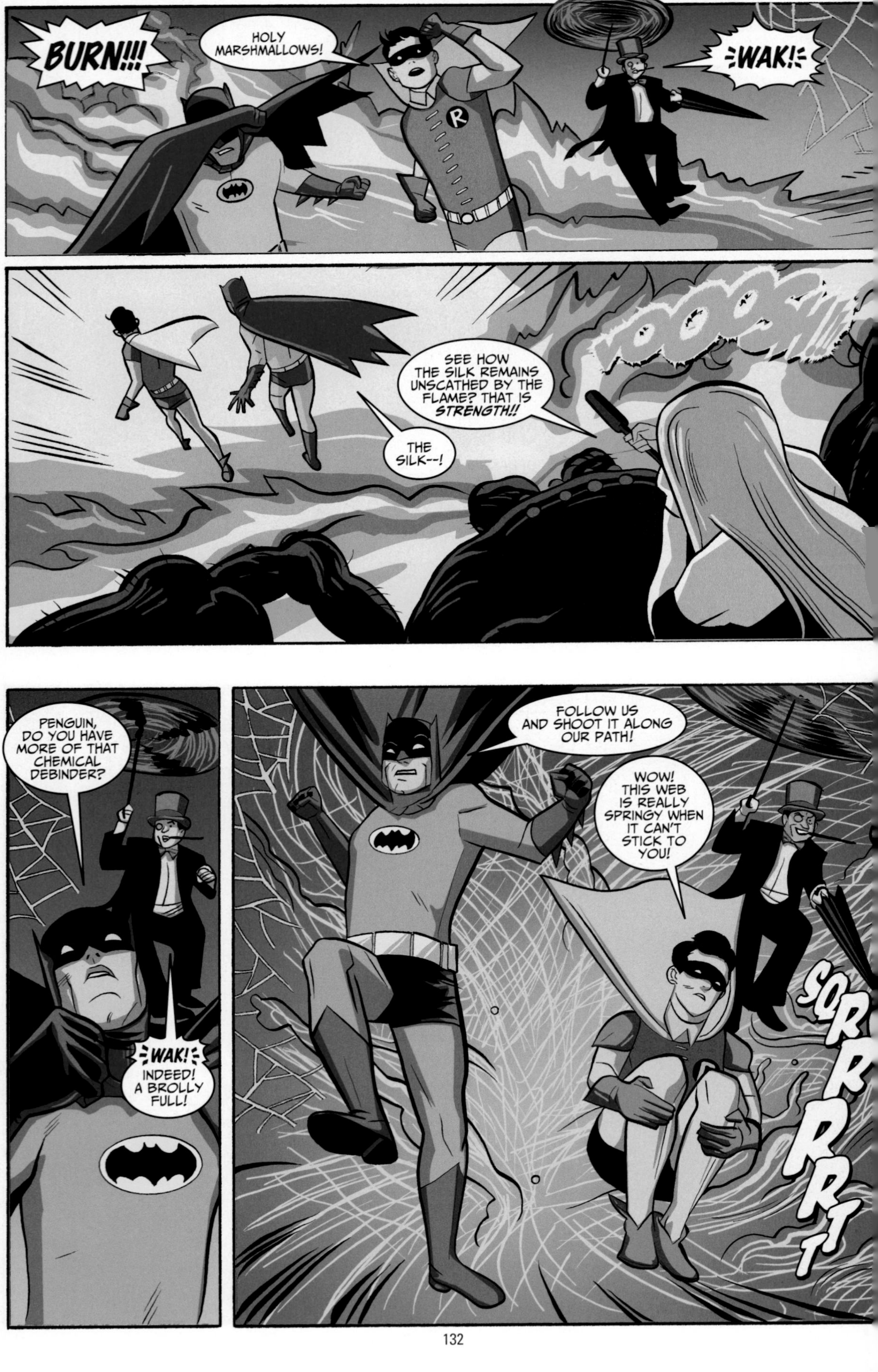

BURN!!!
HOLY MARSHMALLOWS!
WAK!
VOOOSH!!!
SEE HOW THE SILK REMAINS UNSCATHED BY THE FLAME? THAT IS STRENGTH!!
THE SILK--!
PENGUIN, DO YOU HAVE MORE OF THAT CHEMICAL DEBINDER?
WAK! INDEED! A BROLLY FULL!
FOLLOW US AND SHOOT IT ALONG OUR PATH!
WOW! THIS WEB IS REALLY SPRINGY WHEN IT CAN'T STICK TO YOU!
SQRRRRT

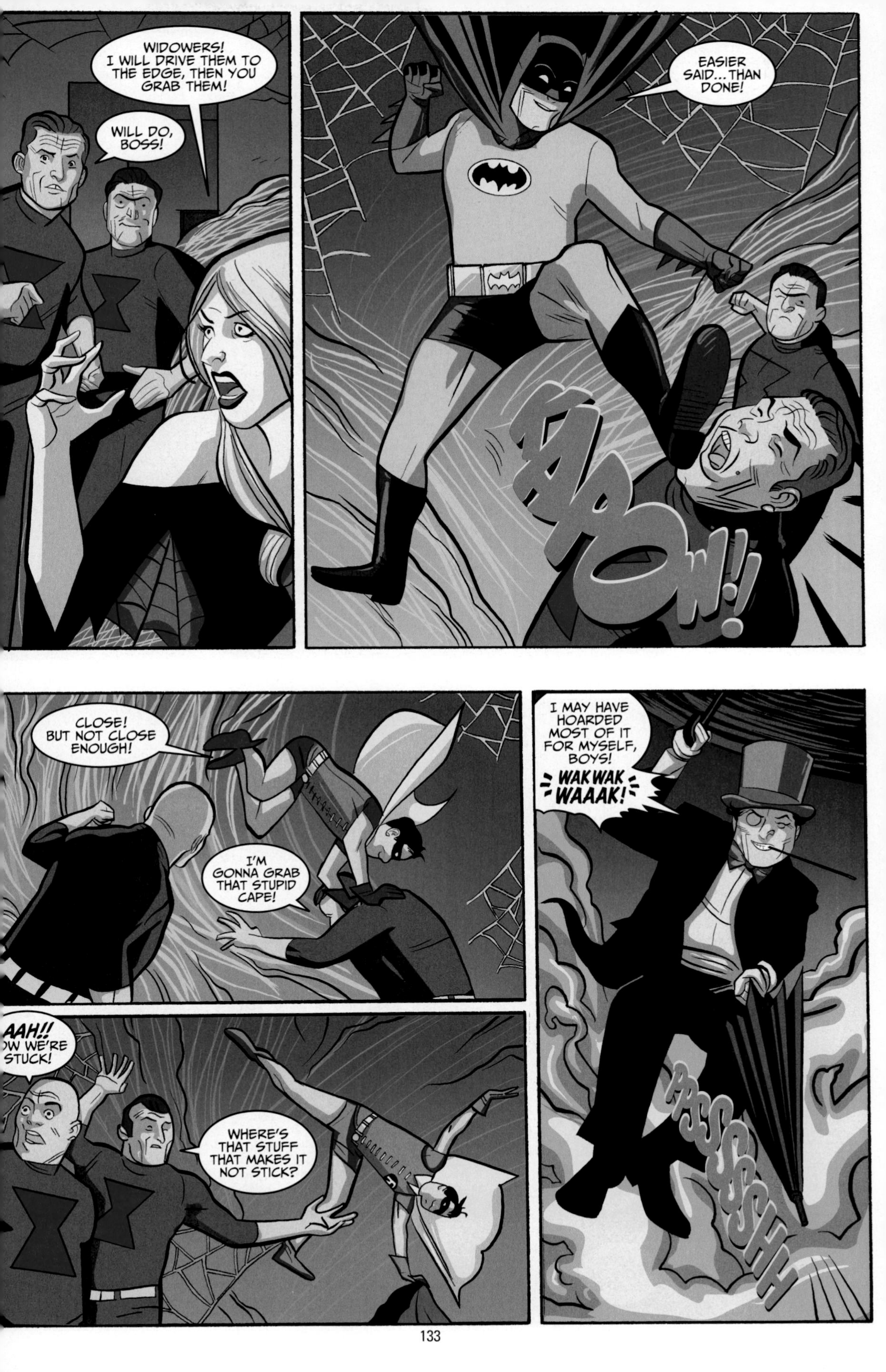
WIDOWERS! I WILL DRIVE THEM TO THE EDGE, THEN YOU GRAB THEM!
WILL DO, BOSS!
EASIER SAID... THAN DONE!
KAPOW!!
CLOSE! BUT NOT CLOSE ENOUGH!
I'M GONNA GRAB THAT STUPID CAPE!
I MAY HAVE HOARDED MOST OF IT FOR MYSELF, BOYS!
WAKWAK WAAAK!
PSSSSSHH
AAH!! OW WE'RE STUCK!
WHERE'S THAT STUFF THAT MAKES IT NOT STICK?

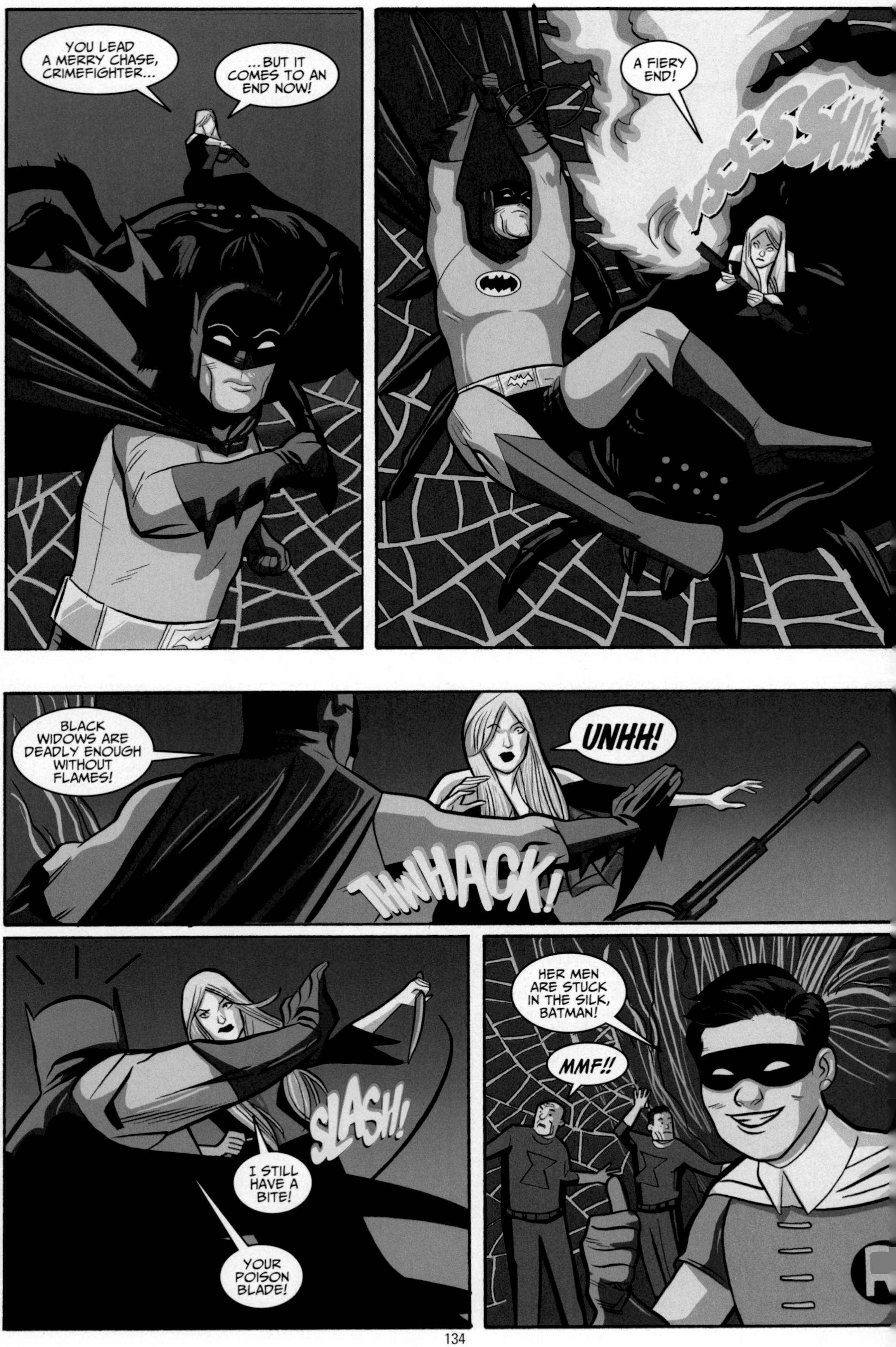
YOU LEAD A MERRY CHASE, CRIMEFIGHTER...
...BUT IT COMES TO AN END NOW!
A FIERY END!
VSSSSSSH!!!
BLACK WIDOWS ARE DEADLY ENOUGH WITHOUT FLAMES!
UNHH!
THWHACK!
I STILL HAVE A BITE!
SLASH!
YOUR POISON BLADE!
HER MEN ARE STUCK IN THE SILK, BATMAN!
MMF!!

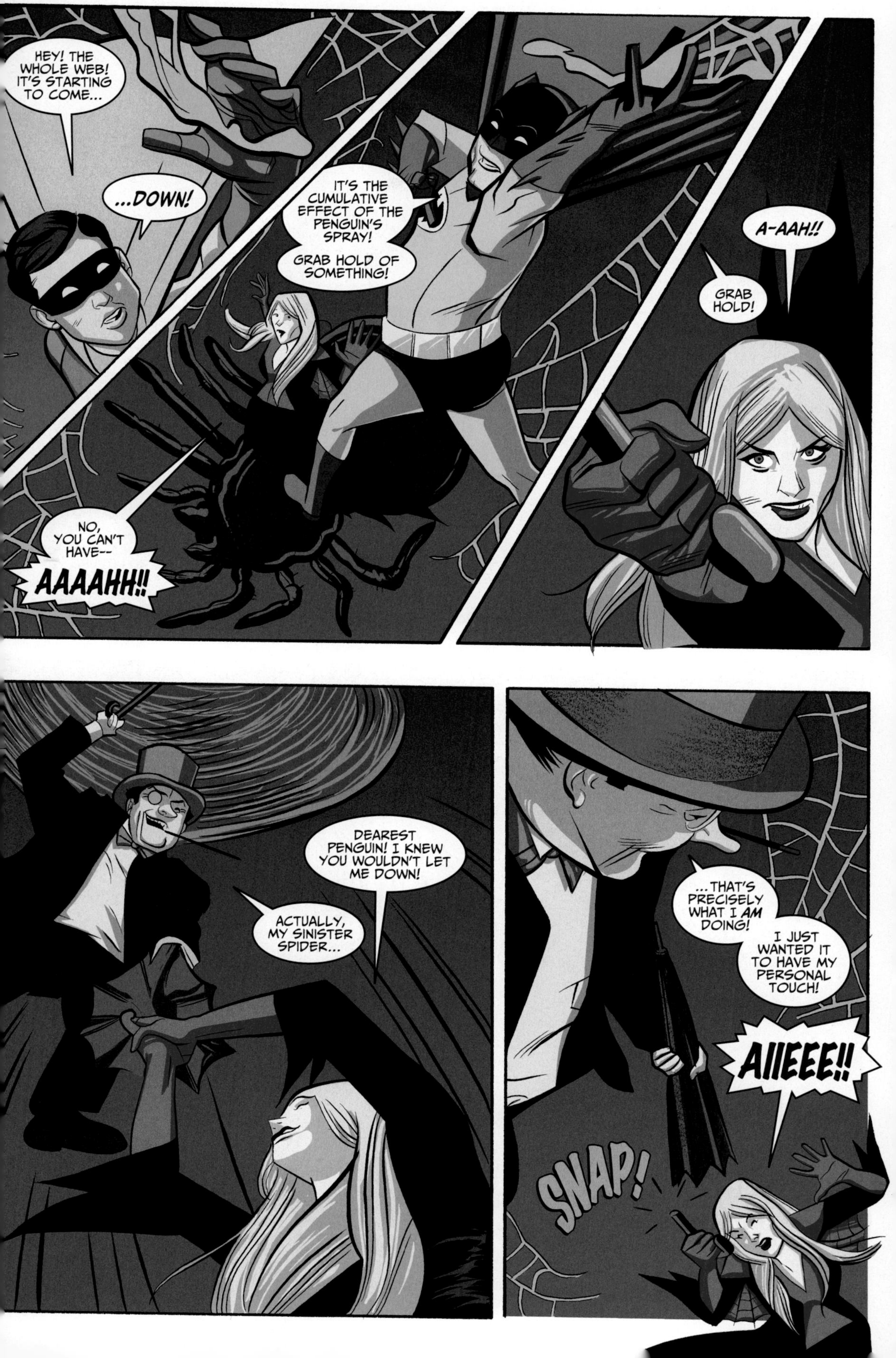
HEY! THE WHOLE WEB! IT'S STARTING TO COME...
...DOWN!
IT'S THE CUMULATIVE EFFECT OF THE PENGUIN'S SPRAY!
GRAB HOLD OF SOMETHING!
NO, YOU CAN'T HAVE--
AAAAHH!!
A-AAH!!
GRAB HOLD!
DEAREST PENGUIN! I KNEW YOU WOULDN'T LET ME DOWN!
ACTUALLY, MY SINISTER SPIDER...
...THAT'S PRECISELY WHAT I AM DOING!
I JUST WANTED IT TO HAVE MY PERSONAL TOUCH!
AIIEEE!!
SNAP!

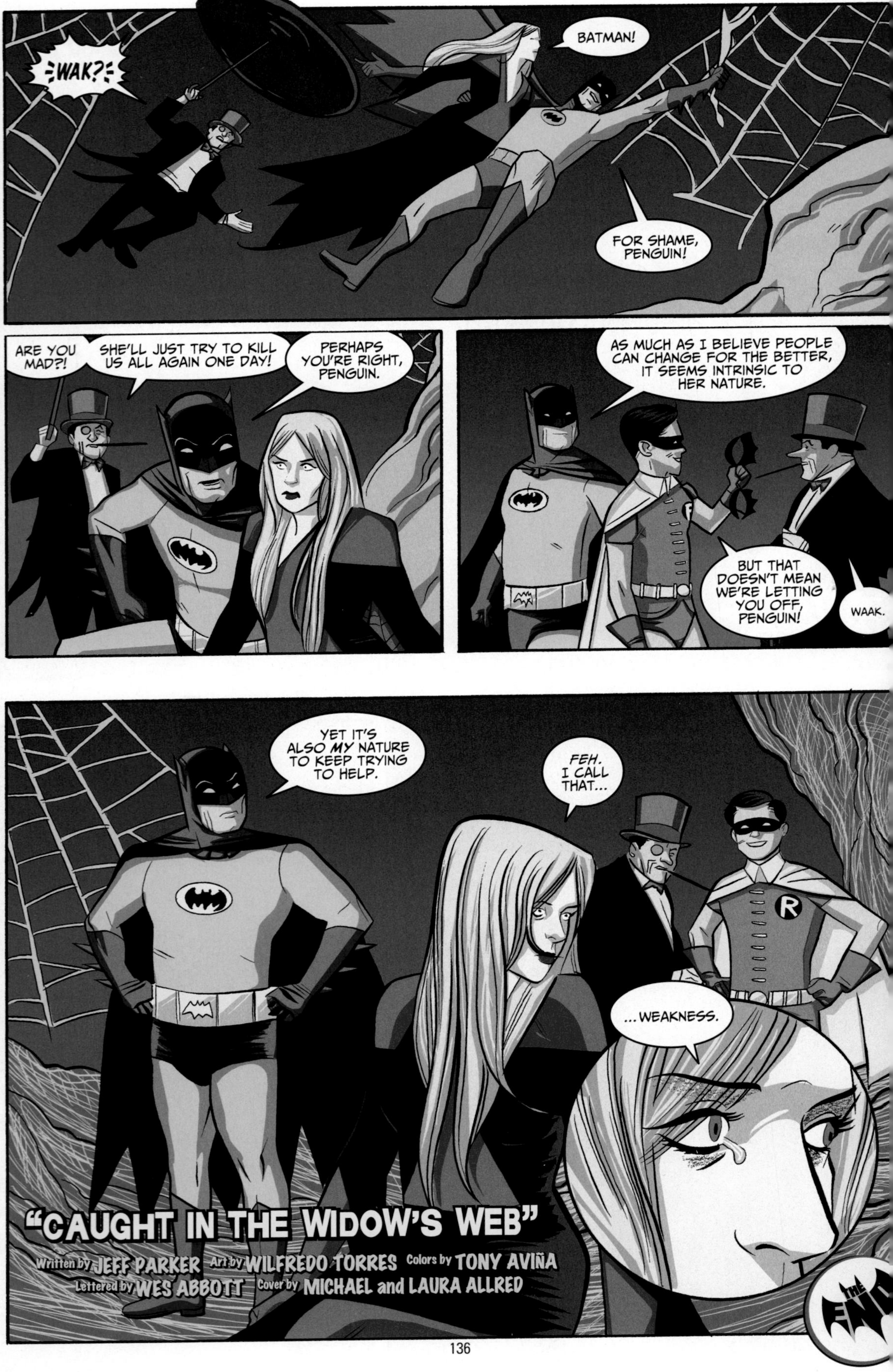
WAK?
BATMAN!
FOR SHAME, PENGUIN!
ARE YOU MAD?!
SHE'LL JUST TRY TO KILL US ALL AGAIN ONE DAY!
PERHAPS YOU'RE RIGHT, PENGUIN.
AS MUCH AS I BELIEVE PEOPLE CAN CHANGE FOR THE BETTER, IT SEEMS INTRINSIC TO HER NATURE.
BUT THAT DOESN'T MEAN WE'RE LETTING YOU OFF, PENGUIN!
WAAK.
YET IT'S ALSO *MY* NATURE TO KEEP TRYING TO HELP.
FEH. I CALL THAT...
...WEAKNESS.
"CAUGHT IN THE WIDOW'S WEB"
Written by JEFF PARKER Art by WILFREDO TORRES Colors by TONY AVIÑA
Lettered by WES ABBOTT Cover by MICHAEL and LAURA ALLRED

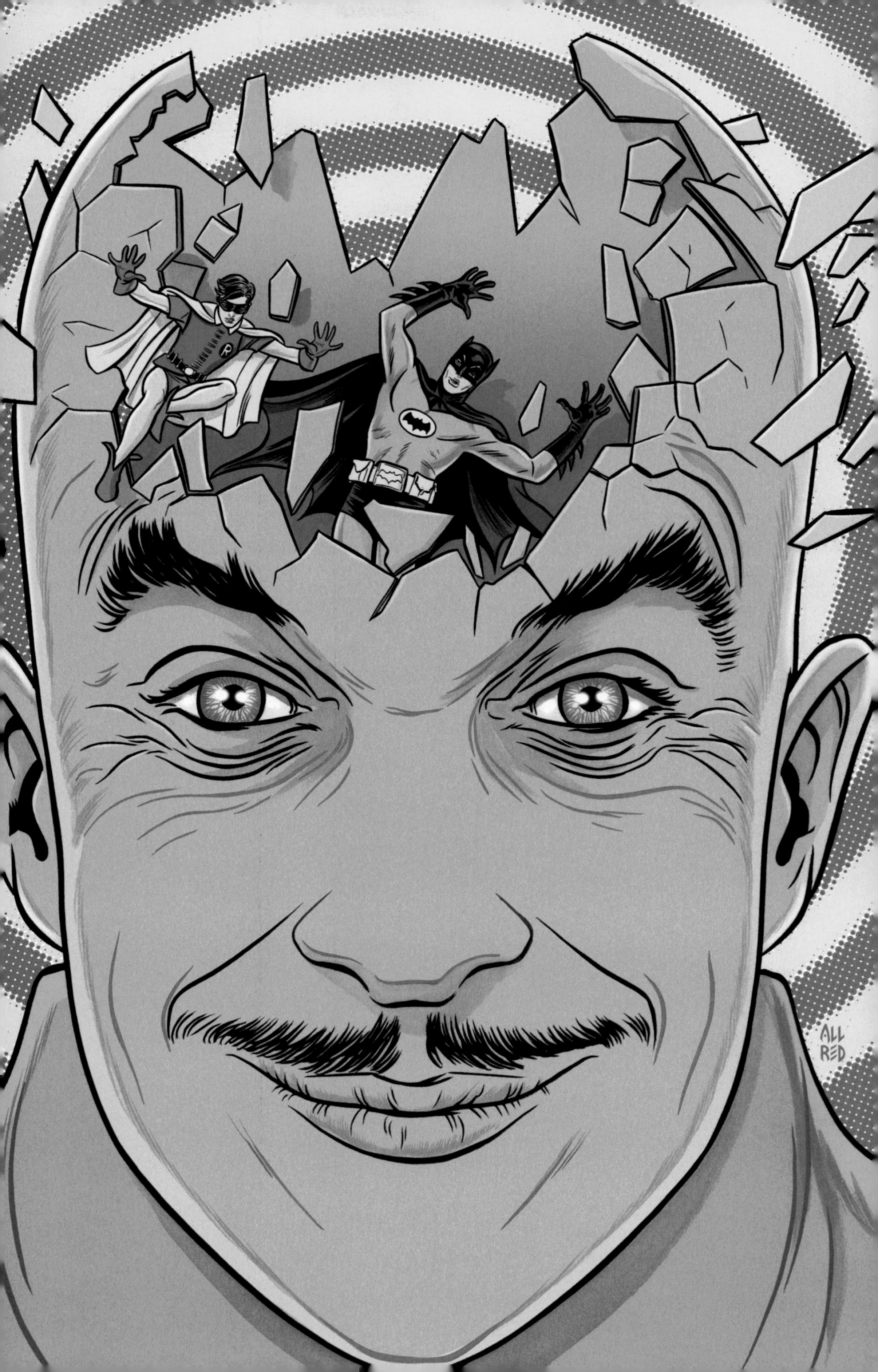
ALL
RED

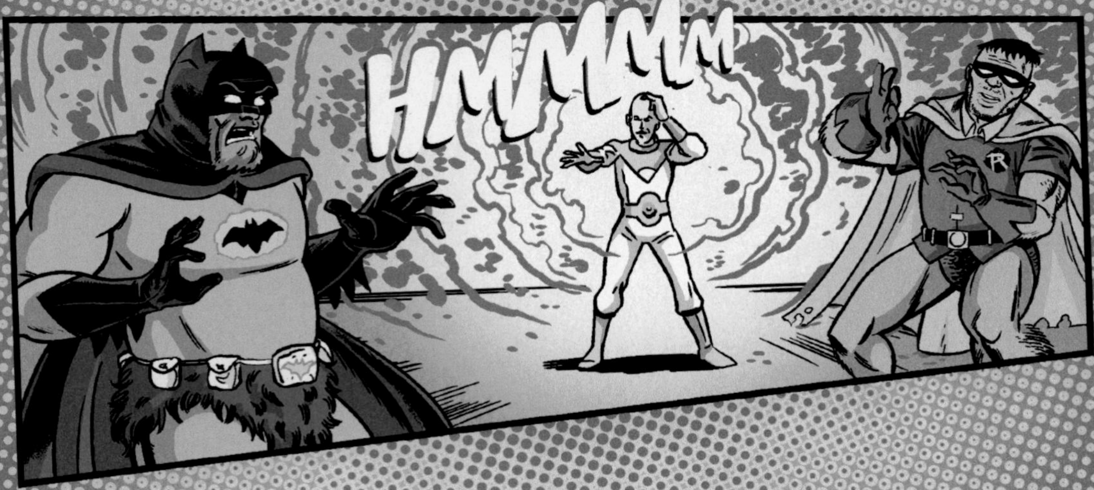
HMMMMM

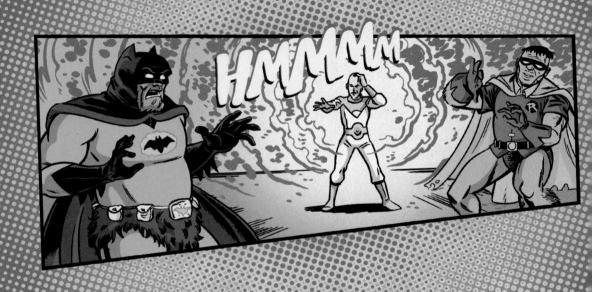

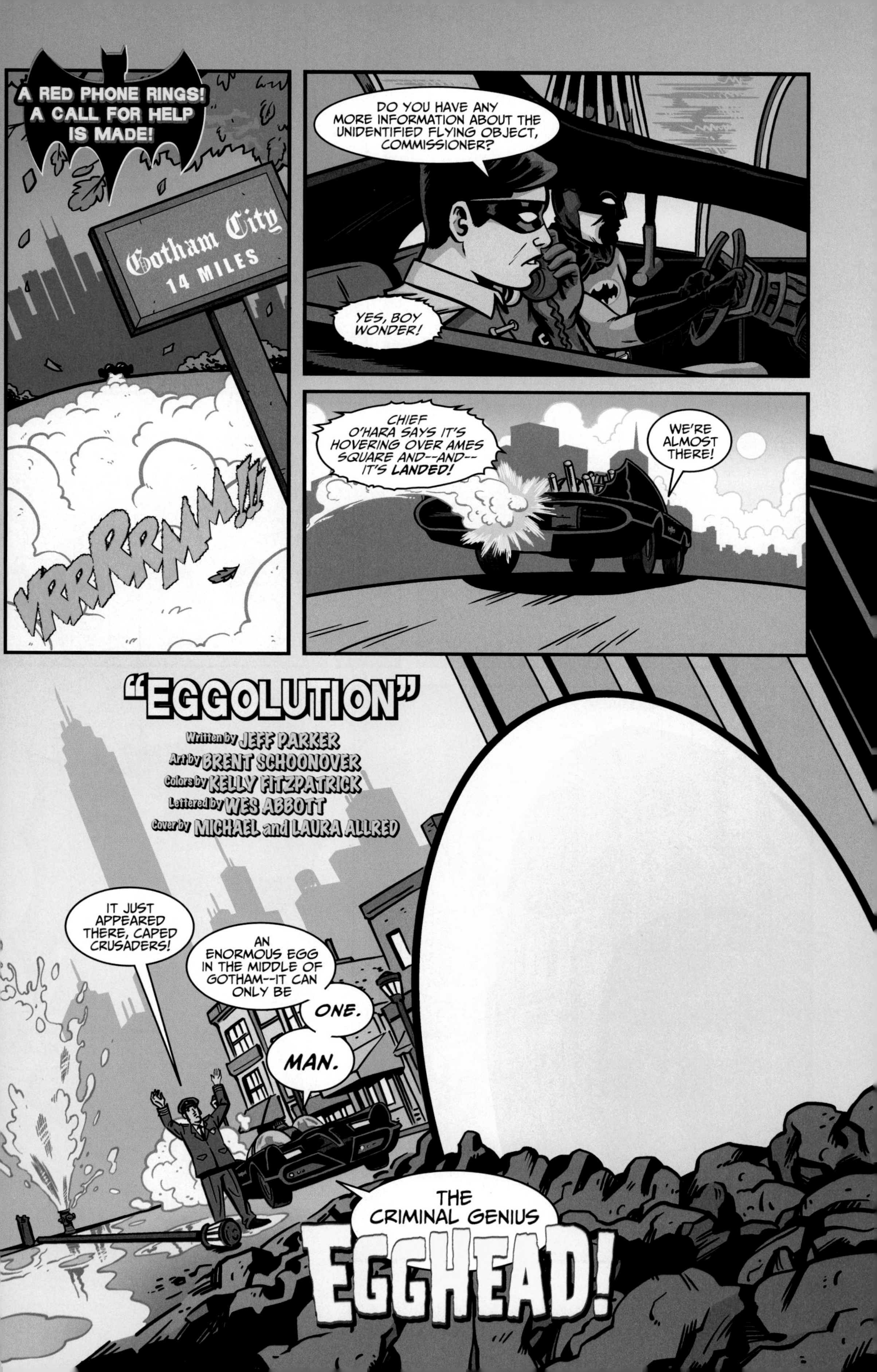
A RED PHONE RINGS! A CALL FOR HELP IS MADE!
Gotham City
14 MILES
VRRRRAMM!!!
DO YOU HAVE ANY MORE INFORMATION ABOUT THE UNIDENTIFIED FLYING OBJECT, COMMISSIONER?
YES, BOY WONDER!
CHIEF O'HARA SAYS IT'S HOVERING OVER AMES SQUARE AND--AND-- IT'S LANDED!
WE'RE ALMOST THERE!
"EGGOLUTION"
Written by JEFF PARKER
Art by BRENT SCHOONOVER
Colors by KELLY FITZPATRICK
Lettered by WES ABBOTT
Cover by MICHAEL and LAURA ALLRED
IT JUST APPEARED THERE, CAPED CRUSADERS!
AN ENORMOUS EGG IN THE MIDDLE OF GOTHAM--IT CAN ONLY BE
ONE.
MAN.
THE CRIMINAL GENIUS
EGGHEAD!

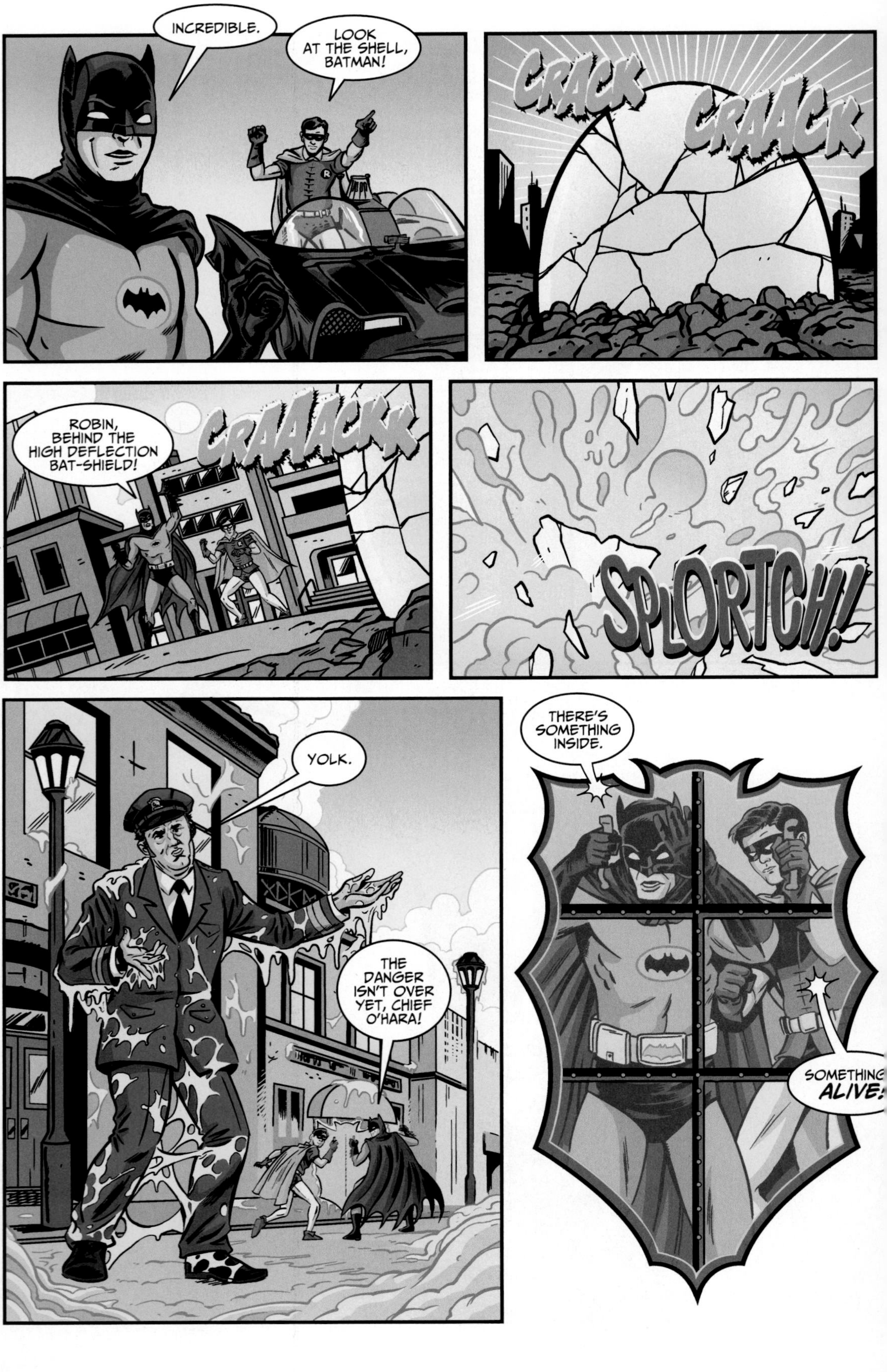

INCREDIBLE.
LOOK AT THE SHELL, BATMAN!
CRACK
CRAACK
ROBIN, BEHIND THE HIGH DEFLECTION BAT-SHIELD!
CRAAACKK
SPLORTCH!!
YOLK.
THE DANGER ISN'T OVER YET, CHIEF O'HARA!
THERE'S SOMETHING INSIDE.
SOMETHING ALIVE!

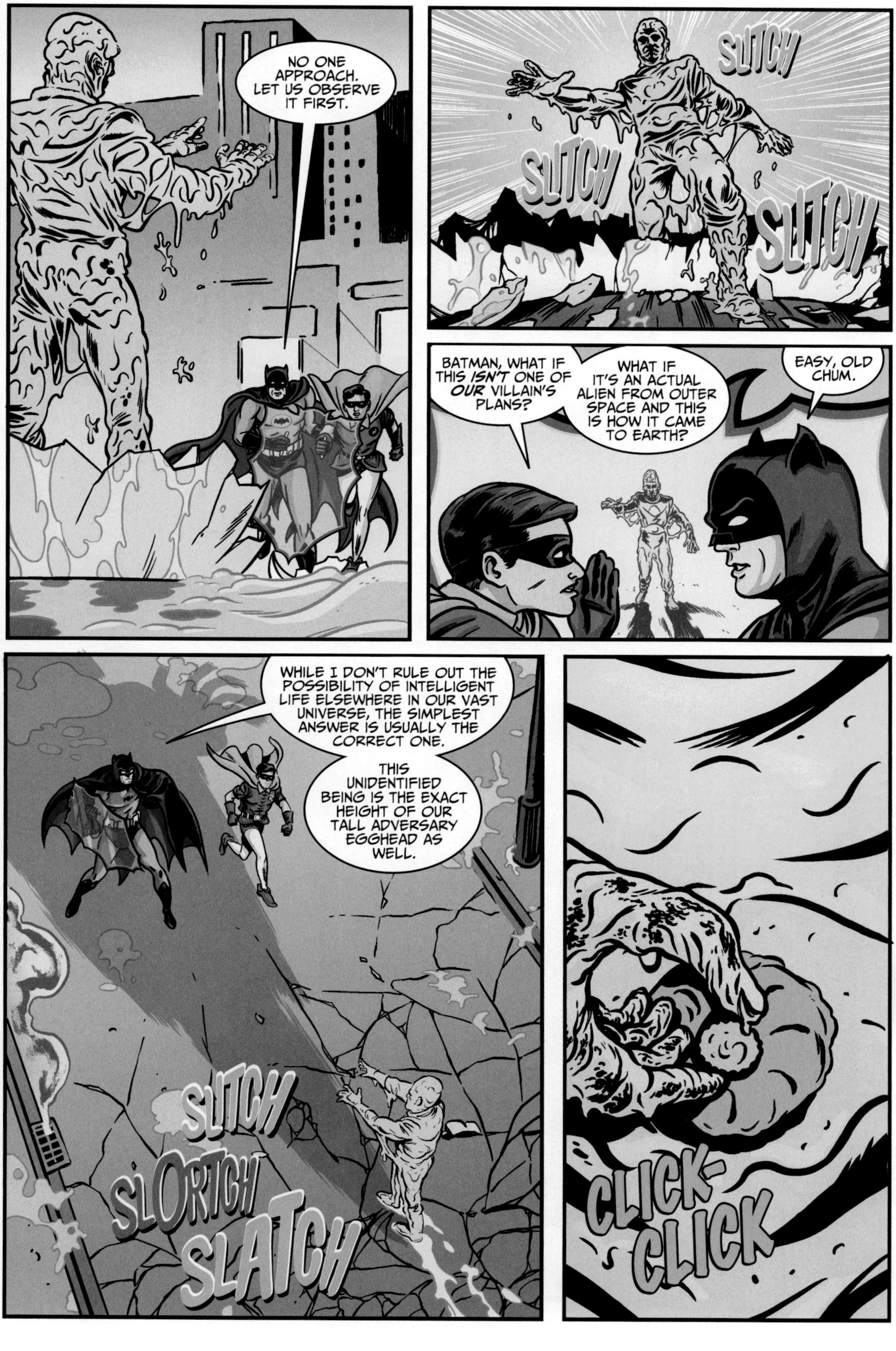
NO ONE APPROACH. LET US OBSERVE IT FIRST.
SLITCH
SLITCH
SLITCH
BATMAN, WHAT IF THIS *ISN'T* ONE OF *OUR* VILLAIN'S PLANS?
WHAT IF IT'S AN ACTUAL ALIEN FROM OUTER SPACE AND THIS IS HOW IT CAME TO EARTH?
EASY, OLD CHUM.
WHILE I DON'T RULE OUT THE POSSIBILITY OF INTELLIGENT LIFE ELSEWHERE IN OUR VAST UNIVERSE, THE SIMPLEST ANSWER IS USUALLY THE CORRECT ONE.
THIS UNIDENTIFIED BEING IS THE EXACT HEIGHT OF OUR TALL ADVERSARY EGGHEAD AS WELL.
SLITCH
SLORTCH
SLATCH
CLICK-CLICK

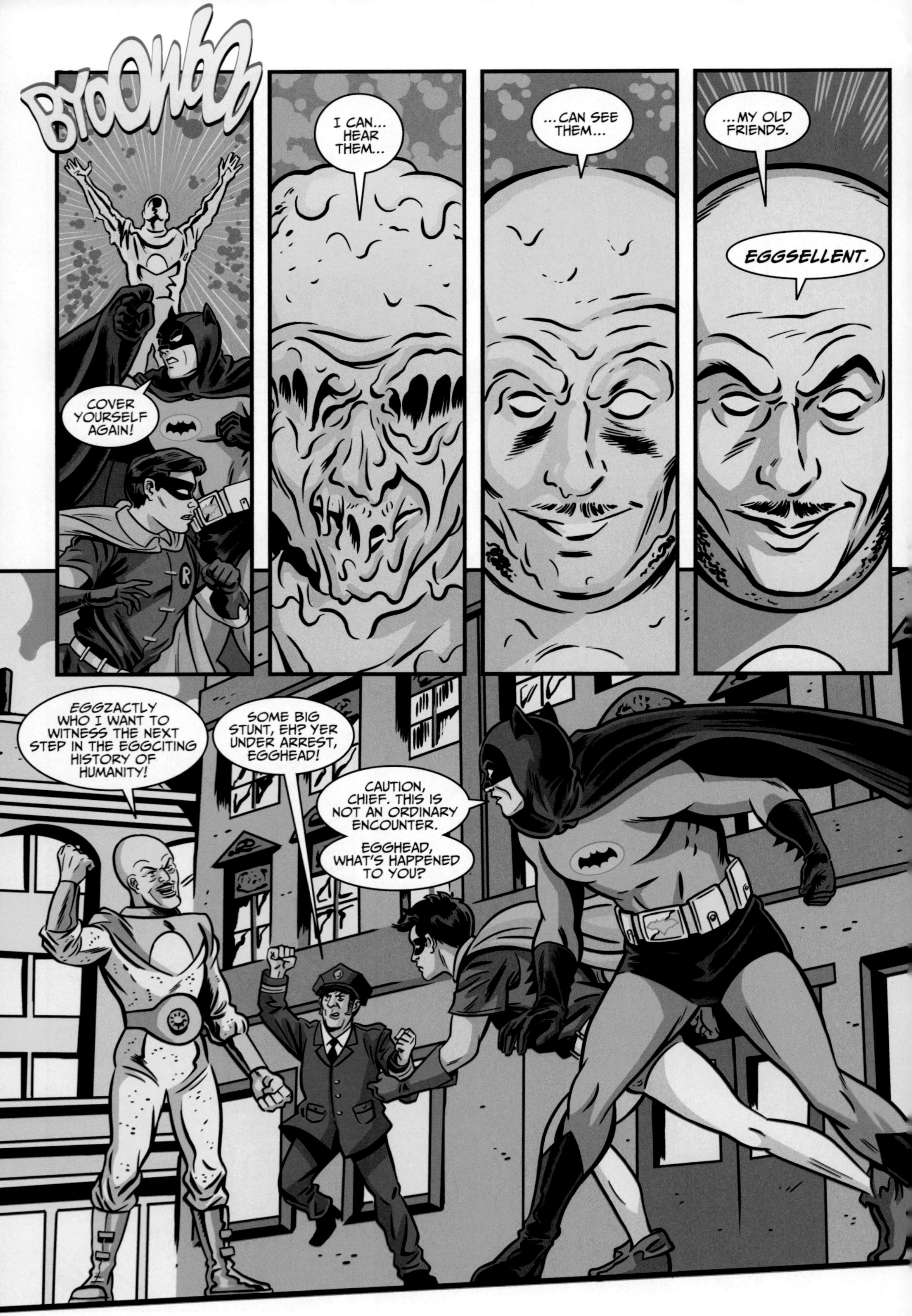
BYOONBO
COVER YOURSELF AGAIN!
I CAN... HEAR THEM...
...CAN SEE THEM...
...MY OLD FRIENDS.
EGGSELLENT.
EGGZACTLY WHO I WANT TO WITNESS THE NEXT STEP IN THE EGGCITING HISTORY OF HUMANITY!
SOME BIG STUNT, EH? YER UNDER ARREST, EGGHEAD!
CAUTION, CHIEF. THIS IS NOT AN ORDINARY ENCOUNTER.
EGGHEAD, WHAT'S HAPPENED TO YOU?

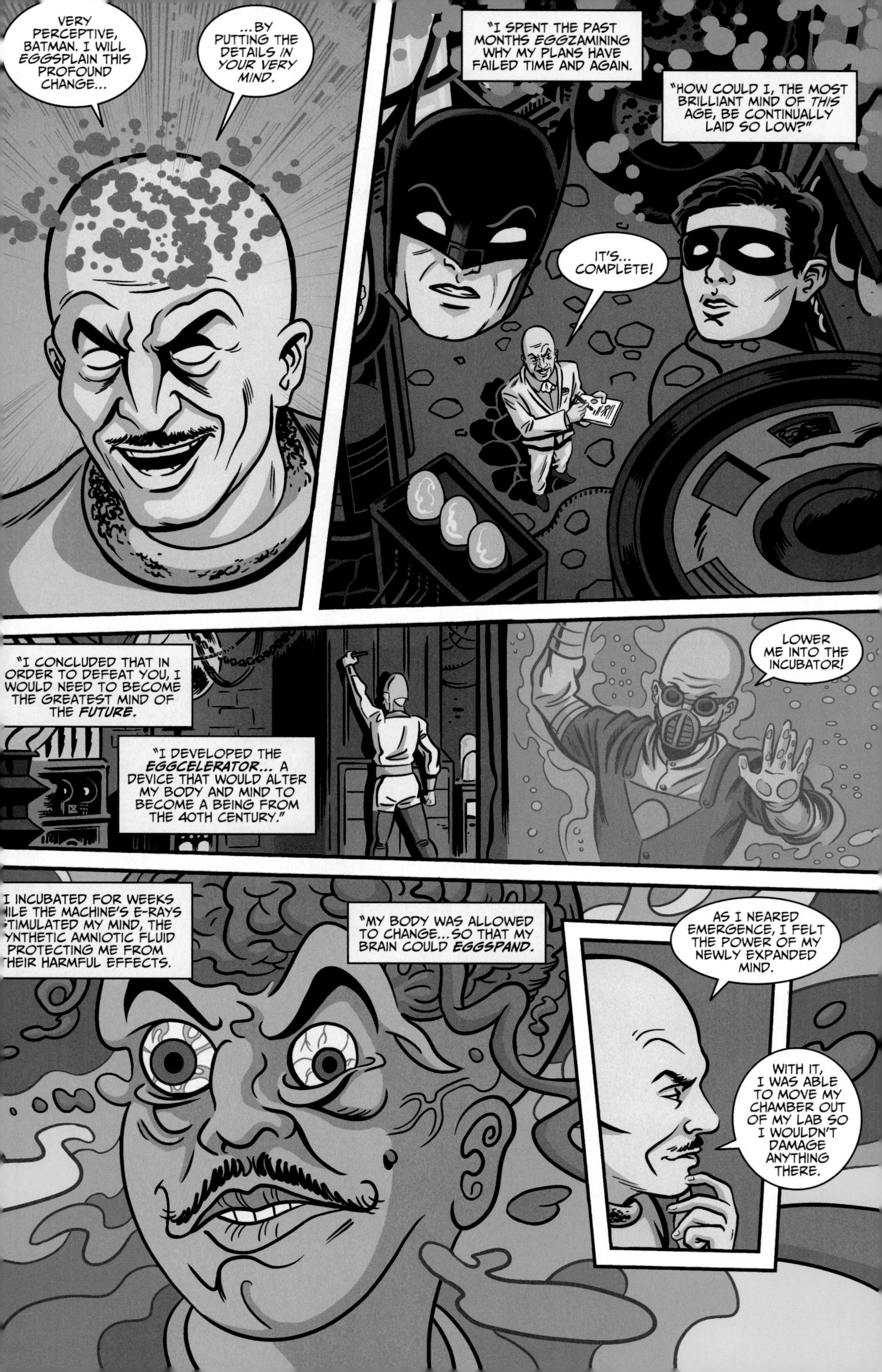
VERY PERCEPTIVE, BATMAN. I WILL *EGGSPLAIN* THIS PROFOUND CHANGE...
...BY PUTTING THE DETAILS *IN YOUR VERY MIND.*
"I SPENT THE PAST MONTHS *EGGZAMINING* WHY MY PLANS HAVE FAILED TIME AND AGAIN.
"HOW COULD I, THE MOST BRILLIANT MIND OF *THIS* AGE, BE CONTINUALLY LAID SO LOW?"
IT'S... COMPLETE!
"I CONCLUDED THAT IN ORDER TO DEFEAT YOU, I WOULD NEED TO BECOME THE GREATEST MIND OF THE ***FUTURE.***
"I DEVELOPED THE ***EGGCELERATOR...*** A DEVICE THAT WOULD ALTER MY BODY AND MIND TO BECOME A BEING FROM THE 40TH CENTURY."
LOWER ME INTO THE INCUBATOR!
I INCUBATED FOR WEEKS HILE THE MACHINE'S E-RAYS TIMULATED MY MIND, THE YNTHETIC AMNIOTIC FLUID PROTECTING ME FROM THEIR HARMFUL EFFECTS.
"MY BODY WAS ALLOWED TO CHANGE...SO THAT MY BRAIN COULD ***EGGSPAND.***
AS I NEARED EMERGENCE, I FELT THE POWER OF MY NEWLY EXPANDED MIND.
WITH IT, I WAS ABLE TO MOVE MY CHAMBER OUT OF MY LAB SO I WOULDN'T DAMAGE ANYTHING THERE.

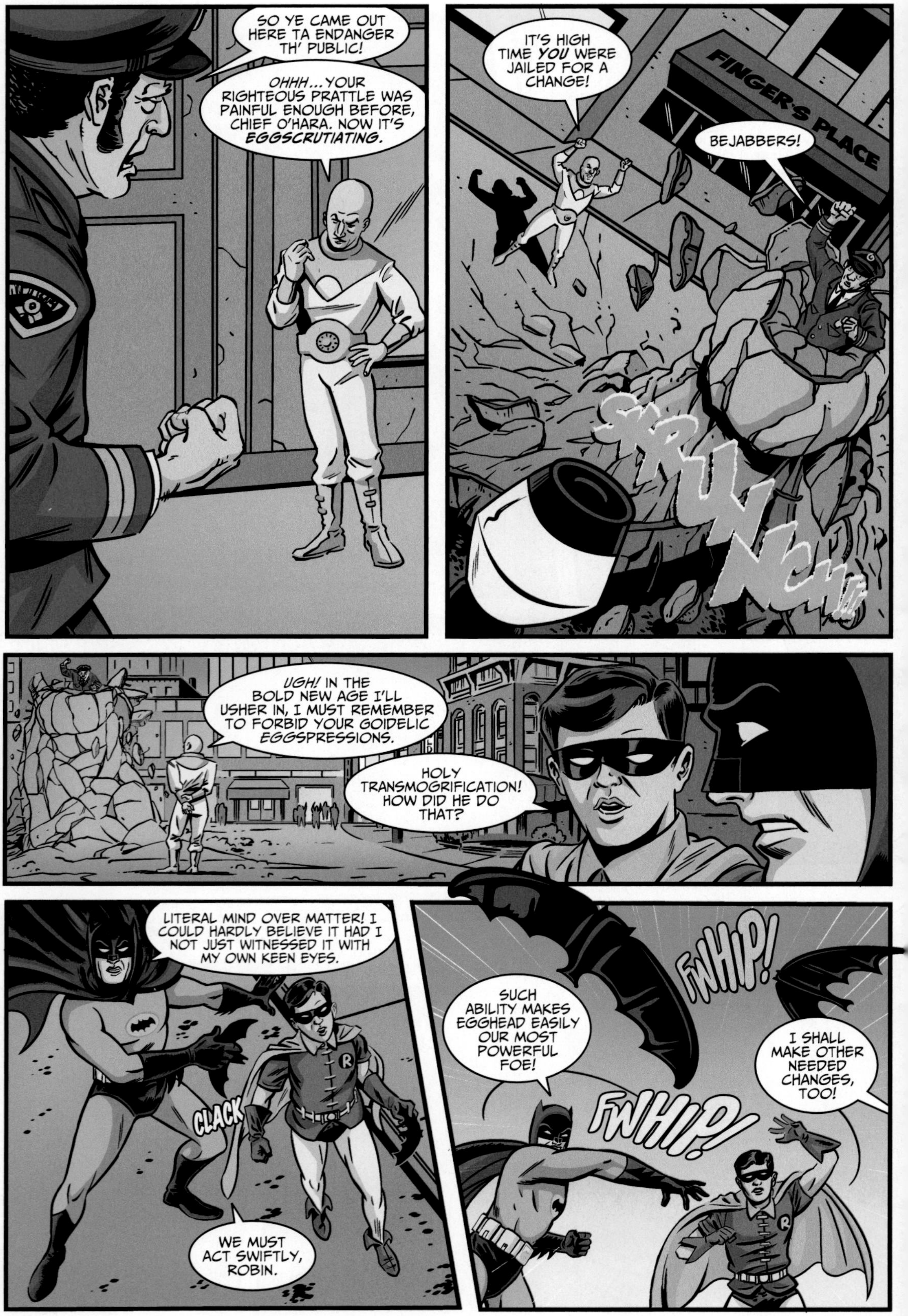
SO YE CAME OUT HERE TA ENDANGER TH' PUBLIC!
OHHH... YOUR RIGHTEOUS PRATTLE WAS PAINFUL ENOUGH BEFORE, CHIEF O'HARA. NOW IT'S EGGSCRUTIATING.
IT'S HIGH TIME YOU WERE JAILED FOR A CHANGE!
FINGER'S PLACE
BEJABBERS!
SKRUNCH!!
UGH! IN THE BOLD NEW AGE I'LL USHER IN, I MUST REMEMBER TO FORBID YOUR GOIDELIC EGGSPRESSIONS.
HOLY TRANSMOGRIFICATION! HOW DID HE DO THAT?
LITERAL MIND OVER MATTER! I COULD HARDLY BELIEVE IT HAD I NOT JUST WITNESSED IT WITH MY OWN KEEN EYES.
CLACK
WE MUST ACT SWIFTLY, ROBIN.
FWHIP!
SUCH ABILITY MAKES EGGHEAD EASILY OUR MOST POWERFUL FOE!
I SHALL MAKE OTHER NEEDED CHANGES, TOO!
FWHIP!

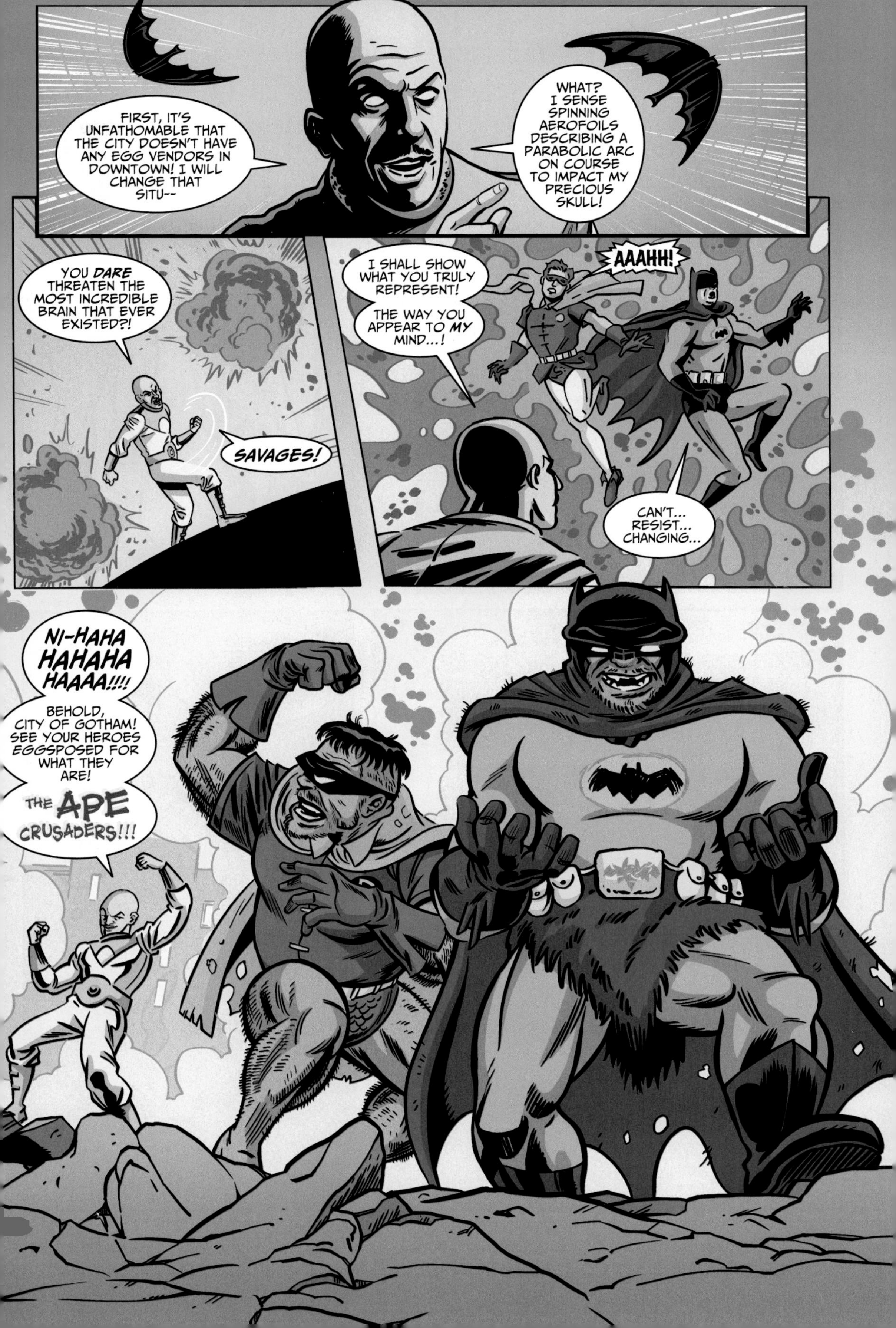
FIRST, IT'S UNFATHOMABLE THAT THE CITY DOESN'T HAVE ANY EGG VENDORS IN DOWNTOWN! I WILL CHANGE THAT SITU--
WHAT? I SENSE SPINNING AEROFOILS DESCRIBING A PARABOLIC ARC ON COURSE TO IMPACT MY PRECIOUS SKULL!
YOU DARE THREATEN THE MOST INCREDIBLE BRAIN THAT EVER EXISTED?!
SAVAGES!
I SHALL SHOW WHAT YOU TRULY REPRESENT!
THE WAY YOU APPEAR TO MY MIND...!
AAAHH!
CAN'T... RESIST... CHANGING...
NI-HAHA HAHAHA HAAAA!!!!
BEHOLD, CITY OF GOTHAM! SEE YOUR HEROES EGGSPOSED FOR WHAT THEY ARE!
THE APE CRUSADERS!!!

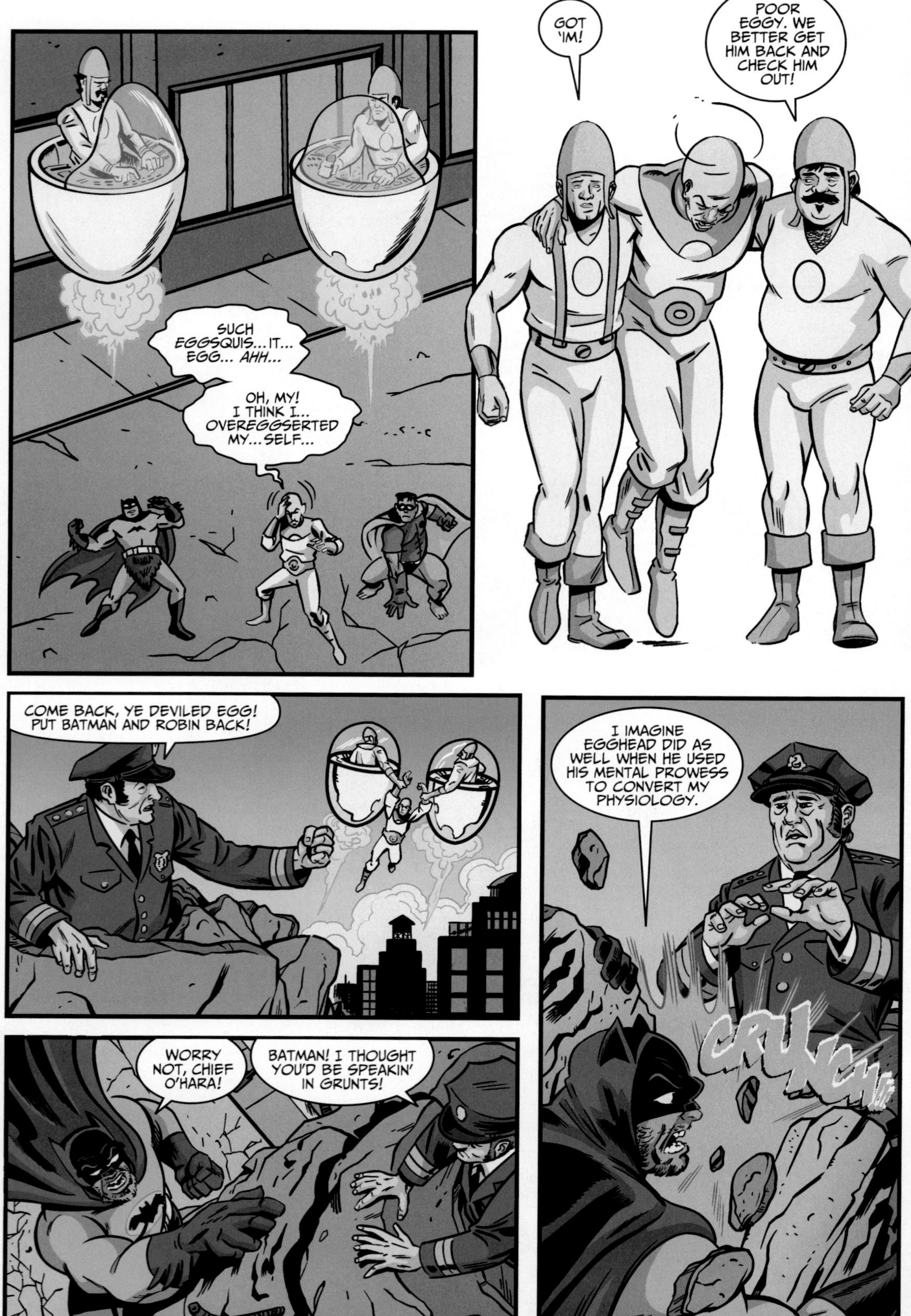
SUCH EGGSQUIS...IT... EGG... AHH...
OH, MY! I THINK I... OVEREGGSERTED MY...SELF...
GOT 'IM!
POOR EGGY. WE BETTER GET HIM BACK AND CHECK HIM OUT!
COME BACK, YE DEVILED EGG! PUT BATMAN AND ROBIN BACK!
WORRY NOT, CHIEF O'HARA!
BATMAN! I THOUGHT YOU'D BE SPEAKIN' IN GRUNTS!
I IMAGINE EGGHEAD DID AS WELL WHEN HE USED HIS MENTAL PROWESS TO CONVERT MY PHYSIOLOGY.
CRUNCH!

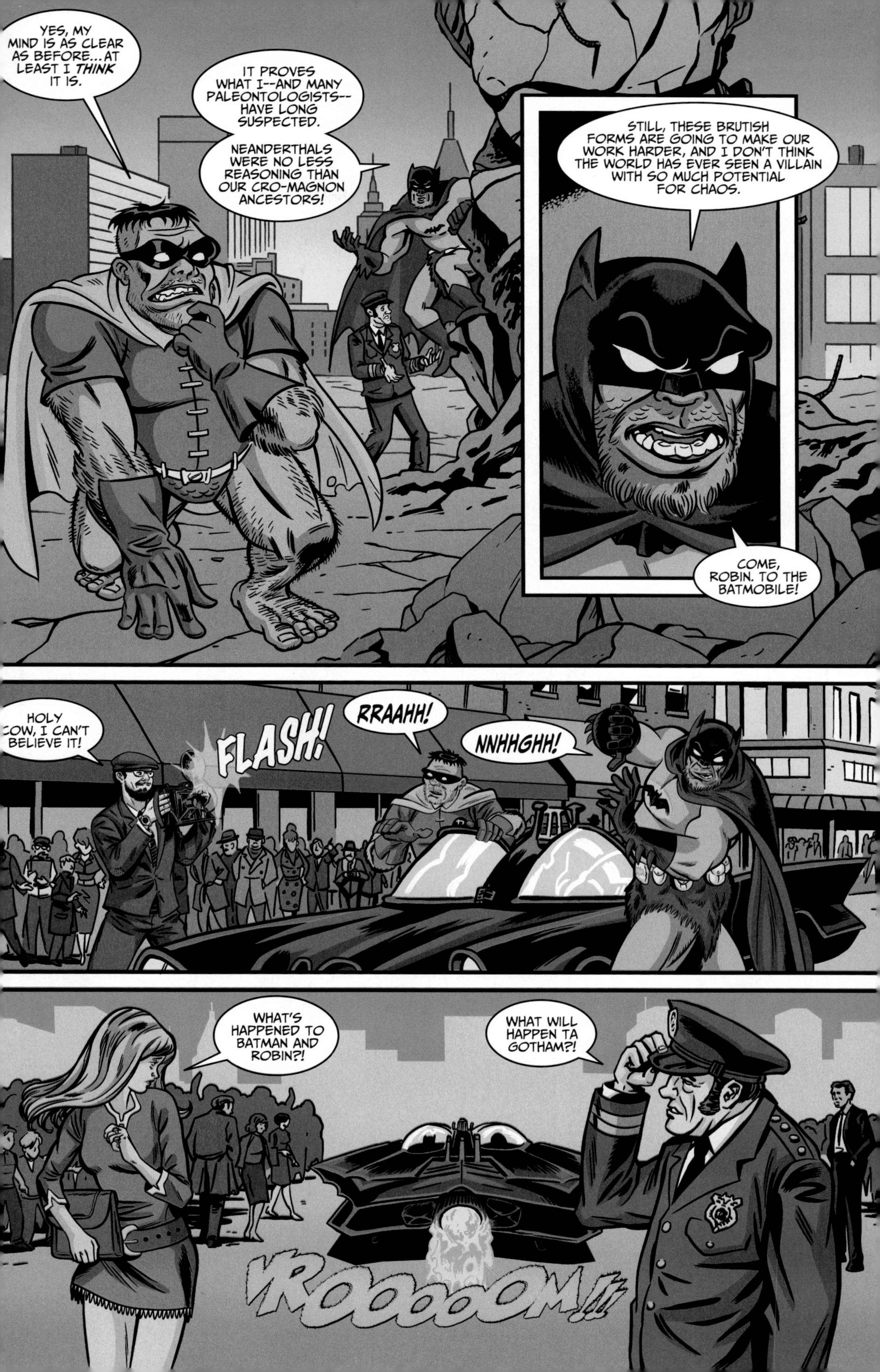
YES, MY MIND IS AS CLEAR AS BEFORE...AT LEAST I *THINK* IT IS.
IT PROVES WHAT I--AND MANY PALEONTOLOGISTS--HAVE LONG SUSPECTED.
NEANDERTHALS WERE NO LESS REASONING THAN OUR CRO-MAGNON ANCESTORS!
STILL, THESE BRUTISH FORMS ARE GOING TO MAKE OUR WORK HARDER, AND I DON'T THINK THE WORLD HAS EVER SEEN A VILLAIN WITH SO MUCH POTENTIAL FOR CHAOS.
COME, ROBIN. TO THE BATMOBILE!
HOLY COW, I CAN'T BELIEVE IT!
FLASH!
RRAAHH!
NNHHGHH!
WHAT'S HAPPENED TO BATMAN AND ROBIN?!
WHAT WILL HAPPEN TA GOTHAM?!
VROOOOOOM!!

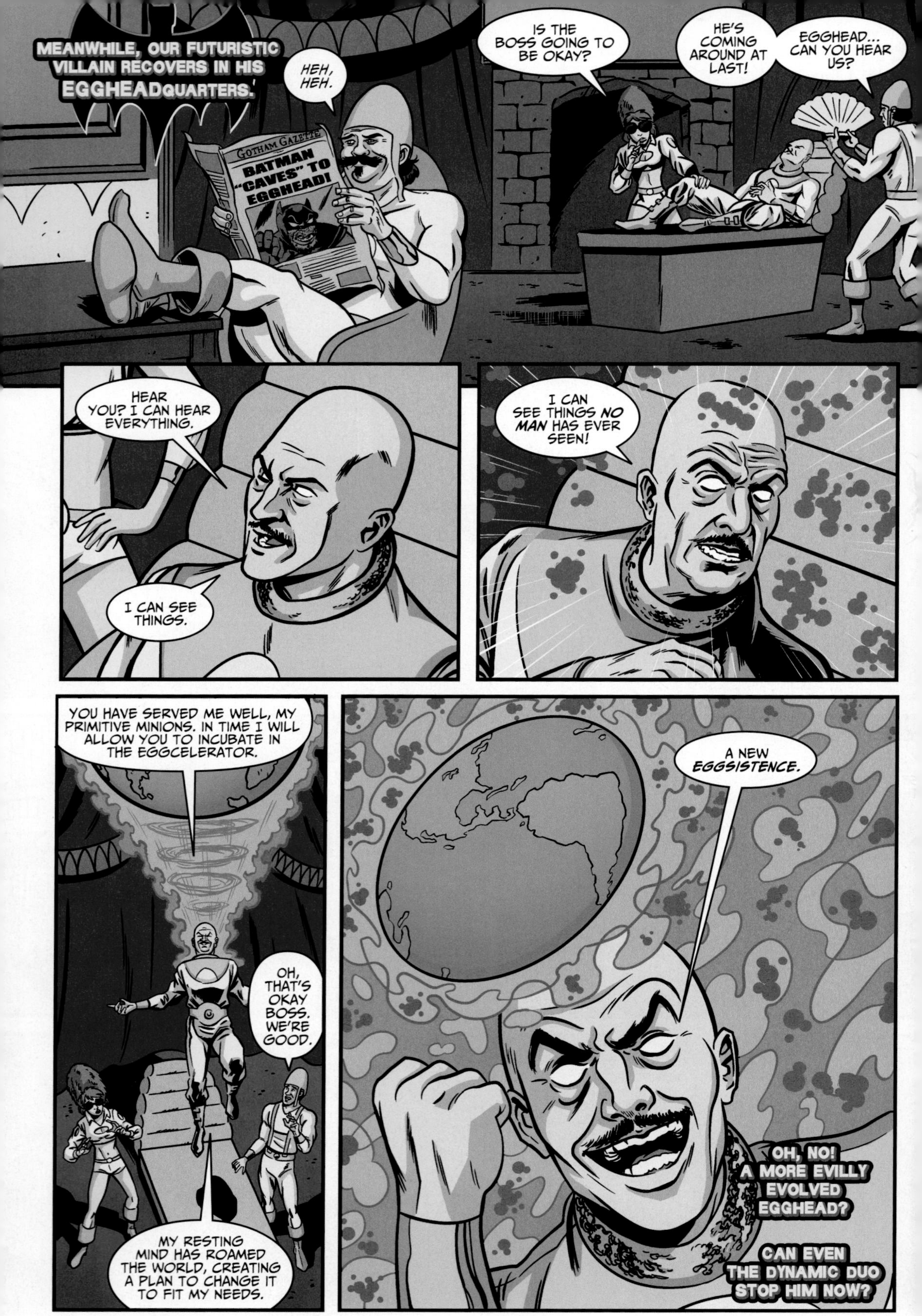
MEANWHILE, OUR FUTURISTIC VILLAIN RECOVERS IN HIS EGGHEADQUARTERS.
HEH, HEH.
GOTHAM GAZETTE
BATMAN "CAVES" TO EGGHEAD!
IS THE BOSS GOING TO BE OKAY?
HE'S COMING AROUND AT LAST!
EGGHEAD... CAN YOU HEAR US?
HEAR YOU? I CAN HEAR EVERYTHING.
I CAN SEE THINGS.
I CAN SEE THINGS NO MAN HAS EVER SEEN!
YOU HAVE SERVED ME WELL, MY PRIMITIVE MINIONS. IN TIME I WILL ALLOW YOU TO INCUBATE IN THE EGGCELERATOR.
OH, THAT'S OKAY BOSS. WE'RE GOOD.
MY RESTING MIND HAS ROAMED THE WORLD, CREATING A PLAN TO CHANGE IT TO FIT MY NEEDS.
A NEW EGGSISTENCE.
OH, NO! A MORE EVILLY EVOLVED EGGHEAD?
CAN EVEN THE DYNAMIC DUO STOP HIM NOW?

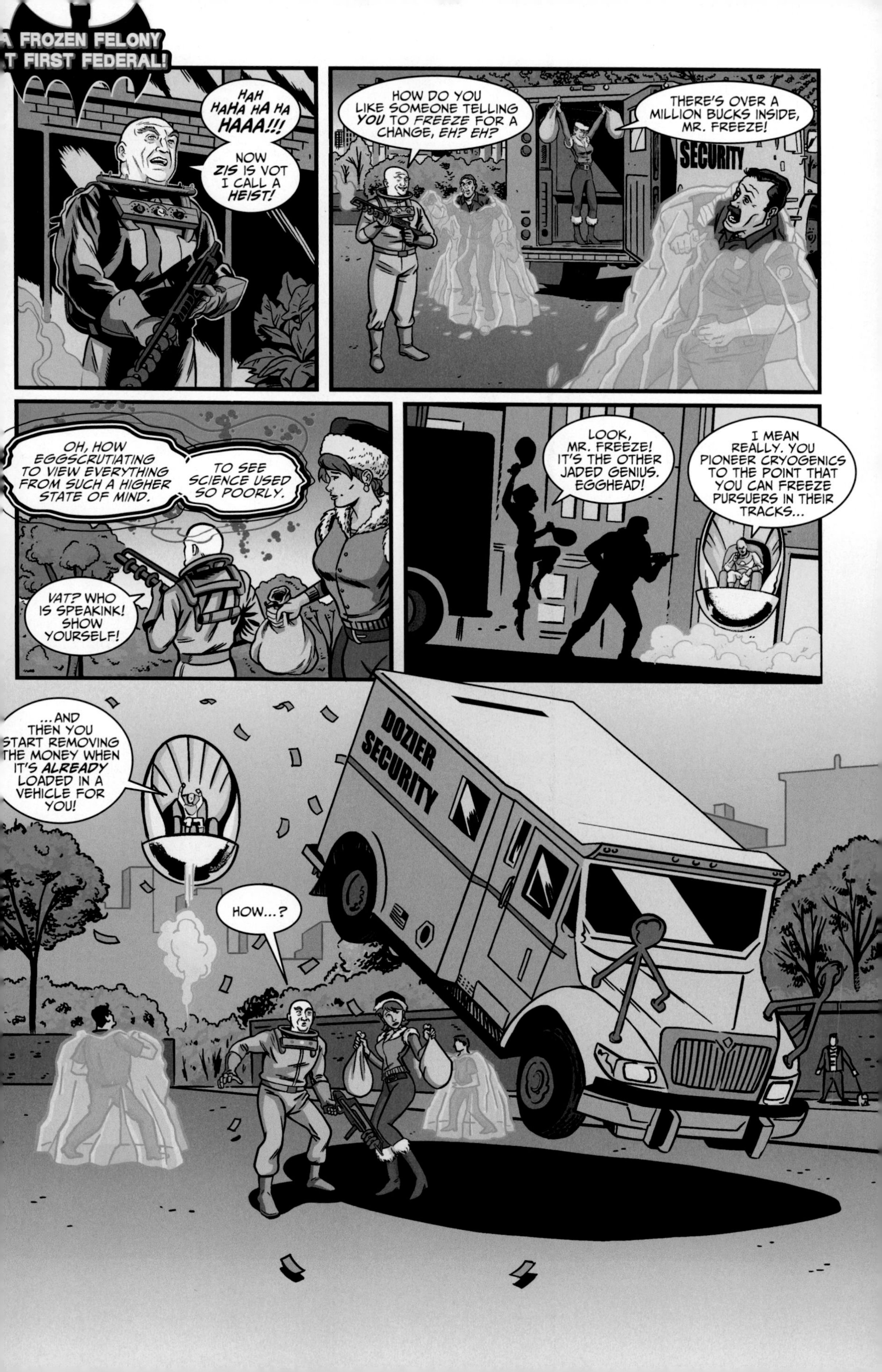
A FROZEN FELONY AT FIRST FEDERAL!
HAH HAHA HA HA HAAA!!!
NOW ZIS IS VOT I CALL A HEIST!
HOW DO YOU LIKE SOMEONE TELLING YOU TO FREEZE FOR A CHANGE, EH? EH?
THERE'S OVER A MILLION BUCKS INSIDE, MR. FREEZE!
SECURITY
OH, HOW EGGSCRUTIATING TO VIEW EVERYTHING FROM SUCH A HIGHER STATE OF MIND.
TO SEE SCIENCE USED SO POORLY.
VAT? WHO IS SPEAKINK! SHOW YOURSELF!
LOOK, MR. FREEZE! IT'S THE OTHER JADED GENIUS. EGGHEAD!
I MEAN REALLY. YOU PIONEER CRYOGENICS TO THE POINT THAT YOU CAN FREEZE PURSUERS IN THEIR TRACKS...
...AND THEN YOU START REMOVING THE MONEY WHEN IT'S ALREADY LOADED IN A VEHICLE FOR YOU!
DOZIER SECURITY
HOW...?

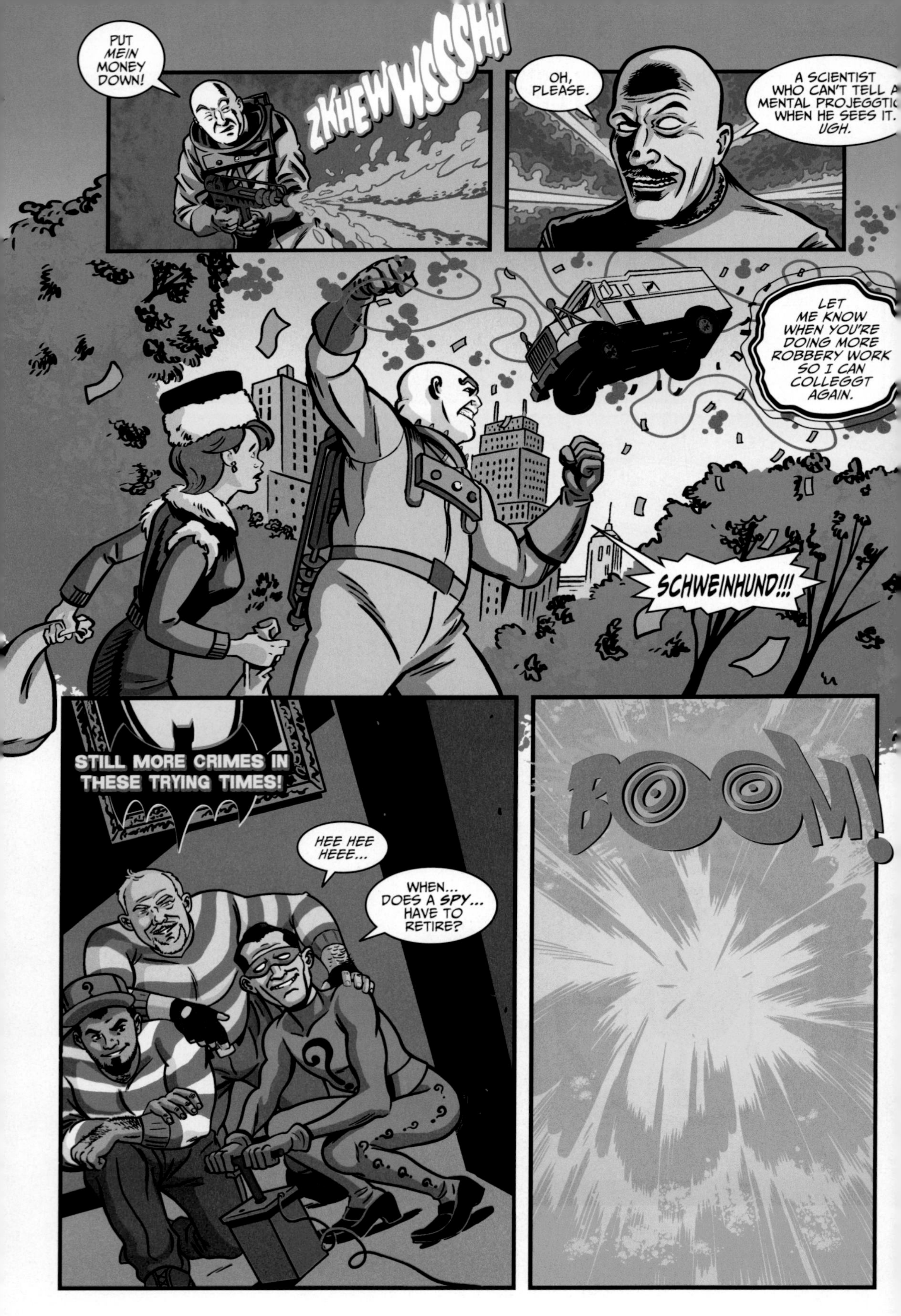
PUT MEIN MONEY DOWN!
ZKHEWWSSSHH
OH, PLEASE.
A SCIENTIST WHO CAN'T TELL A MENTAL PROJEGGTIO WHEN HE SEES IT. UGH.
LET ME KNOW WHEN YOU'RE DOING MORE ROBBERY WORK SO I CAN COLLEGGT AGAIN.
SCHWEINHUND!!!
STILL MORE CRIMES IN THESE TRYING TIMES!
HEE HEE HEEE...
WHEN... DOES A SPY... HAVE TO RETIRE?
BOOM!

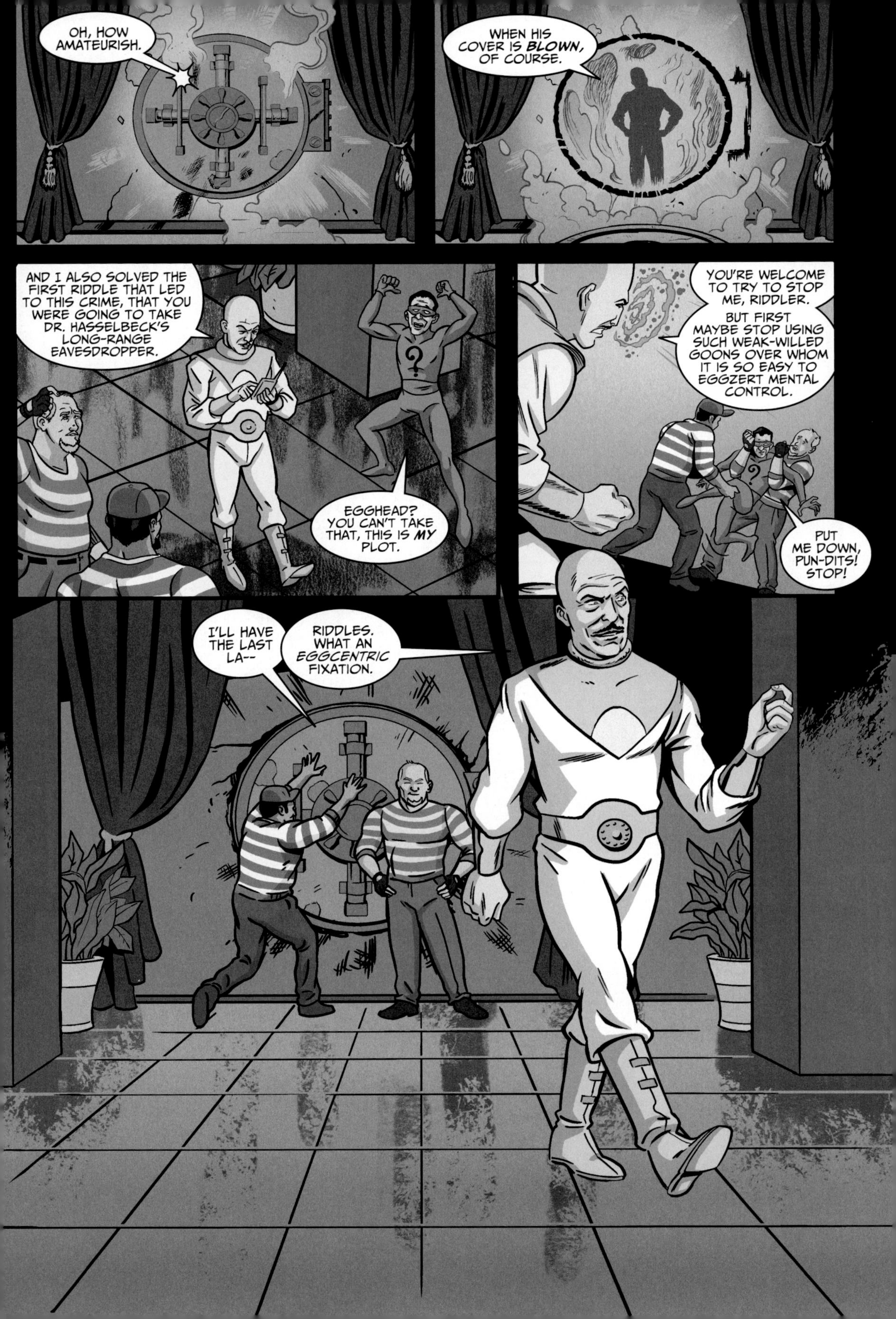
OH, HOW AMATEURISH.
WHEN HIS COVER IS BLOWN, OF COURSE.
AND I ALSO SOLVED THE FIRST RIDDLE THAT LED TO THIS CRIME, THAT YOU WERE GOING TO TAKE DR. HASSELBECK'S LONG-RANGE EAVESDROPPER.
EGGHEAD? YOU CAN'T TAKE THAT, THIS IS MY PLOT.
YOU'RE WELCOME TO TRY TO STOP ME, RIDDLER.
BUT FIRST MAYBE STOP USING SUCH WEAK-WILLED GOONS OVER WHOM IT IS SO EASY TO EGGZERT MENTAL CONTROL.
PUT ME DOWN, PUN-DITS! STOP!
I'LL HAVE THE LAST LA--
RIDDLES. WHAT AN EGGCENTRIC FIXATION.

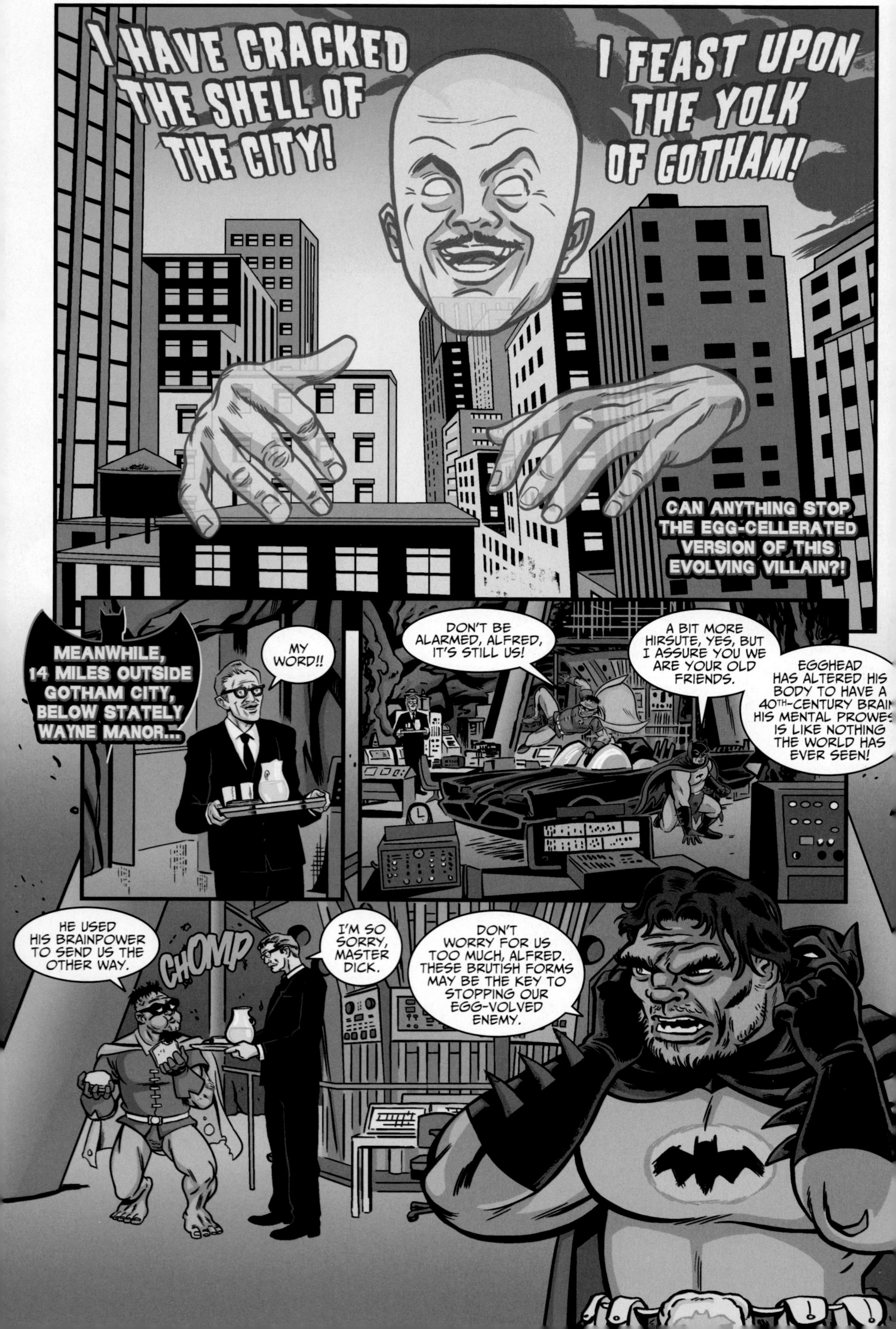
I HAVE CRACKED THE SHELL OF THE CITY!
I FEAST UPON THE YOLK OF GOTHAM!
CAN ANYTHING STOP THE EGG-CELLERATED VERSION OF THIS EVOLVING VILLAIN?!
MEANWHILE, 14 MILES OUTSIDE GOTHAM CITY, BELOW STATELY WAYNE MANOR...
MY WORD!!
DON'T BE ALARMED, ALFRED, IT'S STILL US!
A BIT MORE HIRSUTE, YES, BUT I ASSURE YOU WE ARE YOUR OLD FRIENDS.
EGGHEAD HAS ALTERED HIS BODY TO HAVE A 40TH-CENTURY BRAI HIS MENTAL PROWES IS LIKE NOTHING THE WORLD HAS EVER SEEN!
HE USED HIS BRAINPOWER TO SEND US THE OTHER WAY.
CHOMP
I'M SO SORRY, MASTER DICK.
DON'T WORRY FOR US TOO MUCH, ALFRED. THESE BRUTISH FORMS MAY BE THE KEY TO STOPPING OUR EGG-VOLVED ENEMY.

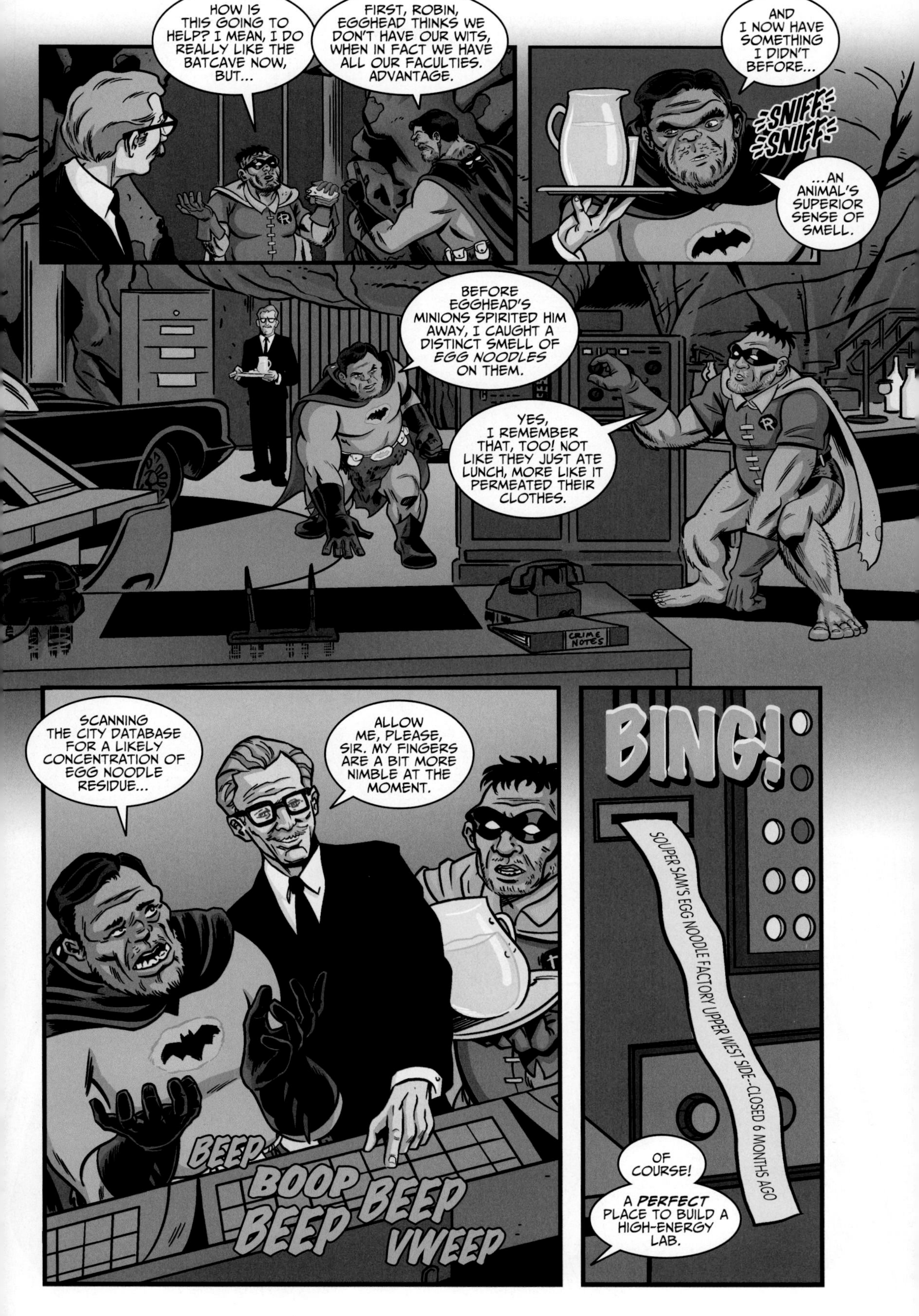
HOW IS THIS GOING TO HELP? I MEAN, I DO REALLY LIKE THE BATCAVE NOW, BUT...
FIRST, ROBIN, EGGHEAD THINKS WE DON'T HAVE OUR WITS, WHEN IN FACT WE HAVE ALL OUR FACULTIES. ADVANTAGE.
AND I NOW HAVE SOMETHING I DIDN'T BEFORE...
SNIFF SNIFF
...AN ANIMAL'S SUPERIOR SENSE OF SMELL.
BEFORE EGGHEAD'S MINIONS SPIRITED HIM AWAY, I CAUGHT A DISTINCT SMELL OF EGG NOODLES ON THEM.
YES, I REMEMBER THAT, TOO! NOT LIKE THEY JUST ATE LUNCH, MORE LIKE IT PERMEATED THEIR CLOTHES.
CRIME NOTES
SCANNING THE CITY DATABASE FOR A LIKELY CONCENTRATION OF EGG NOODLE RESIDUE...
ALLOW ME, PLEASE, SIR. MY FINGERS ARE A BIT MORE NIMBLE AT THE MOMENT.
BEEP
BOOP
BEEP
BEEP
VWEEP
BING!
SOUPER SAM'S EGG NOODLE FACTORY UPPER WEST SIDE--CLOSED 6 MONTHS AGO
OF COURSE!
A PERFECT PLACE TO BUILD A HIGH-ENERGY LAB.

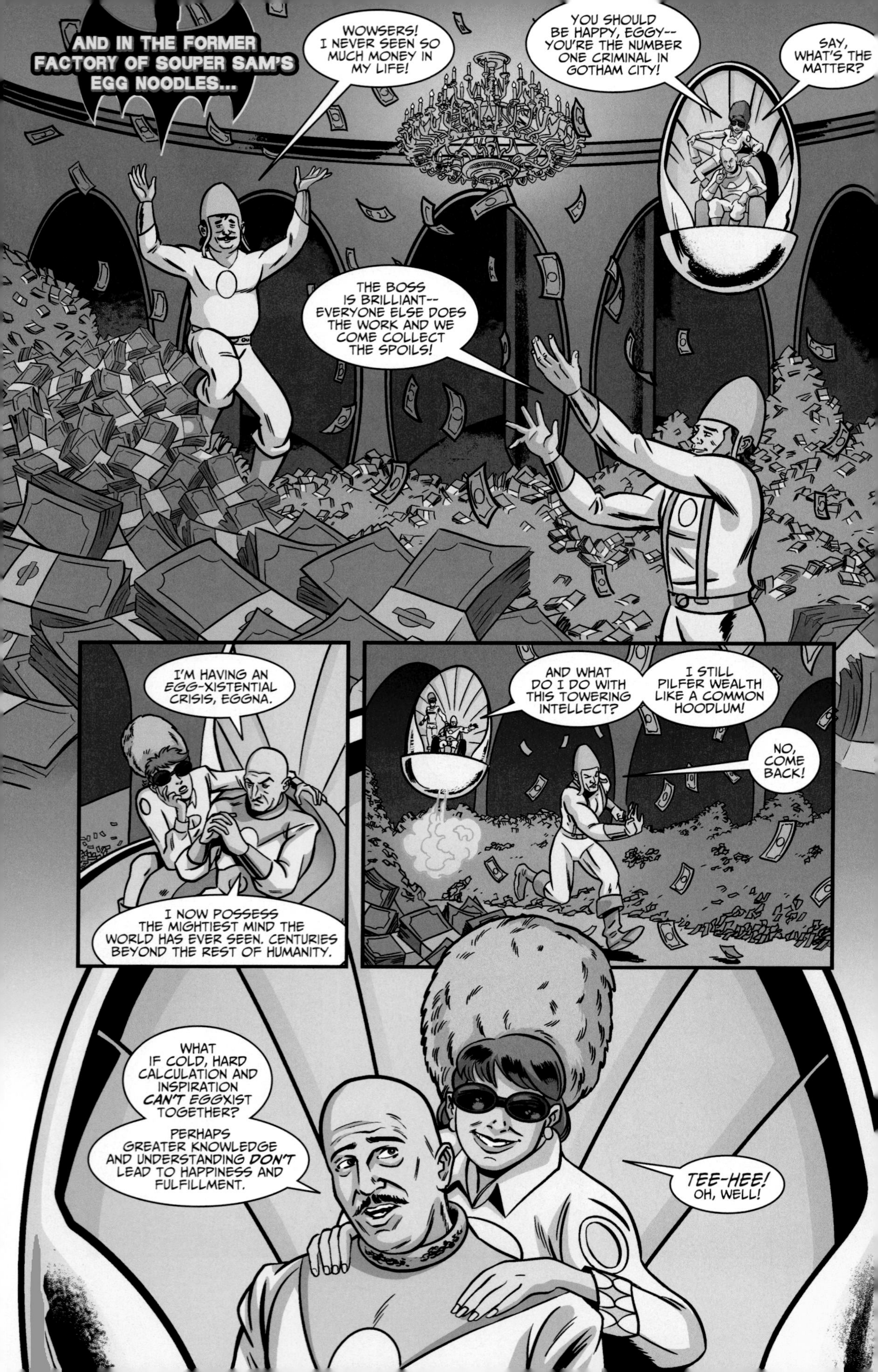
AND IN THE FORMER FACTORY OF SOUPER SAM'S EGG NOODLES...
WOWSERS! I NEVER SEEN SO MUCH MONEY IN MY LIFE!
YOU SHOULD BE HAPPY, EGGY-- YOU'RE THE NUMBER ONE CRIMINAL IN GOTHAM CITY!
SAY, WHAT'S THE MATTER?
THE BOSS IS BRILLIANT-- EVERYONE ELSE DOES THE WORK AND WE COME COLLECT THE SPOILS!
I'M HAVING AN EGG-XISTENTIAL CRISIS, EGGNA.
I NOW POSSESS THE MIGHTIEST MIND THE WORLD HAS EVER SEEN. CENTURIES BEYOND THE REST OF HUMANITY.
AND WHAT DO I DO WITH THIS TOWERING INTELLECT?
I STILL PILFER WEALTH LIKE A COMMON HOODLUM!
NO, COME BACK!
WHAT IF COLD, HARD CALCULATION AND INSPIRATION CAN'T EGGXIST TOGETHER?
PERHAPS GREATER KNOWLEDGE AND UNDERSTANDING DON'T LEAD TO HAPPINESS AND FULFILLMENT.
TEE-HEE! OH, WELL!

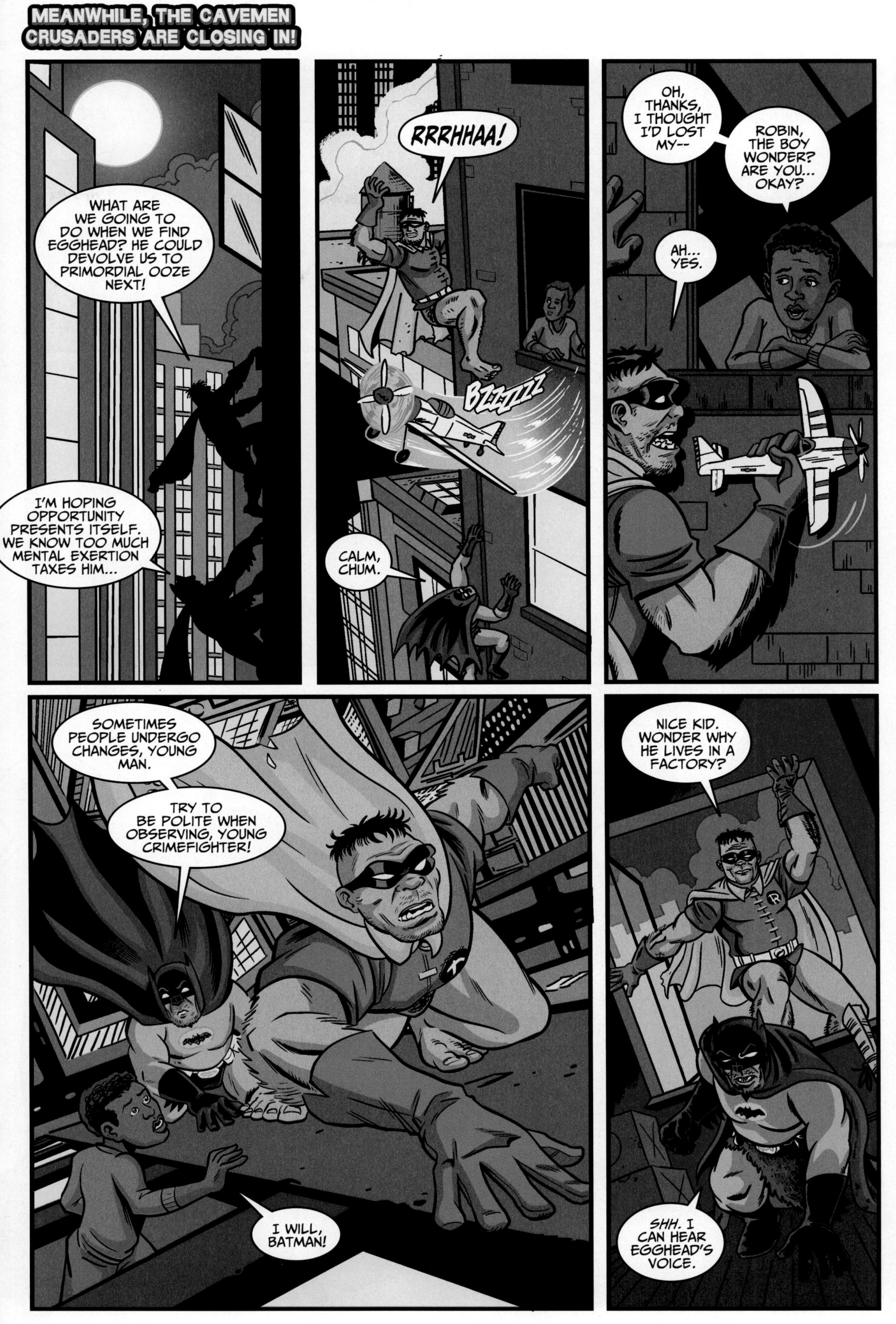
MEANWHILE, THE CAVEMEN CRUSADERS ARE CLOSING IN!
WHAT ARE WE GOING TO DO WHEN WE FIND EGGHEAD? HE COULD DEVOLVE US TO PRIMORDIAL OOZE NEXT!
I'M HOPING OPPORTUNITY PRESENTS ITSELF. WE KNOW TOO MUCH MENTAL EXERTION TAXES HIM...
RRRHHAA!
BZZZZZZ
CALM, CHUM.
OH, THANKS, I THOUGHT I'D LOST MY--
ROBIN, THE BOY WONDER? ARE YOU... OKAY?
AH... YES.
SOMETIMES PEOPLE UNDERGO CHANGES, YOUNG MAN.
TRY TO BE POLITE WHEN OBSERVING, YOUNG CRIMEFIGHTER!
I WILL, BATMAN!
NICE KID. WONDER WHY HE LIVES IN A FACTORY?
SHH. I CAN HEAR EGGHEAD'S VOICE.

ULTIMATELY I'M STILL BUT A CRIMINAL. I HAVE IT ALL WITHIN MY GRASP AND NONE OF IT MATTERS!

IT'S A PYRRHIC VICTORY AT BEST. OHH!

SOUNDS LIKE A WIN TO ME!

FOLLOW MY LEAD, ROBIN.

NO, IMBECILE, IT'S A VICTORY THAT DOESN'T COUNT! OH, WHY DID I DO THIS TO MYSELF?

IT WAS BAD ENOUGH BEFORE, BUT AT LEAST...

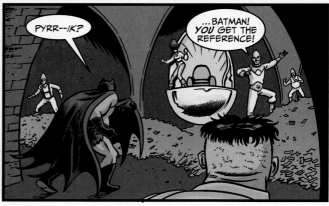

PYRR--IK?

...BATMAN! YOU GET THE REFERENCE!

REF-- RINSE!

OOK!! HA, HA!

NO. NO.

NO!!

CRUEL IRONY!

MY MOST WORTHY FOIL, I'VE REDUCED YOU TO A PRATTLING PRIMATE!

EGGS GOOD!

PROTECT THE BOSS-- GET 'IM!

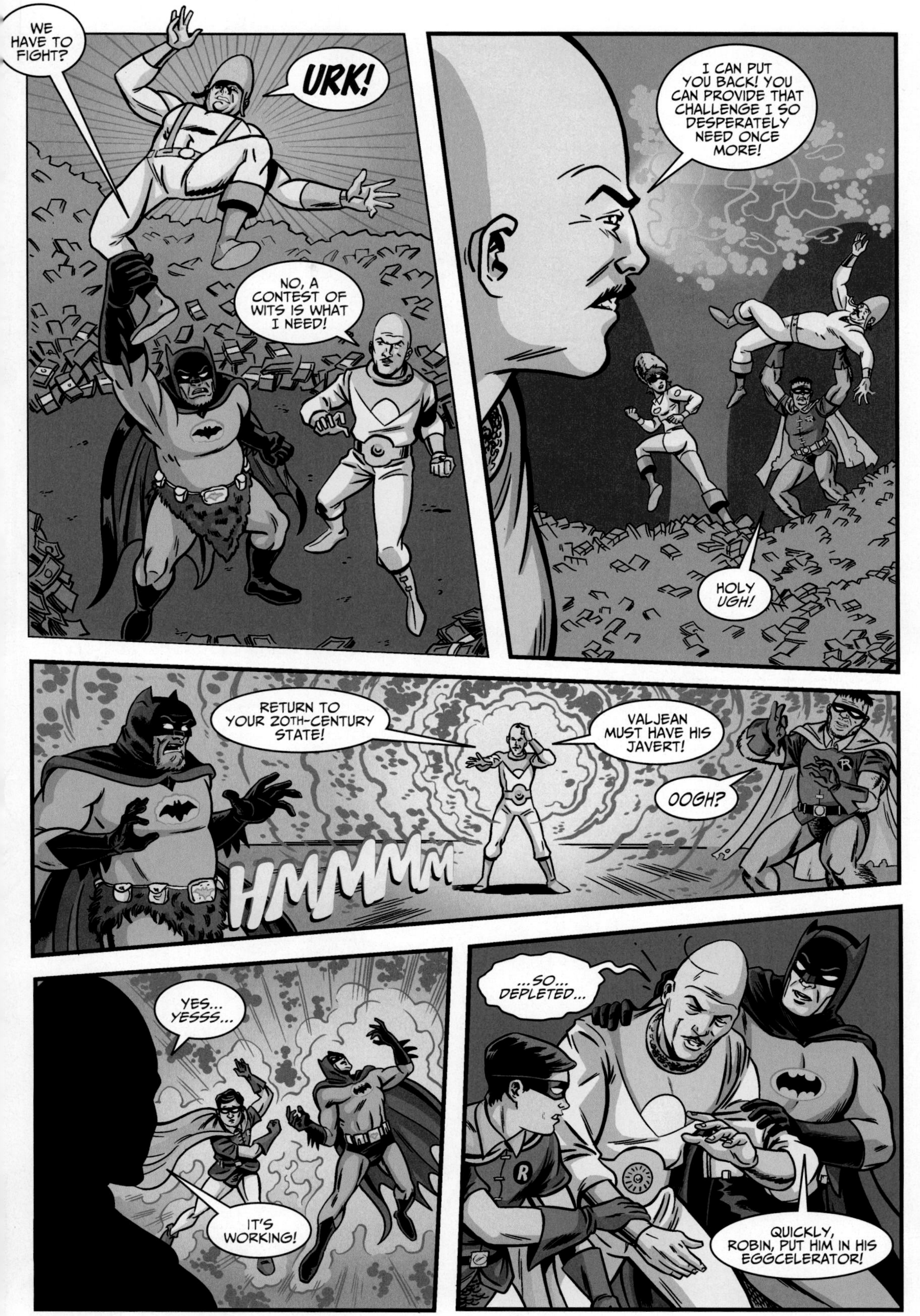
WE HAVE TO FIGHT?
URK!
NO, A CONTEST OF WITS IS WHAT I NEED!
I CAN PUT YOU BACK! YOU CAN PROVIDE THAT CHALLENGE I SO DESPERATELY NEED ONCE MORE!
HOLY UGH!
RETURN TO YOUR 20TH-CENTURY STATE!
VALJEAN MUST HAVE HIS JAVERT!
OOGH?
HMMMM
YES... YESSS...
IT'S WORKING!
...SO... DEPLETED...
QUICKLY, ROBIN, PUT HIM IN HIS EGGCELERATOR!

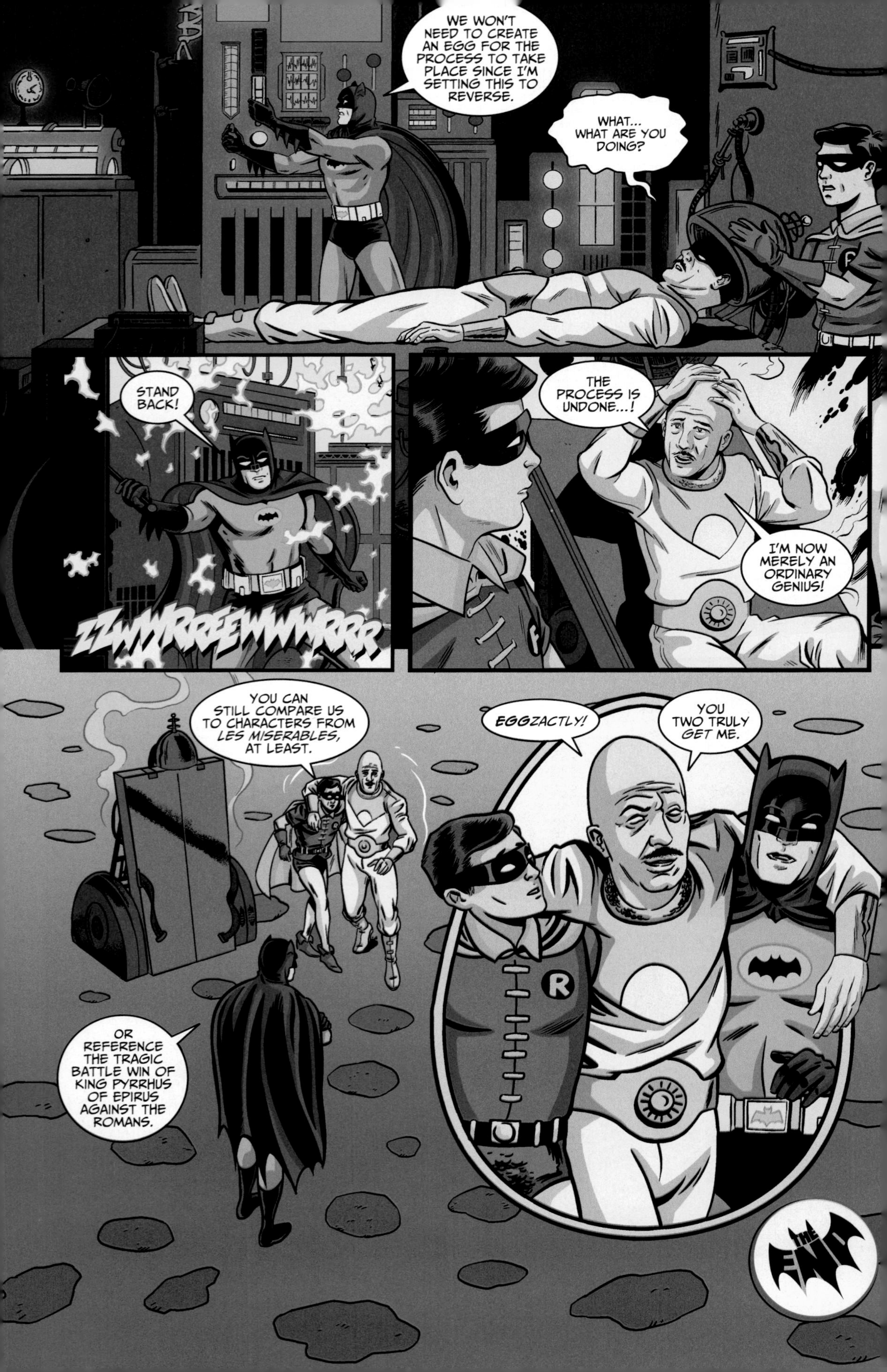
WE WON'T NEED TO CREATE AN EGG FOR THE PROCESS TO TAKE PLACE SINCE I'M SETTING THIS TO REVERSE.
WHAT... WHAT ARE YOU DOING?
STAND BACK!
ZZWWRREEWWWRRR
THE PROCESS IS UNDONE...!
I'M NOW MERELY AN ORDINARY GENIUS!
YOU CAN STILL COMPARE US TO CHARACTERS FROM LES MISERABLES, AT LEAST.
OR REFERENCE THE TRAGIC BATTLE WIN OF KING PYRRHUS OF EPIRUS AGAINST THE ROMANS.
EGGZACTLY!
YOU TWO TRULY GET ME.
THE END

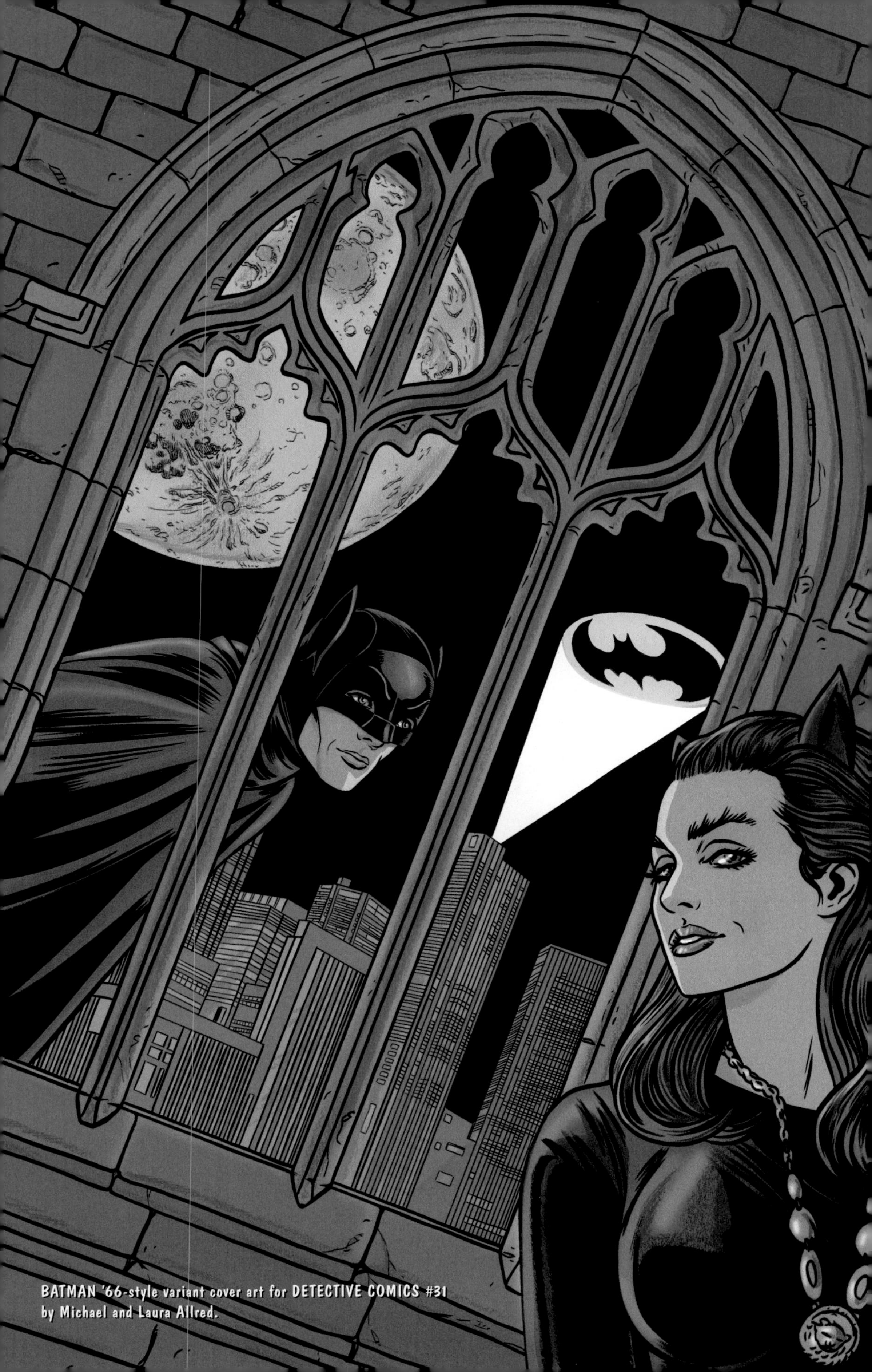

BATMAN '66-style variant cover art for DETECTIVE COMICS #31 by Michael and Laura Allred.

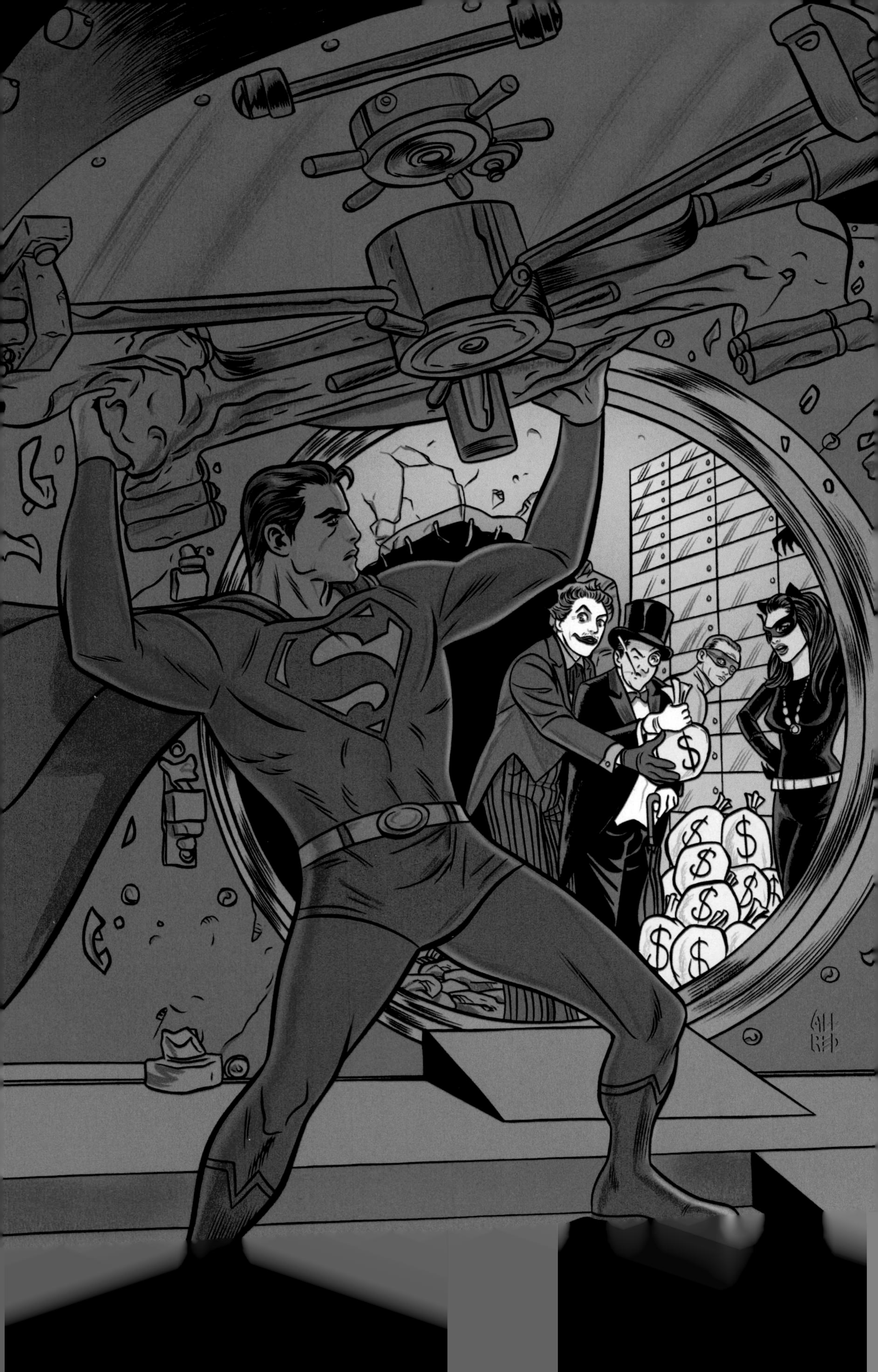

BATMAN '66-style variant cover art for AQUAMAN #31
by Michael and Laura Allred.

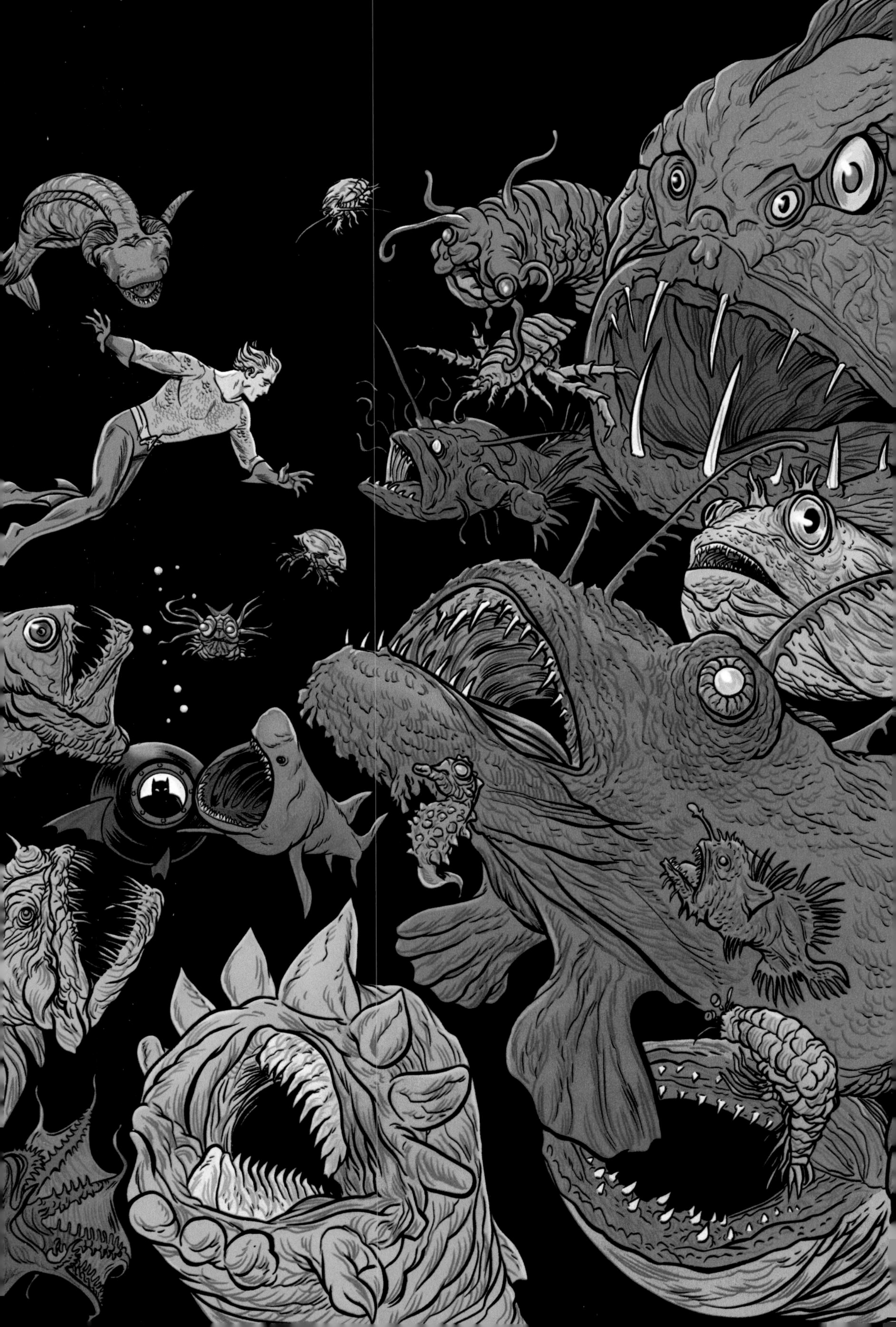

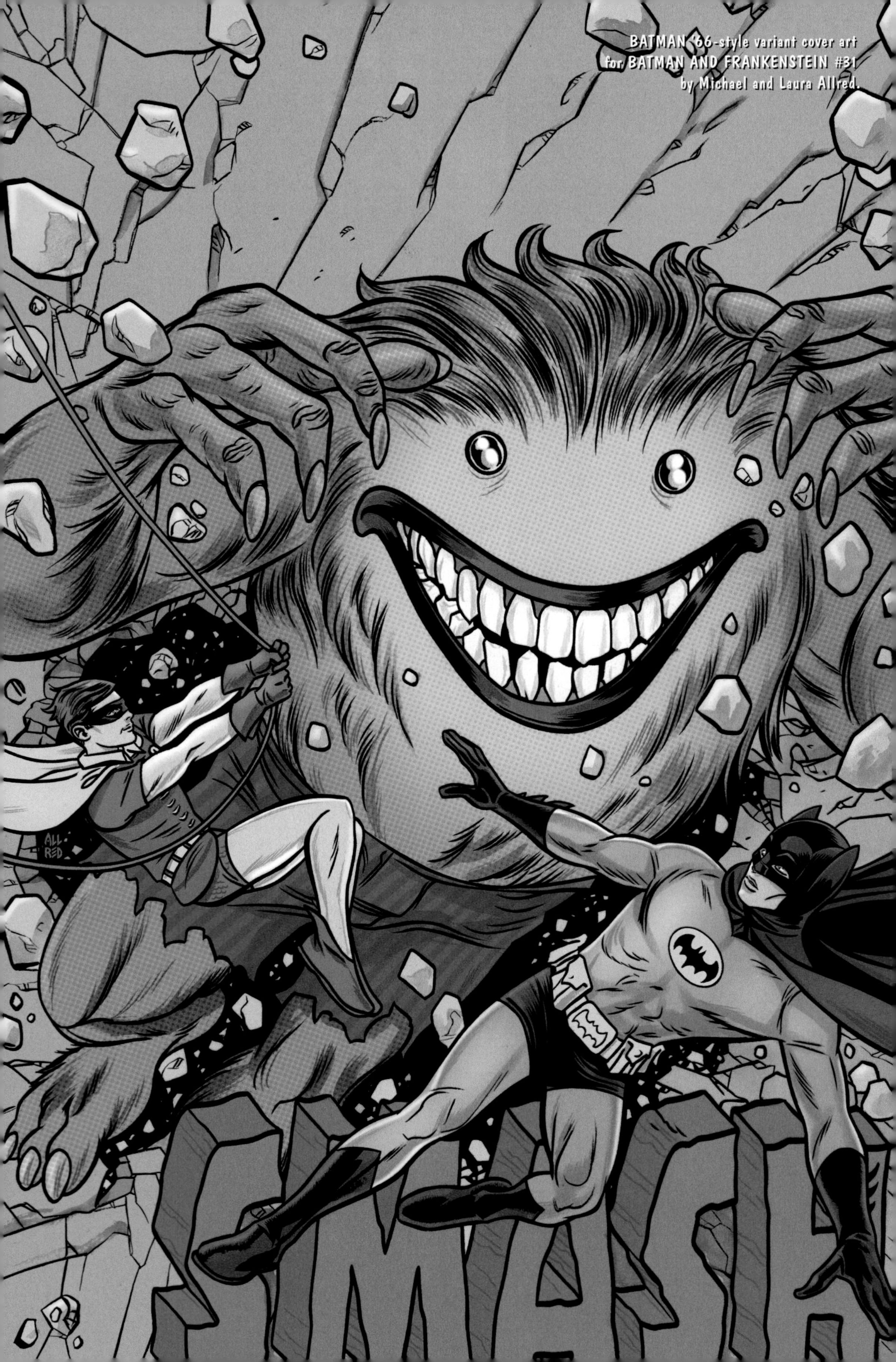
ALL
RED

BATMAN '66-style variant cover art
for BATMAN AND FRANKENSTEIN #31
by Michael and Laura Allred.

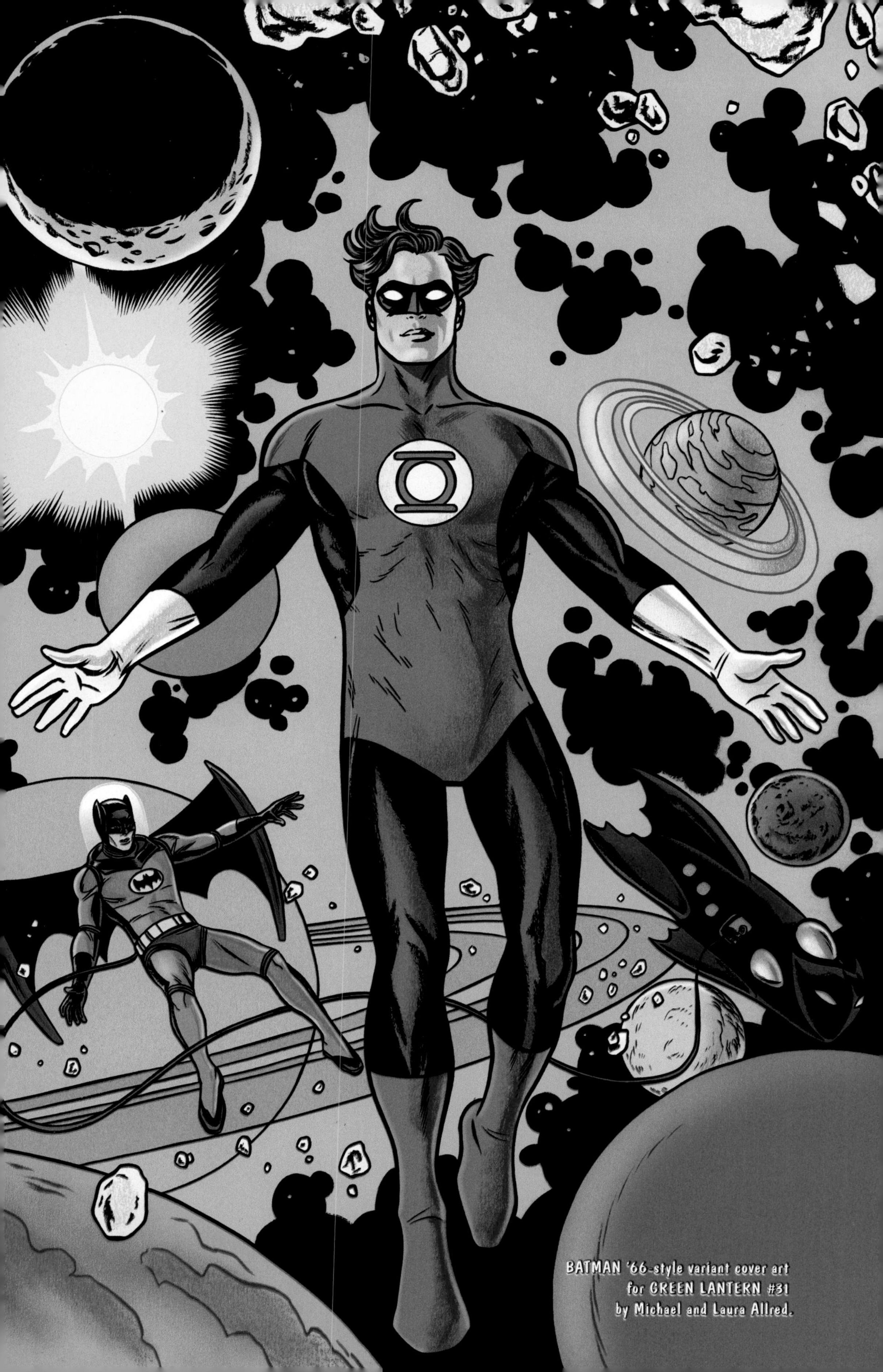

BATMAN '66-style variant cover art
for GREEN LANTERN #31
by Michael and Laura Allred.

BATMAN '66-style variant cover art
for HARLEY QUINN #6
by Michael and Laura Allred.

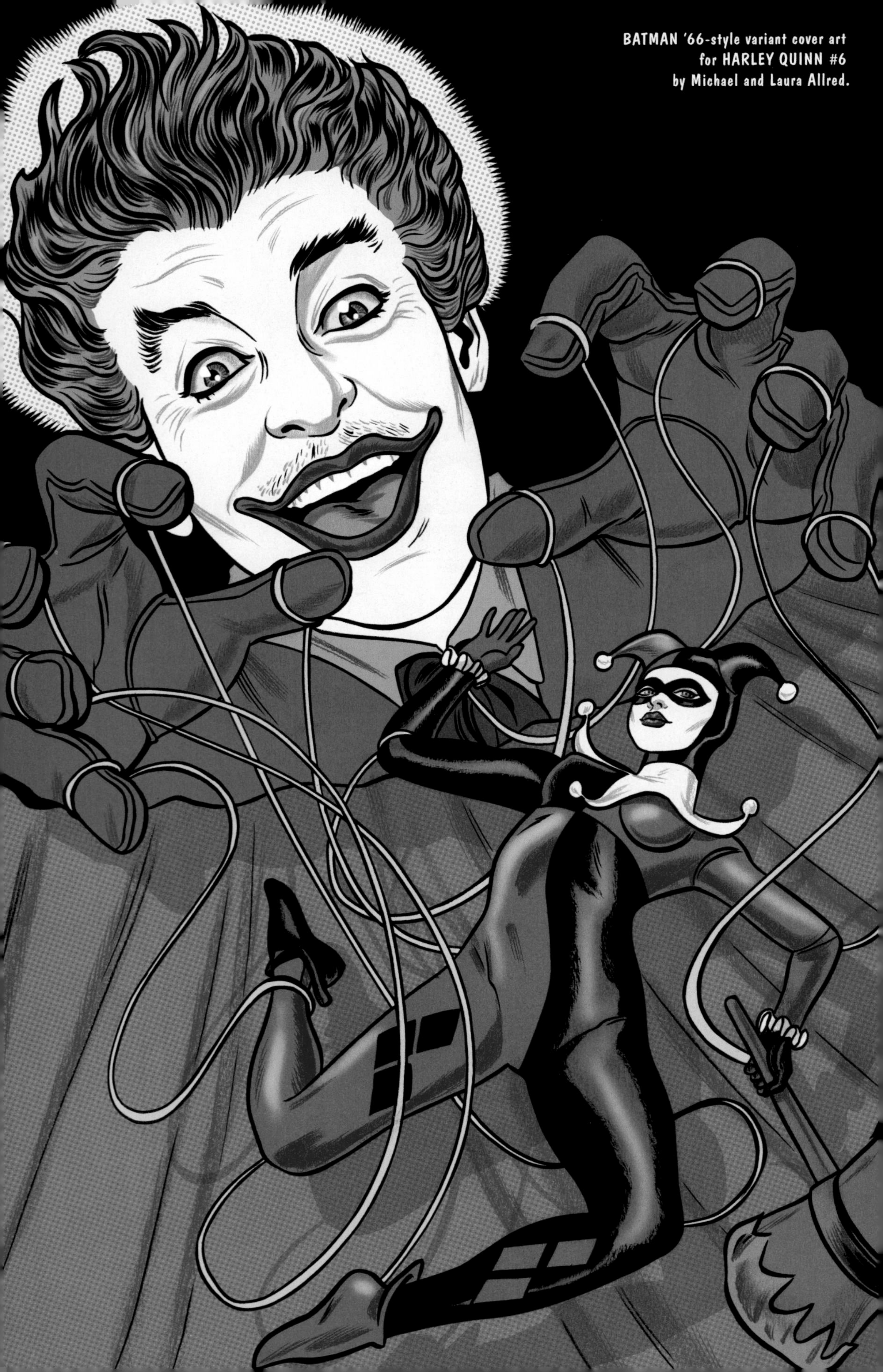

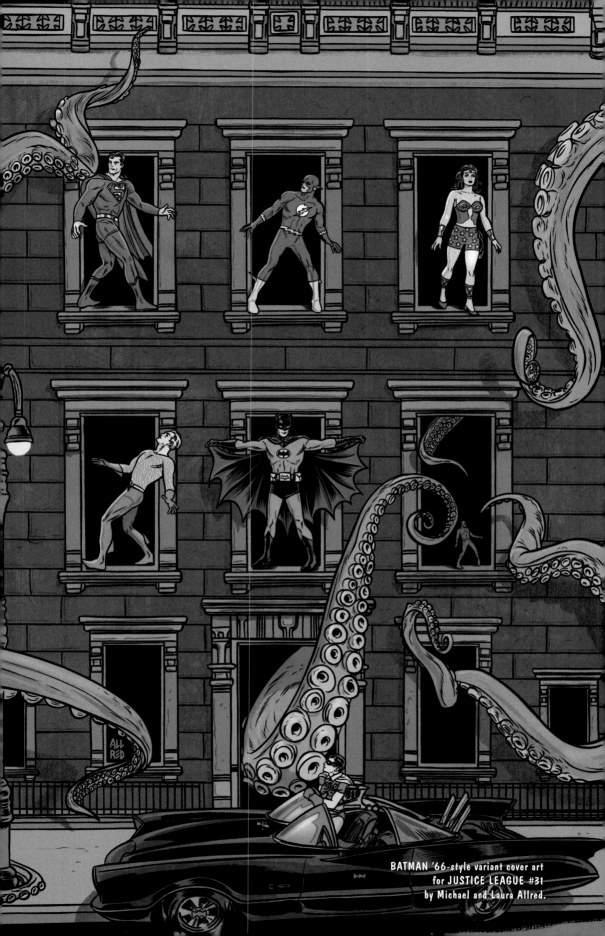

BATMAN '66-style variant cover art
for JUSTICE LEAGUE #31
by Michael and Laura Allred.

BATMAN '66-style variant cover art for THE FLASH #31
by Michael and Laura Allred.

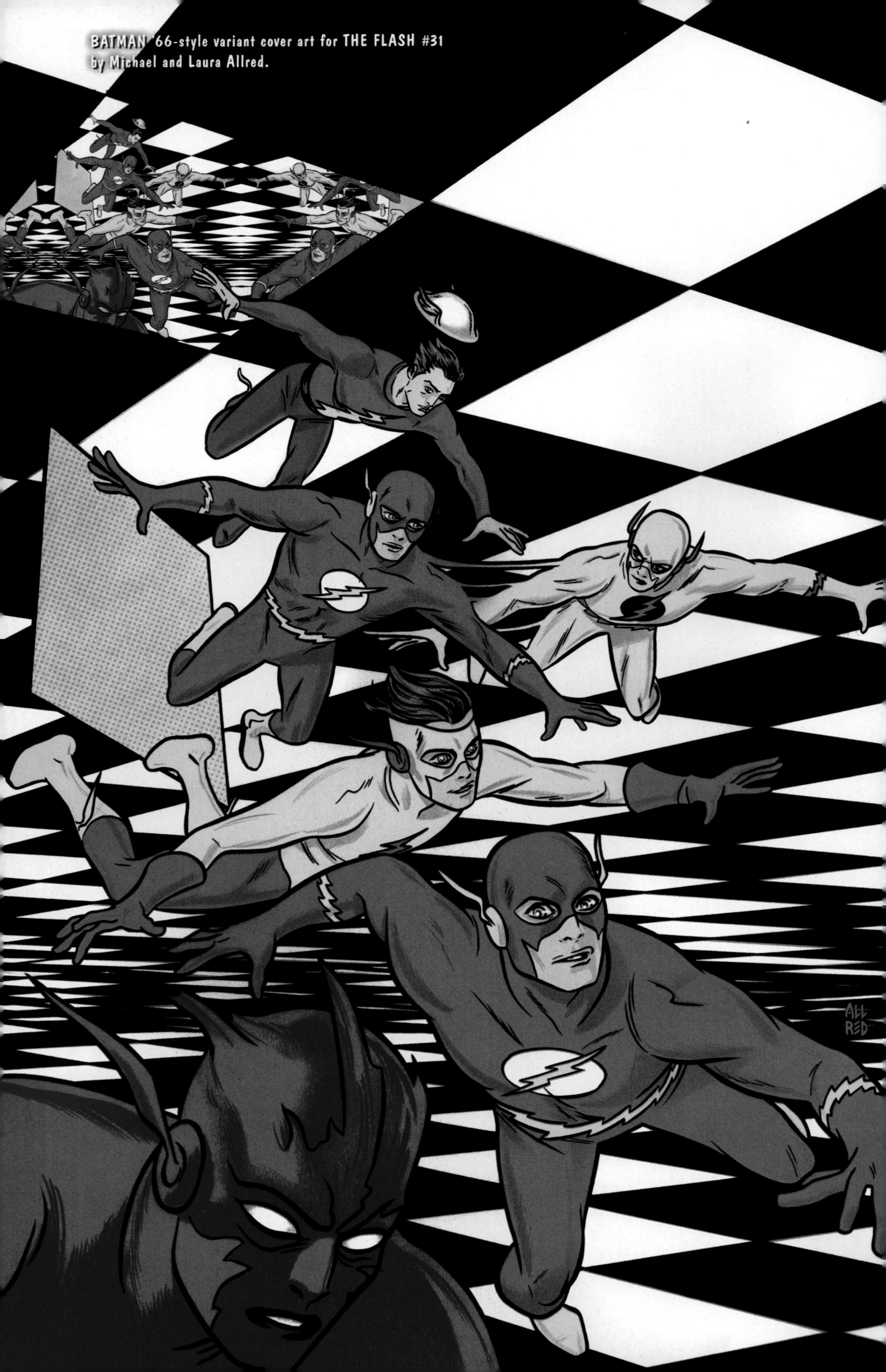
ALLRED

BATMAN '66-style variant cover art
for SUPERMAN/WONDER WOMAN #8
by Michael and Laura Allred.

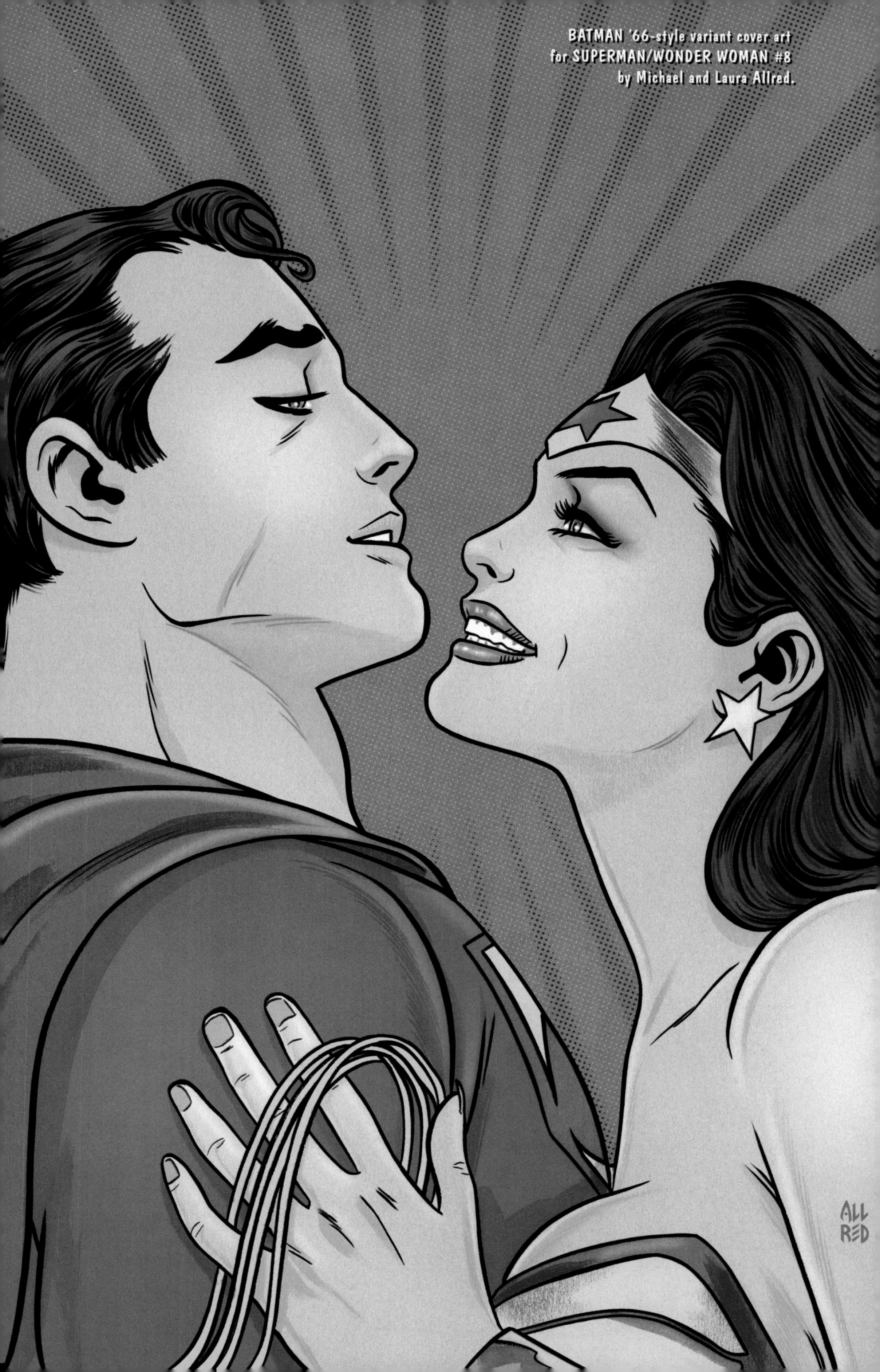
ALLRED

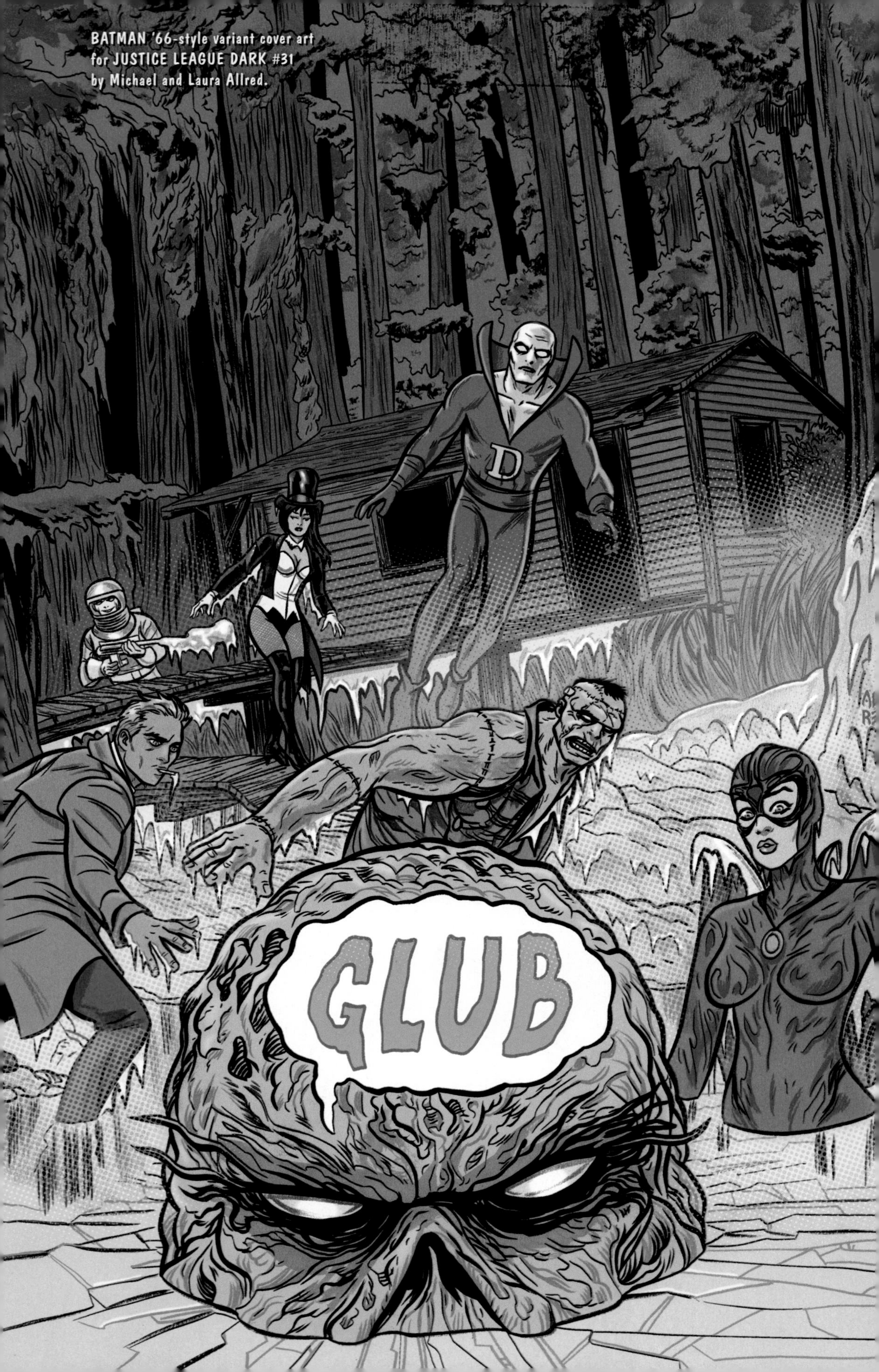
GLUB

BATMAN '66-style variant cover art for JUSTICE LEAGUE DARK #31 by Michael and Laura Allred.